EARLY CHRISTIAN
LITERATURE

Christians in the formative period of their religion, from the mid-first to early third centuries, sought new ways of relating their lives to the dominant society that surrounded them. As doctrine and practice became established, hostility from the wider world was often extreme. Christians used many literary forms to strengthen their own self-definition. Prominent among these were the Apologies as well as the semi-fictional Apocryphal Acts and Martyr Acts. These forms used the existing literary patterns of Greco-Roman society to present distinctively Christian ideas, attitudes and adventures.

In this thoroughgoing study, Helen Rhee shows how the forms of classical genre were adapted to present the superiority of Christian monotheism; the superiority of Christian sexual morality; and Christian (dis)loyalty to the Empire. These propagandistic writings shaped the theological, moral and political trajectories of Christian faith and contributed largely to the definition of orthodoxy.

This outstanding work of scholarship explores issues of cultural identity in an area which has hitherto lacked definition. In clear prose the author presents arguments that will be of equal interest to the student of early Christianity and of Greco-Roman literary culture and civilization.

Helen Rhee is Assistant Professor of World Christianity at Westmont College, Santa Barbara, California. She researches on the second- and third-century Christian literature, focusing on the diverging Christian self-identities in relation to Greco-Roman culture and society.

EARLY CHRISTIAN LITERATURE

Christ and culture in the second and third centuries

Helen Rhee

Dear Julia Woo,

I thank for God's steadfast love for and faithfulness to you! May the Lord show himself to you in a deeper way and you continue to grow in Christ.

In Christ,

Helen Rhee

Routledge
Taylor & Francis Group

LONDON AND NEW YORK

First published 2005
by Routledge
2 Park Square, Milton Park, Abingdon, Oxon OX14 4RN

Simultaneously published in the USA and Canada
by Routledge
270 Madison Ave, New York, NY 10016

Routledge is an imprint of the Taylor & Francis Group

© 2005 Helen Rhee

Typeset in Garamond by
Florence Production Ltd, Stoodleigh, Devon
Printed and bound in Great Britain by
TJ International Ltd, Padstow, Cornwall

British Library Cataloguing in Publication Data
A catalogue record for this book is available from the British Library

Library of Congress Cataloging in Publication Data
A catalog record for this book has been requested

ISBN 0–415–35488–9 (pbk)
ISBN 0–415–35487–0 (hbk)

TO MY BELOVED FAMILY

CONTENTS

CONTENTS

ACKNOWLEDGMENTS

This book grew out of my Ph.D. dissertation submitted to the Center for Advanced Theological Studies at the School of Theology, Fuller Theological Seminary. My gratitude first goes to my supervisor, Dr David M. Scholer, for his breadth and depth of scholarship in Patristics and New Testament, and for his valuable friendship and relentless support in the midst of his medical struggles. I thank my second reader, Dr Cecil M. Robeck, Jr, for his consistent encouragement and timely suggestions throughout my study, especially deepening my critical appreciation for the early Christian martyrs. I would also like to thank my external reader, Dr Everett Ferguson in Abilene Christian University, for offering me constructive comments and helpful suggestions.

Moreover, I wish to thank Dr S. Scott Bartchy at the University of California, Los Angeles, for reading and providing insightful suggestions on Chapter 3. I am grateful to Dr Mary Hope Griffin for sending me her unpublished dissertation on early Christian martyrdom. Other distinguished scholars – Judith Perkins, Gail P.C. Streete and Dennis MacDonald – sent me their papers that were read at the annual meetings of the Society of Biblical Literature.

I also want to extend my thanks to Dr James Bradley, with whom I had the joy and privilege of working as a teaching assistant for many quarters at Fuller. I would like to acknowledge other faculty and staff at Fuller Theological Seminary who have offered me valuable assistance and services: Dr Glen Stassen (for helping me understand R. Niebuhr correctly), Dr Robert Hurteau and Dr Anne Collier-Freed (as current and former program directors of the CATS), Jeannette Scholer (as a director of academic programs and for her loving care), and all the fabulous staff of McAlister Library (for their excellent and laborious work).

My appreciation goes further to my new colleagues at Westmont College who have received me with kindness and have shown genuine support for and interest in this project.

My thanks are incomplete without mentioning the remarkable editorial team of Routledge. Particularly, Richard Stoneman made this project possible and provided me with his sound judgment and expertise, and Rachel Stein took care of all the practical matters of publication with fine professionalism, as did Diana Chambers at Florence Production.

Finally, words are not enough to express my thanks to my family, to whom this book is dedicated. I owe a huge debt of love to my parents, Thankyou and Won Ja Rhee, my beloved grandmother, Kap Boon Kim, my two brothers, Joseph and Danny, and my sister-in-law, Sun Hee, for their unconditional support, prayers, and encouragement throughout this process.

ABBREVIATIONS

1 Apol.	*First Apology*
2 Apol.	*Second Apology*
1 Clem.	*First Clement*
3 Cor.	*Third Corinthians*
Acts Andr.	*Acts of Andrew*
Acts John	*Acts of John*
Acts Just.	*Acts of Justin and Companions*
Acts Paul	*Acts of Paul*
Acts Paul Thec.	*Acts of Paul and Thecla*
Acts Pet.	*Acts of Peter*
Acts Scill.	*Acts of Scillitan Martyrs*
Acts Thom.	*Acts of Thomas*
ACW	Ancient Christian Writers
ANRW	*Aufstieg und Niedergang der römischen Welt*
Apol.	*Apology*
ATR	*Anglican Theological Review*
Autol.	*Ad Autolycum*
BJRL	*Bulletin of the John Rylands Library of Manchester*
Cels.	*Contra Celsum (Against Celsus)*
CH	*Church History*
Dial.	*Dialogue with Trypho*
Diogn.	*Epistle to Diognetus*
DSS	Dead Sea Scrolls
Ep.	*Epistle*
ETL	*Ephemerides theologicae lovanienses*
Exh. cast.	*Exhortation to Chastity*
Haer.	*Against Heresies*
Herm. Mand.	*Shepherd of Hermas, Mandate*
Herm. Vis.	*Shepherd of Hermas, Vision*
Hist. eccl.	*Ecclesiastical History*

HTR	*Harvard Theological Review*
JAAR	*Journal of the American Academy of Religion*
JBL	*Journal of Biblical Literature*
JECS	*Journal of Early Christian Studies*
JEH	*Journal of Ecclesiastical History*
JFSR	*Journal of Feminist Studies in Religion*
JHC	*Journal of Higher Criticism*
JRH	*Journal of Religious History*
JRS	*Journal of Roman Studies*
JSSR	*Journal for the Study of New Testament*
JTS	*Journal of Theological Studies*
Laud. Const.	*De laudibus Constantini* (*Praise of Constantine*)
LCL	Loeb Classical Library
Leg.	*Legatio pro Christianis* (*Plea for the Christians*)
Marc.	*Against Marcion*
Mart. Andr.	*Martyrdom of Andrew*
Mart. Apol.	*Martyrdom of Apollonius*
Mart. Carp.	*Martyrdom of Carpus, Papylus, and Agathonicê*
Mart. Lyons	*Letter of the Churches of Lyons and Vienne*
Mart. Perp.	*Martyrdom of Perpetua and Felicitas*
Mart. Pol.	*Martyrdom of Polycarp*
Mart. Potam.	*Martyrdom of Potamiaena and Basilides*
Mart. Ptol.	*Martyrdom of Ptolemaeus and Lucius*
Nat.	*Ad natione* (*To the Heathen*)
Nat. d.	*De natura deorum*
NTA	*New Testament Apocrypha*
NTS	*New Testament Studies*
Oct.	*Octavius*
OECT	Oxford Early Christian Texts
Or.	*Oratio ad Graecos* (*Oration to the Greeks*)
Praescr.	*Prescription Against Heretics*
Prax.	*Against Praxeas*
Protr.	*Protreptikos* (*Exhortation to the Greeks*)
QE	*Questions and Answers on Exodus*
QS	*Rule of the Community*
RAC	*Reallexikon für Antike und Christentum*
REAug	*Revue des études augustiniennes*
ResQ	*Restoration Quarterly*
RHPR	*Revue d'histoire et de philosophie religieuses*
SBL	Society of Biblical Literature
SecCent	*The Second Century*
SMSR	*Studi e materiali di storia delle religioni*

Spec. Laws	*On the Special Laws*
StPatr	*Studia Patristica*
Strom.	*Stromata (Miscellanies)*
StTheol	*Studia Theologica*
Tim.	*Timaeus*
Ux.	*Ad uxorem (To His Wife)*
VC	*Vigiliae Christianae*
Worse	*That the Worse Attacks the Better*
ZKG	*Zeitschrift für Kirchengeschichte*
ZNTW	*Zeitschrift für die neutestamentliche Wissenschaft*

INTRODUCTION

Broadly speaking, this work is a comparative and cultural study of how different groups of early Christians related themselves to their surrounding dominant society – the Greco-Roman society and culture. The specific topic concerns the early Christians' self-definition and self-representation in the context of pagan–Christian conflict reflected in literatures from the mid-second to the early third century (*c.*150–225 CE), namely, the Apologies, *Apocryphal Acts of the Apostles*, and pre-Decian Martyr Acts. Christianity in this period grew in multi-faceted forms on the one hand and developed core doctrine and practice on the other. As it made a visible inroad into Greco-Roman society, Christianity faced both the external threat of pagan hostility and sporadic persecutions as well as the internal threat of competing doctrines and radical movements that contended for universal acceptance, and yet jeopardized its unity and survival.

With the exception of gnostic writings (Nag Hammadi) and the anti-gnostic works of Irenaeus, these particular bodies of literature as a whole represent the emerging Christian literary culture of the time and thus provide a distinct picture of the Christian self-identities under formative construction. Modern scholarship has almost exclusively concentrated on each "genre" of those writings and rightly on the individual works within each genre on their own terms. The value of a scholarly focus on each corpus of the Christian Apologies, Apocryphal Acts, and Martyr Acts, and on works such as Justin Martyr's *Dialogue with Trypho*, *Acts of Paul*, and the *Martyrdom of Polycarp* is beyond doubt.

However, taken as a whole, there has been an uneven disparity in the treatment of these literary corpora. Overall, Patristic scholars have long favored the Apologies over the other two for their "historical and theological values" and emphasized their theological

1

contribution to early Christianity in systematic and philosophical discourses. Early church historians largely neglected the Apocryphal Acts because of the latter's apparent fictional character and the resulting suspicion of their historical reliability. The Apocryphal Acts received rather greater attention from New Testament scholars as part of the New Testament Apocrypha. The Patristic treatment of the Martyr Acts also concentrated more or less either on the historicity of the documents as the "proofs" of Christian persecutions and martyrdom or on the construction of the theology of martyrdom.

My basic premise in this study is to treat all three corpora as both "historical" and literary works. I do not approach the Apologies as purely "historical" pieces; neither do I treat the Apocryphal Acts and Martyr Acts as purely "literary" pieces. The purpose of this work is to reduce the "historical" gaps among these literatures and present them as "equally" (historically and socially) significant in constructing the complex Christian self-definitions and ideals in the second and third centuries that were decisive for subsequent Christian history. In this way, I will attempt modestly to fill in the scholarly gap in an analytical and comprehensive comparative study.

The extant Greek apologetic works for this study include Justin Martyr's *First Apology*, *Second Apology*, and *Dialogue with Trypho* (c.155–60 CE), *Oration to the Greeks* by Tatian of Syria (c.155–77 CE), *Plea for the Christians* (*Legatio pro Christianis*) by Athenagoras of Athens (c.176–7 CE), *To Autolycus* (*Ad Autolycum*) by Theophilus of Antioch (c.180–5 CE), and *Exhortation to the Greeks* (*Protrepticus*) and *Miscellanies* (*Stromata*) by Clement of Alexandria (c.192–210 CE).[1] In addition, some fragments from the Apologies of Melito of Sardis (c.176–7 CE)[2] and Apollinaris of Hierapolis (c.176 CE?)[3] have been preserved by Eusebius. Major Latin Apologies include Tertullian's *Apology* (c.197 CE) and *Octavius* by Minucius Felix (c.200 CE?) of North Africa.

The Apocryphal Acts consist of the five oldest, major Acts, each one named after an individual apostle – *Acts of John*, *Acts of Paul*, *Acts of Peter*, *Acts of Andrew*, and *Acts of Thomas*. The texts of the first four *Acts* are incomplete and were reconstructed from various fragments and later adaptations of parts of the original Greek texts; only the *Acts of Thomas* survives in complete text in Greek, although it was probably originally written in Syriac. All written from the mid-second to the early third century (c.150–220 CE) by anonymous authors, the order of the list may indicate the chronological sequence of the works, which show definite intertextual relationships in literary dependence, thematic motifs, and possible common traditions.[4] In terms of their provenance, only the *Acts of Paul* has more or less secure evidence in Asia Minor through Tertullian's testimony (*c*.200 CE).[5] However, it is generally accepted that the *Acts of Thomas* came from the region near Edessa, where a rich bilingual culture thrived as a center of commerce and of East Syrian Christianity. The *Acts of John* may have come from Syria, too, or Alexandria, which is supposed to be a probable place for the *Acts of Andrew* as well; for the *Acts of Peter*, Asia Minor is a likely place of origin.[6]

The literary presentations of martyrdom did not appear until the middle of the second century[7] despite the fact that, following Jesus of Nazareth, Christians had died for their faith from the inception of Christianity (e.g. Stephen, James, Antipas, those who were executed by Pliny, and Ignatius of Antioch). The Martyr Acts in this work consist of the extant pre-Decian Martyr Acts which chronologically fit the era of our study (*c*.150–220 CE). Herbert Musurillo considers nine accounts as the most historically reliable, important, and instructive:[8] *Martyrdom of Polycarp*; *Martyrdom of Carpus, Papylus, and Agathonicê*; *Martyrdom of Ptolemaeus and Lucius*; *Acts of Justin and Companions*; *Martyrs of Lyons and Vienne*; *Martyrdom of Apollonius*; *Martyrdom of Potamiaena and Basilides*; and the Latin works from North Africa, *Acts of the Scillitan Martyrs* and *Martyrdom of Perpetua and Felicitas*. Among these nine, Eusebius preserved in his own collection of martyrs the accounts of Polycarp,[9] Carpus, Papylus and Agathonicê,[10] Potamiaena and Basilides,[11] Apollonius (in a considerably different form),[12] and the *Letter of the Church of Lyons and Vienne* (Eusebius is the only source for this Martyr Act),[13] as well as the quoted accounts of Ptolemaeus from Justin's *Second Apology*.[14]

Scholars have recognized that each genre contains discernible themes and concerns that classify them as a general unit. The Apologies as a whole not only defended "orthodox" Christianity against pagan charges, but also expounded Christian doctrine and practice in a way that could appeal to their pagan adversaries on philosophical grounds. While refuting the popular accusations of atheism, immorality, and disloyalty of Christians, they presented Christianity as the genuine heir of Greco-Roman civilization and ideals.[15]

Each of the Apocryphal Acts shares a similar plot line and exhibits intertextual evidences which warrant the basic unity, reporting the travels, miracles, preaching, persecutions, and martyrdom (death in

3

the case of John) of a particular apostle; the apostles' central message is sexual continence which becomes the grounds for persecution. The narrative form and structure betray their affinity with the ancient novel in general, including the Greek ideal romances, with a focus on historical figures, biographical character, the travel motif, adventures and trials, miracles and the marvelous, and the chastity theme.[16]

The Martyr Acts, which come in two literary forms of the *passiones* or *martyria* and the *acta* or *gesta*, are bound by the theme and emerging theology of martyrdom and the heroism of martyrs. The martyrdom/passions are accounts of the last days and the death of the martyr(s), and the acts of the martyrs recount their trials before the political authorities, purporting to be the records of the court proceedings.[17]

There are synchronic relations among these literary bodies in that all of them uniquely emerged and flourished within the contemporaneous period of the mid-second and early third centuries. Moreover, these remarkable texts share to some extent their geographical origins, coming from the Greek East – Greece, Asia Minor, Egypt, and Syria – and Latin North Africa. Nevertheless, despite their similar provenance and time frame, and despite their shared Christian assumptions and social-historical and philosophical milieu of the time, they present radically different, if not contradictory, Christian self-portraits to the surrounding hostile world. The Apologies essentially sought to present Christianity in harmony with Greco-Roman civilization and were endorsed by the later orthodox tradition; the Apocryphal Acts represented Christianity as the antithesis of the established Greco-Roman society and were rejected by the orthodox church; the Martyr Acts, inherently counter-cultural by genre, also portrayed Christianity in resistance to the established authorities of the Empire but were warmly embraced by the orthodox tradition. Hence, they form a triangular relation in their approach to the dominant culture and their reception by the Great Church.

Here, one may recall Richard Niebuhr's typology of Christ and culture. In his influential *Christ and Culture* (1951), Niebuhr presented five types of Christian ethics in relation to culture – Christ against culture, Christ of culture, Christ above culture, Christ and culture in paradox, and Christ the transformer of culture. The first three types in particular are pertinent to this study and thus call for a brief explanation. First, the "Christ against culture" type is defined as the "New Law" type.[18] Seeing themselves as a new people with a new law, Christians in this type perceive holiness as the heart of their ethics and emphasize the fundamental opposition between Christ and culture. At the other end of the spectrum is the "Christ of culture" type, defined as the "Natural Law" or the "Accommodationist" type.[19] Seeing themselves as a part of the social and cultural heritage that must be transmitted and preserved, these Christians recognize the fundamental agreement and harmony between Christ and culture. The third type, "Christ above culture,"[20] rejects those extremes and affirms both Christ and culture by recognizing a gap between them, and yet synthesizing loyalty to Christ and appreciation of culture..

In light of these typologies, it becomes evident, at least on the surface, that the Apologies represent the "Christ of culture" and "Christ above culture" type and that the Apocryphal Acts and Martyr Acts to some extent represent the "Christ against culture" type. What Niebuhr's study lacks, however, is a more dynamic definition and clear reference points of "culture" in that historical and literary context; and there needs to be an understanding of the selective nature of rejection and/or affirmation of "culture," as Niebuhr's critics have pointed out.[21] Furthermore, each type allows room for exceptions and is not an exclusive category. This study will present early Christians' triangular relations to culture in specific categories reflected in those literatures, modifying Niebuhr's typology; it will involve not only historical and theological study, but also sociological, literary, and rhetorical analyses of the primary texts.

Other methodological issues involve unity and diversity in each type of literature, fiction and history, and points of reference. First, in dealing with the given topic, this research is based on the widely recognized unity in each body of literature rather than the individual distinctiveness or diversity within each genre, as briefly discussed above. Where necessary, this study will certainly give proper attention to the unique theological arguments, styles, and emphases of the individual Apologists (e.g. Justin's Logos Christology, Tatian's encratism, and Tertullian's use of history). When needed, it will point out the distinctive portrayal of each apostle in terms of miracles, struggles against pagan authorities, soteriology, martyrdom (or death), and varying degrees of gnostic and current philosophical elements in each of the Apocryphal Acts. Finally, this study will recognize the different experiences of the male martyrs and the female martyrs depicted in the Martyr Acts. Nonetheless, this work is justifiably concerned with the overarching unity and uniqueness of each genre of literature as a whole in its Christian self-definitions against the dominant pagan society.

The issue of genre will be treated more extensively in Chapter 1, but a brief comment is necessary here. Genre is of critical importance for all three bodies of literature in determining their literary purpose and audience, but it is especially so for the Apocryphal Acts in relation to their historical reliability. It is generally accepted that the Apocryphal Acts most closely resemble the Hellenistic (Greco-Roman) novel, and scholars sometimes categorize them as the "Christian fiction."[22] However, their fictional character does not necessarily preclude the fact that what those Acts represent is true; their genre does not undermine their representation of truth. Glen Bowersock, in his *Fiction as History: Nero to Julian* (1994), has shown that in the Hellenistic literature the "fictional" truth was as true as the "historical" truth and that fiction should be seen not only within the context of history but as a part of the continuum of history itself. In this regard, the Apocryphal Acts present the reality and truth of *their* Christianity in a novelistic genre and faithfully reflect the current theological milieu through the central figure of the apostle as the bearer of a particular tradition of Christianity. Their social setting provides a "historical" and realistic outlook on contemporary Greco-Roman society, Christianity, and the conflict between them.

This "truth" or "factual" claim of a fictional genre can be extended to the Martyr Acts. H. Musurillo chose the twenty-eight Martyr Acts as the ones "most [historically] reliable."[23] While he acknowledges the "thin line" between history and fiction and the redactional process in some of the Martyr Acts,[24] these Acts reflect the historical testimony and faithfulness in Christian conflicts with pagan authorities.

This study will proceed in Chapter 1 with a historical overview of the Christian interaction with Greco-Roman society, including the growth of Christianity and the contemporary pagan polemics and persecutions against Christians, which provide the context of those aforementioned literatures. In this context, each of the three bodies of literature will be reintroduced with regard to its literary genre, aim, function, audience, and relation to other genres of Greco-Roman literature. This historical and cultural overview will also present the history of critical scholarship and outline the triangular relation at the end of the chapter.

This work posits the three modes of Christian self-portraits which the Apologies, Apocryphal Acts, and Martyr Acts constructed and within which they diverged: the superiority of belief in and worship of the Christian God; the superiority of Christian sexual morality; and Christian loyalty to the Empire. Each category of these self-portraits is a response to the corresponding pagan charges against Christians – religious (atheism), moral/social (immorality and social deviancy), and political (disloyalty and treason) – and will be treated in Chapters 2, 3, and 4, respectively.

In Chapter 2, I will discuss the presentation of Christian monotheism, which sets up the clearest boundary against Greco-Roman polytheism. The worship of the one transcendent God who created and rules the universe and of his Son demarcates the true worshippers from the false worshippers. Yet this boundary is permeable by one's conversion.[25] These three bodies of literature, each in their own way, present Christian monotheism as something superior and true. By leaving what is inferior and false and joining what is true and superior, one can receive exclusive and yet universal salvation and fulfill the ideal of Christian monotheism.

In Chapter 3, I turn to the moral/social representation, in which Christian asceticism, particularly with regard to sex, defines Christian practice and moral behaviors in relation to Greco-Roman sexual morality. While claiming Christian innovations in sexual morality and ethics, these literary bodies build Christian sexual ethics (i.e. virginity and chaste marriage) upon the foundations of Greco-Roman moral philosophy and the conservative social ethos on the one hand and against established social norm and mores on the other.

Lastly, Chapter 4 will present the political self-portraits, where the distinction of religious and political loyalty becomes crucially significant for all three literary corpora. They recognize the superiority of the heavenly kingdom of God to the earthly kingdom (i.e. Roman Empire); however, they differ from one another in Christians' allegiance toward the earthly kingdom. Their contrasting political attitudes set the lasting agenda and impact on the issue of the "unity of Church and State" and the Christian innovation of the "separation of Church and State."

The Christian ideals that all of them present and define are unabashedly universal in claim and scope, but it is the very universal ideals that disclose a deliberate selectivity in drawing the boundaries. As Judith Lieu reminds us, "boundaries involve selection out of both similarity and difference, and promote interchange as well as distancing."[26] A selective and interactive construction and consciousness permeate each body of literature.

While "united" in facing the outside world and sharing the "Christian" solidarity and cause, each version of Christian self-identity differs and even opposes one another as to the degree to which Christianity (as God's ultimate revelation to humanity) should adopt or reject the dominant culture of which they were a part. This Christian idealism, universalism, and selectivity poses an obvious tension, embracing both inclusive and exclusive claims.

Finally, this study recognizes the propagandist and apologetic nature of all of these bodies of literature, which were prompted by the need to define and defend their own understanding of Christianity in the given harsh historical and culture reality, and thus the partial character and limited scope of their presentations. However, because of the latter characteristic, their points of comparison and contrast become even more remarkable and significant with theological, social, and political implications. While these literary corpora may simply witness to the diverse representations of faith within the second- and third-century Christian milieu, they mark a watershed in the direction of the Great Church as their triangular relations point to the growing competition and chasm between later orthodoxy and heterodoxy.

the interior and west coast even up to the Black Sea. In Greece, Athens, as well as Corinth under Bishop Dionysius, saw solid ecclesiastical development.[1] In Egypt the gnostic mission might have been more successful than "orthodox" Christianity.[2] However, in Alexandria, about the year 190 CE, Bishop Demetrius was leading an already sizable "orthodox" congregation, and the catechetical school, led first by Pantaenus and then Clement, attracted a substantial number of educated Greeks. In Syria, while promising mission work among the upper-class pagans continued in Antioch under Serapion, Christianity spread to Nisibis and Edessa, which became centers of Syriac Christianity, and then further to Persia.[3]

In the West, Christianity advanced further in Italy, Gaul, and North Africa. The greatest growth took place in Rome with the rise of the Roman See and hierarchical development, and with the flowering of divergent Christian teachings. The Church in Rome attracted prominent Christian teachers of every camp, especially from the East, including Cerdo, Marcion, and Valentinus on the one hand, and Polycarp, Justin, Tatian, and Hegesippus on the other. In Gaul a well-established Christian community in Lyons and Vienne is attested to in the famous account of martyrdom (177 CE)[4] and by the work of Bishop Irenaeus, who also reports churches in Germany and Iberia.[5] In North Africa, Carthage was a main center for Christianity where a substantial number of Christians was also evidenced by the extensive catechetical and literary work of Tertullian (c.200 CE); Christianity was also growing in Numidia and Tunisia, and, about 220 CE, Bishop Agrippinus could summon seventy bishops to a local synod.[6] In the West, North Africa was the only area in this period that could be compared with the mission and vitality of Asia Minor and Syria in the East.[7]

In terms of number, a recent study provided a rough framework estimating the number of Christians to be about 40,000 in 150 CE (0.07 percent) and about 760,000 in the Empire by 225 CE, 1.27 percent of the total population of the Empire.[8] Although insignificant in absolute numbers, this period marked the first leap of significant growth in Christianity, confirmed by its geographic spread in its literary and non-literary sources. Christian expansion was not limited to geography and numbers, however; Christians advanced socially as well. As already hinted, some major missionary activities were directed to the members of the upper class during this time, especially in Alexandria, Syria, and North Africa; and converts to Christianity came from various social strata. Despite pagan critic Celsus' scorn that Christianity attracted only the

10

uneducated, slaves, outcasts, and women,[9] the Christian social make-up resembled in fact the typical social pyramid of the Roman Empire (majority in the lower class), with a significant minority from elite and sub-elite groups. Particularly prominent were the conversions of upper-class women[10] and Christians' remarkable orientation to literary texts and activities, which indicated some fair number of Christians from the top 10 percent of Roman society.[11]

Christianity at this time grew in all its diverse forms and expressions on the one hand, and witnessed the emergence of a missionary "orthodoxy" with its hierarchy, sacred Scripture, liturgy, and discipline throughout the whole Mediterranean basin on the other.[12] The issue of diversity and unity in the Church was marked by its important internal movements and controversies that outlined its boundaries and identity as "a positive starting point" in terms of its major doctrinal and structural developments in this and later periods. Regarding the regional diversity, without strictly defined boundaries between the orthodox and unorthodox, the Asiatic churches, the Syrian churches, the Egyptian churches, the Roman churches, and the North African churches each had their own traditions. "Orthodoxy" at this time was to be considered more as "what is acceptable in churches which satisfy the criteria of a true church" rather than "doctrinal norms and standardized institutional structure" as opposed to heresy, which was the development from the mid-third century on.[13] However, three major groups deeply affected the nascent Church and threatened its unity and "orthodoxy," producing an "internal identity crisis": Marcionism and Valentinian gnosticism flourished in Rome and Alexandria, pressing the emerging doctrinal tradition; and the New Prophecy (Montanism) flourished in Asia, threatening the emerging ecclesiastical structure. The unifying factors that formed a pattern of emerging "orthodoxy" were first of all the emerging "New Testament canon" as the four Gospels and the letters of Paul gained authoritative stature and built a common bond among Christians of different theological stripes across large geographic and cultural rifts.[14] This emerging canon safeguarded not only unity but also a range of acceptable diversity centering on the identity of Jesus the human and the exalted Christ.[15] Then, the development of the Rule of Faith, which summarized central Christian beliefs, provided the common themes of missionary preaching based on the tradition by the apostolic succession. Finally, the growing institutional structure of the Church, centered on the bishops with the development of a common liturgy, e.g. baptism and the Lord's Supper, reinforced the sense of unity, order, and identity especially against the deviant "heretics." During this "age of bishops," the Church experienced considerable growth in organization, property, and authority and anticipated the accelerated growth in the rest of the third century.

Christian interaction with Greco-Roman society

Externally, Christian self-definition and identity was inevitably molded from Christians' interactions with the dominant Greco-Roman society. Christian self-definition in relation to Judaism is outside the scope of this study. It will be treated indirectly when relevant to the topic of this study, since the main focus deals with the formation of Christian identity and self-representation in relation to the Greco-Roman "pagan" culture in the Roman Empire. In response to the rapid growth of Christianity, the majority of pagans who came into contact with the movement reacted with fear, contempt, and hostility. The "new" religion with universal claims appeared superstitious, irrational, and dangerous to the good and peace of the Empire. Public prejudices at times resulted in local violence against Christians, and learned aristocrats began to take them seriously enough to launch major intellectual attacks on them and their doctrines. The pagan perception of and periodic opposition to Christians formed "a negative starting point," which provided the situation to which the latter reacted and formed the categories in which they shaped their own self-understanding.[16]

In the early second century, as evidenced in the famous letter of Pliny to Trajan, Christians were denounced as Christians and punished by their confession of the *nomen christianorum* in association with alleged crimes accompanied by the Name. In the course of his investigation, Pliny ordered a "sacrifice-test" for a proof of their innocence; only those who recanted, conformed to the worship of the gods and the emperor, and cursed Christ were pardoned. Although he found no specific crime of Christians, he declared Christianity a "depraved and excessive superstition" (*superstitio prava, immodica*).[17] Describing the fire in Rome under Nero, Pliny's contemporary Tacitus attached to Christians the charge of "hatred of the human race" (*odio humani generis*) and the stigma of a "pernicious superstition" (*superstitio exitiabilis*).[18] Suetonius, also writing about Nero, regarded Christians as "a class of men given to a new and mischievous superstition" (*genus hominum superstitionis novae ac maleficae*).[19] These three distinguished men of the senatorial rank perceived Christianity as a "superstition" in association with

12

Christians' guilt and punishment.[20] These earliest examples reveal that, while the Name itself was punishable, anti-social stigma and crime (*flagitia*) had been already connected with the Name as well.

Superstition, a term in general usage that designated the so-called irrational and fanatical religious groups or practices alien to Rome, rendered itself contrary to the high religious and ethical ideals of Rome. It meant in essence irreligion and impiety, leading to a denial of the gods, i.e. atheism, as opposed to true piety, whose fruit was "to worship God according to the tradition of one's fathers."[21] Superstition was a contagious disease of the mind (*morbus mentis*) and a perversion of true religion; thus it posed a danger to society and a threat to piety, the greatest human virtue, which lay at the foundation of the Roman way of life (*Romanitas*).[22] In this context, superstition and piety were defined with respect to the specific acts of public devotion to the traditional gods of Greco-Roman society, and they brought about opposite consequences in the way the Romans lived – the former brought insanity, immorality, and egoism; the latter brought reason, virtue, and love of community and fatherland (*patria*).

In the Greco-Roman world, where there was a fundamental unity in religion, society, and politics, the established idea of *pax deorum* provided its ideological basis.[23] *Pax deorum*, a sacred contractual relationship between gods and people, preserved the essential unity between religion and politics and governed the basic rules of life in the Empire: the order, success, and prosperity of the Empire would be maintained so long as the worship of the Roman gods continued by means of appropriate cults. *Pax deorum* was the bedrock and goal of *Romanitas*, and this *Romanitas* stood in continuity with the past and stood for the past, i.e. its ancestral tradition (*mos maiorum*). *Mos maiorum* was "the bond and foundation of society, a common fund of wisdom amassed in the course of centuries" that controlled the way the Greeks and Romans thought.[24] The ancient customs, especially in religion, guaranteed the personal, familial, and political security and protection and functioned as the firm stronghold in the midst of and against the infiltration of the countless new and dubious religious and social practices. Thus, the truth of religion was measured by its antiquity and usefulness (*utilitas*) for the existing social order of the Empire; piety embraced both the sense of loyalty to the traditional customs of Rome and public devotion to the gods in traditional cultic acts.[25] Then, while true religion, whose fruit was piety, respected and worked in harmony with *mos maiorum*, superstition (a false religion), whose outcome was atheism with regard to the traditional divinities, inevitably disturbed and deviated from the *mos maiorum*.

Given this cultural mold, it is not surprising that the Christians in the second and early third centuries attracted intense hostility and criticism from their pagan neighbors. All the vices of super-stition were ascribed to Christianity with its ominous Name. In the mid-second century, as the church expanded its mission into urban culture, Christians' neglect of the traditional gods became increas-ingly noticeable and was frequently blamed for local disasters. A disputed rescript of Antoninus to the Council of Asia indicates the Christians having been denounced as "atheists" and a cause of evil in the society and mentions the provincials' anger against them following the severe earthquake in Asian provinces (*c*.152 CE).[26] In the reign of Marcus Aurelius (*c*.165 CE), the great plague, which eventually devastated the entire eastern and central parts of the Empire, was followed by local persecutions of the Christians. Tertullian's sarcastic sneer, though not without exaggeration, still reflected the pungent reality at the end of the century:

> If the Tiber rises to the city walls, if the Nile does not cover the flood-plains, if the heavens don't move or if the earth does, if there is a famine or a plague, the roar is at once: "The Christians to the lion!" Really! All of them to one lion?[27]

This charge of atheism (Christians' denial of the traditional gods), which had been a familiar accusation against the Jews in the East, was now turned against Christians and lay at the core of enmity toward them.[28] It generated intense anxiety and fear of gods' wrath among the pagans and identified Christians as a direct enemy of the *pax deorum* and *mos maiorum* with full social and politi-cal implications; enemies of the gods were the enemies of the people and of the Empire. Hence, Justin in his Apologies (*c*.150–5 CE) singled out "atheism" as the most serious anti-Christian slander.[29] In Philadelphia (*c*.155–60 CE), a group of eleven Christians were brutally tortured and sent down to Smyrna to be thrown to the beasts at the Provincial Games, and this led to the popular demand for the arrest and martyrdom of Polycarp, bishop of Smyrna.[30] Polycarp's confession of his Christian identity aroused such "uncon-trollable wrath" from Jews and pagans that they condemned him as "the destroyer of our gods, who teaches many neither to offer sacrifice nor to worship."[31] The same charge was repeated in Lucian's

Alexander the False Prophet, when Alexander, a quack, labeled as atheists the Christians and Epicureans who were his adversaries (38; cf. 25). In Carthage, as late as the turn of the century, Christians were marked down as "law-breakers" of ancestral tradition because of their failure to worship the gods.[32] This accusation was the strongest obstacle that the Apologists had to confront, refute, and overcome in order to establish Christian monotheism in harmony with the polytheistic Greco-Roman society (see the next chapter).

Other charges soon accompanied the essentially religious charge of atheism. The accusations of Cornelius Fronto, Marcus Aurelius' tutor, preserved by Minucius Felix, were undoubtedly scandalous: worship of a donkey's head, ritual murder of an infant, cannibalism, and incestuous and promiscuous unions on feast days.[33] Practice of black magic, a prominent feature of superstition, constituted another serious social charge; to the pagan eyes, certain Christian rituals and practices such as exorcism and praying "in the name of Jesus," speaking in tongues, and the sign of the cross could have been hardly distinguishable from magical rites.[34] Furthermore, Christian secret assembly, non-participation in the imperial cult, and radical apocalypticism created public suspicion of the subversiveness of Christianity as a political threat to the Empire. These moral and political charges against Christians were particularly prominent during this period and were taken seriously by both pagans and Christians.

In the late second century, a number of pagan intellectuals and aristocratic elites took notice of Christians and began to criticize the "new faith" from their conservative philosophical standpoint.[35] To the eyes of the Greek satirist Lucian, Christians appeared as some kind of Jewish mystery sect[36] and as gullible simpletons who were easily fooled by charlatans (γοής), such as Peregrinus, who dramatically cremated himself at Olympia in 165 CE. Prior to becoming a Cynic, Peregrinus learned the "marvelous wisdom of the Christians" in Palestine and became their prophet (προφήτης), synagogue leader (ξυναγωγεύς), and biblical interpreter (ἐξηγητής). When he was thrown into prison, Christians called him "a new Socrates" and lavished their care on him in such a way that he amassed great wealth from those "poor wretches." Christians' guilt lay at their "once for all" denial of the Greek gods (atheism), worshiping their "first lawgiver," "the crucified sophist," and accepting his doctrines "by faith alone"; thus they allegedly despised all things, including death, and believed in immortality. What is noticeable in this description is Lucian's (sarcastic) characterization

15

of Christians in philosophical terms such as "wisdom," "new Socrates," and "sophist," and recognition of their moral convictions, though they were too credulous and insignificant to deserve any serious attention more than as naive fanatics.[37]

In his four brief references to Christians, Galen, Marcus Aurelius' court physician, significantly classified "the followers of Moses and Christ" as a "school" of philosophy and accorded them moral virtues of philosophers in their contempt of death and self-control and discipline in food, drink, and sex.[38] To him, however, Christian "philosophy" was subject to dogmatism and fideism, drawing its faith not from "any demonstrable argument" but from "parables"; and Christians' ethical standards without rational basis basically made them "philosophers without philosophy," a biting criticism measured by a Greco-Roman intellectual standard. The criticism of simple fideism echoes Lucian's jibe that Christians receive their doctrines "without any definite evidence," and Marcus Aurelius' contrast of the "reasoned and dignified decision" of Stoics with the "obstinate opposition" and theatricality of Christians in their attitude toward death.[39] Marcus Aurelius, a Stoic philosopher-emperor and a devout traditionalist, was hostile toward any religious innovation and all social deviants.[40] To the minds of these educated pagans, Christians appeared, though no longer as heinous criminals or cannibals and now even as inferior "philosophers," still as misguided fanatics of irrationality; they provoked their own doom, deviated from the social norm, and publicly despised the very gods to whom the Empire owed its security.

The first systematic literary indictment of Christianity came from a Platonist named Celsus. His work *True Doctrine* (ἀληθὴς λόγος) was written in the period 177–80 CE, when the Christian apologetic activity was at its peak, possibly as an intelligent pagan retort to the Apologies of Justin earlier.[41] Although Celsus' original work is lost, about 70 percent of it is recovered in Origen's *Contra Celsum* (*Against Celsus*) written about seventy years later.[42] In his formidable attack on Christianity, he attempted to undermine the Christian doctrines and stance against the Greco-Roman philosophy and values on the one hand, and to demonstrate the superiority of the traditional polytheism and the Greek *paideia* upon which the whole Greco-Roman culture was founded on the other.[43]

Celsus' philosophical and theological criticisms of Christian doctrines were fundamentally based on the Platonic notion of divine transcendence and immutability; they targeted the Christian claim of exclusive monotheism, especially in relation to the doctrines of incarnation and resurrection and worship of Jesus. His rational monotheism combined a belief in the Supreme God, incorporeal and impassible, with an affirmation of traditional gods as the intermediaries, including the Demiurge, who created the physical world (henotheism). He rejected the biblical account of creation of the world and humankind and regarded the anthropomorphic portrait of God in the books of Moses (Old Testament) as utterly blasphemous (e.g. 4.50; 6.49–63). The Supreme God cannot be in touch with the physical world, and God's nature is not such that he can undergo change or alteration from perfection to corruption (4.14). In this sense, the idea of incarnation – God or Son of God descending into earth in a mortal body – is not only irrational but also unnecessary. Faith in bodily resurrection as opposed to immortality of soul is equally detestable and theologically impossible; it is a misunderstanding of reincarnation (7.32), and God cannot do what is contrary to nature.

Celsus held that Jesus, whom Christians worship as the Son of God Incarnate, was in fact a wicked sorcerer who had learned magic in Egypt by which he performed miracles no more extraordinary than those of Egyptian sorcerers (1.6, 68, 71; 2.32). He was born as a mere man and died shamefully on the cross as a mere man; virgin birth and resurrection stories were fabricated myth (1.28; 2.58). Jesus in his words or deeds was not unique at all; many Greek gods and heroes performed superior miracles and deserve greater honor than Jesus (1.67; 3.3). Therefore, ascribing divinity to Jesus was unacceptable and even inconsistent to Christians' claim of One God. These doctrines not only revealed Christians' deficiency of reason but also exposed their faint distortion and falsification of the classical Greek tradition and philosophy; Christian teachings were a pale corruption of the ἀληθὴς λόγος handed down from antiquity.

Celsus' social and political criticisms focused on the danger that the Christians posed as a group to the traditional Greco-Roman values and culture. From the outset, he declared Christians the open enemy of the Greco-Roman society – a secret, illegal, and revolutionary sect, bound by oaths, with intent to subvert the established order (1.1). Having no tradition of their own, they apostatized from Judaism with its worst features, namely, radical monotheism and sectarian exclusivism, and sacrilegiously abandoned the ancestral custom (*mos maiorum*) and worship of the gods of the society. As like attracts like, their appeal to the social outcasts and abominable sinners disclosed their own moral bankruptcy

(3.50–9, 64, 76); they drove away the intelligent and attracted only the uneducated and wretched women with simple fideism (1.27; 3.18); they destroyed the families and disrupted social structure by pitting children against their parents (3.55). They also practiced magic and rebelled against the Empire by refusing to honor God and his daemons and by worshiping a dead man (7.68). Finally, Celsus called Christians to obey the emperor, to return to the ancestral customs, and to participate in the civic life and show public responsibility in support of and for the common good of the society (8.63–75).

Celsus' attack on Christians was not merely based on popular rumors but based on logical reasoning and careful study of their Scripture and doctrines. His rejection of Christianity was rooted in his religious conviction, social outlook, and intellectual tradition that were intricately united in paganism.[44] It was this unity that the contemporary educated circle shared and upheld, and it was this unity that Christians seriously threatened – it was felt that they indeed deserved due punishment for their evil.

Under the reign of Marcus Aurelius (161–80 CE), all these accusations and polemics found a vent in local persecutions and pogroms, especially in connection with the eruption of the recurring misfortunes of the constant wars and natural disasters in the Eastern provinces. "At this time," wrote Eusebius, "there were the greatest persecutions excited in Asia."[45] According to Athenagoras, in Athens, Christians were being hunted, plundered, and robbed unjustly,[46] and Eusebius reports the martyrdoms of three bishops in the 160s in Athens, Laodicea, and Phyrigia.[47] In Rome, after a trial by a city prefect, Urbicus, the Apologist Justin was put to death with other Christians (163–7 CE).[48]

The most vivid account of the local persecution under Marcus Aurelius came from Lyons and Vienne in Gaul.[49] A substantially sized Christian community there had consisted of merchants from Asia and Phrygia and included a broad social spectrum from Roman upper-class citizens to slaves. In the summer of 177 CE, during the festival of the imperial cult, sudden mob rage unleashed itself on the Christians who were supposed to be guilty of atheism, incest, and cannibalism. After suffering from robbery, imprisonment, torture, stoning, and a series of social sanctions, the Christians were driven by the mob to the governor's tribunal. They were suspected of treason, and their alleged crimes were confirmed by the false confessions of their slaves under torture. Then, the governor, by the emperor's directive, followed the precedent set by Trajan: the apostates were to be freed but those who persisted were to be condemned to death by beasts or beheading. The account singles out the heroism of a slave girl, Blandina, and a youth, Ponticus, who were the last to die in the amphitheater, and reports some forty-eight martyrs, including those who perished in prison. Even after death, their bodies remained exposed and were burned and scattered in the Rhône River with scorn for the Christian doctrine of resurrection.

Behind this pagan hostility and violence against Christians, especially in Asia, there might have been in fact another force. Eschatological hopes and apocalypticism have always been part of Christianity, particularly in Asia. However, with the speedy advance of the New Prophecy[50] and a series of misfortunes and crises experienced during Marcus Aurelius' reign, prophetic and eschatological faith kindled the latent forces in Christianity at this period.[51] The revelations and prophecies of this movement focused on the imminent return of Christ with the signs of the universal "wars and political convulsions."[52] This eschatological attitude exalted the glory of martyrdom and demanded strict rigorism in ordinary Christian life, most notably renunciation of marriage and regulated fastings. Although the importance of fasting and readiness for martyrdom, as well as exhortation to high moral standards in marriage, had always been standard themes of Christian preaching, the New Prophecy stretched its limit and formed a movement of protest against "compromise with the world and the continued institutionalization of the Church";[53] at the same time, it was a "fierce reaction against a decade of sporadic repression and persecution."[54] Its anti-Roman stance and radical proposal to do away with Hellenistic culture on which the Empire stood, could easily elicit more serious suspicion and severe attack from the populace with greater intensity. With its rapid spread to the other parts of the Empire, particularly Rome and North Africa, the New Prophecy became a "threat" to the peace of the Church and of the Empire.

After a time of relative peace under Commodus (180–93 CE), between 195 and 212 CE there were sporadic persecutions of various intensities in several parts of the Empire.[55] In 203 CE Septimus Severus issued a general edict prohibiting conversion to Judaism or Christianity. Although this edict had rather a short duration, its impact was considerably felt among the upper-class converts, and it provided a precedent for future official actions.

The existing reports of persecution came from four of the main cities of the Empire: Alexandria, Carthage, Rome, and Corinth.[56] In Alexandria, Clement, who fled from the city, reported "roastings, impalings and beheadings" of Christians;[57] victims included Origen's father Leonides and a number of students of the catechetical school, which Clement had been leading.[58] In Carthage, Tertullian reported tortures, rackings, burnings, and condemnations of Christians.[59] The famous martyrdom of noblewoman, Perpetua, and a slave, Felicitas, together with four other catechumens, took place in the amphitheater in March 203.[60] The account of their martyrdom clearly depicted the total disruption of family life and tradition that a conversion to Christianity could bring about as well as the vehement hostility the crowd displayed toward Christians. In Rome, Hippolytus described brutality of angry mobs turning on the Christians and recounted a case of a noble Christian woman in Corinth who was accused of blasphemy against the emperors and gods and was condemned to a brothel and later to death.[61] This precarious state of Christianity under the threat of popular accusations and subsequent condemnation by the authorities (however limited and sporadic it had been), along with Christians' perceptions of persecutions, defined and redefined their mode of self-representation and attitude toward the dominant Greco-Roman society and culture.

Literature of the second century: the Apologies, Apocryphal Acts, and Martyr Acts

In this historical context, second-century Christianity witnessed a most unique literary phenomenon – the concurrent emergence of the Apologies, Apocryphal Acts, and Martyr Acts. If the first half of the second century saw rather faint Christian literary activity (measured by the extant collections – the *Apostolic Fathers*, some so-called Apocryphal Gospels, and some of the Nag Hammadi literature), by comparison, the second half witnessed a plethora of literature that appealed to and engaged with the Greco-Roman values and culture in an attempt to define and present the formative Christian "self." These three bodies of literature were the product of the prevailing Greco-Roman literary culture and were deeply rooted in that cultural soil. The general acceptance of classical and contemporary Greek culture by the Romans from the second century BCE had been conspicuous in the Roman literary tradition.[62] Educational curricula as well as literary and rhetorical theory and practice followed Greek models, and Latin literature was constructed through the Greek methods and in clear reference to the Greek literature. The substantial assimilation of this intellectual inheritance, though never completely achieved, provided a sufficient literary context for the Christians to express and propagate their beliefs in culturally intelligible terms. The writers of these literary corpora employed the current Greco-Roman literary genres, rhetorical techniques, and conceptual frameworks and endeavored to interpret the Christian message, lifestyle, and attitude in search of and in light of their new identity as a "third race" in the established society and culture.

Their synchronic relation and common context provide an opportunity and rationale for an analytical comparative study of these three bodies of literature. In what follows, basic issues of their literary genre, context, audience, and purpose in view of the history of scholarship will be treated. Instead of focusing on the individual works in each category and despite some specific diversities among those works, emphasis is placed on the recognized unity in each corpus and the similarity to and difference from one another as a general unit.

Apologies

Contemporary with and parallel to gnosticism and Marcionism, the Apologists represented a movement that was concerned with Christian identity in relation to the dominant Hellenistic culture, their predecessor and rival, Old Israel, and the Roman authorities in political and social realms. The growth of gnosticism, Jewish hostility, pagan charges, and periodic persecutions prompted them not only to defend the "orthodox" Christianity from pagan calumnies and thus obtain just treatment of Christians, but also to present this Christian position in such a way that could convince their adversaries on rational and philosophical grounds.[63] In defense of Christianity, they refuted the popular accusations of atheism, immorality, and disloyalty of Christians and turned the table on the pagan accusers by attacking their polytheism and immorality. Taking a positive approach, they set forth Christianity as the realization of the ideal Greco-Roman civilization. To this small group of educated Greek and Latin-speaking Christians, Greco-Roman culture was of serious concern. Their language, rhetoric, thought, and education were all deeply steeped in contemporary Hellenistic culture. In their writings, they explicitly and implicitly

21

exhibited a profound appreciation of and belief in that culture.[64] In their "open letters" addressed to the emperors or to the pagan intellectuals and authorities, they sought to establish the bridge between Christianity and Greco-Roman society through a medium of philosophy.

Justin addressed his *First Apology* to the Emperor Antoninus Pius, his two adopted sons, Marcus Aurelius and Lucius Verus, addressed as "philosophers," and the Roman senate, earnestly appealing for justice and fair treatment on behalf of Christians in response to the anti-Christian violence in Asia, possibly including the martyrdom of Polycarp.[65] His so-called *Second Apology* is now considered a part or "appendix" of the *First Apology* occasioned by the then-recent execution of several Christians in Rome by the urban prefect Urbicus. In the *Dialogue with Trypho*, which contains a two-day dialogue with a learned Jew Trypho, Justin extended his apologetic point especially on the Christian claim of Jewish Scripture and the fulfillment of prophecy in Christ.

Some twenty years later, remarkable apologetic activity was concentrated in the years 176–8 CE. Athenagoras, Melito, and Apollinaris all addressed their apologies to Marcus Aurelius, particularly stressing Christians' loyalty to the Emperor and the Empire. Robert Grant identified as the pivotal events the imperial crisis of the revolt of Avidius Cassius (which involved religious fanaticism and apocalyptic fever) and the imperial tour of the East in 175–6 that in turn spurred the Apologists to "prove" their suspected loyalty and innocence to the philosopher-Emperor.[66]

The date of Tatian's *Oratio ad Graecos*, a harsh diatribe against the Greco-Roman culture, ranges from the 150s to the late 170s CE. Tatian's reference to the Cynic Crescens' fatal plot against Justin and Tatian himself (19.1), assuming Justin is still alive, may indicate the early date (150–60 CE) prior to Justin's death.[67] However, Robert Grant argues for the later date (*c*.177 CE), linking Tatian's reference to philosophers' salary (19.1) with the backdrop of Marcus Aurelius' establishment of the chairs of philosophy and rhetoric in Athens in the fall of 176.[68] During the early years of Commodus (*c*.180 CE), Theophilus wrote three books to a certain high-ranking official named Autolycus while some residue of persecutions seemed still to be lingering on.

Some fifteen years later, Clement in Alexandria composed his *Protreptikos* for the educated Greeks and *Stromata*, a loose "patchwork" of Christian and Greco-Roman teachings, in the early third century. On the other side of Africa, when Septimus Severus took the imperial throne after a bloody civil war against Albinus (197 CE), Tertullian at Carthage addressed *Ad nationes* to the pagans in general and *Apology* to the Roman provincial governors, again with painstaking effort in denouncing the pagan allegations and stressing Christians' loyalty to the Emperor.[69] Finally, without any specific circumstance or addressee mentioned, Minucius Felix's *Octavius* presents a dialogue between the Christian Octavius, an advocate from overseas who had died prior to the composition of the work, and the educated pagan Caecilius from Cirta in Numidia, and the latter's conversion at the end.

As one might have noticed, the second-century "Apologies" were not uniform in literary types and addressees. This fact brings up the issue of the genre and purpose of the "apology." The terms "apology" and "apologetics," while commonly applied from Eusebius onward to those particular Christian works of this period that attempted to defend Christianity from pagan criticisms, need to be reconsidered with respect to their purpose in the context of the Greco-Roman rhetoric and literature. Greco-Roman rhetoric was basically divided into the three kinds – forensic (judicial), deliberative (persuasive), and epideictic (demonstrative) – and an apology had its origin as forensic speech in the court. However, the Apologists utilized various literary genres, traditions, rhetoric, and arguments for purposes beyond just legal defense. For one thing, they all knew that the Christian Name alone made one liable to death as ruled by Trajan and that therefore delivering legal apologies would face significant limitation since Christians had no legal standing to appeal unless they would apostatize; their aim in writing the "apologetic" works had to be more than a judicial defense in a narrow sense.[70]

Questioning the general assumption that those "apologies" were written as forensic speeches both in form and purpose can start from the self-references of the authors. Justin described his own work as a *prosphonesis*, "address,"[71] *enteuxis* or *biblidion*, "petition," and an exegesis, "explanation"; Athenagoras' "defense" (ἀπολογία) of Christian teaching was titled a *presbeia (legatio)*, "embassy," much like Philo's *Legatio ad Gaium* on behalf of Jews in Alexandria before the Emperor Caligula; Theophilus referred to his first book as a *homilia*, "instruction," and the second one as a *syngramma*, "treatise"; Clement explicitly titled his work *Protreptikos*, which was patterned after the classical protreptic genre as a missionary track of philosophy. Hence, modern scholars have recognized this inconsistency of categorizing and interpreting those "apologies" in a strict legal sense. Guided by the rhetorical manual of Menander,[72] they have attempted to identify some of their forms not in forensic sense but with deliberative or epideictic speeches as follows: Justin's *First Apology* as the *prosphonetikos logos*, "address of request"; Athenagoras' *Presbeia (Legatio)* as the *logos presbeutikos*, "ambassador's speech,"[73] or *libelli*, "apologetic petition";[74] and Tatian's *Oratio* as the *logos syntaktikos*, "farewell discourse."[75] Paul Keresztes identified Justin's Apologies as "deliberative speeches, in the fashion of advice and protreptic approach" and Tertullian's *Apology* as a epideictic discourse in a "display" of the special injustice of the Christian trials and pagan hostility for the future vindication of Christians and winning of the good will of the Roman authorities.[76]

In fact, what has been emerging in the discussion of contemporary scholarship is a broad consensus concerning the protreptic character of these "apologies" of second-century Christianity. Having classical philosophy and rhetoric as its primary setting, the λόγος προτρεπτικός is "a genre of literature that attempts to persuade students to pursue a proposed way-of-life."[77] In rhetorical setting, it refers to two sides of deliberative speech: *protreptikos*, "persuasion," and *apotreptikos*, "dissuasion"; in philosophical context, *protreptikos* is also paired with *elenchus*, "censure," of epideictic speech, and forms one method of both encouragement and rebuke to lead one to the truth.[78] The two basic parts of protreptic as a literary genre, according to Philo of Larissa, consist of the demonstration (*endeiktike*) of value and benefit of philosophy on the one hand and the refutation (*apelegktike*) of the views of those adversaries who attack, accuse, and misrepresent this philosophy on the other.[79] Thus, *logos protreptikos* makes use of all three forms of speech: deliberative, epideictic, and forensic;[80] in reality, typical "apologetic" features, such as the response to objections in refutation and defense of the particular truth claims are common to this genre. It is also important to note that the *logos protreptikos* contained an element of fluidity between oral and written discourses and was comprised of different written forms, such as discourses, letters, and dialogues.[81] Indeed, the influential extant (fragmentary) protreptics exhibit various forms: Plato's *Euthydemus*, the earliest surviving one, is a dialogue; Aristotle's *Protrepticus* is a discourse; and Seneca's *Ep. 90* is a letter.

Mark Jordan, from his own analysis of Plato's *Euthydemus* and Aristotle's *Protrepticus*, finds the tripartite structure of ancient protreptic;[82] David Aune further outlines three fundamental features of the genre: (1) a negative section focusing on the critique of rival sources of knowledge, ways of living, or schools of thought which reject philosophy; (2) a positive section in which the truth claims of philosophical knowledge, ways of living, and schools of thought are presented, praised, and defended; and (3), finally, an optional section, *protreptikos*, consisting of a personal appeal to the hearer inviting the immediate acceptance of the exhortation.[83] This structure corresponds to the goal of protreptic, which is to win converts to a particular philosophy by demonstrating its superiority and exposing the errors of all competing alternatives.[84] In light of these studies, the genre of protreptic is rightly understood not from the literary forms or even rhetorical styles per se but in light of the "rhetorical situation," the "hearer's moment of choice before ways-of-life."[85] Hence, protreptics should be understood as "just those works that aim to bring about the firm choice of a lived way to wisdom – however different the form of those works and their notions of wisdom might be."[86]

In the Hellenistic period, philosophical schools not only offered a coherent system of metaphysics but also provided moral and religious ideals and ways of life (*bios*), attracting followers and converts not unlike modern religious movements.[87] The philosophical conversion, which involved both cognitive and behavioral commitment in adopting the philosophical way of life, included several levels: the love of wisdom in general; the choice of a particular philosophical school over others; and the persistent discipline in advanced study.[88] The philosophers were seen as "exemplars" of those particular ways of life and practical wisdom and acted as "preachers" or "missionaries" of their respective schools; characteristically, various schools tried to attract adherents by making protreptic speeches in which they exposed the flaws of other philosophies and demonstrated and recommended their unique truth claims as the only way to happiness. In his satire, *Philosophies for Sale*, Lucian portrays the contemporary "hawking of philosophy" in rhetorical competition in the major cities of the Empire, which was a distinctive feature of Greek philosophical life by the second century.

Judaism and Christianity took on this long-standing philosophical and literary tradition as a contemporary activity;[89] both Jewish and Christian apologists fully adopted and appropriated this literary genre and practice to win their converts. At least three centuries prior to the birth of Christianity, Judaism presented itself and appeared to outsiders as a philosophy.[90] Despite persistent anti-Semitism in antiquity, a number of Greek intellectuals, including

Theophrastus (Aristotle's disciple), Megasthenes, and Clearchus of Soli, regarded Jews as "a race of philosophers"[91] and in the second century CE, physician Galen described Judaism as the philosophical "school of Moses." Aristobulus of Alexandria, a predecessor of Philo, proposed that Greek philosophers learned from Moses, an argument frequently taken up by the later Jewish and Christian apologists.[92]

Moreover, Hellenistic Judaism produced a number of protreptic works with apologetic themes: the Jewish *Sibylline Oracles*, the *Letter of Aristeas* in the second century BCE, and the *Wisdom of Solomon* in the first century BCE. More importantly, Josephus' *Against Apion* and *Jewish Antiquities* of the first century CE served as the representative literary propaganda and apologies for Judaism. Josephus not only presented the different Jewish sects as philosophical schools[93] and ancient Jewish notables such as Abraham and Moses as philosophers, but also portrayed his spiritual journey and choice of Pharisaism in the pattern of a typical Hellenistic account of philosophical conversion.[94] Furthermore, a considerable portion of Philo's works had this protreptic goal in mind: *Hypothetica* (or *Apology on behalf of Jews*), *Life of Moses*, the *Decalogue*, and the *Special Laws*. In these works, Philo interpreted the Septuagint (especially Pentateuch) and Jewish traditions in light of Middle Platonism and considered the Logos as an intermediary between God and the world. He presented the central activity of synagogues as the study of philosophy,[95] asserted Jewish monotheism in terms of a Middle Platonic notion with criticism of pagan idolatry, and justified the Decalogue as the supreme ethical standard. As Josephus and Philo defended Jews against the charges of misanthropy, superstition, and ethical inferiority resulting from questionable idiosyncratic customs (e.g. circumcision and observance of Sabbath), they put forth Judaism as respectable philosophy – ancient, civilized, and intellectually fulfilling – with hope of winning proselytes especially from the upper-class gentiles. This presentation of Judaism in the categories of Hellenistic philosophy served both protreptic and apologetic functions in a variety of literary forms.[96]

The Christian Apologists undoubtedly inherited the double tradition of Hellenism and (Hellenistic) Judaism and consciously turned them to their advantage in communicating their message and shaping a Christian identity. In the struggle against the popular pagan perception of Christianity as superstition with a host of religious, moral, and political calumnies (which were the transferred charges from Judaism), they adopted the protreptic genre and presented Christianity as superior philosophy to that of the Greeks.[97] Beginning with Justin Martyr, using a conventional philosophical and rhetorical framework, the Apologists attempted to reinterpret their theology and tradition, to define their relation to the unfriendly outsiders, and to fashion the way they communicated with them. Thus Justin portrayed his conversion to Christianity as a conversion to philosophy (as Josephus had done) and continued to wear philosopher's garb.[98] This kind of gesture in turn was noticed by Greek intellectuals such as Lucian, Galen, and even angry Celsus, however inferior that "philosophy" might be. The exhortation to turn to Christianity as true philosophy was followed by the rest of the Christian Apologists who ultimately claimed an ownership of the Greek and Roman classical past — the cultural and intellectual property and stronghold of their pagan opponents. At the same time, they borrowed from Jewish predecessors such typical apologetic themes and strategies as defense of monotheism, attack on idolatry, antiquity of Moses, high ethical standards of the adherents, and loyalty to the dominant authority. Therefore, presentations of Christian philosophy in their apologies served not only to defend Christian faith by refuting the pagan accusations but also to win their educated opponents over to Christianity by presenting the positive tenets of its doctrine and practices.

A couple of examples may illustrate the representative protreptic *topoi* and structure of the Christian apologies. In Justin's *Dialogue with Trypho*, Justin starts with a premise that "philosophy is the greatest and most honorable possession before God, to whom it leads us and alone commends us" (2.1). Then, after describing his philosophical pilgrimage as a Stoic, a Peripatetic, a Pythagorean, and finally a Platonist, he recounts his meeting with an old man; the latter first dissuaded Justin of Platonism (3.1–6.2), attempted to persuade him that Christianity (Hebrew Scripture) was the true philosophy, and then appealed to him for a response which led him to conversion (7.1–9.3). This kind of structure is expanded in the rest of the book, in which Justin issues similar invitations to Trypho at the beginning and the end of the dialogue (8.2; 142.1), which sets forth the Divine Sonship of Logos-Christ in dual respects — fulfillment of Hebrew prophecy and climax of human reason — in allegorical interpretation of Scripture.

In Minucius Felix's *Octavius*, another philosophical dialogue is taking place. The protreptic *topoi* are enclosed in a double structure: first in each of the speeches — Caecilius' case for supremacy of Roman religion and custom (6–12) and Octavius' case for superiority of

Christianity (16–38); then in the work as a whole, as Caecilius embraces Christianity at the end (40). Caecilius' case for traditional Roman religion comes from his philosophical skepticism and the value he holds in *mos maiorum*, and he attacks Christianity with familiar charges of atheism, cannibalism, incest, and superstitious beliefs. Octavius' reply, steeped in appeal to Roman classical tradition, common reason, and Stoicism, rebuts those charges, condemns Roman mythology and polytheism, and highlights monotheism, divine providence, immortality, and the lofty ethical standards of Christians in the language of Cicero and Seneca. Octavius explains Christianity as the true philosophy, which has the truth (*veritas*) and wisdom (*sapientis*) for which the philosophers have been seeking (38.5–7). It is significant that in this presentation there is little reference to Scripture or any Christian writing and that Caecilius' abrupt conversion is described as an intellectual choice recognizing his error and Octavius' triumph in the debate.

Seen from the perspective of *protreptikos*, it is not surprising that the Apologists addressed their works to the "philosopher"-Emperors Antoninus Pius and Marcus Aurelius and to individual pagan elites, Greeks in general, or Roman authorities. Regrettably, aided by Tertullian's complaint that Christian literature was read only by those already Christians,[99] some modern scholars have regarded these works as literary fictions[100] and dismissed the expressed addresses as a mere rhetorical device for the actual audience – Christians.[101] However, a brief survey of the literary genre, purpose, and content confirms the intended wider pagan (especially the educated) audience of these works as well as internal Christian consumption.[102]

Historically and socially, the Apologists themselves were both people of the old Greco-Roman culture, rooted and educated in the classical tradition on the one hand, and people of a new community, committed to its radical truth and ways of life which they regarded as the fulfillment of the human ideal but which were misunderstood and persecuted by the majority on the other. They stood on an existential borderline of the two ways of being, "overlapping parts of both areas but not fully identifiable with either part of the whole," but in desperate need of some way of reconciliation in view of the precarious state of the new community.[103] Apologists understood themselves as representatives of their minority group, guides for the community, and ambassadors on its behalf toward the dominant and hostile Greco-Roman society.[104] In an effort to bridge the gap, they operated within the structures of what was religiously and socially acceptable in the Greco-Roman society and sought to achieve the triple aim in their works: to defend Christianity against pagan accusations, to persuade and convert the (educated) pagan audience, and to strengthen believers' faith in and commitment to the truth and way of life they had already adopted. With this apologetic, missionary, and didactic/edificatory goal, they interpreted Christianity with the language of the outsider and defined and redefined the Christian identity vis-à-vis Greco-Roman culture. What they chose to defend, propagate, and explain represented what they wanted to identify with and distinguish themselves from in the dominant culture as Christians and would eventually change the way in which the Christians formulated their tradition and related to the society.

Apocryphal Acts

Contemporaneous with the rise of the apologetics, there emerged another "movement" within Christianity to represent another particular Christian self-definition – the *Apocryphal Acts of the Apostles*. While each of the Acts (*Acts of John*, *Acts of Paul*, *Acts of Peter*, *Acts of Andrew*, and *Acts of Thomas*) is distinctive in style, content, and theological perspective, they have justifiably been treated as a corpus in scholarly discussions in terms of their plot line, themes, purpose, and genre.[105] Each of the Acts narrates the remarkable missionary career of a particular apostle, which consists of his travels, adventures, miracles, speeches, persecutions, and death (martyrdom); the central message of the apostle's preaching is sexual continence, which results in conversions and sexual abstinence of the high-ranking women and subsequent persecutions by their husbands who are in positions of authority. Each of the Acts except the *Acts of John* ends the narrative with the martyrdom of the apostle (natural death in case of John) that constitutes the climax of his ministry and the ultimate happy ending. As early as the late third century, these five Acts were gathered as a corpus by the Manicheans in place of the canonical (Lucan) Acts,[106] and since then they were transmitted as a collection into the time of Photius (ninth century) in spite of an individual work's separate history of transmission prior to and alongside the collection.[107]

Evidently, the Apocryphal Acts employed a number of sources, techniques, and forms. For models within the Christian tradition, a few scholars have recently stressed affinity between the Apocryphal Acts and the canonical Gospel narratives. François Bovon regards the Gospel of John as a literary model of the Acts, especially in terms of the account of travel and pleasure of couples consisting of an apostle and a converted woman.[108] Richard Pervo judges the Gospel of Mark, the first Christian gospel, as the nearest antecedent of the Acts[109] and also sees the *Acts of John* as an attempt to interpret the Gospel of John.[110]

More concretely, the Lucan Acts appear to have provided for writers of the Apocryphal Acts a narrative and theological model and inspiration to varying degrees.[111] In general, the structure of the Lucan Acts revolving around the missionary activity of an apostle in the post-resurrection setting presents a narrative unity and model; it includes episodic travel narratives with speeches and (often wondrous) deeds of an apostle, which all the Apocryphal Acts follow to a certain degree, especially the *Acts of Paul* and the *Acts of Andrew* more closely.[112] The focus on the missionary activity of an apostle in all the Acts reveals a biographical character in a special sense "determined by the Christian concept of the role of an apostle in salvation history."[113] Among the five, the *Acts of Paul* resembles the Lucan Acts the most for an obvious reason: it narrates the many missionary journeys of Paul – this is the most prominent characteristic of the Lucan Acts; and their relationship to each other has spawned intense debates among scholars.[114] Although the *Acts of Peter* is different from the Lucan Acts and the rest of the Apocryphal Acts in that it reports only one journey by Peter from Jerusalem to Rome, its main section is a dramatic expansion of Peter's confrontation of Simon Magus in canonical Acts 8. In addition, rather an unexpected similarity is shown between the Lucan Acts and the *Acts of John* in the imitation of the Lucan "we-passages" in the latter's otherwise enigmatic third-person narrative.[115] Theologically, the triumph and power of God, Jesus, and his apostles over evil and temporal power forms the main concern of both Lucan and Apocryphal Acts.[116]

These similarities, however, do not conceal significant differences between them when examined more closely. The biographical character is much more outstanding in the Apocryphal Acts than in the Lucan Acts as each of the Acts focuses on a single apostle and ends with his death (martyrdom). The apostolic miracles in the Apocryphal Acts are more incredible and dramatic in scale and effect, and the apostle's status and role much more elevated; the fantastic and fabulous episodes in the Apocryphal Acts far outweigh those of the Lucan Acts.[117] Even the *Acts of Paul* reveals a striking lack of parallels with the Lucan Acts: there is no correlation between them in Paul's itinerary, specific incidents, and other characters. Rather, it shows an interesting correspondence with the Pastoral Epistles.[118] Thus the Apocryphal Acts disclose a rather limited relationship with and influence by the Lucan Acts.

The question of the Acts' genre in a broader Greco-Roman literary context has been a perennial topic in scholarly discussions. On the surface, scholars have had a consensus in classifying the Apocryphal Acts as a genre of ancient novel – as Christian fictions.[119] However, on the definition, nature, purpose, forms, and origins of the ancient novel itself, there has been a bewildering range of differences and variations in proposed theories, especially because the ancients had no genre of novel as such. Since the magisterial study of Erwin Rohde in 1876,[120] the genre of the ancient novel has been represented by the five extant Greek novels of the imperial age – Chariton's *Chaereas and Callirhoe*, Xenophon's *Ephesiaca*, Longus' *Daphnis and Chloe*, Achilleus Tatius' *Leucippe and Clitophon*, and Heliodoros' *Eithiopika*. These five "ideal romances," roughly contemporary with the period of the Apocryphal Acts (*c*.50–300 CE), form a corpus with a schematic plot line and recurrent themes of two young handsome lovers whose fidelity to each other triumphs through separations, incredible trials, and perilous adventures; they finally arrive at a happy reunion in marriage. Rohde argued for the genre of the novel as a product of the Second Sophistic in the early imperial era and presented the Hellenistic erotic poetry and travel narratives as the origins of the novel. However, the discovery of the *Ninus Romance*, a fully developed erotic romance written probably in the first century BCE, challenged his theory and chronological scheme.

Rohde's narrow evolutionary view on the origin and nature of the novel has been challenged over the years. Scholars such as Ben Perry argued for the broad nature and origin of the novel and saw the development of the ancient novel as a response to assert individual selfhood in the wake of vast social, political, and cultural changes such as the transition from the individual Greek city-states to centralized Hellenistic kingdoms and empires.[121] He also recognized the novel in two historical phases: pre-Sophistic novels prior to the emergence of the five erotic romances written in simple *koine* (e.g. *Ninus* and *Alexander Romance*) and Sophistic novels for those five romances as well as others that reveal considerable sophistication in language and content, which flourished during the Second Sophistic era of the second century CE. Reardon extended Perry's analysis with the notion of "personal myth" that the novel represented (in contrast to the "social myth" of New Comedy and the "political myth" of Greek tragedy). As the protagonists solved problems, achieved goals, or discovered their identity through trials, adventures, and love, the novels focused on the human experiences of love and salvation.[122] Whereas Rohde and Perry regarded entertainment as the sole purpose of the novel, Reardon saw the significance of religious beliefs and values in interpreting the novels, similar to what Kerenyi had proposed earlier – that the novels functioned like the mystery religions to satisfy the cultural desires and religious needs of the people.[123]

However, these analyses have been mostly confined to the five "canonical" romances in the imperial age. Graham Anderson, considering the genre of the ancient novel much more diverse, challenged this approach and brought a number of religious, historical, and other types into examination. He argued for the oriental (Near Eastern) origin of the novel from Sumerian love tales in place of Hellenistic origin and attempted to expand its classification.[124] Although his argument for oriental origin is not without problems, its possibility also encouraged some scholars to see interactions between Greek and other ethnic traditions, such as Jewish traditions, Egyptian traditions from the papyrus remains, and influences of Syrian tradition. Novels in the Hellenistic age represented exceptionally pluralistic and multi-cultural perspectives. Scholars in fact came to recognize that the novel in general "is too complex a phenomenon to be reduced to a single impetus,"[125] and is rather "a form characterized by its elasticity, its ability to enter into dialogue with and absorb virtually any other literature."[126] Ancient novels drew on and included epic poetry, historiography, New Comedy, legends, local folklore, rhetorical topography, epistolography, and biography.

Consequently, Pervo provides a fairly inclusive definition of the novel:

> A relatively lengthy work of prose fiction depicting or deriding certain ideals through an entertaining presentation of the lives and experiences of a person or persons whose activity transcends the limits of ordinary living as known to its implied readers.[127]

What defines the novel is the combination of themes, motifs, modes, style, and structure.[128] Typical themes include politics, patriotism, religion, wisdom, and fidelity; recurrent motifs contain travel, adventure, excitement, warfare, aretalogy, court life, intrigue, and rhetoric.[129] Modes indicate subgenres of novel, which provide further categorizations in terms of tone, setting, style, and manner.[130] Among them, the historical novels deal with prominent historical or legendary figures in politics, philosophy, or religion with historiographical style and techniques; they include national hero romances (first coined by M. Braun[131]), such as the *Alexander Romance*, *Cyropaideia*, and the *Ninus Romance*, and biographical novels (or "novelistic biography"), such as *Life of Secundus* and Philostratus' *Life of Apollonius of Tyana*. The comic novels include Lucian's *Ass*, and two Latin works, Apuleius' *Metamorphoses* and Petronius' *Satyricon*; the five Greek erotic novels are often referred to as the ideal romances.[132]

In fact, to one degree or another, most of the ancient novels were historical, as Pervo reminds us,[133] for there existed no clear borderline between fiction and history in the ancient literary world as the moderns understand today. In the Greco-Roman world, while the notion "fiction" (πλάσμα) did not entail total fabrication so much as a creative shaping of material especially in rewriting the past,[134] the concept "history" (ἰστορία) could also mean the plot, "the story as it was known and told," as well as a serious investigation or research.[135] According to Roman philosopher Sextus Empiricus, the historical narratives include three kinds: history, fiction, and myth.[136] History is presentation of things that actually happened; fiction, of things that did not happen but resemble what really happened; and myth, of things that did not happen and are false.[137] The boundary between fiction and reality is hazy and fuzzy; both history and fiction actually present "truth" in recasting of the past; thus fiction is to be seen not only within the context of history but as a part of the continuum of history itself.[138] Novels, including ideal romances, first appeared in historical garb, and, in this sense, they should be seen as historical accounts of varying degrees.

Historical novels as a subgenre particularly deserve special attention with respect to their place in the historical continuum. Historical novels as mentioned above belong to the pre-Sophistic novels written in unadorned *koine* for a general audience and follow a biographical scheme as they focus on the extraordinary lives (βιοί) and deeds (ἀρεταί) of a protagonist. Drawing upon history, legend, local folktales, and oral sources, national hero novels – products of the Hellenistic period – center on the romanticized portrait of great historical or legendary rulers such as Alexander, Ninus, Sesonchosis, Nectanebus, and even Moses. These heroes represented the cultural identity and pride and embodied the ideological ideal of the ethnic group they belonged to against the dominant ruling power: Alexander for Greeks, Ninus for Babylonians, Seconchosis and Nectanebus for Egyptians, and Moses for Jews. Their twin themes were politics and patriotism, which functioned to raise a group consciousness and assert minority culture in a pluralistic and syncretistic environment.[139] Prominent in the exploits of those heroes was an aretalogical motif, which was closely related to the religious concerns such as oracles, revelations, miracles, and providence – the motif by which the heroes were ultimately vindicated. These narratives were read as "history" and also shared some fluidity in the manuscript tradition as they usually existed in multiple recensions with continual retelling of the past well into the early Roman imperial age. Hence, the national novels defended the traditional culture in the context of the new through the medium of the new.[140]

The other type of historical novel – biographical – overlaps with the genre of Greco-Roman biography and especially novelistic biography, and as such needs to be treated in relation to that genre. Like the ancient novel, ancient biography is an inclusive genre that employs novellas, speeches, and dialogues.[141] Distinguished from historiography, it rather shares the place of the historical novel in the continuum of history as "a halfway house between history and oratory."[142] Whereas biographies of politicians and generals tended to be closer to actual political history, lives of philosophers were often idealized and romanticized for the purpose of propaganda against competing schools of philosophy.[143] It appears that, if the national hero novels focused on the lives of political figures with creative use of history, biographical novels took as their target the lives of philosophers. It is illustrative that the *Life of Apollonius* (early third century CE) by Philostratus and the *Life of Secundus* (late second century CE), both products of the Second Sophistic and concurrent with the Apocryphal Acts, have been considered as both biographical novel and novelistic biography. In the *Life of Apollonius*, Apollonius, a Pythagorean philosopher during the reign of Domitian, embodies the ideal holy man as the pious ascetic, wonderworker, charismatic revealer of truth, and martyr. This portrayal emerges in the midst of travels, wondrous adventures, religious controversies, and erotic subplots with remarkable aretalogical feats of prophesying, exorcism, healing, and resurrection. The *Life of Secundus* depicts another Pythagorean philosopher under Hadrian both as an ideal ascetic who overcomes a sensational sexual test and as a martyr who keeps his vow of silence against the

Emperor's command to speak. In both cases, the typical erotic themes function to foil the ascetic ideal of the philosophers, and the motif of heroic martyrdom, in parallel with the pagan Martyr Acts and the Christian Martyr Acts, including martyrdom of the apostles, serves the propagandist aim.

Jewish novels can be understood in this context of historical novel. According to Lawrence M. Wills, ancient Jewish novels can be divided into three types.[144] First, the "national hero novellas" deal with the exploits of the ancient heroes such as Abraham, Moses, and Joseph. A chief example of this type is the work of Artapanus, who wrote in Egypt around 200 BCE, though only fragments survive in Eusebius' report of Alexander Polyhistor's universal history. These fragments on Abraham, Moses, and Joseph show "a biographical focus with apologetic interests and admiration of the wondrous"[145] and have been aptly compared to the *Ninus* and *Alexander Romances*. Here the biblical narratives were retold and reshaped with creative expansions and unexpected turns. Moses, for instance, was represented as serving the Egyptians not only as a military general but also as a religious innovator who established the animal cults, instructed Orpheus, and thus benefited humanity. The exploits supplied by Artapanus were intended to refute anti-Semitic charges and Egyptian condescension and to be read as "true" history.

Second, "novellas" (short novels), treated the figures who were insignificant or even unknown in the traditional Jewish history, such as Esther, Daniel, Susanna, Tobit, Judith, Joseph, and Aseneth. Although their "historical" references such as "Darius the Mede" in Daniel or "Nebuchadnezzar, king of the Assyrians" in Judith are incorrect and other references are replete with historical errors, they present and claim an appearance of historical verisimilitude. These Jewish novellas proper can be also "national hero novellas" in the sense that they particularly heighten the sense of Jewish pride in the midst of foreign threat and conflict, and that the scope of the action is "turned inward upon one or two protagonists who bear the burden of their extended family, and by extension, of Jews in general."[146] Moreover, most of them utilize a political background and employ court and erotic themes, also popular in Greek romantic novels, and reveal the strong influence of the latter, as evidenced by the first-century CE story of the marriage of the Patriarch Joseph to an Egyptian woman Aseneth.

Finally, "historical novellas" deal with historical figures of the recent past in a way that was again received as historically true, such as *Third Maccabees*, and the *Tobiad Romance* and *Royal Family of Adiabene* in Josephus' *Antiquities* (12.4.1–11 and 20.2.1–4.3, respectively).[147]

The history of the Jewish novel from *c*.200 BCE to *c*.200 CE shows the influence of Greek romance: the prominence of women, the increased use of erotic themes, baroque plots, domestic values, exotic settings, fascination with miracles, and manipulation of emotions.[148] However, while utilizing those motifs and settings, the Jewish novels sought to maintain Jewish boundaries by communicating the Jewish ideals (thoughts and behaviors), however Hellenized they might be.[149] Jewish novelists did not create their characters but took from Scripture, history, legend, and myth, and the leading characters were usually exceptional models of Jewish piety.[150] Indeed, the characteristic moral of those stories was that those heroes and heroines won

> because of, not in spite of, their fidelity to traditional observances and beliefs. God is on the side of the faithful, providence aids the righteous while punishing the wicked, and all ends well for those who follow the true path.[151]

While this message of the Jewish novel certainly had an edificatory as well as popular entertainment purpose, it was also apologetic and propagandist in thrust as the novels dealt with the very issues and problems that were raised by Jews maintaining their traditional ethnic and religious boundaries.[152] Therefore, the Jewish novels shared in the concern of the Jewish Apologists as they appealed to Jewish consciousness and identity through the creative and imaginative rewriting of the past.

In light of this brief survey on the ancient novel, the classification of the Apocryphal Acts as a true ancient novel needs to be qualified in a sense that the novel as a genre extends beyond the ideal romances and is an inclusive genre that employs diverse literary motifs and forms, such as letters, poetry, dialogues, speeches, etc. While certainly showing their affinities with the ideal romances, the Apocryphal Acts stand closer to the historical novels, adapting the characteristics of national hero romances and biographical novels (novelistic biography).[153] They especially follow the Jewish precedent, focusing on the missionary career of the apostle with an apologetic and propagandistic aim on behalf of a particular group or religious ethos.[154] They are "historical" works not in terms of factual precision but, rather, creative use of history by retelling the tradition of the apostles and their public exploits with both message and entertainment in mind. The Acts' retelling of the past is projected in the contemporary social and theological milieu, providing the "historical" outlook into the then-current Greco-Roman society, as well as contemporary Christianity with a proclivity toward dualistic theology and encratism, and the issues arising out of their contact and conflict with each other. To this end, the anonymous author(s) of each of the Acts wove a host of different traditions and materials into the single unifying work, including letters (e.g. the so-called the *Third Corinthians* in the *Acts of Paul*), hymns (e.g. the Hymn of Christ in the *Acts of John*; the Wedding Hymn and the Hymn of the Pearl in the *Acts of Thomas*), local folktales (e.g. the Thecla legend incorporated as the *Acts of Paul and Thecla* in the *Acts of Paul*), and individual martyrdom accounts.

The general characterization of the Apocryphal Acts as a Christian parallel to or variation of the Greek novel (i.e. the five ideal romances) gained strength earlier through Rosa Söder, who identified the five novelistic elements or motifs that are shared by the Apocryphal Acts: travel motif, aretalogy (supernatural power of the hero), teratology (fabulous representation of event, world, or characters), propaganda (tendentious element in speeches), and erotic elements.[155] Furthermore, some recent studies poignantly examined the transformation or reversal of the erotic theme[156] of the ideal romances – sexual fidelity and consummation in marriage – in each of the Apocryphal Acts in the continence stories of upper-class women who forsake their husbands (or fiancé) and renounce their conjugal responsibilities to follow the apostle's teaching, most famously in the *Acts of Paul and Thecla*. These features are certainly significant points of contact and parallel;[157] however, similar motifs alone do not account for a characterization or model, and the fundamentally biographical and missionary focus of the Acts delimits the ideal romances as the main literary model for the Acts.

The Apocryphal Acts were popular in character. There were differences in the degree of literary sophistication among the Acts, the *Acts of Thomas* being the most refined work in both literary and theological depth, followed by the *Acts of Andrew*. However, those differences among the Acts are not so great as the disparity between the pre-Sophistic and Sophistic novels and among the Sophistic novels themselves. The corpus as a whole exhibits the literary techniques and style below the level of the surviving Sophistic romances and resembles the more popular, less literary level of the pre- and non-Sophistic novels.[158] The traditional assumption of the ancient novel as popular literature with wider circulation and particular appeal to distinct groups such as juveniles, women, and those of lower status has been challenged by recent studies of the readership based on the surviving papyrus texts and fragments which are relatively small in number and reveal higher literary quality, which presupposes a cultivated audience.[159] When both views are taken seriously, these studies may indicate that, instead of a set social group of readers, there were different levels of audience based on the literary sophistry rather than the themes or motifs of the works which are shared across the literary levels. It is also not unreasonable to assume women as part of the target audience whose ideal images presented by the novelists corresponded to the aspirations of women in the Greco-Roman world.[160] In case of the Apocryphal Acts, their popular character is evidenced not only in literary quality but also in their preoccupation with and resort to manifestation of superior power in theological confrontations.[161] The blossom of the Acts during the heyday of the Sophistic ideal romances indicates the similar taste and needs of the audience or even possibly a shared one, including those of women; their needs might have been "fulfilled" in both ideal romances and Apocryphal Acts but in contrasting terms.[162]

The popularity of the Acts throughout the Church in time and place is evidenced by the various early and later versions and also by widespread patristic references despite repeated condemnations by the Church, especially after their incorporation into the Manichean collection. The extant manuscripts exist in Greek, Latin, Coptic, Syriac, Ethiopic, Armenian, Georgian, and other languages, and each of the Acts has a very fluid and complex textual and transmission history. In the case of the *Acts of Paul*, Paul's correspondence with the Corinthians, the *Acts of Paul and Thecla*, and the *Martyrdom of Paul* were circulated separately from the early period on, and all the other apostolic martyrdom accounts enjoyed a separate circulation history.

The Apocryphal Acts were intended to attract and persuade their audience – both pagans and Christians. They appealed to the outsiders who might have enjoyed the similar novelistic literature and were also intended to edify and entertain established believers. The Acts are replete with stories of conversion with a missionary thrust. Particularly, they sought to influence readers toward a particular understanding of Christianity. The central figure of each of the Acts is an apostle, represented as the bearer of a particular tradition of Christianity.[163] The kind of Christianity these Acts try to communicate to the readers is bound up with the person of the apostle – his speeches, actions, and death. He functions as a divine man (θεῖος ἀνήρ) who embodies the Christian ideal and reveals the Christian truth. This apostle is in constant confrontation with the pagan world full of evil spirits and idolatry, and demonstrates the power and triumph of the one true God by miracles, asceticism, and martyrdom. The Christianity of the apostle is in utter contrast with the beliefs, ways, and power of the Greco-Roman world. This anti-social stance is further reinforced in the Christian version of "chastity" preached by the apostles that disrupts the marriage bond and in their incessant conflict with civil and religious authorities. The Apocryphal Acts came into being when various movements within Christianity interacted with the dominant, often hostile world; in addition to the obvious entertainment value, the Acts shared, on a different level, in the apologetic, missionary, and edificatory concerns of the contemporary Christian Apologists. However, in contrast to the Apologists, the Acts rejected the traditional social and cultural ideals in favor of new ones, attempted to reshape the established assumptions in light of the new, and represented this attitude as the defining feature of Christian self-definition.[164]

Martyr Acts

Finally, the Martyr Acts represent the third movement in Christians' search for self-definition and collective boundaries. The Christian contempt of death and enthusiasm for martyrdom were the best-known features of Christianity to the contemporary pagans, the mass, and the elites alike (as mentioned earlier), since Christian martyrdom was a part of the Roman urban public spectacles with high visibility and great emotional charge.

Traditionally, Martyr Acts have been categorized into two literary types: the *passiones* or *martyria* and the *acta* or *gesta*. The martyrdom/passions refer to descriptive accounts of the last events and the death of the martyr, apparently by eyewitnesses or contemporaries, and the *acta* of the martyrs consist of purported official records of their court trials before the authorities (*commentarii*).[165] However, this classification is not rigid, for *acta* usually include simple descriptions of martyrs' deaths, and martyrdom/passions normally contain parts of courtroom discourses. Actually, the Martyr Acts employ diverse literary forms such as letters, narratives, paraeneses, visions, etc. *The Martyrdom of Polycarp* and the *Martyrs of Lyons and Vienne* are both letters written to the specific recipients by the churches in Smyrna and in Lugdunum respectively that contain detailed narratives and paraeneses on martyrdom. The *Acts of Justin* and the *Acts of the Scillitan Martyrs* are the *acta* proper in a form of court records (*commentarii*). The rest of the Martyr Acts are the narrative proper with short court proceeding accounts that range from the simple work like *Martyrdom of Carpus, Papylus, and Agathonicê* to complex pieces such as *Martyrdom of Perpetua and Felicitas*, which incorporates a martyr's personal diary and visions with the clear intention to be read aloud in church (1.1, 5; 21.5).

The Martyr Acts describe and celebrate, sometimes with gruesome detail and arresting images, the undaunted faith, noble endurance, and incredible valor of Christians arrested, imprisoned, tried, tortured, and brutally executed by the Roman authorities. The martyrs are the heroes of the Church whose death stands as a witness to their unshakeable allegiance to Christ. They are noble athletes (ἀθλητής)[166] who are engaged in a supernatural combat (ἀγών) against the Devil beyond the earthly struggle against the crowd or governors. They are the partakers of Christ in his sufferings and the imitators of Christ in his death, who is the protomartyr or the first martyr of Christianity in his self-giving death on the cross.

All of these themes are explicit in the earliest account of a Christian martyrdom, *The Martyrdom of Polycarp*, a congregational letter from Smyrna to the church in Philomelium in response to the latter's request for a detailed account of the aged bishop Polycarp's martyrdom that took place between 155 and 160 CE.[167] Recognized as an "authentic" contemporary account, it became the model for what would become a popular genre of literature, Martyr Acts, as it set forth "a martyrdom in accord with the gospel" (1.1) through Polycarp's example and bore the earliest testimony to the cult of the martyrs in the church (17.1–18.3).[168] Here the words "martyr" (μαρτύς) and "martyrdom" (μαρτύριον), in the definite sense of witnessing to Christ by dying at the hands of a hostile secular authority, first appear.[169] Only those who die in accordance with God's will are the true martyrs who are the imitators of the Lord (1.2; 19.1) and partakers of Christ (6.2) in his death. The twin theme of *imitatores Christi* and athletic heroism governs not only this piece but also all the subsequent Martyr Acts.

In light of these literary motifs and modes of presentation, "how far are these accounts, the [pre-Decian] *acta martyrium*, to be regarded as either contemporary or accurate records?"[170] The question of authenticity and historical value of the Martyr Acts has been an important concern for scholars. Unlike the case of the apostolic martyrdom accounts in the Apocryphal Acts, most scholars accept the authenticity or historicity of these selected Martyr Acts with a certain level of confidence. Timothy Barnes, in his classic study on this issue, affirmed that six out of nine Acts (except the *Martyrdom of Carpus, Papylus, and Agathonicê*; the *Martyrdom of Apollonius*; and the *Martyrdom of Potamiaena and Basilides*) preserve "as accurate a report of what happened as may be expected from a contemporary."[171] Hippolyte Delehaye, offering a system of classification for the degree of authenticity and historical reliability, placed Polycarp, the Martyrs of Lyons, and Perpetua in the category of the reliable eyewitness accounts, and Justin and the Scillitan Martyrs in the category of the official written reports of the interrogation (*acta proconsularia*).[172] This, however, does not mean that they are innocent histories merely telling the events "as they really were." Glen Bowersock saw the Martyr Acts as a whole resembling Greek fiction in both style and composition and standing in a similar historical continuum with the Gospels (which in his view represent the development of the imperial historical fiction), in combining fictional expansion with historical substance.[173] Gary Bisbee, using a form-critical method, demonstrated that the *commentarius* form of *acta* did not correspond to the actual court *commentarii* but were edited works to meet the needs and agenda of Christian communities. He redefines "authentic" account as "a text that is not necessarily the historical original but a text that is demonstrably derived from a historical original," especially in light of the multiple recensions for some of the accounts.[174] One must remember that the Martyr Acts present a version of truth that was necessary and significant to their authors rather than a complete story;[175] for it was more important for the Christian community which martyrs were authentic rather than which written texts were authentic.[176] Therefore, "the *acta* of an authentic martyr were *de facto* authentic" and functioned "to demonstrate the authenticity of the martyr";[177] the historical value of the Martyr Acts was closely related to the apologetic purpose of the Acts.

Tracing the origin and the background of Christian martyrdom and martyrology in the larger Jewish and Greco-Roman context has solicited lively scholarly discussions over the years. The view of the Jewish context as the primary locus of origin and influence can be represented by W.H.C. Frend, who, in his classic *Martyrdom and Persecution in the Early Church* (1965), has set the development of Christian martyrdom and *acta martyria* solidly in the Jewish (especially the Maccabean) tradition. According to Frend, the origin of the concept of martyrdom began in the deutero-Isaiah and the (post-exilic) prophetic tradition with the idea of a suffering witness to God in the person of the Suffering Servant and concurrent with the rise of the Jewish eschatological and apocalyptic tradition; these traditions represented the Jews as the "martyr people" suffering vicariously for the whole humanity.[178] Then, the Maccabean tradition became the direct predecessor of the Christian martyrdom and martyrology with the following major developments: the idea and practice of martyrdom, defined as "personal witness to the truth of Law against the forces of heathenism, involving the suffering and even death of the witness";[179] the hope of personal reward and resurrection of the faithful (i.e. martyrs) and vengeance on the apostates and persecuting powers beyond death;[180] and the transfer of the secular struggle to a cosmic level as the contest between God's agents (i.e. martyrs) and the demonic powers.[181] Therefore, he declares the Second Maccabees as the "first Acts of Martyrs";[182] then, with the explicit development of the idea that martyrs' blood brings vicarious atonement for people in the Fourth Maccabees (6.29; 17.22), the Jews in post-Maccabean times, both in Palestine and the Dispersion, "accepted and taught the permanent glory of victorious suffering by the great prophetic heroes of Judaism."[183] The Christians took on, continued, and superseded the Jewish ideals and practices with the life and death of Jesus and their own heroes.[184]

This approach, however, was recently challenged by Bowersock, who in his *Martyrdom and Rome* (1995) asserted that martyrdom was something alien to both Greeks and Jews and "entirely new" with the rise of Christianity, especially in Asia Minor in the second, third, and fourth centuries CE.[185] According to him

> Christianity owed its martyrs to the *mores* and structure of the Roman empire, not to the indigenous character of the Semitic Near East where Christianity was born . . . like the very word, "martyr" itself, martyrdom had nothing to do with Judaism or with Palestine. It had everything to do with the Graeco-Roman world, its traditions, its language, and its cultural tastes[186]

running its course in "the great urban spaces of the agora and amphitheater, the principal settings for public discourse and for public spectacle."[187]

Bowersock dismisses any significant connection between Christian martyrdom and the death of Socrates on the one hand and between Christian martyrdom and the stories of Eleazar and the mother with her seven sons in the Maccabean tradition on the other. The portrayal of Socrates as a kind of pre-Christian martyr is only retrospective after the later development of the full-blown concept of martyrdom. Even if the early Church used him as an example, Bowersock claims, it is rather a rhetorical argument for a pagan audience, definitely not in the Christian sense of a martyr.[188] The accounts of Eleazar and the mother with her seven sons in the Second Maccabees and its dramatic elaboration in the Fourth Maccabees, as the case of the alleged martyrdoms at Masada in the first century or of Rabbi Akiva in the second, are again a retrospective construction of a later age, subsequent to the first Christian martyrdoms.[189] The words "martyr" or "martyrdom" never appear in the Maccabean books, and the composition of the Fourth Maccabees points to the late first century CE (after the destruction of the Temple in 70 CE), contemporaneous with the birth of the gospels and other Christian documents that later became the New Testament.[190] Those two stories in the books of the Maccabees indicate not the Jewish influence and model for Christian martyrdom but rather the Christian interest in and aspiration for constructing their own concept of martyrdom.[191]

In the midst of these opposing poles, Daniel Boyarin (1999) agrees with Bowersock in his chronological arguments and with Frend in acknowledging the Jewish influence. Yet he questions the fundamental assumption shared by both Frend and Bowersock, "namely, that Judaism and Christianity are two separate entities," as though a person can speak of either one or the other as the point of origin of the idea and practice of martyrdom.[192] Instead, Boyarin presents a more complex and intertwined picture of the Jewish and Christian relations in late antiquity. He proposes martyrdom as a developing "'discourse' about dying for God that [is] added on to the fundamental constituent of preferring death to compliance and that together, in the end, produce[s] that sense of something entirely new"[193] through "a tangled process of innovation and learning, competition and sharing of themes, motifs, and practices" between the two communities from the second to the fourth centuries CE.[194] Thus, the process of and influence on "making of martyrdom" was not unilateral but mutual and has ultimately become a part and parcel of the Jewish and Christian movements toward more separate self-definition. Hence, the crime for which the martyrs were killed was understood as having to do with their essence as Christian or as Jew per se (i.e. their identity) and not as punishment for any specific "criminal" acts; the public declaration of Christian Name for Christians or of belief in one God for Jews was itself now the cause of torture and death. This was indeed new with the *Martyrdom of Polycarp* in the case of Christian texts and new with the stories about Rabbi Akiva, Polycarp's contemporary, for Jews.[195] Furthermore, as the death of the martyr was conceived as a religious fulfillment per se for the first time during this period, for Jews, martyrdom was a fulfillment of the commandment to "love the Lord with all one's soul," on the one hand, while, for Christians, beginning with Ignatius, martyrdom was a central aspect of the experience of imitation of Christ on the other.[196]

In light of this concise overview of major scholarship, it is clear that Christian martyrdom and martyrology came into being in the rich cradle of both Jewish and Greco-Roman tradition of noble death and cultural systems. It is undeniable that the Jewish notions of final judgment, resurrection of the dead, both righteous and wicked, divine vindication and vengeance, and vicarious suffering noticed as early as the deutero-Isaiah and throughout the Second Temple literature (especially in the apocalyptic tradition such as Daniel) provided at least in part a conceptual framework of Christian interpretation of the death of Jesus and the subsequent idea of martyrdom. Although the term "martyr" occurs in neither the pre-Christian Second Maccabees (c.120–100 BCE) nor the Fourth Maccabees (c.70–100 CE), those ideas are well attested to in the Second Maccabees with the role of the martyr as the model for all Jews suffering for their faithfulness to the Lord and Torah with posthumous glory (6.12–7.42). In the Fourth Maccabees the conquering heroism of the martyr is highlighted with the image of a noble athlete (17.11–16) whose voluntary death is a ransom and brings atonement for sin of the whole nation and purification of the fatherland (17.21). Its numerous points of contact and parallels in literary motifs and language with the letters of Ignatius, the *Martyrdom of Polycarp*, and the Eusebian *Letter of Martyrs in Lyons* have attracted a great deal of scholarly attention.[197]

However, as van Henten reminds us, this continuity of ideas does not mean a linear growth of Christian Martyr Acts out of its Jewish source.[198] In fact, those corresponding motifs rather point to the larger Greco-Roman common tradition.[199] It needs to be stressed that the books of the Maccabees are the product of

Hellenistic Judaism, and especially the impact of Hellenistic (Stoic) philosophy on the Fourth Maccabees is noteworthy; the example of the martyrs demonstrates the essentially philosophical thesis of the work: "devout reason is sovereign over the emotions" (1.1). The motifs such as the portrayal of martyrdom as a military contest, or as an athletic contest with the crown as symbol of victory, the joyful perception of the suffering, contempt for the physical pain or tortures, and the effectual death of the martyrs have parallels in Greek and Greco-Roman funerary orations, encomium, philosophical discourses, novels, and biographies.[200] Both Jewish and Christian making of martyrdom, however different the end result would be, was influenced by the ideals of voluntary death in Cynic-Stoic philosophy[201] and perhaps by Roman practice of *devotio* and death for the fatherland.[202] The "philosophic martyr" tradition inspired by the heroism of Socrates was cherished by the Stoics such as Cicero, Seneca, Epictetus, Plutarch, and Marcus Aurelius, who accorded the moral virtues of freedom, nobility, and dignity to voluntary death for a rational principle in defiance of tyranny or patriotic cause. Although Lucian's account of flamboyant Cynic Peregrinus' (who had once been a Christian) dramatic display of self-immolation at Olympia in 165 CE is full of pungent sarcasm and satire, Epictetus thought highly of him. Moreover, it was the Cynics and Stoics who used the old athletic terminology in diatribal presentation of the true contest (ἀγών) for virtue.[203]

Besides the philosophical tradition, the Roman tradition of military and gladiatorial *sacramentum* as a way of redeeming one's lost honor through heroic self-destruction provides the Greco-Roman context for Christian martyrdom.[204] Here a connection lies in the significance of the role of the martyrs in the Roman penal system and public games as well, who re-enacted the mythological role-play in the dramatic display of public executions in arenas and amphitheaters.[205] The "fatal charades" by criminals or martyrs were a popular form of entertainment, and those public spectacles of martyrdom in cities thus fit within a pre-existing social order of the Empire that shaped them.[206]

In these public spectacles, martyrs made "an ultimate statement of commitment to the group and what the group represented."[207] The *acta martyria* deal with two primary concerns: a demand to sacrifice/swear allegiance to the gods and the emperors and the question, "Are you a Christian?"[208] These two concerns are closely related in such a way that the answer to the question of Christian identity always involves a refusal to partake in pagan ritual and to give allegiance to the pagan gods/emperors. The climax in the Martyr Acts then is the final confession of the martyr made in public: "I am a Christian."[209] As Ekkehart Mühlenberg observes in those texts, "while death is part of the confession, death or manner of dying has no value of its own apart from the confession."[210] It is this final confession that unites the martyr with "all the sojourners of the holy and catholic church everywhere"[211] and serves to draw the Christian "group identity and self-definition."[212] The Christian Martyr Acts present martyrdom as the supreme religious value for the group and tells the "collective stories" of dying for God in and with all of their collective cultural traditions: Socrates, Maccabees, the Roman generals' *devotio*, Greek tragedies and their heroes, gladiators, games, and athletes, philosophers, and Jesus on the cross.[213] In this way, the Martyr Acts culturally legitimize the martyrs' death and define the Christian identity and ethos represented by their words and deeds to those who would oppose them – the Jews, Roman authorities, and pagan crowds in general.

If we accept the thesis of Bowersock and Boyarin that Christian martyrdom was a "new" phenomenon in the second century CE within Greco-Roman and Jewish cultural legacy, it is evident that public executions of Christians needed an explicatory context both for outsiders and for insiders as well.[214] The fact that martyrdom was used as a positive "demonstration of religious truth" is beyond doubt,[215] and the Martyr Acts shared some common literary elements in describing martyrs' heroism[216] with a theological thrust of witnessing to God over and against pagan gods. Thus, martyrology carried strong missionary messages to the outsiders, and martyrs constituted "strong 'apologies' for the faith to pagan audiences"[217] resulting in conversions.[218] In a world where people were seized by "a sort of fascination with death . . . surrounding voluntary death in legend and life, a desire for theatrical prominence, the very widespread idea of the body as a prison for the soul, and pessimism,"[219] and where different religious and philosophical schools contended over the merit of their respective "martyrdoms,"[220] the Christian Martyr Acts placed an exclusive claim on theirs as the only "authentic" martyrdom to the one true God as opposed to any other causes or beings, and imparted a powerful and indelible impression to pagan minds. Apologist Justin, who himself would be martyred for his faith, was as a pagan profoundly impressed by the scene of Christian martyrdom.[221] This missionary or propagandistic purpose of the Martyr Acts is further seen in the martyrs' exploit of the trial scenes by presenting Christian truth and apology to the authorities and exhorting them to earnest hearing and conversion.[222] To the insiders, Martyr Acts certainly provided a teaching on the true nature of martyrdom and an inspiration and a heroic model to follow or at least to commemorate. Thus, the Martyr Acts joined in the threefold concern of the Apologists and the Apocryphal Acts: missionary, apologetic, and didactic/edificatory.

The martyrs transformed the stigma of deviance into a badge of honor.[223] Just as the apostles in the Apocryphal Acts, martyrs struggled against the persecutors who personified the demonic powers but overcame them not with the sword but with blood. Just as the apostles, they loomed larger than life as the exemplars of faith and the embodiment of Christian ideals – ostensibly spiritual perfectionists along with the ascetics. Their desire and contempt for death and defiance to the Roman authorities set themselves against the established culture and society and denied the socio-political paradigm of power. The Martyr Acts, so deeply embedded in the life and spectacles of the Greco-Roman world, put forth the Christian resistance to the life this world offers for glory in the next.

Triangular relationship

The late second- and early third-century Apologies, Apocryphal Acts, and Martyr Acts were propagandistic literature anticipated by Hellenistic Judaism and thoroughly embedded in the Greco-Roman religious, social, and cultural environment. They were to present the gospel – the core Christian message that made Christianity distinctive in character, exclusive in claim, and universal in scope – to the Greco-Roman world and define it in relation to that polytheistic and syncretistic world; with that, they were to present their own understanding of new Christian identity to the old world and define it in relation to that world, where the concept of "new" was often held in suspicion and doubt. In such literature, "the self-identity of the missionary community is intertwined with its understanding of its mission and the formation of its propaganda"[224] and apology to the dominant established outsiders which in turn strengthens the collective sense of unity and group boundaries of the insiders. The expression and consolidation of the Christian self-identity as "a new race," "a third race," is most clearly seen in these literatures in this particular period as each of them tried to come to terms with the larger culture with a unique and yet interconnected message.

While these three bodies of work all share the general Christian assumptions and theological milieu of the time, with varying degrees of fictional elements and shapings by common apologetic concerns, they all portray Christian idealism in different aspects with distinct attitudes toward the prevailing culture and form a triangular relation in their presentation and approach. For the Apologists, Christian idealism consists of its philosophical truth and way of life mediated by the Divine Logos whereas the Apocryphal Acts define Christianity in terms of its superior power and radical encratism demonstrated by the apostles; the Martyr Acts delineate Christian ideals and identity as the superior sacrifice and imitation of Christ exhibited by the martyrs. The Apologists found remarkable continuity and harmony between the old creation and the new; they saw in Greco-Roman culture and philosophy the final stage of the *telos* of civilization, only to be fulfilled by Christianity, the true philosophy. The Apocryphal Acts found radical discontinuity and tension between the existing world of corruption and evil and the celestial world of purity and spirit they sought. They created their alternate symbolic world of perfection in conflict with the conventional Greco-Roman society and culture, rejecting marriage and family life and seeking an ascetic lifestyle and death. The Martyr Acts certainly posed an undeniable struggle between following Christ and following Caesar, who personified the Empire, Satan's puppet. Like the Apocryphal Acts, they portrayed their heroes threatening the existing authority in defiance and gladly choosing death as the only option to life, and thus they created a spiritual power struggle. The Martyr Acts also found common ground with the Apologists, who embraced the martyrs as the heroes and heroines of Christian philosophy and virtue; martyrs fulfilled the ultimate divine ideal. However, though they were honored, celebrated, and remembered in their contests, they were also to be defined and identified "in accord with God's will" and their charismatic power to be contained within the Church.

In this triangular relation, the Apologies, Apocryphal Acts, and Martyr Acts develop three modes of Christian self-portrayal within which they diverged: superiority of Christian monotheism; superiority of Christian sexual morality; and Christian loyalty to the Empire. Each category of these self-definitions will be treated respectively in the following chapters. In their divergent self-representations, they expounded the diverse versions of the Christian canon of belief and practice in relation to Greco-Roman culture.

2

THE SUPERIORITY OF CHRISTIAN MONOTHEISM

The most pronounced theme in the Apologies, Apocryphal Acts, and Martyr Acts is the superiority of Christian monotheism. Since the charges of atheism caused the most hostile reaction from pagans and posed the most serious threat to Christian existence, it was only appropriate for Christians to prioritize this issue and set forth a clear delineation of the Christian belief in and worship of God. In one sense, the essence of the Christian apologetics and propaganda was to answer the question, "Who is the God of Christians and how do they worship him?"[1] in a manner intelligible and credible to the Greco-Roman audience of the day. In asserting the superiority of Christian monotheism, these texts also had to deal with its theological and practical implications such as the issues of God's nature and relationship to the world, Christology, Christian relation to traditional Greco-Roman polytheism, and antiquity and/or radical novelty of Christian belief. In this way, each of the literary bodies outlined the doctrinal self-definition of Christianity with characteristic emphasis and silence on some distinctive issues. Along with what they defined, how they defined their monotheism was of significant importance for apologetic purpose, and this self-definition was to direct the subsequent theological trajectories of the early Church. First, the Apologists associated themselves with the classical philosophical tradition against popular religion and fundamentally presented Christianity as true philosophy, thus claiming it as the genuine successor and the final destiny of the Greco-Roman civilization. Second, the Apocryphal Acts primarily presented Christianity as true power, ascribing with the power of judgment upon the pagan culture on which Greco-Roman education (παιδεία) was based. Finally, the Martyr Acts mainly presented Christianity as true piety through the portrayal of public sacrifice in martyrdom as true sacrifice versus that of pagans. In this chapter we will

49

focus on how the three literary bodies develop these portraits of Christian monotheism and claim its superiority based upon their self-definitions.

Apologies: Christianity as true philosophy

In order to claim the superiority of Christian monotheism, the Apologists first concentrated their energy on establishing common ground with the Greek philosophical tradition. They strove to show that Christianity was in harmony with the best of what had been thought, taught, and said. The Apologists' most important task in that endeavor was to demonstrate their competence, showing that the reasoned discourses of the Christian message were in accord with the contemporary philosophical categories and concepts. Given the Jewish precedent, this involved building a convincing synthesis of Christian faith and Hellenistic reason and developing the philosophical and rational doctrine of God.[2] Therefore, the case for Christian monotheism would start with the case for philosophical monotheism.

Christian monotheism: the transcendent God

To begin with, the Apologists upheld the unity of God in Middle Platonism,[3] which has to do with a particular interpretation of Plato influenced by Peripatetic logic, Stoic ethics, and Neo-Pythagorean mysticism. From the outset, it is important to remember that, when the Apologists refer to Plato and his texts, it is the Plato and Plato's texts not necessarily of the original Academy but of this eclectic Middle Platonism already compiled and used by the philosophers of the day;[4] the Apologists followed the contemporary interpretation of Plato and his works. The same is true with Homer in this period. In interpreting the Homeric poems, Middle Platonism inherited the allegorical traditions of Stoics (more cosmological) and Pythagoreans (more moralistic) and "transformed" Homer into "a prophet of monotheism and of the immortality of soul";[5] thus, the Homer to whom the Apologists refer is the allegorized Homer of Middle Platonism.

The Apologists stressed Christian monotheism in accord with the Platonic notion of God's transcendence and employed the current terms of the negative theology of Middle Platonism.[6] According to the influential Middle Platonist Alcinous, who is a contemporary of Justin, since God is wholly other, above all matter, and free from any boundaries and limitations or anything that humans can know, any statement that attempts to describe God is inadequate and thus to be expressed only in a "negative" way.[7] Following this view, Justin praises Plato for his teaching that the transcendent God is unknowable, unchangeable, passionless, incorporeal, and incorruptible. The God whom Christians worship is the very God who is unbegotten (ἀγέννητος) without beginning or end;[8] who is ineffable (ἀνωνόμαστος), impossible to be named or described;[9] who is invisible (ἀόρατος) without shape or form;[10] and who is in need of nothing (ἀνενδεής), neither blood nor libation;[11] he is the Unknowable and the First Cause distant from the world. Athenagoras, Tatian, and Theophilus readily join Justin in asserting God's transcendence in a similar way. According to Athenagoras, Christians worship one transcendent God who is distinguished from matter, "uncreated (ἀγέννητος), eternal, invisible (ἀόρατος), impassible, incomprehensible (ἀκατάληπτος) and infinite (ἀχώρητος)."[12] He is "Light inaccessible, Himself a universe of perfection and beauty, superior to the exigencies of change and decay, uncaused by anything outside of Himself."[13] Likewise, Tatian[14] contends that "the perfect God" is ineffable (ἀνωνόμαστος), incorporeal, fleshless, invisible (ἀόρατος), intangible, impalpable, and entirely free of needs (ἀνενδεής).[15] Then, Theophilus presents God's transcendence with forceful eloquence: the immutable God is "in glory uncontainable (ἀχώρητος), in greatness incomprehensible (ἀκατάληπτος), in loftiness inconceivable, in wisdom unteachable, in goodness inimitable, in beneficence inexpressible."[16] The Latin Apologist Minucius Felix declares the same truth concerning God's nature: God is too great to be named or comprehended by the human sense or intellect, "for he is beyond all sense, infinite, measureless, his dimensions known to himself alone."[17]

The four types of Greek expressions stand out among God's transcendent attributes: first, the term that expresses that God has no beginning – unbegotten or uncreated (ἀγέννητος); second, the words that express that God is beyond any human appellation or comprehension – ἀνωνόμαστος, ἀκατονόμαστος, ἀκατάληπτος; third, the terms that express that God is not bound by space, form, or senses – ἀχώρητος, ἀόρατος; finally, the terms that express God's utter self-sufficiency, such as ἀνενδεής or ἀπροσδεής. These particular terms belonged to the rather distinct vocabulary of the Middle Platonic negative theology and recall their intense appropriation by the Jewish Apologists (especially Philo and to some extent

Josephus) in the context of their defense for monotheism against popular paganism and idolatry.[18]

Since the transcendent God is unbegotten, he is the Father and Maker of the universe. The phrase, "Father and Maker of the universe (ποιητὴς καὶ πατὴρ τοῦ παντός)," comes from Plato's *Timaeus* 28c, which is one of the most popular texts of Middle Platonism. The text in question relates to the impossibility of finding and articulating God, the Father and Maker of the universe. While in original Plato the phrase refers to the Demiurge, who is different from the Good, in Middle Platonism the two are identified; the Creator is none other than the supreme God.[19] This phrase not only was the standard expression of God by Middle Platonists but also became the Christian Apologists' favorite designation of God as the Creator.[20] Justin, Athenagoras, and Clement frequently use this title and its variation to speak of God: the "Father of the universe,"[21] the "Maker of the universe,"[22] and/or the "Father and Maker of the universe (all)."[23] The eternal God is sovereign over the universe that he created, and this universe is absolutely contingent upon him for existence.[24] Moreover, they all cite this passage, drawing the philosopher's support for monotheism and the incomprehensibility of God the Creator.[25] Hence, following the quote, Athenagoras immediately comments, "Here he [Plato] understands the uncreated and eternal God to be one."[26]

It was convenient for the Apologists then to link Platonic fatherhood with creation and creation with biblical sources. The "Father of all"[27] is the Creator God of Genesis and the Heavenly Father of the Gospels. God created the world in his goodness for humanity so that he might bring them to share in his life and immortality.[28] He has guided his people in every age and finally sent his Son Christ according to his will to save the corrupt and wicked world. Apparently, Justin does not see any significant inconsistency between the Platonic God and the biblical God. He reads the Platonic creation myth in *Timaeus* as parallel to the Genesis account of creation.[29] Justin declares that "in the beginning He [God] of His goodness (cf. *Tim.* 29c), for people's sake, formed all things out of unformed matter (δημιουργῆσαι αὐτὸν ἐξ ἀμόρφου)."[30] Later he complements this statement by asserting that "it was from our teachers – we mean from the Logos through the prophets – that Plato took his statement that God made the Universe by changing formless matter (ὕλη ἄμορφος)."[31] Although Justin quotes Genesis 1.1–2 to support this claim, Justin's point recalls in fact not the creation *ex nihilo*[32] in the "biblical" sense but the Platonic notion of creation from formless matter (cf. *Tim.* 51a) influenced again by Alcinous.[33] Clement of Alexandria has a similar viewpoint when he speaks of the creation "out of nothing."[34] In each of the three times he mentions it, he uses not ἐκ οὐκ ὄντος but ἐκ μὴ ὄντος – creation not from absolute non-existence but from relative non-being or unformed matter[35] – and correlates the Genesis account with *Timaeus*, though with greater sensitivity and flair than Justin.[36] This Platonic nuance is more explicit in Athenagoras' *Legatio*, where he, while completely silent on Genesis, describes the creation as ordering of pre-existent yet undifferentiated matter by the Divine Artificer (δημιουργός) using the analogy of the artisan and the artisan's material (15.2).

When we come to Tatian and Theophilus, we have a clearer articulation of the creation *ex nihilo*.[37] Tatian seems to present the creation in two stages. First, the Logos, "begotten in the beginning in turn begot (ἐν ἀρχῇ γεννηθεὶς ἀντεγέννησε) our creation by fabricating matter (τὴν ὕλη δημιουργήσας)."[38] This "matter is not without beginning like God, nor because of having beginning is it also of equal power with God; it was originated and brought into being by none other, ... by the sole creator of all that is."[39] Lest God's omnipotence be compromised, Tatian asserts that matter itself is not pre-existent but produced by God. Then, the second stage consists of the raw and unformed matter being separated into parts and organized in order.[40] The visible universe emerges from a differentiation (διάκρισις) and transformation of matter into intelligible reality by the Logos' activity.[41] Here reliance on the Platonic model of creation as forming or ordering of matter is still apparent, but Tatian's point is also clear that God created matter prior to its ordering although he does not add the expression, "out of nothing."

An unequivocal affirmation of the creation *ex nihilo* comes from Theophilus who declares, "God *made* everything *out of what did not exist* [2 Macc. 7.28], bringing it into existence" (τὰ πάντα ὁ θεὸς ἐποίησεν ἐξ οὐκ ὄντων εἰς τὸ εἶναι).[42] For Theophilus, this affirmation of the creation *ex nihilo* confirms the sovereignty of God as supreme Creator and discloses a remarkable discrepancy in the Platonic paradigm, the very area about which Justin and Clement felt uneasy in their attempt to reconcile with Genesis 1: "Plato and his followers acknowledge that God is uncreated, the Father and Maker of the universe; next they assume that uncreated matter is also God, and say that matter was coeval with God."[43] If God and matter are both uncreated and immutable, the unique sovereignty of God is at risk; there is nothing extraordinary about God's nature if God made the world out of pre-existent matter.[44] Thus, Theophilus confronts and departs from the Platonic system of creation and redefines the philosophical vocabulary of creation used by the Apologists.[45] In fact, the creation *ex nihilo* only became an issue when Christians began to reflect on the origin of the cosmos in a serious interaction with Greek thought (as exemplified in Hellenistic Judaism).[46] For Theophilus, the transcendent "God is not a Framer or even a begetter of matter, but a giver of being in its widest sense."[47] While Justin and Clement tended to read the biblical notion of creation into Plato's *Timaeus*, Theophilus stayed with "literal" biblical understanding; however, all the Apologists relied on the Greek philosophical concepts, terminology, and arguments to the Christian end – to articulate God as the sovereign Creator.

The Apologists then bring in a list of notable supporters of monotheism from the Greek classical tradition (παιδεῖα). For example, Homer prophetically advocated the "doctrine of a single ruler of the universe (μοναρχία)" with a saying, "A multitude of masters is no good thing. Let there be one master (εἷς κοίρανος),"[48] which is explicitly alluded to by Tatian.[49] Athenagoras' list of monotheist sages is extensive, including: tragedians such as Euripides[50] and Sophocles, who acknowledged only "one God, who formed the heaven and the broad earth";[51] philosophers such as Plato, Aristotle, and the Stoics; and Pythagoreans such as Lysis, Opsimus, and Philolaus, who taught that God was one and above matter.[52] He draws their fragments from the doxographical collections which were popular in Middle Platonism. Minucius Felix appeals for the rational and spiritual character of the one God to a long list of philosophers, including Thales of Miletus, Diogenes of Apollonia, Anaxagoras, Pythagoras, Xenophanes, Democritus, Aristotle, Zeno, Cleanthes, Chrysippus, Xenophon, and Plato,[53] and closes the section with this statement: "The position is pretty much the same as our own; we too recognize God, and call him the parent of all."[54] Thus, these testimonies by the Greek notables confirm not only the transcendence and unity of the Creator God but also the claim that "Christians of to-day are philosophers, or that philosophers of old were already Christians."[55]

Certainly this Creator "Father of all," worshiped by poets and philosophers, and now Christians, is invisible to human eyes and unknowable by physical senses,[56] but he can be, in fact, should be, perceived by mind alone, as Plato affirms.[57] This teaching, which is again quoted from Alcinous and Maximus of Tyre, is the prevailing argument of the Apologists, especially against popular paganism.[58]

Athenagoras claims that the transcendent God can be "contemplated only by thought and reason"[59] and "apprehended by mind and reason alone,"[60] "whereas matter is created and perishable."[61] They earnestly appeal the knowledge of God to reason and intellect. For Theophilus, knowing God by reason first involves seeing the invisible God with the eyes of the soul purified from sin.[62] The witness of the human soul to the one true God is as such that Tertullian can exclaim, "O the witness of the soul, in its very nature Christian!"[63] The knowledge of God also entails recognizing God through his providence and works. Just as the design of the great universe is the product of the divine reason, human beings are endowed with speech and reason.[64] Therefore, by observing the creation and the orderly design of the universe, one must reason that "the pilot of the universe is God."[65] Athenagoras, Tatian, Tertullian, and Minucius Felix concur with this argument from design, which is derived from Stoicism.[66]

Furthermore, since God is the Creator who is transcendent and incorporeal, he is not to be worshiped with material offerings of his creation like the gods of the polytheists.[67] God is absolutely self-sufficient; he does not need sacrifices.[68] God is a spiritual being, so our worship should be rational and spiritual, far from blood, libation, or temples with altars; rather, our "acceptable sacrifice is a good spirit and a pure mind and a conscience without guile."[69] Again, in the context of polemic against pagan sacrifice, Apologists underscore the rational "bloodless" (ἀναίμακτος) sacrifices of Christians, which consist of praise and thanksgiving, prayer, eucharist, and virtuous and righteous life.[70] In this way, following the poets and philosophers, Christians too proclaim the one God to be but mind, reason, and spirit.[71]

Christian monotheism: the divine Logos

The chief problem which challenged the Apologists was the relationship between the transcendent God and the Son of God – the agent of divine activity in the world: how to safeguard Christian monotheism while still maintaining a balance with philosophical monotheism. As in the case of God's transcendence, they turned to what had been already available to them: the concept and doctrine of the Logos. The doctrine of the Logos had an established pedigree in the Greco-Roman world. Following the pre-Socratic philosopher Heraclitus, Stoics thought of the Logos as the rational principle or law of the universe according to which people should act and live.[72] They also regarded it in a pantheistic way as the formative principles of particular things, which are parts of God.[73]

In the Middle Platonism, this Logos, the supreme principle, was identified as the Logos of God, through which God works and manifests himself along with other powers; it is both transcendent and immanent. In this Logos are "the Platonic Ideas, the archetypes of all created things, the 'architect's plan' of creation."[74] In the Septuagint, the Logos appears as the Word of God in creation and as the message of the prophets by which God communicates his will to his people.[75] Here the Logos as God's Word represents spoken and active communication rather than abstract concept.[76] In the Jewish Wisdom literature, Wisdom is not only a divine attribute but also a mysterious entity distinct from God, an entity who was the first of the creation and was in the beginning with God as his agent in creation.[77] Then, it is in Philo that the Middle Platonic idea of Logos as the Ideas in the Mind of God encounters the Jewish Wisdom tradition. In Philo, the Logos is identified with the intelligible world, the ideas, the wisdom, and the powers of God in a more impersonal sense, and also as Second God, First-born of God, Son of God, Angel and Apostle – in more personal terms.[78] Philo speaks of the Logos as the instrument of God in the creation of the world and mentions the *logoi spermatikoi* as the models and creative principles of the physical world.[79] The Christian Fourth Gospel declares that the divine pre-existent Logos was made flesh, and the Incarnate Logos is identified with the person Jesus Christ in support of messianic theology (John 1.1–4).

In this rich milieu of understanding the Logos and in light of their conviction in the unity of God, the Apologists highlighted the divine metaphysical nature and cosmological function of the Logos-Son.[80] As Daniélou has observed, we can discern in their writings two states or stages of the Logos:

> the one where it exists eternally in God as his thought and counsel, but without a separate subsistent entity of its own, the other where it is brought forth, or begotten, so that it acquires such an entity before the creation of the universe, and as a means to that end.[81]

First, the Son as the Logos of God is the mind of God, represents the rational intelligible thoughts of God, and thus shares essential unity with God. For Athenagoras, the Son of God is "the Logos of the Father in Ideal Form and Energizing Power."[82] In Clement, the Logos is identical with the mind of God that contains his thoughts or ideas.[83] Here the Logos-Son is linked with the Platonic Idea, which in Alcinous is indistinguishable from divine thought.[84] Athenagoras further speaks of the Son as mind, reason [word] and wisdom (νοῦς, λόγος, σοφία) of the Father;[85] he is the "totality of God's intelligence or thought and all the Son's rational activity is God's."[86] In this sense, the unity of God is not diminished by the fact that God has a Son; rather, "the Father and Son are one" because the Son of God is the very mind and reason of the Father united by spirit.[87]

Second, in the transcendent God there inherently exists the Son as a creative power "which contains *in potentia* the whole creation," and this Son was begotten from the Father especially for the work of creation.[88] The Son of God is referred to by various equivalent titles with no clear distinction: Logos (λόγος), Power (δύναμις), Spirit (πνεῦμα), Wisdom (σοφία), etc.[89] According to Justin, "God has begotten of Himself a certain rational Power (λογικὴ δύναμις) as a Beginning (ἀρχή)[90] before all other creatures," and the Holy Spirit designates this Power by various titles: the Glory of the Lord, Son, Wisdom, Angel, God, Lord, or Logos.[91] This Logos, the first-born (ὁ πρωτότοκος)[92] of God, a second God, and the true, supreme, and unique Son of God,[93] is understood only by the spirit (πνεῦμα) and power (δύναμις) of God.[94] Here the Logos-Son as the Power is related to the Platonic world-soul, νοητὸς κόσμος, which is begotten by and distinct from the First God (πρῶτος θεός).[95] As the "Power (δύναμις) of the ineffable Father,"[96] and "the Only begotten of the Father of the universe,"[97] the Logos-Son created (ἔκτισε) and ordered (ἐκόσμησε) all things.[98] The Logos is God's sole instrument in the work of creation. His character as God's power and his status as the Only Begotten of the Father are uniquely associated with his function as God's exclusive agent in the creation.[99] This role of the Logos-Son as God's power in fashioning and ordering the universe again adopts Philo's thought on the Logos and constitutes an important cosmological argument for the subsequent Apologists.[100]

In this state, the generation of the Logos is a spiritual generation, not by section (ἀποκοπη) but by partition (μερισμός) from the Father,[101] which means that the pre-existent Logos-Son still shares a unity with the Father in substance (οὐσία) but is distinct in name, number, function, and personality (ὑποστάσις).[102] The analogies come from both nature and human speech: many fires are kindled from one torch;[103] the light of the sun on earth is indivisible from the sun in the skies;[104] and, when speaking, a speaker is not deprived of thought through transmission of speech.[105] According to Theophilus, God had his Logos, always innate (ἐνδιάθετος) in the heart of God, as his "Counselor, his own Mind and Intelligence," but made him external (προφορικός) as the firstborn of all creation for the purpose of creation.[106] Theophilus applies to the Divine Logos the Stoic terms ἐνδιάθετος (inner thought – immanent) and προφορικός (uttered speech – expressed) used by Philo and other philosophers for human thought and speech; they correspond to the Latin *ratio* (Reason) and *sermo* (Word) as applied to Logos by Tertullian.[107]

In these analogies, while the Apologists stress the Son's unity with the Father, they also point out his distinction from and subordination to the Father in economy – generated from the Father for the work of creation and revelation, the Son is subject to the Father's will and thought. Thus, the theophanies in the "Old Testament" are attributed not to the Father but to the Son, for the Father of the universe is unconfined (ἀχώρητός), whereas the Son is "sent by God and is present in a place" where he is heard and seen.[108] By implication, the Son is apparently χώρητός in contrast to the Father and operates in space and time. The Logos-Son is the revelation and manifestation of the ineffable and invisible Father and as the messenger of God[109] bridges the impassable gulf between the transcendent God and the created world and makes this unknowable God known to the world.

In Justin and Clement of Alexandria, the role of the Divine Logos as the universal revealer of the Father and divine truth is underlined especially in relation to Greek philosophy. It is not coincidental that these two Apologists, who are most conciliatory toward Greek philosophy, are extensively engaged in this theological endeavor. For Justin, the Divine Logos is the Sower, the "Word that sows the seed" (λόγος σπερματικός) of divine knowledge (i.e. monotheism) on the one hand,[110] and in every person there is an implanted seed of Logos (σπέρμα τοῦ λόγου)[111] on the other.[112] Hence, human reason is participation in the Logos and represents the "seed of Logos" (i.e. fragmentary knowledge of the divine);[113] at the same time, the Logos is the object and the norm of that knowledge and thus engages in a special act of sowing his divine revelation and principle into certain people, i.e. a few philosophers.[114] Therefore, these philosophers, namely, Socrates, Heraclitus, and Plato, who received what the Logos sowed, lived according to Logos and thus uttered something good (καλῶς) and comprehended the divine.[115]

In that sense they can even be called "Christian." Justin can extol philosophy as follows:

> Philosophy is indeed one's greatest possession, and is most precious in the sight of God, to whom it alone leads us and to whom it unites us, and they in truth are holy men who have applied themselves to philosophy.[116]

However, even these philosophers knew the Logos, the Truth, only partially (ἀπὸ μέρους) and dimly (ἀμυδρῶς), for they did not receive the whole Logos, which is Christ;[117] only in Christ is revealed the fullness of the truth. Thus, Justin strikes a balance between the certain merit of and truth in Greek philosophy and its limited boundary and imperfection lest he undermines his own argument concerning the harmony of Greek philosophy with Christian monotheism.

Clement follows Justin on this line of thought and develops it further. As the Mind of God, the Divine Logos is the image (εἰκών) of God, and an image of the Logos is the mind in the human being; therefore, the human being is created in the image of God and thus of the logos on account of human reason.[118] Since there is a natural kinship between the universal Logos-Son and the human mind, the Greek philosophers have discovered and grasped a certain measure of the divine knowledge and truth by natural reason. Moreover, God inspired some philosophers by dropping particles of the Logos into their minds,[119] and they, under divine inspiration, declared "the one only true God."[120] On this divine inspiration of philosophers, Clement is more explicit and uses the image of rainfall in connection with the dissemination of the seeds.[121] Although Clement does not refer to Justin's λόγος σπερματικός in describing the origin of Greek philosophy under the activity of the Lord (i.e. Logos), he does refer to the Gospel parable of the Sower as Justin does.[122] Furthermore, like Justin, he recognizes the value of Greek philosophy and even its divine origin and at the same time delineates its partial nature in attaining the truth in contrast to the whole knowledge of the Incarnate Logos, Christ. Again, he frames the revelatory role of the Logos in a way that keeps balance between his theological conviction and his appreciation and appropriation of Greek philosophy for Christian monotheism.

How is the Divine Logos-Son related to the person Jesus Christ, then? Certainly, for Justin and Clement, Jesus Christ is the historical embodiment of the eternal Logos-Son, the full manifestation and the power of the transcendent Father, and thus the whole of the divine truth. Justin goes into detail in presenting earthly ministries and teachings of Jesus and does not hesitate to speak of the virgin birth, incarnation, passion, and resurrection of Christ.[123] With an apparent neglect of the philosophical problem entailed in these doctrines, he finds similarities from the Greek tradition for those Gospel stories about Christ. They are nothing new in comparison with the sons of Zeus who suffered; like Hermes, Jesus is the Word of God and teacher of all; like Perseus, Jesus was born of a virgin; like Asclepius, Jesus healed the lame, the paralytic, and the blind and raised the dead.[124] Justin describes Christ as a philosopher (Socrates); he is "no sophist,"[125] but the Teacher of the way to "happiness"[126] and, embodying the right reason, teaches the "doctrine of divine virtue."[127] The incarnation of the Logos in Christ was according to God's grand plan in history, and, thus, Jesus Christ, the Incarnate Logos whom Christians worship next to the Father, is the same Divine Logos who is pre-existent with the Father; hence, Christianity is not historically novel but is as ancient as the Divine Logos itself.[128]

It is noteworthy, however, that, in Athenagoras', Tatian's, and Theophilus' works, the cosmological nature of the Logos-Son has hardly any bearing on the person of Jesus, whom Minucius Felix never mentions in *Octavius*.[129] Athenagoras cites a portion of the Sermon on the Mount as traditional Christian teachings without mentioning the name of the founder.[130] Tatian's and Theophilus' focus on the cosmological Logos emphasizes the eternal timeless character of Christian philosophy in place of its historical character.[131] Tatian's mention of the incarnation, that "God has been born in the form of man," does not specifically refer to Jesus and is in defense of its possibility in comparison with ridiculous pagan mythology.[132] Theophilus' quotes from the Gospel of Matthew do not name Jesus and are mainly confined to moral teaching as in the case of Athenagoras.[133] In Minucius Felix's *Octavius*, in response to the pagan charge of Christian "worship of a malefactor and his cross" (29.2), Christian Octavius gives an unqualified repudiation: "Crosses again we neither worship nor set our hopes on" (29.6). There is no reference to the virgin birth, the incarnation, the passion, or the resurrection of Christ in their Apologies.

The reason for this striking absence of the missionary *kerygma* of the early Church concerning the person and passion of Christ may be attributed to the regional diversity especially for Tatian and Theophilus, who represented East Syrian Christianity and Jewish

Christianity in Antioch respectively. More significantly, it may be ascribed to the apologetic nature and purpose of their works. As one may recall, the most vehement areas of attack on the Christian doctrine by the pagan contemporary Celsus centered around the person of Jesus and concentrated on those very points on which these Apologists kept their silence. In an attempt to present Christianity as true philosophy to the educated pagans, the Apologists developed the philosophical *kerygma*, which would appear relevant, reasonable, and acceptable, particularly to their audience. The presentation of this "alternative" *kerygma* influenced the course of Christian theology and its controversies, as well as the formation of orthodox theology.

Polemic against paganism

If establishing a harmony between Christian monotheism and Greek philosophical monotheism is a positive strategy, the Apologists' vehement polemic against popular polytheism and myth forms a negative strategy in the *protreptikos logos*. Since both philosophers and Christians acknowledge the one true God, it is absurd that Christians are considered "atheists." They ostentatiously identify themselves with the Academy and other philosophers using the established philosophical criticism of popular paganism.

Their attack on pagan religion and myth targets several different but related categories of the so-called gods of paganism.[134] We may take a cue from Tertullian's criticism of Varro's threefold classification of gods in *Ad nationes* (2.1–8) and adopt it for our purpose.[135] Varro's classification consists of: (1) nature gods treated by the philosophers; (2) the gods of myths propagated by the poets; and (3) national/ethnic gods. Tertullian's point is to show that none of them is a real god. First, Tertullian points out that the allegedly divine elements of nature, including the heavenly bodies, are subject to change as opposed to the immutable true God. While the sun is often put to eclipse, the moon goes through monthly changes.[136] Surveying the history of Greek religion, Clement of Alexandria shows that the worship of the universe – heavens, angels, sun, moon, stars, and planets – is the starting point of grave idolatry, for it is a worship of not God but his work.[137] He then discusses the pre-Socratic philosophers who supposed the elements, such as water, air, fire, and earth to be the first principles. Though the philosophers' merit lies in eliminating the immoral gods of myth, their worship of the material principles, which they learned from barbarians anyway, is ludicrous and fails to acknowledge the transcendent spiritual God. Therefore, he says, "these men were really atheists (ἄθεοι)" for their worship of matter.[138] In this, one sees the standard Christian objection to pagan religion, which is repeated by all the Apologists throughout the period: idolatry – worship of creature rather than the Creator.[139]

Second, as for the gods of myth, Tertullian's condemnation is based on the theory of the pagan theologian Euhemerus that the alleged gods were once merely mortals.[140] The bestowal of deity after death was a method of rewarding the distinguished human beings so that their memory might be honored and perpetuated, so pagans said.[141] Tertullian argues that such honors are a cheap prostitution of God's infinite grace and mercy,[142] and he mocks them by saying that, if one needs the help of another to be a god, it is beneath one's dignity![143] In fact, if one reviews the supposed merits of the pagan gods, they deserve not apotheosis but infernal punishment; they commit incest with parents or sisters, seduce wives, rape virgins, defile boys, kill, steal, and deceive.[144] With the aid of the Academy's attack on the Homeric gods and poets, the Apologists thus focus on the corporeal nature and scandalous immorality of the gods.[145] The genealogy of those gods given by Orpheus, Homer, and Hesiod shows that they are mortal and perishable beings with bodies, passions, and bodily needs.[146] Philosophers such as Socrates and Plato have already regarded the old myths of the anthropomorphic gods as false and corrupting[147] because they were filled with vices and absurdities such as adultery, lust, drunkenness,[148] thefts, murders, and castrations.[149] In fact, these entire myths are a product of "the aberrations, follies, and excesses of a disordered mind" i.e. the poets who invented them.[150] If these ridiculous fables are false, the gods do not exist; if they are true, then they no longer exist since they came into being from non-existence.[151]

Third, concerning national and ethnic gods, Tertullian highlights the multiplicity of names and functions of the gods among various races.[152] In *Legatio*, Athenagoras points out that the pagans are in disagreement about their own gods because there are so many deities whose worship is only confined to their own cities: Athenians set up Celeus and Metaeira; the Trojans bring forward Hector; and the Carthaginians, Hamilcar and the like (14.1). While the gods of Greece and other nations are made of stone, wood, and other material substance, Egyptians worship a multitude of animals, and the plurality of types of Zeus testifies against his real existence.[153]

Again, these gods are nothing but mere images and worthless idols made by human hands;[154] they are gods only by human will and human acts of dedication.[155]

Behind the worship of the idols and all those abominations and absurdities of the pagan gods and rites stand the demons, which are really the fallen angels.[156] They foster superstitions, instigate deceit, enslave humans with magical tricks, work toward people's destruction, blind their minds from the light of the truth, and call them away from the true God to material things.[157] In reality, the pagan gods (both gods of myth and national gods) are "the wicked and impious demons,"[158] the same beings who orchestrated the condemnation of Socrates who by true reason tried to deliver people from the demons.[159] In order to deceive and lead astray the human race, the demons parody the Christian teachings and rites: Bellerophon, Perseus, Heracles, and Asclepius are the caricatures of Christ's incarnation, virgin birth, and healing;[160] ritual washings are a mimicry of baptism;[161] and the Mithraic mysteries are an imitation of the Eucharist.[162] However, their attempts are only foolish and irrational: How can one worship the created matter rather than the Creator? How can one worship the mortal gods, just as needy, emotional, and vicious as human beings? How can one worship irrational animals and lifeless images and idols made by human hands? After all, how can one worship the demons, which work for one's own ruin? It follows that it is only absurd to worship the pagan gods and insane to participate in the traditional cults. The Apologists thus appeal to reason for rejection of paganism;[163] no one should be blinded by the stupid customs of traditional polytheism.[164] Since the nature of the paganism has been exposed, a person with "power of reasoning and understanding" should firmly reject it;[165] only atheists would persist in paganism.

Therefore, the notion of "atheism" must be redefined, not with respect to the pagan gods who are in fact mere demons but with respect to "the most true God" who is "free from all impurity."[166] Christians are not atheists but worshipers of the true God since they distinguish God from matter and recognize "the Maker of the universe and the Word proceeding from him as God."[167] According to this definition, the real atheists turn out to be the Greeks and Romans who are enslaved by their worship of demons and idols. "By your worship of a lie," Tertullian reproaches them, "by your neglect of the true religion of the true God – and more than that – by your assault upon it, [you] commit against the true God [the] crime of real irreligion (*crimen verae inreligionsitatis*)."[168] Then, he reveals the evil and injustice of their "irreligion"; their "atheism" not only ignores the true God but also takes away "freedom of religion" and forbids a person "choice of deity, so that I may not worship whom I would, but am forced to worship whom I would not."[169] Tertullian protests the "coercive" nature of pagan worship and demands "freedom of religion," for "the true religion of the true God," i.e. Christianity, inspires worship not by force but by reason and freedom.[170] Similarly, Clement of Alexandria urges the Greeks to abandon the custom and to rationally "choose the better things (αἱρούμεθα τὰ βελτίονα), that is, God instead of the evil one, and [to] prefer wisdom to idolatry."[171] In this way, the Apologists not only redefine "atheism" but also advocate religious freedom by a rational choice in contrast to irrational compulsion and absurd customs in pagan worship.

The Apologists' polemic against pagan religion and myth is now extended to the philosophers and Greco-Roman culture in general – for they, even the most distinguished of their rank, had some kind of connection with the idolatry. Although they show painstaking effort in drawing the compatibility of Christianity with Greek philosophy and though they think and operate within the language of that philosophy, the Apologists, Justin and Clement included, do not ignore its limits and shortcomings and do pass judgment upon it. Although the philosophers achieved by reason some great insights about the unity of God,[172] having only partial knowledge, they fell into many errors and contradictions. Plato erred in supposing transmigration of the soul and its immortality as a natural inherent right;[173] the Stoic pantheism and materialism contradict each other since they believed that the elements of the physical world would perish at the conflagration.[174] Aristotle's error lies in identifying the transcendent Father with the world-soul and contradicting his own doctrine that providence does not extend down to the sublunary sphere.[175] The philosophers' multiple and conflicting theories about God and the universe only point to their lack of true understanding; in that way they distort and corrupt the truth.[176] By their self-contradiction, they demolish their own doctrines, and "if they spoke about the gods, they later taught atheism."[177] All of the Apologists were in agreement that "no philosopher had discovered the truth in its purity and perfection; and further . . . no philosopher was in a position to demonstrate with certainty the truth which he had discovered, or to spread it far and wide."[178] Thus, even the best of the Greek philosophical teachings are only "the seed and imitation of truth," and the precise error of the philosophers is "to think that they possessed the whole, when in fact they had only a part."[179]

Tatian, Theophilus, Clement, and Tertullian go further. They stress that whatever truth those philosophers had discovered was in actuality borrowed from the "barbarian writings," i.e. Jewish Scriptures; even then those philosophers distorted the truth with their false interpretations.[180] Indeed, for Tatian, not only philosophy but "everything that the Greeks regard as their own 'inventions' (εὑρέσεις) are really 'imitations' (μιμήσεις), for the Greeks themselves were dependent on the barbarians for their customs and practices."[181] He proves his point by citing a catalogue of barbarian inventors and inventions, which points to their historical precedence to Greek "imitations."[182] Clement echoes Tatian's point by saying, "Non-Greeks [Barbarians] invented not only philosophy but practically every form of technical skill (τέχνη)," and provides his own list of barbarian inventors.[183] However, Tatian's polemic runs deeper. He violently reproves the lives and doctrines of the Greek philosophers as a whole, ridiculing philosophy as folly and rhetoric as frivolity.[184] He categorically rejects the whole Greek literary discipline (παιδεῖα) and civilization in which he was nurtured and of which he himself is the very product − irony, indeed.

Against the fragmentary and peripheral understanding of the poets and philosophers, the Apologists posed the prophets of the Jewish Scripture who wrote under God's direct and full inspiration; the limitation of human reason and comprehension, i.e. Greek philosophy, only points to the need for divine revelation.[185] Prophetic wisdom differs from human wisdom; Christian doctrine is superior to "all human teaching" because of its revelatory character.[186] Even for Justin and Clement, the philosophers mainly relied on themselves and only some received the "seeds" or "drops" of divine inspiration, but the prophets of old spoke of God and the divine things by the revelation of the Logos and the Prophetic Spirit of God.[187] These prophets proclaimed the one Creator God and the coming of Christ long before the fulfilled events, and taught humanity to abstain from idolatry.[188] In contrast to the poets and philosophers, the prophets spoke *in complete agreement and harmony by one and the same Spirit* about the monarchy of God, the origin of the world, and the creation of humanity.[189] Hence, the voices of the prophets affirm the Christian arguments.[190] Christian faith is not deficient of reason as falsely accused, but revelation is still the higher and surer guide to God's truth.

Antiquity of Christian belief

The highlight of the Apologists' case for the superiority of Christian monotheism focuses on their chronological and historiographical arguments which would demonstrate the antiquity of Christian belief. Fundamental to any truth claim in the Greco-Roman world, in fact, in any ancient world, was the authority of antiquity. Both pagan polemicists and Christian Apologists admitted the value of the past and the critical importance of establishing its sacred sanction for their respective religions.[191] Celsus' caricature of Christianity as a novel (thus phony and counterfeit) imitation of the ancient Greek philosophical tradition may well have been a rejoinder to Justin's lengthy apology for Judeo-Christian antiquity and also a catalyst for the contemporary and subsequent surge of Christian apologies.[192] Then, the Apologists' arguments for historical priority were not only essential to the claim to Christian superiority but also a vital part of the literary tradition of the day.[193] Their arguments involved the interrelated themes of the antiquity of Moses and the Jewish Scriptures, argument from prophecy, and Christian interpretation of history.[194]

First, the remote antiquity of Moses was a well-established topic in Hellenistic Jewish apologetics and even in Greco-Roman literary traditions. Picking up that theme, the Apologists unanimously (except for Athenagoras who is strangely silent about this) affirmed that Moses was more ancient than all the Greek poets and philosophers and that their writings borrowed from and depended on those of Moses. As mentioned above, the Apologists' appeal to the Hebrew prophets was based on their supernatural and ancient character. Moses was the first of the prophets[195] and, according to Justin:

> is more ancient than all the Greek writers. And everything that both philosophers and poets have said concerning the immortality of the soul, or punishments after death, or contemplation of heavenly things, or doctrines like these, they have received such hints from the prophets as have enabled them to understand and expound these things.[196]

Justin, who was a Christian pioneer of this claim, presents his evidence for Moses' priority with more literary data rather than historical data.[197] Apparently setting the date of Moses as five thousand years before Christ,[198] Justin presents his literary proof mainly with reference to Plato, which consists of a series of passages from Plato that are (in his opinion) imitations of what Moses taught.[199] For example, concerning the creation, Plato learned from Moses (Gen. 1.1–3) that the universe came into being by the Logos of God out of formless matter.[200] And "in the physiological discussion concerning the Son of God in Plato's *Timaeus*, when he says, 'He placed him like a *Chi* in the universe,' he borrowed similarly from Moses."[201] After quoting the account of Moses' bronze snake in Numbers 21.6–9, Justin continues: "Plato, reading these things and not accurately understanding, nor realizing that it was the figure of a cross, but thinking it was a *Chi*, said that the power next to the first God was placed *Chi-wise* in the universe."[202]

The subsequent Apologists attempted to establish the validity of the priority of Moses with chronological research. For Justin's pupil Tatian, the reference person is Homer, and his point is to prove that Christian "history is not only earlier than Greek culture, but even than the invention of writings."[203] According to Tatian, "Homer was not only no later than the Trojan War, but lived at the very time of war," based on the various estimations of Greek writers.[204] Then, with his research from the histories of Chaldeans, Phoenicians, and Egyptians,[205] Tatian declares that Moses was not only older than the fall of Troy but even antedated the foundation of Troy.[206] To be exact, Moses lived four hundred years before the Trojan War, and, what is more, Moses is older than pre-Homeric writers and even "older than heroes, cities and demons!"[207] Tatian's chronology was certainly original and was used and cited by Clement, Tertullian, Origen, and Eusebius.[208]

Theophilus' chronology attempts to be even more precise and comprehensive. After presenting his theological exegesis of Genesis 4 and 11 as the Christian paradigm of cultural history at the end of Book 2 (2.29–32), in Book 3, Theophilus sets out to offer a "scientific" world chronology since God's creation of the world.[209] His chronology intends to prove "that our [Christian] doctrine is neither modern nor mythical but more ancient and true than all the poets and historians."[210] First, he sets up the biblical account of the Deluge against the Greek myth of Deucalion and Platonic theory of recurrent cataclysms.[211] Then, he shows Moses' date nine hundred years prior to the Trojan War with respect to Manetho's chronology of Egyptian kings[212] and correlates the date of Solomon's Temple with the Phoenician chronology.[213] Finally, he presents the biblical chronology from Adam to Cyrus as the "true history" of the world with an addition of Roman history from Cyrus to Marcus Aurelius.

The total number of years from the creation of the world comes out to be 5,695, the number which he proudly submits.[214] This confirms that Greek and Roman civilization is pale in comparison to the biblical history of culture.

For the Apologists, the point of proving the antiquity of Moses is to demonstrate "the antiquity of the prophetic writings and the divine nature of our [Christian] message."[215] Their aim is to show that true wisdom and philosophy are to be found in Scripture, which properly belongs to Christians, and that "the Greeks got it right only when they borrowed from the older literature of the Hebrews,"[216] "the storehouse for all later wisdom."[217] The dependence on Moses in Justin becomes "theft" and "plagiarism" in Tatian, Theophilus, and Clement with a more polemical edge.[218] The Greeks took the ancient prophetic wisdom of Moses and corrupted it with poor imitation, but Christianity finally restored the divine truth and brought it to perfection and fullness.

The Apologists' historical arguments provide a distinctive Christian interpretation of human history in universal scope. They relate the origin of Christianity to the pre-existent activity of the Logos, and its history to the creation of the world and the revelations of the same Logos and the Spirit to Moses and other prophets throughout history. Therefore, what appears most recent (i.e. Christianity) is in fact most ancient;[219] Christians are in possession of the history of the whole world. This claim to antiquity enables them to assert that whatever truth has been discovered and said among all people, including the Greeks and the Jews, belongs to Christians. This view of history legitimizes the "Christian" interpretation and appropriation of the Jewish Scripture, though their reasoning is circular. Hence, they presuppose the continuity of salvation history between the Old and New Israel (the Church), between the Old Covenant and the New.[220] After all, Moses is "our prophet,"[221] the Hebrew Scriptures are "our books,"[222] and the Hebrews are "our forefathers," claims Theophilus.[223] For the Apologists, it is the prophecies of the Scriptures and their fulfillment that places Christian philosophy in the continuum of biblical history. For Tatian and Theophilus, the argument from prophecy is more connected to the role of the Divine Logos in Jewish history with only implicit allusions to the Christ event;[224] in that regard, the continuity is explained through the Hebrew Scriptures rather than through the person of Christ.

For Justin, Tertullian, and Clement, the argument from prophecy centers on the Christ event. They also conceive of the divine activity of the Logos in and through history from the time of creation as occurring through the prophets of Old Israel. However, the pinnacle of it all is the life, death, and resurrection of Jesus Christ – the heart of God's salvific plan in history (οἰκονομία). For Justin, the Logos who was manifested to the ancient Jewish patriarchs came to prophets and gave them the messages about himself. Thus, the "Old Testament" is full of such soteriological "types" (τύπος) of Christ as Noah, Jacob, Moses, and Joshua,[225] and such "symbols" (σύμβολον) as the Pascal lamb, the scapegoat, and Rahab's scarlet rope.[226] His continuous activity finds a climax in the unique event of his incarnation that had been predicted by a succession of inspired prophets since Moses. Christ's virgin birth, humiliation, crucifixion, and resurrection fulfilled all the divine prophecies about him[227] and brought about complete restoration of what had gone wrong – a doctrine which anticipates Irenaeus' famous "recapitulation" theme.[228] Thus in relation to Jews, Christ, the "Eternal Law," is the fulfillment of the Law of Moses and prophecies, and consequently also the "New Testament for the whole world"[229] – the culmination of the salvation and the whole dispensation which God had planned. In relation to Greeks, Christ, the whole Logos, is

> the principle of unity gathering into one the scattered fragments of truth divided among the different schools of Greek philosophy, the one who brings potentiality to actuality, and the teacher who extends truth beyond a narrow elite to uneducated and educated alike.[230]

Clement places the unique event of the incarnation of the Logos "within the universal context of divine purpose and human destiny," under the single principle of educating humanity back to God.[231] Therefore, Greek philosophy, like the Hebrew Scripture for Jews, functions as a "tutor" for Greeks to prepare them to receive the Christian message, the "true philosophy";[232] and with the "Old Testament" it forms part of tributaries flowing into a perennial river of Christianity.[233]

Christianity as true philosophy

Since the fundamental goal of philosophy is to lead one into true knowledge of God, the world, and one's destiny,[234] Christianity, which has comprehended and embodied the whole truth of God and his salvation, "is in itself an educational discipline (παιδεία), a philosophy superior to anything that the Greeks can offer."[235] Thus, both Justin and Tatian, while being poles apart in their attitude toward Greek philosophy, are still able to claim Christianity as true philosophy, a true way of salvation.[236] Both Tatian and Clement of Alexandria, again standing at opposing ends of the spectrum in their attitude toward Greco-Roman culture, exhort the Greeks to turn to Christianity as true philosophy, a fulfillment of human aspiration. Even Tertullian, whose apparent contempt for philosophy is elsewhere often noted,[237] is consistent in his *Apology* in describing the Christian religion as a philosophical school (*secta*) – united in wisdom learned from a Divine Teacher.[238] In this way, Christianity is not only in harmony with the highest teachings of the philosophers but supersedes Greek philosophy as the true philosophy, as the true beacon for the Greco-Roman civilization.

Power and miracles

Having established Christianity as true philosophy, the Apologists were wary of appealing to miracles as evidence of the superiority of Christian monotheism. Although miracles were important to them as Christians, the Apologists were all too well aware that the market for miracles in the contemporary Greco-Roman world was already inundated.[239] Everyone – across the different religions, social groups, and even philosophies – claimed to perform miracles (e.g. Apollonius of Tyana), and claims of miracles had little appeal to validate one's cause in the eyes of the educated. The Apologists were also sensitive to the fact that miracles were often associated with magic, a generally scandalous and seditious charge from which the learned Christians in particular wanted to dissociate their faith, especially in light of the contemporary predicament of Christianity. Ordinary people could be confused in distinguishing divine from demonic wonders, and one of the popular charges against Christianity was (black) magic. In addition, Celsus' accusation of Christ as a wicked magician (γόης) who worked his δυνάμεις by γοητεία was too close to home.[240] Hence, their argument from miracle is only peripheral and guarded by philosophical skepticism.

The Apologists mention contemporary miracles of exorcism, healing, and resurrection – the most representative types from the Gospel accounts. The power of God is primarily exercised in the name of the Christ Crucified. At his name demons shudder[241] and confess their identity,[242] and it is through his name that Christians conquer and drive out demons and evil spirits[243] and heal the sick.[244] Tatian attributes the healing power to the Divine

Logos and God.[245] He emphasizes the contrast between the genuine healing by the superior power of God and the ineffectual dependence on human medicine, magic (spells and potions), and drugs, which are all ascribed to demonic trickery. Justin also attributes magic to demonic activity and cites magical arts (μαγικαῖς τέχναις) as something that Christians have left behind and overcome upon becoming Christian.[246] Moreover, he labels the "mighty works" of Simon Magus as magic wrought by demons to deceive people.[247] Thus, he draws a firm boundary (or as much of one as he can) between Christian miracles (i.e. supernatural phenomena wrought by God), and pagan and heretical magic (i.e. supernatural phenomena wrought by demons).[248]

Finally, the power of God manifests itself most clearly in the phenomenon of resurrection. Nonetheless, the Apologists discuss the resurrection from a more philosophical rather than a phenomenological standpoint. Regarding resurrection, they point to the absolute power of God on the one hand, and to the philosophical reasonableness on the other; for, being aware of the philosophical problem of resurrection (especially in Platonism), they attempt to overcome that problem.[249] In their apologies, resurrection does not focus on the *present* resuscitation of the flesh but the *eschatological* restoration of the body, which constitutes part of God's final judgment with the Second Coming of Christ.[250] There is a parallel between creation and resurrection,[251] and as part of the eschatological events, it points to the supreme power of God.[252]

Apocryphal Acts: Christianity as true power

In contrast to the Apologists, the last subject, namely, miracles as proof of Christian monotheism and of the superiority of Christian faith, receives central attention in the Apocryphal Acts. In the popular Greco-Roman world, the idea of divinity was conceived in terms of manifestation of power, and the culture's obsession with divine power was expressed by people's fascination with supernatural wonders and those who performed or claimed to perform them. As briefly mentioned, miracles and magic, which were hardly distinguishable from the witness' standpoint, were the "universal elements" in that world.[253] The truth claims of various religions, then, exploited this saturated market of miracles and magic and competed for popular allegiance or conversion, demonstrating their "greater miracles" on the one hand and labeling the rival's miracles as magic on the other.[254] The display of the extraordinary as the essence of power, whether perceived as miracle or magic, provided the most tangible point of contact with the divine and the most powerful mode of persuasion concerning the divine. Therefore, "the supposed miracles done by these gods and the literary propaganda which made them known and enhanced their value" were keys to winning converts to new religions, concludes A.D. Nock.[255]

The Apocryphal Acts, product of the culture and age, underscore the religious value of miracle as the verification of the superiority of the Christian God and the means of conversion to Christian monotheism. Here Christianity is principally set forth in terms of power over the diabolic counterfeit power of the pagan world; harmony or co-existence cannot be conceived, only the existence of the superior and thus authentic power in the inevitable confrontation. In the Acts, the superiority of the Christian God, demonstrated again and again by his supernatural power over pagan gods, demons, diseases, and death, elicits conversion of the individuals, households, and crowds.[256]

Christian monotheism: greater power through miracles and judgments

The theme of the Acts is laid out by the declaration of Peter as he is about to confront Simon Magus who claims that he is the power of God: "I came not only for the sake of convincing you with words that he whom I preach is the Christ, but by reason of miraculous deeds and powers I exhort you by faith in Jesus Christ."[257] Throughout the Apocryphal Acts, it is the power of God in the persecuted apostle that establishes the superiority of Christian monotheism over pagan polytheism. With a strong overtone of the confrontation theme, these Acts dramatize the visible demonstration of God's power; they typically choose as a narrative setting the public theater or arena where a massive crowd can witness the power of Christian God. In the *Acts of Paul* at Ephesus, Paul is thrown into the amphitheater to fight against a beast because of the local hostility toward his preaching of the one God, Christ Jesus, against numerous pagan "gods" (7). However, the lion he meets at the theater is the very lion he has baptized, and at the governor's attempt to do away with both of them, a violent hailstorm from heaven strikes the whole crowd and rescues Paul and the lion. As a result, the multitude acknowledges the Christian God as the true God and cries out, "Save us, O God, save us, O God of the man who fought with the beasts!" (7). At Sidon, again persecuted by the locals, Paul prays to God for his deliverance and judgment, and "Apollo the god of the Sidonians" with half of his temple collapses (5). Paul's God, Christ Jesus, is the only true God of salvation because of the manifestation of his superior power over the pagan gods, whereas the pagan gods are mere idols of "stone and wood and can neither take food nor see nor hear, nor even stand" (7).

A more telling scene comes from John's confrontation with the Ephesians at the temple of Artemis in the *Acts of John*. The whole scene is quite symbolic: the contest between John, the "servant of the only God," and the Ephesians, proud worshippers of the celebrated Artemis, is held in the temple of Artemis – the strong-hold of pagan worship in antiquity. The author intensifies the conflict scene by portraying John consciously wearing black in con-trast to everyone in the temple in white garments (38). While the Ephesians attempt to seize and kill the apostle, John indicts the Ephesians for their hostility to "true piety" in the Christian God and for their stubbornness in the "old idolatry" (39). He brings his case directly to them:

> Behold, here I stand. You all assert that Artemis is powerful. Pray to her, that I alone die . . . If you do not wish to die, let me convince you of your idolatry. . . . So that you may desist from your old error. Be now converted by my God or I will die at the hands of your goddess. For I will pray in your presence to my God . . . who are [is] God above all so-called gods.
>
> (39–41)

In response to John's prayer, God's judgment falls immediately: the altar of Artemis is split into pieces, the temple is destroyed, and the priest is struck to death. Then, the crowd exclaims:

> There is only one God, that of John, only one God who has compassion for us; for you alone are God; now we have become converted, since we saw your miraculous deeds. Have mercy upon us, God, according to your will, and deliver us from our great error.
>
> (42)

As the Ephesians recognize the superior power of John's God over that of Artemis, they identify him as the only God to whom they should pledge their allegiance. The deity with greater power is the only true God who is able to rescue them from their error and preserve their lives. Certainly, there is fear of divine retribution involved in this acknowledgment; so, rising from the ground, they hurry to destroy the rest of the temple and confess, "We know that the God of John is the only one, and henceforth we worship him" (44). As Ramsey MacMullen argues, the portrayal of Christianity in the Apocryphal Acts repeatedly shows that it is its power that proves the validity of its claim of exclusive monotheism and that leads to conversion of the pagan witnesses.[258] The intertwined theme of judgment over pagan gods by the Christian God and of simultaneous conversion to the true God runs through all five Apocryphal Acts.

The presentation of Christianity as the superior power continues in the numerous exorcisms and healings performed by the apostles, and they invariably effect conversions as well. The Apocryphal Acts portray this world as bewitched and dominated by the hostile forces of demons; Satan, the chief Devil, who appears in many forms,[259] is constantly watching to deceive people with idolatry and transient illusions of the temporal world, preventing them from following the true God of Christians, and hampering any liberation by the believer from this world of senses.[260] Hence, John in his confrontation with the Ephesians sees demons behind the deception of worship of Artemis, and invokes the authority of God to drive out idols, demons, and unclean spirits as a single entity in parallel with the destruction of the temple.[261] In the *Acts of Thomas*, a link between pagan polytheism and demons, and Christian judgment on them, is more apparent. At the command of Apostle Thomas not to enter into human dwellings, demons boast of their safe haven in the idols, pagan rites, and sacrifices. Then the apostle pronounces the judgment on the pagan religions: "They shall now be destroyed with their deeds" (77); with that word the demons suddenly disappear. In the *Acts of Andrew*, the author juxtaposes Andrew's powerful exorcism from a beloved slave of the proconsul's brother Stratocles with the helplessness of magicians. Andrew attributes the magicians' inability to their association with demons – since magicians and demons have kindred relations, they cannot drive each other out (2–4); thus, besides idolatry (pagan religions), like the Apologists, the Apocryphal Acts single out magic as demonic activity per se in contrast to Christian miracles.

As the apostles cast out these adversaries, it is always by the name of Jesus Christ who is "more powerful than all powers."[262] The characteristic belief of these Acts is professed by a demon whom

74

Judas Thomas exorcises from a woman: "I fear the name of him [Jesus] who has protected you."[263] At the same time, the power of the apostles is directly authenticated by the effect of this name of the Lord[264] as the demons cry out in a manner reminiscent of the exorcisms of the Synoptics, "What have we to do with you, apostle of the Most High?"[265] Overall, the portrayals of the apostles' exorcisms closely resemble Jesus' exorcisms in the Synoptic accounts: as the apostles confront the demons, they humiliate them, make them acknowledge the (almost divine) identity of the apostles, cry for mercy, confess their secrets and evil activities, and leave in haste.[266] As MacMullen observes, this kind of handling of demons by the apostles

> served a purpose quite essential to the Christian definition of monotheism: it made physically (or dramatically) visible the superiority of the Christian's patron Power over all others. One and only was God. The rest were *daimones* demonstrably, and therefore already familiar to the audience as nasty, lower powers that no one would want to worship anyway.[267]

The combination of exorcism and healing also manifests the superior power of God. In the Apocryphal Acts, demons are often portrayed as causing physical illness, and exorcism, physical healing, and spiritual healing are intertwined and interconnected. The famous *Epitome* of the *Acts of Andrew* (*Laudatio*) by Gregory of Tours recounts only the miracles, of which the majority constitute exorcism and healing, including raising up of the dead. In one brief episode, when Andrew sees a man with wife and son, all blind, he declares, "Truly this is the work of the devil, for he has blinded them in mind and body" (32).[268] As Andrew restores their physical eyes, he also calls on the name of Jesus Christ to "unlock the darkness of [their] minds," resulting in their conversion and the conversion of many witnesses (32).

In the *Acts of John*, John's healing of the old women (30–6) is particularly illustrative of the triangular relationship of demonic power in illness, physical healing, and conversion. John commands women over sixty years of age to be cared for in the whole city of Ephesus. When he finds out that all of them except four women are sick, he regards this phenomenon as a wicked mockery of the Ephesians by the devil and plans a public spectacle of healing in the theater specifically to convert people to Christ, the God whom

75

John preaches. On the next day, as the whole city gathers in the theater, John first speaks to the whole city and to Andronicus, a *strategos*, who thought John's promise of healing "impossible and incredible." John's message is an encratic indictment of the Ephesians' unbelief and slavish bondage to the treasures, pleasures, and lust of this world and is also a call to repentance and conversion. The text then abruptly states, "Having thus spoken, John healed all their diseases by the power of God" (36). Here the demonic work in illness is taken seriously and the purpose of physical healing is directly linked to the "care for the souls" (34); the manifestation of the power of God is for the sake of spiritual healing – the exclusive worship of the true God of the apostle.

In a summary fashion, the *Acts of Thomas* speaks of Thomas' fame that "spread over all the cities and villages, and all who had sick persons or such as were troubled by unclean spirits brought them to him . . . and he healed all by the power of the Lord" (59). Then those healed and freed from demons praise Jesus and decide to follow him: "Glory to you, Jesus who in like manner has given healing to all through your servant and apostle Thomas . . . we pray that we may become members of your flock and be counted among your sheep. Receive us, therefore, O Lord" (59). Again, the *Acts of Peter* states that a multitude of Romans "brought the sick to him [Peter] on the Sabbath and asked him to treat them. And many paralytics and podagrous were healed, and those who had two- and four-day fevers and other diseases, and believed in the name of Jesus Christ" (31). Jesus Christ, whose power is mediated through the apostles, overcomes demons and diseases, and people respond to this power by worshiping Jesus as the only true God.

Most of all, it is the numerous miracles of resurrection that play the most prominent role in this theme. Unlike its treatment by the Apologists, resurrection in the Apocryphal Acts is not primarily concerned with Christ but with human beings and centers on the physical resuscitation of life as a definite present reality more than as a future reality.[269] Reflecting the current second-century emphasis on the corporeal resurrection, this understanding of resurrection as the present physical transformation from death to life is the strongest proof of God's superior power – power over death, which was thought to be the ultimate enemy of creation. Therefore, the frequent resurrection stories attest to the true life and efficacious power of the one living God the Creator and also point to the spiritual resurrection; thus resurrection becomes the surest means to bring about conversion. Andrew raises to life at least ten people

(*Laudatio*) and in one occasion, raises 39 drowned bodies (24)! John raises to life four people (*Acts John* 23, 51, 75, 80) and empowers others to perform the same miracle (24, 47, 82ff.). Peter raises two youths (*Acts Pet.* 27–8) and a gardener's daughter (*Ps.– Titus*), and empowers another to raise a youth (26). Paul raises five people, including Nero's cup-bearer (*Acts Paul* 2, 4, 8, 11), and, finally, Thomas raises three (*Acts Thom.* 33, 81) and empowers one to raise others (54).

In these five Apocryphal Acts, every resurrection event is followed by conversion except in two cases. First, in the *Acts of John*, Fortunatus, Andronicus' wicked servant, wishes to have remained dead and, running away from John, dies again soon after he is raised (83, 86); his act is attributed to his "unchangeable" nature as devil's child (83). Second, in the *Acts of Peter*, the gardener's daughter is "killed" and raised by Peter's prayer.[270] Here, the girl's death by Peter's prayer is seen as God's blessing in disguise for her soul, and her resurrection demanded by her distrustful father actually results in her "shamelessness in the flesh." These two accounts reveal that resurrections in and of themselves do not automatically result in conversions. However, they still show that physical resurrections carry spiritual consequences – even in a negative way. In all other cases, there is a clear correlation between resurrection and conversion, that resurrections always bring about spiritual rebirth. In the *Acts of John*, at John's exhortation to faith and eternal life, the resurrected priest of Artemis immediately believes in "the Lord Jesus" and follows John (47). When John raises an old man killed by his son, he says to him, "If you rise up to the same life, you would be better to remain dead. But rise up to a better" (52); and the old man immediately believes in the Lord. Physical resurrection not only testifies to the power of the supreme God, but, as such, it invariably carries a spiritual significance with it and leads to spiritual new birth offered by the same God.[271]

In Gregory's *Epitome*, a particular story of the confrontation between Andrew and the proconsul Virinus at Thessalonica illustrates in a comprehensive manner the schematic pattern of the demonstration of God's power followed by the conversion of the recipients and the onlookers (18). Here Andrew is denounced before the proconsul as destroying the established order in that Andrew preached the destruction of the temples, rites, and all the ancient laws, and that people should worship only one God, whose servant he is. He is arrested by the proconsul's soldiers on a charge of sorcery (*magus*) for his "contempt for [their] gods," but one of the proconsul's soldiers is possessed by a demon and falls dead. Andrew raises him to life but as reward is thrown into a fight with beasts, in which the animals do not touch him but a leopard instead kills the proconsul's son. Again, Andrew immediately brings him back to life, declaring to the people that "Christ is the true God" whose power conquers demons, beasts, and death. In this scene, the people praise God and reply to the confounded proconsul that they "have received the word of God, and forsaking their idols, worship the true God." The collective forces of the pagan world – idols, demons, worldly authorities, and death – fall flat at the power of the only true God, and people turn to him on account of his superior power mediated through his apostle.

In the *Acts of Peter*, resurrection is at the center of a competing power struggle between Peter's and Simon's God, for their dramatic showdown in *Forum Iulium* focuses on their attempt to raise the dead (25–8). The prefect Agrippa places one of his slaves before them. Simon kills him with a simple whisper. As Peter proceeds to raise the young slave, he declares, "Since my God and Lord Jesus Christ is now tempted among you, he is doing many signs and miracles through me to turn you from your sins" (26). When the lad is restored to life, the multitude responds with acclaim similar to the one from the *Acts of John*: "There is only one God, the God of Peter" (26). In response to the petition of an aged widow, Peter goes on to raise her son, and that again evokes a similar confession from the crowd: "You, God the Saviour, you, God of Peter, invisible God and Saviour" (27). Finally, a senator's mother requests that Peter raise her son, too. Peter then asks the multitude to be the judge and challenges Simon to restore the son. Simon on his part incites the crowd to cast Peter out of the city when he succeeds. However, Simon succeeds only in making the son move his head and open his eyes. Peter exposes it as a magical sham and Simon to be a "sorcerer" (*magus*) (28) and a "messenger of the devil" (32). Raised by Peter, the senator says to him, "I beg you . . . let us go to our Lord Jesus." Then elated Peter pleads with the crowd:

> Romans, thus the dead are awakened . . . they live for so long as it pleases God. But now I turn to you who came to see the spectacle. If you repent now from your sins and from all your man-made gods and from all uncleanness and lust, you shall receive the communion of Christ in faith so that you may obtain life for eternity.
>
> (28)

The resurrection in a contest of miracles is pivotal in ascertaining the power of the one true God and leads to the conversion of the youth and the witnesses. The defeated Simon finally flies away but falls down because of Peter's prayer and breaks his leg in three places. One of Simon's friends poignantly points out the illusion of Simon's God: "Simon, if God's power is broken, shall not that God, whose power you are, be darkened?" (32). Subsequently, people, including this friend, quickly flock to Peter and "believe in Christ." Therefore, the true God is proven to be the God of Peter who regains all the converts from Simon through his "great and wonderful sign" (9) – the wonder of resurrection.

Christian monotheism: philosophy and revelation

In this context, as the apostles' miracles demonstrate the superiority of Christian monotheism, apostles' speeches also reveal the nature of the Christian God. The apostles' miracles are usually accompanied by their messages about the God whose power wrought those wonders and what believing in that God entails. Much of the apostles' messages are strongly affected by a certain dualism of current philosophical schools and religions, especially by the Platonic "body/soul or matter/spirit" dichotomy and the Judeo-Christian eschatological or apocalyptic "this world/next world" tension.

Like the works of the Apologists, the Apocryphal Acts emphasize God's transcendence with Middle Platonic negative descriptions: God is unbegotten (ἀγέννητος), ineffable, incorrupt, invisible (ἀόρατος), invincible (ἀκράτητος), and unchangeable (ἀμετάτρεπτος); he is eternal, holy, pure, merciful, and beautiful.[272] John speaks of God as the only Creator, "the immense, the unspeakable (ἄφραστος), the incomprehensible, to whom all worldly power is subject, before whom every authority bows."[273] Certainly, this Creator God is referred to as the Father Almighty and the Father of the only begotten Son Jesus Christ in the "orthodox" sense.[274] However, in the *Acts of John* and the *Acts of Andrew*, this one transcendent God is explicitly identified as Jesus Christ and vice versa. At the farewell speech, John speaks of the "good God ... the compassionate, the merciful, the holy, the undefiled, the immaterial, the only, the one, the immutable" as "our God Jesus Christ" (107) and praises "God Jesus" as "Father of the supernatural, ruler of those in heaven, law of things ethereal, the course of things in the air" (112).

In the *Acts of Andrew*, too, there is no God other than Jesus Christ. The different predicates of God are used for Jesus interchangeably as if they were the same deity: Lord, God, Jesus, Master, unbegotten, light, life, Father, brother, majesty, above the heavens, merciful, compassionate, deliverer, the better, the beautiful, righteous, the One.[275] Christ is the one God and one Lord;[276] Jesus is never called the "Son of God" in this *Acts*. This unity of God that recognizes no distinction between God, the Lord, and Christ has been called "Christomonism" or "Unitarianism of the Second Person" and reflects the contemporary development of monarchianism (modalistic monarchianism) in that it accepts only one divine person – Jesus Christ as the very appearance of the Father God himself.[277] However, whereas modalism still affirmed the real incarnation and passion of Jesus, Christomonism denied their validity.[278]

Even in the other Acts (the *Acts of Paul*, *Acts of Peter*, and *Acts of Thomas*), where the Godhead is differentiated as the Father, Son, and the Holy Spirit in the "orthodox" sense, often the one true God whom the apostles preach and represent is identified as the Lord Jesus Christ, especially in the context of miracles and conversions.[279] The apostles perform signs and wonders on behalf of and in the name of "Jesus Christ," and people respond by believing in the "Lord Jesus" as the only God. When the apostles refer to God in speeches, it can mean either the Father or the Son (Jesus Christ), and the divine references and titles may be deliberately ambiguous.[280] In this sense, these Acts also presuppose the unity of the Godhead as they name the Christian God of superior power Jesus Christ and inadvertently accept "Christomonism" by blurring the Father–Son distinction in Godhead.

The corollary to this kind of unity of God is the elevation of the divinity of Christ even at the expense of his humanity (at times). The Apocryphal Acts are more Christocentric than theocentric. The Christology of the Apocryphal Acts in general, even where they affirm Christ's humanity, presupposes and stresses the divine nature of Jesus Christ. Jesus Christ, "the Son of the living God"[281] is above all "God Jesus Christ,"[282] and the "Lord Jesus Christ"[283] – the Lord of life, death, and the whole world. He is the "new God" of the respective apostles, the Hidden One, alien to this fallen world.[284] It should be noted that "Christ" in these Acts is not used as a title but a name; they do not follow the gnostic distinction between earthly Jesus and divine Christ but exalt the divine Jesus Christ as one person.[285] It is significant that Simon's attack on Peter's God focuses on reducing Jesus Christ to a mere human, "the son of a carpenter . . . whose family is from Judaea"; he provokes the Romans, "Men of Rome, is a God born? Is he crucified? Whoever has a master is no God" – a statement that they agree with.[286] It is Simon's challenge that leads to the climactic contest of miracles with Peter in the *Forum*, and Peter's concern is to safeguard the divinity of Christ through the demonstration of his power. Simon's charge in fact reflects both pagan and Jewish accusations in the second century against the person of Jesus and the Christian worship of Christ; the exalted Christ's divine glory in these Acts reflects a prevalent Christian apologetic response and missionary *kerygma*.[287] As mentioned, this emphasis on the divine nature and cosmic stature of Jesus Christ corresponds to the portrayal of the Christian God as the supreme power and the triumphant God and to the fundamentally spiritualizing and encratic stance of the Acts.

The Acts exhibit their "high" Christology in the following ways. First, the divine and cosmic Christ is expressed by docetism, which comes from radical forms of spirit/matter dualism in some Acts. Flesh simply serves as an occasion or a channel for the display of a power that transcends the flesh and thus comes from the divine sphere.[288] Undoubtedly, docetic Christology appears most strongly where Christomonism occurs. The section 87–104 in the *Acts of John*, including cc. 94–102, an interpolation clearly gnostic in character, presents a distinctly cosmic Christ. This section starts with Drusiana's confusion with the polymorphy of Christ and consists of John's lengthy answer to the nature of Christ, which includes: the polymorphy of Christ (88–93); The Hymn of Christ (94–6); and the revelation of the mystery of the cross (97–104). John's speech presents an alternative "gospel" on the events from the Last Supper through the crucifixion;[289] this "gospel" reveals that "the Lord is not a human being liable to physical vicissitude and suffering but the unchangeable and invincible God."[290] John describes the many forms of Christ[291] and discloses that he never saw the Lord blinking his eyes (89) or saw his footprints when walking (93). Then, the docetic Christology unfolds more fully in cc. 94–102, which contain esoteric revelations concerning the Lord's mysterious hymn and dance and the cross of light, explained by the Lord exclusively to John.

In this section (94–102), the key to the Christological mystery and revelation is the cross of light. In a cave on the Mount of Olives, to which John fled from the wooden cross of Calvary, the Lord reveals the cross of light; this, with the cross of wood, points to the two kinds of existence of Christ – heavenly and earthly – and the corresponding two kinds of people on earth, the former superior to the latter. John sees a great multitude *around the cross of light*, one

81

form and one likeness *in the cross*, and hears only the voice of the Lord without a form *above the cross* (98). This suggests that in this vision the Lord simultaneously appears in three ways: as one on the wooden cross, one in the cross of light as the cross itself, and one above the cross invisible to human sight.[292] The horizontal bar of the Lord's cross (the cross of light) divides the divine realm above from the lower world below (99). This feature certainly shows an affinity with Valentinian gnosticism. The multitude down below in the world (Jerusalem) thinks that the Lord suffered on the wooden cross with beating and piercing (97). However, those who belong to the spiritual realm, the gnostics, are to understand that the Lord's true suffering does not involve physical suffering but the "suffering of the divine light in the dark and demonic world";[293] eventually they will be united with the cross of light, the cosmic principle of order and unity – the Lord himself (99).

Similarly (though not necessarily gnostic), in the *Acts of Peter*, the cross ("hidden mystery") points to what is invisible behind the visible, and Christ's passion is to be understood as totally different from what is visible (37). Therefore, the cross is the mystery of salvation, and its meaning is revealed only by Christ, the Logos (38). The cross of light and the cross of mystery stand in opposition to the shameful cross of the canonical Gospels and Paul,[294] and the Christ of the cross of light is contrasted to the Christ of the wooden cross. The docetic cross and the docetic Christ go hand in hand.

This cross of light,[295] which is the revelation of the Lord, is called the Logos, Mind, Jesus, Christ, Door, Way, Bread, Seed, Resurrection, Son, Father, Spirit, Life, Truth, Faith, and Grace (98). In the *Acts of Peter*, a very similar list of Christological predicates appears in Peter's sermon after his explanation of polymorphous Christ: Door, Light, Way, Bread, Water, Life, Resurrection, Seed, Grace, Faith, and Logos (20). Pieter Lalleman points out an interesting parallel in Justin's titles of the Divine Logos in his *Dialogue with Trypho* mentioned in the first section: "God has begotten of Himself a certain rational Power. . . . The Holy Spirit indicates this Power by various titles": the Glory of the Lord, Son, Wisdom, Angel, God, Lord, or Logos (61.1).[296] In these descriptions, the relationship among Christ, Logos, and the cross demands our attention as a view comparable to the Apologists. The cross, called Logos,[297] is a principle of unity and order for the universe, keeping the created world in harmony;[298] whereas its horizontal beam separates the two worlds (spiritual and physical, superior and inferior), its vertical beam unites heaven and earth.[299] The cross and the

Logos, having the same cosmic role and significance, form a poly-morphous revelation of the Lord.[300] Thus, as "the mystery of the whole creation . . . and all things," the cross, Logos, and the Lord reveal the secret of the nature, conversion, and repentance of humankind.[301] In the Apocryphal Acts, however, the Logos, as a manifestation of the God Christ, does not have a separate identity or hypostasis (subsistence) as it does to Justin and the other Apologists.[302] These manifold names, titles, and identities of the Lord indicate that "the divine glory of Christ completely swallows his humanity and death."[303]

Second, the divinity of Christ is distinctively characterized by the metamorphosis and polymorphy of Christ. The metamorphosis or polymorphy of Christ is in fact part of the docetic Christology: since Christ's human form is only an illusion, he is not confined to any single illusory form on earth.[304] According to Lalleman, metamor-phosis, which is very common in Greek religions, means a person or deity taking another form, stature, or age *at any moment consecu-tively*; polymorphy is a specific kind of metamorphosis in which (usually) a deity takes several forms *at the same time* such that this deity can be seen in different forms by different people *all at the same time simultaneously*.[305] In all of the Apocryphal Acts, Christ's metamorphosis recurs in two main ways: the appearance of the Lord in the form of the (respective) apostle;[306] and the appearance of the Lord as a beautiful young man.[307] Both underline the heavenly Christ who transcends the flesh and manifests his supernatural power in the texts: the former in association with depicting the apostles as divine men and exalting their divine roles; and the latter in depicting Christ as a timely supernatural helper to the apostles and other characters.

The polymorphous Christ uniquely appears in the *Acts of John* 87–93 and the *Acts of Peter* 20–1 and is referenced in the *Acts of Thomas* 143 (cf. 153). In the *Acts of John*, Christ's polymorphy is a part of his hidden glory (δόξα), revealed only to John (88, 93). One time, different disciples see Christ in different ages: whereas James, brother of John, sees him as a child, John sees him as a handsome man (88); in another, Jesus appears to John as bald-headed man with a flowing beard while to James as a youth whose beard is just starting (89). Then Christ also assumes shapes that are physically impossible: an unattractive dwarf and huge giant reaching to heaven (89). One time on the mountain of the Transfiguration, when a light is on Christ, John peeks at his back; he sees Christ naked and not at all like a human; his feet are whiter than snow and his head reaches to heaven (90). Moreover, "a doubling of the Lord" occurs.[308] While John is with the Lord on the mountain, Peter and James see another man talking with the Lord, who has "unity which has many faces" (πολυπρόσωπον ἐνότητα); this suggests that another man is a double of the Lord.[309] On another occasion, John sees "another like him [Lord] . . . saying to my Lord" (92): two identical Jesuses in conversation with each other.

Finally, the polymorphous Christ appears not only in different ages and statures, but also in different levels of corporeality through touch.[310] When at table, as John sits on Jesus' knee and embraces him, sometimes his breast is tender and smooth, at other times hard like rock (89). On other occasions, when John attempts to touch Jesus, sometimes the Lord's body is solid and some other times immaterial and bodiless (93). These various aspects of polymorphy confirm the divine and spiritual nature of Christ that defies human comprehension and senses. As Junod and Kaestli have observed, John never tells us the Lord's usual appearance: he is never really a human being but always the immutable God.[311] It is significant that, in the *Acts of John*, Christ's polymorphy takes place during his "earthly life" and thus serves to highlight his divine fullness and eternal glory.

In the *Acts of Peter*, the polymorphy of Christ takes a different nuance. Explaining his account of the Transfiguration tradition, Peter says that each of the witnesses saw Christ in another form as one's capacity permitted (20). For Peter, Christ's majesty, brightness, and voice were indescribable, and he saw the Lord in a form he did not comprehend. In this context, he speaks of God bearing human infirmities and carrying human transgressions (cf. Isa. 53.4) and of the earthly life, suffering, death, and resurrection of the Son Christ as though Christ's taking on a human form itself was part of his polymorphy according to people's capacities. Therefore, "he ate and drank on our account though he was neither hungry nor thirsty" (20). Then, he portrays the Lord as the "Great and Small One, this Beautiful and Ugly One, this Young Man and Old Man, appearing in time, yet utterly invisible in eternity" (20). Afterwards, a company of blind widows, after being healed by a bright light, saw the Lord in different forms: some saw an old man with an indescribable appearance; some saw a young man; others saw a boy tenderly touching their eyes (21). Similar to the *Acts of John*, Christ's polymorphy here has to do with the symbols of light/enlightenment and blindness/giving of sight in the context of the Christological revelation. However, unlike the *Acts of John*, here this revelation of polymorphy is not restricted to the apostle alone but is more inclusive.[312] Peter considers this polymorphy as evidence of Christ's greatness and majesty beyond human understanding and at the same time of Christ's condescension and accommodation to the different capacities of people (21).[313]

In the *Acts of Thomas*, Thomas becomes the bearer of the Transfiguration tradition and Christ's polymorphous revelation of his nature (143).[314] In a discourse with Vazan, King Misdaeus' son and a prospective convert, who asks him what the nature, power, and glory of his God is, Thomas begins with esoteric statements:

> Believe in the Healer of all pains, hidden and manifest. . . .
> He [Christ] is the Father of the height and the Lord and judge of nature. He became the highest from the greatest (παρὰ τοῦ μεγίστου), the only-begotten Son of the depth (βάθος).

Then the statements take a docetic turn:

> And he was called (ἐνομίζετο) son of the virgin Mary and son of the carpenter Joseph; he whose lowliness we beheld with our bodily eyes, whose majesty (μεγαλειοτῆτα), how-ever, we have received by faith and seen in his works (ἐργοις); whose human body we handled with our hands, whose transfigured appearance (ἐνηλλοιωμένην θέαν) we saw with our eyes, whose heavenly form (τύπος), however, we could not see on the mountain.
>
> (143)

Christ *appears* here in three forms: human body, transfigured appear-ance, and heavenly form. His polymorphy corresponds to different levels of understanding Christ: through bodily senses (touch and eyes), enlightened eyes, and beyond human capacity. Christ's glory and majesty are so great that we can only perceive them through his (miraculous) works and by faith. Christ's polymorphy is again the manifestation of his glory (cf. 153) and part of his mystery, his Hidden nature.

What then can be said about the humanity of Christ? Whereas there is hardly any reference to Jesus' incarnation, earthly ministry, physical passion, and resurrection in the *Acts of John* and the *Acts of Andrew*, the reality of those events is assumed and affirmed in those Acts (*Acts of Paul*, *Acts of Peter*, and *Acts of Thomas*) where the doctrinal Christonomism does not explicitly occur. In the so-called *Third Corinthians* in the *Acts of Paul*, the "physical" aspect of the Christ event, including the virgin birth, is clearly laid out with a strong anti-gnostic and anti-docetic message; the author emphasizes that Christ's corporeal resurrection guarantees the corporeal resurrection of the dead in future (3). In the *Acts of Peter*, Peter identifies Christ, born of the Virgin Mary, as "the crucified Nazarene, who died and rose again on the third day" (7). In spite of its harsh condemnation of anything bodily and material, the *Acts of Thomas* upholds the human Jesus as well as the divine Jesus, who was "man, slain, dead, buried" (47) and incorporates many ethical sayings of the historical Jesus, citing mainly from the Sermon on the Mount in the canonical Matthew and the *Gospel of Thomas* (e.g. 28, 36, 53; 136, 147).[315] This Jesus Christ is the promised Messiah of the prophetic writings, and thus these Acts along with the *Acts of Peter* assume continuity with the Old Testament.[316] In these five Acts, nonetheless, Christ's humanity, though real and important, is still seen in light of his divinity. The incarnation itself is a part of Christ's polymorphy in accommodation to people's capacity, and his humanity does not have any real bearing upon the soteriology of the Acts. In this way, Christ's humanity tends to be overshadowed by his eternal spiritual nature.

Apostle as a divine man: the mediator

As one can see, the Christianity represented in the Apocryphal Acts through miracles and speeches is the Christianity of the apostle who acts as an intermediary between the transcendent God and the physical, polluted world.[317] Despite the Christocentric character of the Apocryphal Acts, since Christ's divinity is elevated and the cosmic Christ identified often as the one supreme God, it creates a vacuum in the role of mediator between the transcendent God and the transient world. It is the individual apostle in these Acts who is the mediator between the divine and the fallen world, the role that the Divine Logos assumes as the creator and the revealer in the Apologies.[318] Thus, "the apostles, however much their power may be attributed to Christ, nevertheless occupy center stage in the drama."[319] They are the hero whose words and actions reveal "the effusion of the divine and the supernatural in history."[320] Indeed, the apostles in these Acts respond to the demand and the question of the pagans: "Show us . . . who is your God?"[321]

The apostle's mediating role as a revealer of God's nature and power and the way of salvation takes place in this world of senses, which is corrupt, transient, and deceptive under demonic control; humanity is in bondage of body, ignorance, and slumber under the power of this world.[322] Through the apostle, the merciful God offers humanity salvation, which is an escape or deliverance out of this material world of darkness and carnality.[323] Salvation is not through faith in the Christ event but through acceptance of the apostolic revelation of the divine power, wisdom, and mystery.[324]

For example, in the *Acts of Andrew*, Andrew functions as a Socratic "midwife" who brings forth the "inner man," who is immaterial, immortal, pure, light, and akin (συγγενής) to God (7, 38). As a "messenger of the living God," (8)[325] he is the sower (σπορεύς) of the salvific words in the redeemed (44),[326] and his words act as a mirror to one's soul (47). Andrew is also a redeemed redeemer, for, as he delivers himself out of this world, his own redemption is bound up with others – their obedience to the revelation to "recognize their true nature" (cf. 37–40, 47).[327] He is even portrayed as a philosopher whose "philosophy" is superior to that of pagans (cf. 59); Andrew's discourse with Stratocles, philosopher, makes the latter realize that his "former philosophy" was hollow and is now destitute, useless, and worthless (7). In the contemporary Middle Platonic and Neo-Pythagorean language and concept, Andrew presents Christian faith as eternal, timeless, and true philosophy, which surpasses, supersedes, and passes judgment on all "former religion" and "former philosophy."[328] In this way, he proves himself a divine man (θεῖος ἀνήρ); his overpowering miracles, his supernatural message and revelations, his power of discernment, his metamorphosis, his ascetic life, and his extraordinary and voluntary character of his death – all of them establish the apostle as a divine person who bridges between God and humanity.[329]

Moreover, the apostles receive divine honors and veneration from people,[330] introduce a new God and religion, convert the masses, and gather a group of disciples around themselves.[331] In the Apocryphal Acts, the apostles are the physicians of both souls and bodies – the divine men who are the inimitable mediators and thus hold the key to the sovereign God and his celestial world.

Christian polemic

In these apostolic presentations of Christian monotheism, the polemical tone of the Acts persists. Wherever the apostle goes and whatever he says or does, his presentation of a "new God" is in sharp conflict with the contemporary society and its religious beliefs. The world of the Apocryphal Acts – the world of signs and wonders, dreams and visions, and demons and magic – mirrors in reality the contemporary Greco-Roman world. Greco-Roman society is a heartland of marvelous nostalgia and a hub of riches, power, pleasure, and allurement of the temporal existence, and thus embodies the wicked and corrupt world in error and illusion. The Apocryphal Acts draw the line between those who would follow the apostles and their one God, and those who would follow the Devil in pagan idolatry and bondage to this life: the insiders and the outsiders; and the spiritual and the physical. The Acts' dualistic outlook demands a "we" versus "they" mindset and calls for simultaneous resistance to and judgment on contemporary religion, philosophy, society, and culture whose values do not recognize the power and truth of the one true God. Therefore, the apostle's spiritual power outstrips all enemies and turns them into Christians through various miracles and revelatory speeches; even his martyrdom, the final battle which crowns all the previous conflicts, testifies not to a defeat but to the ultimate power of and glory to the Christian God that He is in control.

Martyr Acts: Christianity as true piety

If the Apologies present Christianity as true philosophy and the Apocryphal Acts represent it as true power, the Martyr Acts portray it as true piety. In the ancient world, the universal language of religious piety (εὐσέβεια, *pietas*) was offering of a sacrifice. The sacred rite of sacrifice was an essential part of the Greco-Roman religion and tradition (*mos maiorum*) and a visible means of public worship to secure *pax deorum* and avert divine wrath. The sacrificial system and structure were well integrated into the urban civic (social and political) life with festivals, athletic games, and imperial cults since the ancient society was fundamentally religious. The content of the offering covered all forms of material sacrifices to the gods and the emperors, including burning of incense, but, most often and most importantly, it involved the killing and burning of animals. In contrast to this pagan piety in the traditional sacrificial system, the Martyr Acts present Christian piety in a radically new and different sacrificial system. As the Apologists claimed, Christians rejected the material sacrifices of the pagans (and the Jews); instead, they insisted on the "spiritual sacrifices" of rational worship to the supreme God.

The Martyr Acts present martyrdom as the supreme sacrifice to the true God and portray Christian monotheism in close connection with this new Christian sacrifice in fundamental conflict with the pagan εὐσέβεια. As Frend observes, "what was εὐσέβεια to the pagan was ἀσέβεια to the Christian and vice versa."[332]

Christian monotheism

In the Martyr Acts, the consistent demand made of Christians at the trials before the Roman authorities is to offer sacrifice to the gods and/or the emperors[333] or to swear by the gods and/or the emperors' genius.[334] It appears that the "sacrifice-test," which had already been used by Pliny in the early second century,[335] had now become the standard measure for the investigation of Christians by the mid-century. The Christian refusal to offer sacrifice, which is seen as irrational and incomprehensible obstinacy by the Roman officials, demonstrates more than their uncompromising persistence and heroism; it unveils the inevitable clash between the two opposing systems of worship: the worship of the one God of Christians and the worship of the many traditional gods of the Empire.[336]

Who the Christians worship determines how they worship and who they are, and, obviously, their exclusive belief in the one true God provides the reason for their refusal to sacrifice. When ordered by the proconsul to sacrifice to the gods, Carpus replies:

> The living do not sacrifice to the dead . . . they [pagan gods] are nothing: made of earth's substance (ὕλη), they are destroyed by time. Whereas our God, who has created the ages, is timeless (ἄχρονος) and he abides eternal (αἰώνιος) and immortal (ἄφθαρτος); ever the same (ἀει), he cannot suffer increment or diminution.[337]

Speratus, one of the Scillitan Martyrs, when faced with the order to swear by the genius of the emperor, declares, "I do not recognize the empire of this world. Rather, I serve that God whom no man has seen, nor can see, with these eyes."[338] Here the character of the Christian God expressed by the martyrs echoes that of the transcendent God articulated by the Apologies and Apocryphal Acts in Middle Platonic negative theology. This rationalistic portrayal of God even in the Martyr Acts points to the general theological tendency in early Christianity.

The God whom Christians worship is "the one, true God, the One existing before all the ages (θεὸς τὸν ὄντα [τὸν] πρὸ αἰώνων), who was not fashioned by human hands, but rather appointed a man among men to be ruler over the earth."[339] As the sole Creator (δημιουργός) of the universe,[340] "God has no name as men have" (ὁ θεὸς ὄνομα οὐκ ἔχει ὡς ἄνθρωπος),[341] and he is the omnipotent and almighty Father (πατὴρ παντοκράτωρ)[342] and the "living and true God, who has power over all flesh."[343] At the consummation of the world, God will execute the "true and eternal judgment (*uerum et perpetuum iudicium*), where there will be no mercy" for the impious, i.e. Roman officials and pagans (and Jews), on the one hand[344] and where there awaits the divine gift of eternal life and the victor's crown for the pious, i.e. Christian martyrs, on the other.[345] There is no other God than this invisible (ἀόρατος) and invincible (ἀνικήτου) God of Christians who deserves their worship and "sacrifice."[346]

God's transcendence and sovereignty is drastically contrasted with the lifeless artificial gods of paganism. The *Martyrdom of Apollonius*, which itself is a sophisticated apology for Christianity, puts forth the truth of the pagan gods in several categories in a manner similar to the Apologists. In response to the proconsul Perennis' urge to worship the gods that the Romans worship, Apollonius asserts that those "gods" are merely "gold or silver, bronze or iron, . . . false gods made of stone or wood, who can neither see nor hear" (14); they are "but the work of craftsmen . . . and have no life of their own" (14). Moreover, pagan gods ridiculously include produce such as garlic and onions, animals such as monkeys and cows, and the gods of myths who were once human beings given divine honors (16–22). Apollonius declares that he only worships the Creator God who "breathed into all men a living soul and daily pours life into all" (15) and that he will not humiliate himself and commit sin by worshiping "what is no better than man and, indeed, inferior to the demons (δαιμόνων)" (16). In fact, as the Apologists and the writers of the Apocryphal Acts all agree, these so-called gods are none other than deceptive demons, and "those who sacrifice to them are like them."[347] Therefore, Christians, who worship the only true life-giving God, cannot sacrifice to the dead idols, creatures, and demons that are subject to the eternal judgment of their God.[348]

This one true God is the Father of Jesus Christ who is the Savior[349] and the Lord.[350] The Martyr Acts, as we will see, are not concerned about the philosophical exposition of the Father–Son relationship in terms of their divine unity and distinction any more than what later emerges as the New Testament. Although Christ is never explicitly identified as "God" and is always clearly distinguished from the Father, his divinity and monotheism are always assumed and taken for granted. Christology in these Acts is deeply connected to soteriology and may reflect the contemporary "orthodox" missionary *kerygma* concerning Christ. As the Son of God,[351] Jesus Christ was foretold by the prophets to come to the world as a "herald of salvation and a teacher of good doctrines";[352] when he came, he delivered humanity from the deceits of the Devil.[353] As mentioned, his divinity is not explained but taken for granted; his incarnation is presupposed and his earthly life is absolutely essential in these Acts. The *Martyrdom of Apollonius* provides a relatively rich exposition of his person, life, and work. The salvific function of Jesus Christ is closely related to his role as a teacher. As the Logos of God, he not only knows all the thoughts of people (5) but also taught people the divine wisdom (36). He taught "who was the God of all things, and what was the purpose of virtue in a life and holiness" (36); he taught to "worship the immortal God alone," to despise death, and to believe in a divine judgment and reward after death (37–8). Jesus, who himself attained a renown for virtue, reasoned with people, taught principles of morality and virtue, and, like Socrates, was condemned by malefactors (41). In this portrayal of Jesus, he is likened to the philosophers and noble men of the past, especially Socrates, and this particular presentation of Jesus, supported by the fine examples of philosophers of the past, mirrors that of Justin and Clement of Alexandria.[354]

The most important aspect of Christ is his passion and death. "By his passion he [Jesus Christ] destroyed the roots of sin," declares Apollonius;[355] he "suffered for the redemption of those who are saved in the entire world" (17.2), writes the author of the *Martyrdom of Polycarp*. Christ's passion effected atonement and redemption of people, and, therefore, his death was seen as an atoning sacrifice.[356] He is not only the "eternal and celestial high priest,"[357] but also a victim, offering himself to God as the perfect sacrifice.[358] Thus, he is the first "martyr" (a witness by death): "the true and faithful witness, the first-born of the dead, and the prince of God's life."[359] It is precisely through his death that he overcame his Adversary (ἀντικείμενος), the Devil, and thus received glory (δόξα).[360] Christ the Sufferer and the Victim is Christ the Victor and "the mighty and invincible Athlete" (μέγαν καὶ ἀκαταγώνιστον ἀθλητής).[361]

In this way, Christ modeled the martyrdom "in accordance with God's will"[362] for the saints to follow and imitate.[363] Moreover, it is Christ who strengthens and empowers his martyrs in their contests (ἀγῶνοι) with the Adversary and who manifests his glory in and through their sufferings.[364] The "glorious Christ . . . represented as actively present in the life of the Church" and the individual martyrs, is "thought of as a heavenly source of life, strength, dynamism, and consolation" to his martyrs, as he is united with them in their struggles and sufferings.[365] This interpretation of Christ's passion and death in the Martyr Acts carried practical implications for late second-century Christians faced with occasional persecutions and sufferings whether real or perceived. It set the theological (Christological) basis for and vindication of Christian suffering and martyrdom; since "Christ suffered and died in the same [physical] way that we do ourselves can our suffering and death imitate his."[366]

Martyrs as the imitators of Christ

Hence, martyrs are the imitators of Christ (μιμηταὶ Χριστοῦ) par excellence.[367] The chief motivation and goal for martyrdom is to become "a partaker of Christ"[368] by sharing in the Lord's suffering.[369] The martyr's death is intimately connected with the Lord's in obedience to the divine will. In this motif of *imitatio Christi*, the Martyr Acts adopted from the Greco-Roman society and Hellenistic Judaism the two most prominent cultural and religious symbols: the athletic contest and the sacrifice, which are often mixed in presentations; martyrs imitate Christ through their athletic contests and self-sacrifices to God.[370]

Martyrs as the imitators of Christ: martyrdom as the contest for Christ

Eusebius, in his preface to the *Martyrs of Lyons* in his *Ecclesiastical History*, explains the nature of their martyrdom chiefly in athletic imageries:

> It is the struggles of the athletes of piety (ἀθληταὶ εὐσέβειας) and their valour which braved so much, trophies (τρόπαιά) won from demons, and victories (νίκαι) against unseen adversaries, and the crowns (στέφανοι) at the end of it all, that it [the following record] will proclaim for everlasting remembrance.
>
> (5)

Following after Christ, "the mighty and invincible Athlete,"[371] the martyrs are engaged in the contest (ἀγών) as the noble athletes (γενναῖοι ἀθληταί) for a crown.[372] Their contest is twofold: the conflict with the pagan opponents, such as the Roman officials and the crowd – the Devil's minions;[373] and the supernatural combat against the Adversary, the Devil himself, just like that of Christ.[374]

In this contest, especially with the Devil, athletic imagery is combined with military imagery; while still called the noble athletes, martyrs are portrayed as God's prized combatants who fight against the angry onslaught and attacks of the enemy (the Devil) and overcome him. Similarly, martyrs as the athletes are also portrayed as the "gladiators for Christ."[375] In fact, the actual events of martyrdom frequently took place as public spectacles in arenas or the amphitheaters, where the athletic and gladiatorial contests were held. Thus, among the Gallic martyrs, Maturus, Sanctus, Blandina, and Attalus were exposed to various tortures and beasts in an amphitheater in a pre-arranged day of gladiatorial games (τῆς τῶν θηριομαχιῶν ἡμέρας).[376] Attalus is said to have entered the arena "as a warrior (ἀγωνιστής) well prepared for the contest,"[377] and other martyrs were made a spectacle (θέαμα) to the world as a substitute for various gladiatorial combats.[378] When none of the animals touched the slave heroine Blandina hung on a post in the form of a cross, she was preserved for another day of the gladiatorial games. This was because

> for her victory in further contests she would make irreversible the condemnation of the crooked serpent, . . . for she had put on Christ, that mighty and invincible athlete, and had overcome the Adversary in many contests, and through her conflict had won the crown of immortality.[379]

In the case of Perpetua, she and her fellow martyrs were supposed to fight with the beasts at the military games (*munere castrensi*) in honor of the Emperor Geta's birthday.[380] On the day before the contest, she had a vision of herself fighting as a man with an Egyptian in the game administered by a huge figure in the attire of a *lanista* (ἀγωνοθέτης, "president of games or spectacles").[381] She defeated the Egyptian and soon recognized this vision as a divine revelation of the true Adversary with whom she would fight and whom she would overcome in her contest (*munus*) of martyrdom.[382] The word, *munus*, used for gladiatorial spectacles, occurs throughout the text to describe the kind of death that Perpetua and her companions would undergo, in which they gain their victory (*uictoria*).[383] Furthermore, Felicitas, who had given birth to a child while in prison but joined Perpetua in the amphitheater for the *munus*, is described as one who "could fight the beasts, going from one blood bath to another, from the midwife to the gladiator (*retiarius*, "net-fighter"), ready to wash after childbirth in a second baptism."[384]

The portrayal of the martyrs as gladiators and their struggles as gladiatorial contests reflects not only the contemporary cultural scene of violence and its influence on Christian literature but also the conscious Christian appropriation of the culture of violence in transforming the image of martyrs.[385] For, in a bitter irony, the despised gladiators (often condemned criminals or slaves) were "glamour figures, culture heroes."[386] The moment they took a solemn oath of violence and death, the *sacramentum gladiatorium*, their fate became a point of honor;[387] and as long as they valiantly kept the oath, they provided one model for "the man of honor," "an ideal type of the soldier-philosopher," for their severe discipline (*askesis*), strength, and bravery.[388] Given that they would fight to death with contempt of life and intense "love of death" (*amor mortis*), they could gain glory from the crowd,[389] for they were offered "another opportunity to redeem [their] honor and display [their] valor before the eyes of the enemy."[390] Therefore, the gladiator was, "in one aspect, a metaphor of empowerment, and the *munus* a ritual of empowerment"; the gladiator's existence provided "a means of gaining honor within a dishonorable situation, and a way of transforming humiliation into self-sacrifice."[391] Christian martyrs depicted as the gladiators were accorded with "the inverse exaltation" similar to the Roman gladiators.[392] The Martyr Acts transformed their status from the reviled obdurate criminals and irreligious atheists to the noble heroes and heroines with unflinching endurance, courage, and valor in the face of death.[393]

The martyrs' attitude toward death can also be characterized by "love of death" as they exhibit seemingly incomprehensible joy and tranquility[394] with thanksgiving[395] and glowing countenance[396] at the prospect of their death – although the motivation and reason for such an attitude are radically different from that of the gladiators. Their love of death was motivated by "escaping the eternal fire" of God's Judgment on the one hand,[397] and by winning "the crown of immortality" (τῆς ἀφθαρσίας στέφανος), the eternal life (their ultimate prize for victory) on the other.[398] Furthermore, with the desire of wanting to imitate Christ, the martyrs had the vision of Christ's glory[399] and Paradise[400] to win their contests.

The *Martyrs of Lyons* draws a sharp contrast among the would-be martyrs between those who made a full confession of their faith "with the greatest enthusiasm" and those "stillborn" who denied it (1.11). The former group was "comforted by the joy of martyrdom, their hope in the promises, their love for Christ, and the Spirit of the Father; whereas the others were greatly tormented by their conscience" and humiliated over their defection (1.34). These two groups correspond to the contrast between those who have been "nobly trained in the Christian discipline" (ἐπειδὴ γνησίως ἐν τῇ Χριστιανῇ συντάξει γεγυμνασμένος ἦν) to witness to Christ, such as Attalus (1.43), and those who are "still untrained, unprepared, and weak, unable to bear the strain of a great conflict" (οἱ ἀνέτοιμοι καὶ ἀγύμναστοι καὶ ἔτι ἀσθενεῖς, ἀγῶνος μεγάλου τόνον ἐνεγκεῖν μὴ δυνάμενοι) (1.11). Then, crucial also to the agonistic theme of the martyrdom was the training for martyrdom,[401] which involved the public confession of faith, "I am a Christian" (Χριστιανός/ ἡ εἰμι; *Christianus/a sum*),[402] and the knowledge of ("orthodox") Christian teaching.[403] This training bore a significant consequence for the "quality" and "effect" of the Church's witness to the hostile world and for the internal example for the future contestants. Thus, the annual celebration of the martyrs' deaths served "both as a memorial for those who have already fought the contest and for the training and preparation of those who will do so one day."[404]

Martyrs as the imitators of Christ: martyrdom as the sacrifice

The second and related element in the *imitatio Christi* motif is that of the self-sacrifice of martyrs; martyrs imitate Christ as the sufferer and the victim of sacrificial offering to God. The interpretation of Christ's passion and death as the atoning sacrifice for others with salvific significance in obedience to God's will is solidly grounded in the New Testament. This early formulation of Christian faith is in turn linked with the Jewish understanding of vicarious suffering and "martyrdom": that the violent deaths of the chosen exemplary servants of God were sacrificially efficacious, starting from the Suffering Servant in Deutero-Isaiah and most visible in the Second Maccabees and the Fourth Maccabees.[405] Here, possibly, we can consider another background: "the Roman model of aristocratic voluntary self-sacrifice," *devotio*.[406] The *devotio* was

the ceremonial dedication by the Roman general Publius Decius Mus in the Samnite Wars (340 BCE) of his body, through a violent death at the hands of the enemy, to the Earth and the gods of the dead, before and in return for the victory of his beleaguered troops.[407]

It was the general's bargain with the hostile Power in the hope that the gods would accept not only the lives of the enemy but also his own life as full payment for the victory of his troops.[408] Livy, Cicero, and Juvenal all regarded Decius Mus as an "expiatory sacrifice (*piaculum*) for the Roman forces that transfers the wrath of the gods (the plague or *pestis*) to himself and to the enemy,"[409] and it led to the belief that the death of the good man was acceptable to the benevolent gods. Therefore, the *"devotio* is *either/or and both* expiatory sacrifice and free gift."[410] The Christian martyr's sacrificial death should be seen in this larger context of expiatory suffering and death of the righteous precisely in sacrificial terms.

This theme of martyr's death as sacrifice is most evident in the *Martyrdom of Polycarp*, which lays out the martyrdom "in accordance with the Gospel" (1.1), that is, "in accordance with God's will" (2.1). The negative example of this is Quintus, who, of his own will, gave himself up but ended up swearing by the pagan gods and offering sacrifice to them (4). The central conflict and testing revolves around the sacrifice – to the pagan gods or the one true God of Christians? In contrast to Quintus, Polycarp, the chosen vessel of God, re-enacts in his own martyrdom the passion and martyrdom of Jesus as an efficacious and acceptable sacrifice to God. Thus, the details of his martyrdom are patterned after the Gospel accounts of Jesus' passion: Polycarp's judge is called Herod (6.2; 8.2); the soldiers arrest him as though he were a brigand (7.1; Matt. 26.55); he enters Smyrna riding a donkey (8.1); and when Polycarp enters his passion, he intercedes for "everyone and for all the churches" in the world (5.1; 8.1; cf. John 17.7–26) and prays, "May God's will be done" (7.1).[411]

Polycarp's refusal to confess, "Caesar is Lord," and to sacrifice (8.2) is coupled with his rejection of animal sacrifice and other aspects of pagan worship (11.1–2). After the governor's verdict, Polycarp "was bound like a noble ram chosen for an oblation from a great flock, a holocaust prepared and made acceptable to God" (14.1; ὥσπερ κριὸς ἐπίσημος ἐκ μεγάλου ποιμνίου εἰς προσφοράν, ὁλοκαύτωμα δεκτὸν τῷ θεῷ ἡτοιμασμένον). Then, he prayed at the stake, "I bless you [God] because you have thought me worthy of this day and this hour, to have a share among the number of the martyrs in the cup of your Christ, for the resurrection unto eternal life. . . . May I be received this day among them before your face as a rich and acceptable sacrifice" (ἐν οἷς προσδεχθείην ἐνώπιόν σου ὅμερον ἐν θυσίᾳ πίονι καὶ προσδεκτῇ) (14.2).[412] His inflamed body subsequently had "such a delightful fragrance" of incense (15.2) and, in the end, his life was taken by the sword; he then shed so much blood that it extinguished the flames (16.1). In this way, Polycarp's sacrifice (i.e. his martyrdom) *overcame* not only the unjust rulers (ἄρχον) but also the Adversary (ὁ ἀντικείμενος), the Evil One, and so won the crown of immortality (19.2). Furthermore, by his own martyrdom, he put a stop to the persecution (1.1), saved not only himself but also all his brothers (1.2), and thus became an exemplar for others to imitate (1.2) in his obedience to God's will. Finally, Polycarp offered himself as a supreme praise offering to God in response to and in imitation of Christ's atoning sacrificial death, as Polycarp's sacrifice was prepared by God himself and performed through the "eternal and celestial high priest, Jesus Christ" (14.3).[413]

The portrayal of martyrdom as sacrifice unto God is also visible in the *Martyrs of Lyons*, again in combination with the athletic metaphors. Maturus and Sanctus, after a long contest of being made a spectacle to the multitude as a substitute for a gladiatorial combat, were in the end sacrificed (ἐτύθησαν) to God (1.40). Attalus and Alexander, too, after gruesome torture and intense contest with the beasts, were finally sacrificed (ἐτύθησαν) (1.51). Lastly, Blandina was also "offered in sacrifice" (ἐτύθη) to God after enduring so much suffering by the beasts and other tortures (1.56). The martyrs' sacrifice was understood to be efficacious in the war against the Demon (2.6) and in bringing about salvation and benefits for the community. By the martyrs' sacrifice "the dead were restored to life through the living; the martyrs brought favour to those who bore no witness" (1.45); those who had denied the faith were "born again" and redeemed to confess Christ (1.46, 48). The martyrs joyously offered their own various types of martyrdom to God as the one crown of victory (1.36), adorned with rich ornaments and the sweet odor of Christ (1.35). Thus, the three aspects of the martyr's sacrifice in the *Martyrdom of Polycarp* echo in these Acts: it brings salvation and forgiveness for themselves and others, defeats the power and schemes of the Adversary, and offers praise and worship to God in response to Christ's own salvific sacrifice. All of these are an integral part and result of imitating Christ, who is the Perfect Martyr and Sacrifice for all.

Christianity as true sacrifice and true piety

Martyrdom was a public act and spectacle, charged with powerful emotions and rich symbolism, and it took place in the middle of urban surroundings and religious rituals, whether as part of an athletic contest or sacrifice. The conspicuous urban setting for martyrdom was significant. The martyrs moved from prison to tribunal, usually located in the agora, the central part of the city, and near the temple in which sacrifice to the Emperor in addition to the gods would be enjoined.[414] In addition, as previously mentioned, the days of martyrdom usually coincided with the major holidays, such as the Great Sabbath (Μέγα Σάββατον)[415] and the Emperor Geta's birthday,[416] on which festivals, games, and sacrificial rituals were expected to take place, attracting large crowds. Then, with this great visibility, the spectacle of martyrdom could make a forceful impact on the audience, resulting in conversions from pagans and secondary martyrdoms from Christians. For example, in the *Martyrdom of Perpetua and Felicitas*, the adjutant Puden became a Christian by the martyrs' display of extraordinary virtues and strength (9.1; 16.4). Also, the soldier Basilides, who led the heroine Potamiaena to her death, professed his Christian faith in public after her noble death and even joined her in martyrdom.[417] Another Christian, Agathonicê, threw herself into the flame when inspired by the vision of Christ at the moment of Carpus' death;[418] and Lucius and an unknown man shared the fate of Ptolemaeus while protesting on his behalf in the trial.[419] Thus, Tertullian's famous statement, "the blood of the martyrs is seed," was not merely rhetorical.[420]

In the form of both athletic contest and sacrificial rite, martyrdom was a public ritual and dramatic "liturgical sacrifice in which the word of Jesus and his kingdom was confessed and acted out, and an offering made that repeated his own."[421] The martyrs, "the athletes of piety," proclaimed loud and clear that Christianity was the true piety over against the pagan piety by virtue of their public confession and self-offering: the supreme sacrifice in imitation of Jesus Christ. If one recalls that the purpose of sacrifice is to restore *pax deorum* and harmony to the community, that is, to reinforce the socio-religious fabric,[422] the Martyr Acts' portrayal of martyrdom and thus of Christianity as true sacrifice indeed turns the table on pagan sacred piety and upsets the entire structure of Greco-Roman religion and society. Christians' daring refusal to participate in pagan sacrifice is juxtaposed with their joyous offering of their prayers, praises, and finally their own lives to the one true God of creation. When Perpetua and her fellow martyrs entered the arena for their combat, she firmly resisted the authorities' attempt to dress them as priests of Saturn (for men) and priestesses of Ceres (for women).[423] For not only was the authorities' attempt a deliberate insult to Christian monotheism but it might have meant using them as both ministers and sacrifice to those gods.[424] These martyrs instead insisted on their "free will" and "freedom" to die as Christians[425] – as pure and noble sacrifice to the true God.

The martyrs publicly testify that the so-called traditional gods to whom pagans offer sacrifice are only dead idols and in fact evil demons, and, therefore, pagan sacrifice is false, ineffective, and a mere semblance of true sacrifice. However, since the Christian God is the only true God, Christian sacrifice, most remarkably in the form of dying for God, is the true sacrifice; hence, Christian worship is the only authentic worship. One has only to remember that one of the functions of martyrdom as a cosmic contest and efficacious sacrifice to God was conquering the Devil, the chief of the pagan gods. Thus, Justin Martyr replies to the prefect's urge to sacrifice: "What person of sound mind . . . would choose to turn from piety (εὐσέβεια) to impiety (ἀσέβεια), from light to darkness, and from the living God to soul-destroying demons?"[426] The object of their worship authenticates the means of their worship (i.e. martyrdom as sacrifice), and this is inversely applied for the pagan gods and pagan worship.

The object of Christian worship also authenticates Christian confession and identity. This presentation of Christianity as true sacrifice to the true God, thus as true piety, validates the Christians with the confession "I am a Christian" as true worshipers in contrast to the falsehood of pagan worship. It is significant and inevitable that this confession of Christian identity immediately follows the martyrs' rejection to partake in pagan sacrifice and their affirmation of Christian monotheism.[427] This confession also unequivocally answers the question, "Are you a Christian?" which usually precedes the demand to offer sacrifice, and thus provides a valid reason for the Roman officials to persecute and execute Christians.[428] Therefore, this confession is a crucial part of martyrs' training[429] and constitutes the most resounding declaration of the Christian self-definition.

Martyrs as mediators

If Christianity is true sacrifice and thus true piety in contrast to pagan piety, the perfect mediator as the perfect sacrificial victim is

Jesus Christ. However, this fact notwithstanding, the Martyr Acts also depict the martyrs as mediators in several aspects. While the martyrs' deaths can never replace that of Christ, as the *imitatores Christi*, their self-sacrifice unto God brings about redemption, victory over the Adversary, and thanksgiving and praise pleasing to God. The martyr's sacrifice is analogous to Christ's sacrifice and therefore is to be understood as the same kind: a sacrifice offered as a ransom to avert the power of the Evil One and effect forgiveness of sin and expiation; "the warfare against the Devil in which Christ had already won the ultimate victory";[430] a sacrifice of perfect worship and obedience to God. "Like Christ, the martyr glorified God simply by his willing self-sacrifice to the cause of dealing with the sin and evil of the world."[431] The martyr was in Christ and Christ was in the martyr. In the person of the suffering martyr, bruised and disfigured by unspeakable tortures, Christ who was suffering in him "achieved great glory, overwhelming the Adversary."[432]

Often included in the redemptive role of the martyrs is their intercession for the individual believers and the Church. As already mentioned, Polycarp, when he learned of his imminent martyrdom, interceded for the "entire Catholic Church."[433] The martyrs of Lyons "gave of their own abundance to those in need [those who had fallen], showing to them a maternal love, shedding many tears on their behalf before the Father."[434] The very Life they obtained through their martyrdom, they shared with fellow believers.[435] Potamiaena, when led by the soldier Basilides to execution, prayed for him that he would join her in martyrdom and thus get a crown by God's grace.[436] Perpetua prayed for her deceased brother Dinocrates' salvation, and the efficacy of her prayer was confirmed through the vision in which Dinocrates appeared all clean, well dressed, and refreshed.[437] Martyrs' prayers were thought efficacious because of their special intimacy with Christ by their imitation of Christ. Thus, through their prayers the martyrs not only brought together disillusioned and demoralized communities but their work also resulted in conversion.[438]

Martyrs also reveal God's presence and power in their contests and sufferings. In the words of Robin Young:

> Because martyrs bore the name of Christ, they were themselves like letters meant to be read by the community and the world, letters from Christ that were recognizably like Christ. Since they were given a pattern for imitation, a

pattern based on an interpretation of the life of Christ, it was crucial that their testimony be true. Like Christ they were the temples where the spirit dwelt, they themselves making the presence of God manifest in the world. They were also visionaries who transmitted their revelations to their supporters.[439]

By virtue of their special relationship and union with Christ, they exhibited supernatural qualities and divine virtues. They felt torture like a cure or nothing;[440] they were the recipients of heavenly visions[441] and were thought to possess supernatural power;[442] in the end, martyrs "were no longer men but angels," the representatives of heaven.[443]

Finally, like the apostles in the Apocryphal Acts, martyrs' mediating role involves teaching Christian truth. However, its content is not the esoteric revelatory kind but the "mainstream" *kerygma* of the Church. Polycarp was not only an eminent martyr but also a great teacher (διδάσκαλος ἐπίσημος);[444] in fact, during his interrogation, the whole crowd of pagans and Jews of Smyrna shouted out aloud: "Here is the teacher of Asia, the father of the Christians, the destroyer of our gods – the one that teaches the multitude not to sacrifice or worship!"[445] The day before the martyrdom, Perpetua and her fellow martyrs taught the mob "God's judgment, stressing the joy they would have in their suffering."[446] As a result of their teaching, "many of them began to believe."[447] The martyr Ptolemaeus was a converted Roman matron's famous "instructor of Christian doctrine (διδάσκαλος τῶν Χριστιανῶν μαθημάτων)."[448] Certainly, Justin Martyr was one of the greatest expounders of "the true doctrines of the Christians (οἱ ἀληθεῖ λόγοι τῶν Χριστιανῶν),"[449] joined by Apollonius whose eloquent apology surely impressed Eusebius.[450] It is noteworthy that there is such emphasis on the martyrs' fame and role as faithful teachers and expositors of the Christian doctrine. Thus, these martyrs were not only sufficiently trained by the "orthodox" Christian teaching in the process but also functioned as the "guarantors of true teaching" of Christian faith.[451]

In all of these roles, martyrs were the ideal exemplars of the Church. Along with the apostles in the Apocryphal Acts, they are the Christian perfectionists and heroic overachievers for God. However, unlike the apostles in the Apocryphal Acts, lest the power of and adoration for martyrs go uncontrolled,[452] their boundaries are also made clear in these Acts. While martyrs are in Christ and Christ is in martyrs, and while martyrs share mystical union with Christ, there is no role confusion or takeover; there is a more clear divine and human demarcation here than in the Apocryphal Acts. Whereas Christ is to be worshiped, martyrs are to be loved.[453] However valiant, heroic, or exalted they are, the martyrs themselves joyously yield the title of martyr to Christ alone[454] and their humility and loyalty to Christ are the prime virtues after all. Martyrs are the ones certainly called and chosen by God, but only to glorify Christ, not themselves. Therefore, with all the honor, admiration, and special status, they do not become divine men taking over Christ (as in the case of the apostles in the Apocryphal Acts), but still remain as the "disciples and imitators of Christ." Martyrs are the mediators – conditioned, contained, and controlled by the Church.

Christian polemic and resistance

Like the Apocryphal Acts, the Martyr Acts' presentation of Christian monotheism obviously carries an apologetic and polemical thrust toward the Greco-Roman society and religion. The portrayal of the Roman officials and pagan crowd as Devil's henchmen, and martyr-dom as a cosmic battle against the Devil, who is embodied by the Roman religious, social, and political system, demonstrates the Acts' apocalyptic perspective. As the noble athletes and sacrificial victims, martyrs felt themselves at war with all the forces of evil when they died for their faith. The martyrs' choice for death was passive resist-ance toward the dominant authority and yet absolute victory over the Devil – which was therefore ultimately a victory over the domin-ant society. Their self-sacrifice, along with their endurance, valor, and strength, testified to the one true God, against the pagan gods to whom the martyrs were forced to sacrifice. Their "strange new cult"[455] redefined true sacrifice and thus true piety in utter conflict with traditional pagan sacrifice and piety. Like the Apocryphal Acts, the Martyr Acts draw a sharp boundary between "we" and "they." Only dying for the true God overpowers pagan impiety and realizes true Christian piety.

Summary and conclusion

By way of concluding this chapter, it may be appropriate to compare and contrast the presentations of Christian monotheism in these corpora of literature. First, all of them asserted the Christian belief in the one true transcendent God in philosophical language. The Christian God is presented in the negative theological terms of

Middle Platonism, which was the dominant school of philosophy of the period. God is portrayed as totally "other" and "spiritual," yet he is the Creator of the material world. A difference, nonetheless, is shown in the way each literature presented this God in relation to the dominant culture. The Apologists are most comprehensive in this rational presentation of the God; for them this philosophical monotheism provides the major point of contact and harmony with the Greco-Roman philosophical tradition and culture, and demonstrates the rational competence of Christian monotheism. In the Apocryphal Acts, the dualism between this pure and transcendent God and the material and polluted world under the influence of the Devil (the Greco-Roman world) is highlighted more. The Martyr Acts, while presenting the transcendent God in the manner of the Apologists, heighten the contrast between the Christian God and the pagan gods to whom the Christians were demanded to sacrifice.

Second, these literatures all struggled to express the nature, status, and role of Jesus Christ in light of their conviction in Christian monotheism (their portrayal of the transcendent God). However, the related but divergent Christology of each literature attests to the rising Christological concern of the early Church which was not doctrinally settled until the fifth century. The Apologists almost unanimously adhered to the Logos-Christology, emphasizing the divine nature and cosmological function of the Son, again appropriating the well-established Middle Platonic notion of the Logos. The Logos, both transcendent and immanent and both united with God and distinguished from God, was the agent of creation and revelation, and thus the mediator of the transcendent God. The Apocryphal Acts stressed the divine unity and elevated the divinity of Christ as well but still in a distinctive way; "Christomonism" appears doctrinally in the *Acts of John* and the *Acts of Andrew* but also indirectly in the rest of the Acts. Christ's humanity, though presupposed, is overshadowed by his divine nature and glory, which are displayed in his docetic and polymorphous appearances with revelations of esoteric mysteries. The Martyr Acts are not interested in the philosophical and cosmological doctrines of Christ; instead, they focus on the person and work of Christ on earth, especially his teaching (as a philosopher) and atoning death on the cross with respect to the soteriological effect that he brought about. His passion and death are absolutely necessary for the Christian faith and the imitation of Christ by the martyrs.

Third, these literary bodies all saw demons behind paganism as its real authors and propagators. Pagan gods are not only creatures and mere idols created by human hands but also demons themselves whose chief is the Devil, who deceives humanity and lures it away from the true God and his truth. They are deeply involved in and influence every aspect of the pagan world: myth, religion, society, and even political authorities. Nonetheless, in the Apologies the treatment of demons is more "philosophical" and rational rather than "practical," as they stress the reasonableness of Christianity as opposed to the unreasonableness and falsehood of pagan religion. In the Apocryphal Acts, the power struggle between God and Satan is real, though the latter is no match for God; demons thrive in this (Greco-Roman) world causing not only spiritual but also physical evils – illness, insanity, apostasy, and even death – that challenge the power of God in practical and tangible ways. In the Martyr Acts, the Devil is the cosmic Adversary of Christ and his imitators (martyrs) and works through the Roman officials and the pagans by persecuting the Church, yet is overcome by Christ and the martyrs through their martyrdom. In the Apocryphal Acts and the Martyr Acts, the tangible demonic activity in the dominant Greco-Roman society is much more pronounced as both take a more polemical stance against its culture in general.

These literatures' presentation of monotheism naturally affected their presentation of Christianity; the Apologies presented Christianity fundamentally as true philosophy, the Apocryphal Acts as true power, the Martyr Acts as true piety. "Salvation" in each respective literature is embracing that respective essence of Christianity through a mediator. In the Apologies, the Divine Logos leads one to the eternal truth and philosophy of Christianity, which originates from God himself through the Logos and is the final fulfillment of Greco-Roman civilization; salvation is the "Truth Encounter." In the Apocryphal Acts, one turns away from the wicked idols to the supreme God whose power and revelation are mediated by the apostles, the divine men; salvation indeed comes through the "Power Encounter." For the Martyr Acts, salvation belongs to those who imitate Christ by participating in his suffering and contest against the Devil and by presenting themselves as a sacrifice acceptable to God in the company of martyrs.

In the end, these three corpora's portrayal of Christian monotheism defined their identity, mode of worship, and their stance within the Church and toward the dominant polytheistic society.

This theological self-definition was critical especially in the church's growing interaction with Greco-Roman culture and her attempt to settle in that soil. The similarities and/or divergences we saw in this chapter will continue as we move on to the moral and social realms of Christian self-definition in the next chapter.

3

THE SUPERIORITY OF
CHRISTIAN SEXUAL
MORALITY

The Christian claim of moral and ethical superiority in response to pagan accusations of immorality and social disruption was in fact the logical outcome of their doctrinal self-definition; for Christians insisted that right living came from right belief. Their superior way of life, they claimed, was the tangible hallmark of their superior belief – their belief in the one transcendent God who is the Judge of the living and the dead. The Apologies, Apocryphal Acts, and Martyr Acts all base their moral self-definition on their theological self-definition. That being the case, the moral mandates in each literature betray the similar but much more divergent and controversial interpretations of what it means to be "in the world but not of the world" as the worshipers of the one true God.

To cover the whole spectrum of moral attitudes and actions described and defined in each type of literature is beyond the scope of this study. Instead, in this chapter, we will concentrate our attention mainly on the issue of sexuality and its moral and social implications in these literary bodies, since it was undoubtedly the most prominent and characteristic area of the Christian claim of moral superiority over Greco-Roman society and simultaneously a point of intense controversy among themselves. However, before we deal with that topic, we will first briefly look at the literatures' shared perspectives on Christian ascetic attitudes and behaviors in general, showing some broad similarities in all three.

Asceticism in general: the controlling paradigm

The essential Christian attitude toward life and the world that all three literary corpora offered to the dominant society was asceticism. In the Greco-Roman world, an ascetic attitude and behavior was by no means unique to Christianity. It had been an ancient moral virtue in varying degrees among the diverse philosophical schools and religious sects of the day. The notion of "asceticism" derived from the term *askesis* (ἄσκησις), denoting military or athletic "training" or "discipline," which eventually emerged to mean various forms of self-renunciation of physical and social needs such as food, wealth, comfort, and sex for philosophical or religious purposes.

(Middle) Platonists, Stoics, and Cynics all embraced certain forms of ascetic ideals that strongly influenced nascent Christianity, which in turn selectively adopted and transformed those ideals into its own. The pervasive Platonic dualism of mutable and mortal body alongside immutable and immortal soul often led to a contempt of the body as opposed to the pure and spiritual soul; due to their inferior and foul nature, bodily or material needs hamper the pursuit of the Good through philosophy, which can be fulfilled when the soul overcomes or escapes its prison, the body. Unlike Platonists, Stoics did not pit body against spirit and accepted the reality of bodily existence; but they ignored the importance of body in pursuit of philosophy as something indifferent (ἀδιάφορον).[1] Both Platonists and Stoics emphasized the supremacy and priority of reason over body, using the power of the mind to subjugate and control the body. Stoics, whose ethical teachings were incorporated in Middle Platonism and provided the ideological and moral backbone of the Empire, taught the virtue of mastering one's desires and attitudes (ἐγκράτεια) by bringing an inner life into conformity with reason, i.e. one's actual course of life ordained by the Logos, and accepted social norms and duties in acquiescence of life according to nature.[2] Stoic asceticism emphasized rational detachment from one's internal passions and desires (ἀπάθεια) and separation of mind from external affairs and circumstances through the discipline of mind (αὐτάρκεια).[3] Cynics, in contrast to Stoics, placed the basis of their virtue in individualism and freedom from a conventional mode of existence, which exhibited its radical ascetic behaviors by limiting the requirements of life to bare essentials; thus, they stressed radical independence from and rejection of the traditional social structures, needs, and values.[4]

The Christian asceticism espoused by all of the three literary bodies with which we are dealing reflects the amalgam of those features. Regardless of the varying degrees of self-denial and negative views of the world, their ascetic worldview and behaviors deal with the tension of how to "be in the world but not of the world."[5]

The general controlling paradigm behind the Christian ascetic attitude toward the world is that of a certain dualism, namely, dualism of this world and the other world, which is motivated by the eschatological and apocalyptic impetus and also by the Platonic dualism of spirit/matter. This world of senses and bodily existence in suffering, pain, and persecutions is incomparable to the world to come, where the Great Judge, God himself, will reward the good (i.e. Christians) and punish the wicked.[6] Because Christians live in expectation of the final judgment, eternal salvation, and resurrection, they endure their present predicament and injustice with virtue and courage, and renounce any temporal pleasure, comfort, and desire with disdain;[7] for they will have to give an account to the Judge for the life they led on earth.[8]

In this paradigm, the most conspicuous example of their ascetic ideal is marked by their attitude toward death, characterized by contempt with praise for martyrdom, which the Apologies, Apocryphal Acts, and Martyr Acts so proudly affirm. Indeed, as evidenced by the pagan comments, whether positive or negative, Christians were known for their contempt of and readiness for death.[9] The unflinching heroism of martyrs elicited inspiration and admiration from the witnesses on the one hand but strong suspicion and condemnation on the other, ironically from the Stoics, who endorsed a voluntary death as an expression of human freedom and dignity.[10] For Christians, death is a "happy ending"[11] for which they render thanks rather than regret or lament;[12] it is a joyful exit to Paradise freed from this life and a vindication of their commitment to the truth they proclaim: "death after death they fear, but death in the present they fear not."[13] Ultimately, ordinary Christians exhibited superior moral discipline not only comparable but even superior to the pagan sages. Thus, Christianity, in the words of Wayne Meeks, "democratized asceticism."[14]

Asceticism: sexual chastity and renunciation

One of the most distinctive aspects of the "democratized asceticism" of Christianity was its claim of sexual purity. The Apologies, Apocryphal Acts, and Martyr Acts all boast of Christian purity in contrast to pagan immorality and fornication (πορνεία); however, the Christian renunciation described in them also attests to a sharp dichotomy between the conservative ascetic ideals and the radical ascetic ideals that had developed since the inception of Christianity. They became the subject of bitter disputes as to their concepts of

108

sexual purity, their positions regarding marriage and family, and their social repercussions and implications even in their attempt to portray the Christian self-definition vis-à-vis the Greco-Roman culture. In the imperial period, these issues of sexuality and marriage became matters of public concern and were intertwined with the traditional and social conventions and mores. For the Apologists, Christian chastity validates the "new but really ancient" religion's harmony with the Stoic ethical ideals and establishes its moral and social respectability in the dominant society. For the writers of the Apocryphal Acts, categorical denial and renunciation of sexuality are essentially linked to the fundamental Christian identity and calling, which reject the conventional social ethos and undermine the established patriarchal structure. Finally, for the writers of the Martyr Acts, the issue of sexuality does relate to the women martyrs, whose familial and social renunciations in terms of the traditional family identity and loyalty represent resistance to the established social order.

Chastity, marriage, and family in Greco-Roman society: ideology and practice

With the change of the Roman political system from republic to monarchy in the first century BCE, there came a coalition of Stoic ethics and the Roman government in a conservative moral ethos for marriage, family, and social order. The Augustan legislation on marriage, the *Lex Iulia de martandis ordinibus* of 18 BCE, and its revision, the *Lex Papia Poppaea* of 9 CE, despite its general failure in practical enforcement and result, set the moral tone in law, religion, and philosophy and remained in effect with some modifications for over two centuries.[15] The legislation made marriage a mandatory responsibility for Roman citizens, for men from the ages of twenty-five to sixty and for women between twenty and fifty.[16] It also required divorced women and widows within that age bracket to remarry within six months and a year, respectively (the *Lex Papia Poppaea* of 9 CE extended the period to eighteen months and two years, respectively).[17] This was intended to promote the procreation of legitimate citizen children – the chief purpose and duty of marriage. From the time of the Republic, the formulaic phrase "for the purpose of producing children" (*liberorum quaerrendum gratia*), which often appears in marriage pacts and literary sources, may have been part of a citizen's declaration to the censors.[18] Therefore, while the legislation rewarded the men and women who had three or

109

more children with political favor and advantage and with tax relief and "right of children" (*ius liberorum*), respectively, political and financial liabilities were levied against childless couples and the unmarried, such as prohibition to inheritance.[19]

Moreover, the conservative tone of the legislation prevailed in regulating legal boundaries of marriage itself. Augustus formalized divorce, which had been effected by simple mutual consent of a couple, by requiring a formal letter and witnesses; he also made any extramarital liaisons (*stuprum*) and adultery public crimes, liable to *accusatio publica*[20] and prohibited marriages between the members of the senatorial class and persons of freed status. All of these legal acts were his attempt to inculcate, especially in the upper class, social and moral responsibilities and the significance of marriage and family for the continuation and welfare of the Empire as part of his restoration of the old Roman ideals and values.

However, not many in the upper class welcomed this series of strict and intrusive measures; the legislation stirred up some strong resistance, particularly from the educated men. Roman satirists such as Juvenal dramatized the horror of marriage and depravity of wives from a clear misogynistic perspective.[21] Above all, there had been a long tradition of an ideal of celibacy and endless debates on the benefits and distractions of marriage among the philosophers, especially concerning their single-minded pursuit of philosophy. According to Clement of Alexandria, whereas Plato and Aristotle saw marriage as a means which provided the immortality of the human race through procreation, Democritus and Epicurus disparaged marriage and childbearing due to unpleasant encumbrances and distractions from more essential matters, i.e. the pursuit of philosophy.[22]

From the second century BCE to the second century CE, the locus of debate on marriage was between Cynics and Stoics.[23] The Cynics, while not avoiding sex itself but valuing radical individualism and self-sufficiency, rejected marriage as a social convention and responsibility. Thus, Diogenes renounced marriage and its attendant duties of being a husband, father, and citizen as distracting (περισπάστως) to the pursuit of philosophy. The ideal Cynic portrayed by the Stoic Epictetus is the one who should be "free from distraction (ἀπερίσπαστον), wholly devoted to the service of God."[24] While the Stoics regarded marriage and childbearing as matters of indifference (*adiaphora*), they argued in favor of marriage as an indispensable and microscopic building block of the city-states and the *kosmos*. Therefore, marriage was in accordance with nature, and,

110

as such, it was incumbent upon all men, including philosophers, as a moral duty to insure the future of the *kosmos*.[25] To those who thought marriage and family a burden and distraction, Antipater of Tarsus in the second century BCE argued that a man should marry a wife precisely to keep himself from the distractions (ἑαυτὸν ἀπερίσπαστον) of managing household and daily necessities.[26]

Indeed, Stoicism of the imperial period, endorsing the Augustan legal, social, and political acts, provided the ideological backbone of marriage and family with a corresponding conservative ideal and ethos of sexual moderation and restraint. According to Musonius Rufus, a respected Stoic of the first century, marriage is according to nature, the foundation for the city and state, and the fundamental unit for the traditional values and order of society, and is therefore essential for civilization.[27] The chief end of marriage is undoubtedly "community of life with a view to the procreation of children."[28] Hence, marriage and procreation of children constitute the central duty (*pietas*) of not only all Roman citizens but also all humanity,[29] and "whoever destroys human marriage destroys the home, the city, and the whole human race."[30] Alluding to the Augustan legislation on rewarding couples for large families and punishing childless couples, Musonius strongly upholds the traditional value in having many children; for that reason, he denounces limiting family size by exposing or abandoning infants.[31] Concerning sexual purity, Musonius sees procreation in marriage as the only legitimate reason for sexual intercourse and regards sex for pleasure as unjust and unlawful.[32] In this regard, he condemns all extramarital sex, such as adultery, homosexuality, and even relations with slaves, not only for women but also for men, as showing lack of self-restraint.[33]

Musonius' stance on marriage is followed by his disciple Hierocles in the early second century, who also speaks of marriage as a civic duty even for philosophers and in harmony with nature for the procreation and nurture of children.[34] Children are valuable assets and helpers to their parents and guarantee the stability of the state; consequently, he also condemns exposing infants. Epictetus, another disciple of Musonius, also regarded citizenship, marriage, begetting children, and worshiping God as social duties incumbent upon all men.[35] These prominent Stoics, Antipater of Tarsus, Musonius, Hierocles, and Epictetus, all stressed the purpose and importance of marriage for procreation and therefore regarded marriage and procreation as a natural, patriotic, and sacred duty, which ensures the continuation of the human race and its immortality.

In addition to its reproductive purpose, the ideal marriage was understood in terms of sacred conjugal union: "the union of male and female, a partnership (*consortium*) in all of life, the conjunction of human and divine law."[36] Numerous references to partnership and support, mutual love and loyalty, and the ideal of happy and harmonious union in popular literature, epitaphs, imperial propaganda, and Stoic teachings about marriage indicate that marriage as a harmonious partnership was "part of a popular ideal as well as public and imperial ideology."[37] Especially prominent in the conjugal ideal of partnership was the notion of *concordia* (harmony), which was frequently celebrated in Antonine coins with symbols of the *dextrarum iunctio* (joining of hands) of imperial couples.[38] Many inscriptions and epitaphs bear testimonies of loving marriages without discord (*sine discrimine, sine offensione, sine ulla querela*).[39]

The Stoics and other educated elites philosophized about and romanticized this harmonious partnership. Musonius Rufus describes the ideal marriage as follows:

> In marriage there must be above all perfect companionship and mutual love of husband and wife, both in health and in sickness and under all conditions, since it was with desire for this as well as for having children that both entered upon marriage. Where, then, this love for each other is perfect and the two share it completely, each striving to outdo the other in devotion, the marriage is ideal and worthy of envy, for such a union is beautiful.[40]

Pliny the Younger, in his letter to Calpurnia Hispulla, the paternal aunt of his young wife Calpurnia (4.19), portrays his marriage as one of harmony (*concordia*) and happiness with mutual love and contentment, which was intended to serve as a model for his readers.[41] The Greek contemporary of Pliny, Plutarch, extols the ideal marriage as an affectionate and harmonious partnership in his famous *Advice to Bride and Groom*, which would be subsequently celebrated in the Christian homilies:

> It is a lovely thing for the wife to sympathize with her husband's concerns and the husband with the wife's, so that, as ropes, by being intertwined, get strength from each other, thus, by the due contribution of goodwill in

corresponding measure by each member, the copartnership may be preserved through the joint action of both.

(140E, 20)

For Plutarch, this kind of conjugal love is a higher form of friendship, though this partnership or friendship is certainly not of equals. The husband's virtue lies in his exercise of authority over his wife as a "guide, philosopher, and teacher in all that is most lovely and divine" (145C, 48). The wife, in turn, is to be submissive to her husband and "have no feeling of her own, but she should join with her husband in seriousness and sportiveness and in soberness and laughter" (140A, 14) and share her husband's gods as well as his friends (140D, 19). Similarly, Pliny, while stressing the moral qualities and public decorum of both husband and wife, expresses the ideal virtue of wife as devotion (*pietas*) to her husband's interests and deference and obedience to him.[42] Thus, the ideal of harmonious partnership also preserves the basic social hierarchy and conforms to the traditional expectations of gender roles.

In this conjugal partnership, two essential virtues of women were highlighted: *castitas* (chastity) and *pudicitia* (modesty, prudence). The former refers to the complete sexual integrity and fidelity within marriage, and the latter connotes the conscience and scrupulousness that keeps a person (woman) from shameful actions, in regard to sexual conduct in particular.[43] The Greek equivalent of these Latin terms is *sōphrosunē*, σωφροσύνη, which is a "virtue proper to a devoted, and fertile, wife, celebrated by the ancients as the female counterpart to male self-mastery."[44] Indeed, the way for a (married) woman to exhibit her virtue and control over passions is through her exercise of σωφροσύνη, which encompasses both *pudicitia* and *castitas* in meaning and usage. Thus, both Pliny and Plutarch underscore *castitas* and σωφροσύνη as the highest virtues of a model wife, whose rewards are her husband's love and *concordia* in marriage.[45]

Marriage and celibacy in the New Testament

The Christian teachings and debates on marriage and celibacy should be seen in this larger cultural and philosophical milieu as we turn to Jesus (in the Synoptics) and Paul on these issues. As noted by Elaine Pagels, both "conservative" and "radical" ascetics in the second century, usually referring to precisely the same texts, claimed the Dominical (or Evangelical) and (Pauline) apostolic authority that they all revered in common.[46] Therefore, we will mention briefly those foundational passages in the New Testament that have carried enormous influence over the ascetic Christian self-definition in this period and thereafter.

Jesus' teaching on marriage is in fact his reply to the Pharisees' question regarding the legal basis for divorce (Mark 10.2–12; NRSV). Alluding to the creation account in Genesis (1.27; 2.24), he affirms monogamy and the fundamental indissolubility of marriage: "the two shall become one flesh. . . . Therefore, what God has joined together, let no one separate" (Mark 10.9). He further explains this by condemning a remarriage of a divorcee, whether a man or a woman, as adultery (Mark 10.11–12). Even the Matthean version, which allows divorce only on the ground of πορνεία, prohibits remarriage as adultery (5.32; 19.9), which is defined much more inclusively in that Gospel (5.28 – one commits adultery in the heart even with a lustful glance). This divine sanction of marriage and prohibition of divorce and remarriage (or strict regula- tion of divorce) are certainly distinctive from the Greco-Roman practices of divorce and remarriage, which were relatively easy and frequent and even required by the law (in the case of remarriage), though the ideal was still lifelong monogamy. Then, in the same Gospel, as the disciples react to his stern teaching of the indissolu- bility of marriage, Jesus introduces an even more radical possibility: "there are eunuchs who have made themselves eunuchs for the sake of the kingdom of heaven" (Matt. 19.12). This is a voluntary, reli- gious, and extraordinary renunciation of marriage, for "not everyone can accept this teaching, but only those to whom it is given. . . . Let anyone accept this who can" (Matt. 19.11–12). While Jesus affirms marriage, he also approves a voluntary renunciation, noting its exceptional character beyond ordinary human capacity. As a matter of fact, the significance of marriage in this age is only pen- ultimate in relation to the ultimate eschatological reality: in that age and in the resurrection from the dead, people will not marry nor will they be given in marriage, for, like angels, they will not die (Luke 20.35–6; cf. Mark 12.25; Matt. 22.30; 24.38–9).

When we come to the issue of marriage and celibacy in Paul, this eschatological motif and concern becomes more dominant. The main text is 1 Corinthians 7, in which he begins with the slogan of the Corinthian "ascetics": "It is good (καλόν) for a man not to touch a woman" (7.1). This is in truth Paul's own view, though he attempts to correct their theology behind the slogan. Although, in general, it is better (κρεῖττον) to marry than to burn with passion (πυροῦσθαι) (7.9), it is certainly better for virgins and widows to remain unmarried just as he is (7.8). In this recommendation, Paul claims (perhaps deliberately) no Dominical authority (7.25) but gives his personal reflections: it is in view of the "impending crisis" (τήν ἐνεστῶσαν ἀνάγκην) (7.26) and for freedom from anxieties (ἀμερίμνους εἶναι) and distractions (ἀπερισπάσμος) (7.32–5). Here Paul uses the very terms used in the Cynic–Stoic debates on marriage and relates them to devotion to the Lord as a reason for continence.[47] Whereas the married are anxious about the affairs of the world and how to please each other, the unmarried are anxious about the affairs of the Lord (7.32–4); it is for their benefit – their "undistracted devotion to the Lord" (εὐπάρεδρον τῷ κυριῳ ἀπερισπάστως) – that the unmarried are to remain continent (7.35).

However, Paul recognizes that celibacy, which has to do with self-control (ἐγκράτεια) of desire, is a gift (χάρισμα) from God (7.7; cf. 7.9, 37)[48] and affirms and recommends marriage to those who have not received this gift as a "prophylaxis" against fornication (πορνεία) for their lack of self-control (ἀκρασία) (7.2, 5).[49] Therefore, once married, the couple should not only remain in marriage according to the Lord's command (7.10) but also exercise "conjugal rights" (i.e. sexual accessibility) in mutual respect and agreement (7.3). Even in case of the "mixed" marriages between Christians and pagans, the Christian partner should not seek divorce or leave the spouse unless the pagan partner wants it (7.12–13). For the believers' primary identity is not their relationship with their unbelieving spouses but their relationship with Christ;[50] thus, the unbelieving spouse as well as children are sanctified through the believing partner in marriage (7.14). Ultimately, the rule of thumb is that everyone should remain in the calling (κλῆσις) of the Lord, i.e. God's call to salvation, regardless of one's worldly status (7.17–24);[51] for the appointed time is short (7.29), and the present form of this world is passing away (7.31). Therefore, even those who have wives should live as though they had none (7.29); and while the one who marries, because of desire, does not sin and does well, the one who does not marry, because of self-control, does well and in fact does better (7.28, 36–8). In the same way, while a widow is free to marry a believer, she is more honored[52] if she remains continent (7.39–40). In this argument, like Jesus in the Synoptics, but unlike the contemporary Stoics (and Jews) on marriage, Paul is unconcerned about procreation or nurture of children as reasons for marriage. For Paul, what determines the expediency of marriage or celibacy is the problem of *porneia* and the concerns of eschatology and single-minded devotion to the Lord, which in effect relativize the significance of both celibacy and marriage, although he prefers celibacy for the very reasons of eschatology and priority of devotion.

In the deutero-Pauline letters we witness the transformation of Paul's teaching, in their conservative attempt to "correct" the "ascetic" interpretation of Paul in 1 Corinthians 7. The letters to the Colossians and Ephesians ignore the issue of celibacy or virginity but assume marriage as a typical lifestyle of believers. In the *Haustafel* of Ephesians, the ideal conjugal relation in wifely submission and husband's love for wife is modeled after the "great mystery" of the Christ–Church relation with the divine sanction of marriage from Genesis 2.24 (cf. 5.21–33). The Pastorals offer a Christian version of the contemporary ideal of marriage and gender roles that recall Plutarch's *Advice to Bride and Groom* and Pliny's letters. They take marriage for granted as the normal condition for the Christian leaders and believers as already shared by Colossians and Ephesians. The overseers and deacons in 1 Timothy and the elders in Titus are required to have monogamous marriages and to manage their households well, i.e. keep their children submissive and wives respectful (1 Tim. 3.2–5, 11–12; Titus 1.5–6). The central qualities of women are submissiveness to their husbands, love for their husbands and children, modesty and chastity (σωφροσύνη), and self-control (1 Tim. 2.9–11; Titus 2.4–5; cf. *1 Clem.* 1.3; 21.6–7). Unlike the Paul of Corinthians, the "Paul" of the Pastorals advises the young widows to "marry, bear children and manage their households" (1 Tim. 5.14). Moreover, this "Paul" declares that a woman will be saved through childbearing (σωθήσεται δὲ διὰ τῆς τεκνογονίας; 1 Tim. 2.15), resulting in a vast array of controversial interpretations in subsequent centuries. In contrast, only false teachings forbid marriage, which God created and is thus to be received with thanksgiving (1 Tim. 4.1–3); for "everything created by God is good, and nothing is to be rejected" (1 Tim. 4.4). About a century later, Clement of Alexandria would pick up this theology of creation as the basis of his argument for the validity of marriage against the radical ascetics.

Apologies: harmony with the established social order

The Apologists invariably maintained that Christian practices derived from divine truth and teachings, for they were based on the doctrines and laws taught not by humans but by the transcendent God through the Logos. In professing the superiority of Christian sexual morality, the Apologists took the same approach as in the previous discussion of Christian monotheism: first, demonstrating the Christian lifestyle as consistent with the best of Greco-Roman sexual ethics against the popular practices; then, moving on to the claim of a higher standard with that basic agreement in mind. As we will see, Christian chastity and continence characterized by the Apologists not only developed the teachings of Jesus and Paul in the tradition of the deutero-Pauline letters but, in that attempt, closely paralleled their Hellenistic counterpart, the sexual ethics of the Stoics.

Christian chastity and marriage

The Apologists assert that the principal characteristic of Christians is their chastity and continent life. Following their predecessors (Rom. 1.24–7; 1 Pet. 4.3; *1 Clem.* 30.1), they characterize pagan sexual practices as replete with adultery, incest, prostitution, homosexuality, and other licentious unions; and they condemn those practices along with abortions and infanticide, which were actually common and legal in Greco-Roman society.[53] Christian transformation is such that, according to Justin, "those who formerly delighted in fornication (πορνεία) now embrace chastity (σωφροσύνη) alone."[54] Indeed, Justin provides an example of a Roman matron, who left her dissolute past and licentious (pagan) husband as a result of Christian teachings.[55] Tertullian, with poignant sarcasm, argues that Christians share everything in common except their wives – the only place where pagans practice partnership.[56] The Apologists stress the rigor and stringency of the Christian sexual codes and purpose of marriage: Christians marry only for the procreation and nurture of children[57] and keep sexual intercourse with only one marriage partner.[58]

This, however, does not correspond to the teachings of Jesus or Paul (of Corinthians) but to the Stoic concept of marriage (cf. "Paul" of the Pastorals) and Musonius' strict sexual code. What seems particularly "Christian" is the Apologists' subsequent declaration

117

of a prohibition of divorce according to the teaching of Jesus (cf. Mark 10.9) and assertion of the validity of a single marriage alone for Christians with a condemnation of a second marriage as adultery (cf. Mark 10.11–12; Matt. 19.9).[59] They claim that, as a matter of fact, Christians are not even allowed to imagine any impure thoughts in their hearts, covet another person's wife, or indulge in a lustful glance, which all amount to adultery as well, according to the Gospel teaching.[60] It is noteworthy that the Apologists invariably quote Matthew 5.28 in this regard and underline the close connection between the offense of the eyes and sexual sins. In liturgical ceremonies, Christians exchange only one kiss as a reverential greeting.[61] The Apologists emphasize self-control and codes of sexual restraint for Christians in light of God's scrutiny and judgment,[62] the attitude and behavior that the Stoics prize for the purpose of "training the instincts to pursue rational goals."[63] Just as the Apologists appealed to human reason and free will for Christian monotheism, their argument for Christian chastity presupposes the human moral capacity to choose good and avoid evil, enlightened by the Logos.[64]

When it comes to the conjugal union, the Apologists' view of ideal marriage elicits even more interesting parallels to the conjugal ideal of the Stoics. The Apologists extol the preservation of monogamy as a Christian virtue.[65] Theophilus especially upholds marriage as a fulfillment of the first divinely inspired prophecy in creation: Adam himself prophesied, "For this reason a man will leave his father and mother and will cleave to his wife, and the two shall be one flesh" (Gen. 2.23–4).[66] This prophecy speaks of the extent of a husband's love for his wife – more than his own father, mother, whole family, and all his relatives; the marital bond is of such nature that husbands often sacrifice their lives for the sake of their wives.[67] Theophilus then sees conjugal love and unity as being ancient on a par with the very creation of humankind and as representing the ideal harmony of the whole created order in its universal fulfillment and significance in all civilizations.

A rather amazing tribute to conjugal union comes from Tertullian in *To His Wife*:

> What kind of yoke is that of two believers, sharing one hope, one desire, one discipline, one and the same service? Both are brethren (*fratres*), both fellow servants (*conserui*); there is no difference of spirit or of flesh. They truly are two in one flesh, and where the flesh is one, the spirit is one

also. Together they pray, together prostrate themselves, together perform their fasts; mutually teaching, mutually exhorting, mutually sustaining. Equally (*pariter*) are both in the Church of God; equally at the banquet of God; equally in straits, in persecutions, in refreshments. . . . When Christ sees and hears such things, he rejoices. To these he sends his own peace. Where two are, he is also there. Where he is, the evil one is not.

(2.8)

In its polemical context of opposing the "mixed" marriages between pagan men and Christian women, this praise of Christian marriage is none other than a Christian version of the conjugal ideal set by the Stoic and Middle Platonic moralists. Despite his rigorist reputation and his preference of celibacy to marriage, Tertullian envisions a (Christian) "marriage *in facie ecclesiae*, and with a special blessing";[68] it is the marriage which "the Church arranges (*conciliat*), the Sacrifice [eucharist] strengthens (*confirmat*), upon which the blessing sets a seal (*obsignat*), at which angels are present as witnesses (*renuntiant*), and to which the Father gives His consent" (*rato habet*).[69] Against Marcion's encratism (cf. the similar view of Tatian), Tertullian regards the sexual union reflected in Adam and Eve complementary rather than contrasting with the spiritual union of Christ and his church (cf. Eph. 5.32).[70] Indeed, "if there is to be no marriage, there is no sanctity."[71]

Finally, it is Clement of Alexandria who fully integrates the Stoic code of sexual chastity and the conjugal ideal with the Christian theology of marriage. For Clement, the doctrine of creation is the foundation of his ethic, including sexuality and marriage, the topics to which he devotes Book 3 of *Stromata*.[72] There he presents two "heretical" views of sexuality and marriage: Carpocratian antinomianism and the encratism of Marcion and Tatian. The Carpocratians idealize and indulge in their hedonistic licentiousness as a mystical communion with God by appealing to "God's universal fairness and equality" and by exploiting Plato's saying on sharing wives in common in *The Republic*.[73] The Encratites, also by exploiting Paul and the Platonic dualism of body/soul, regard marriage and procreation as something evil, corrupt, and mortal, and they practice excessive abstinence against the Creator and his creation, as evidenced in the *Gospel of Egyptians*.[74]

In response, Clement adopts the *via media* of chaste marriage based on the goodness of God's creation, which corresponds to the

119

conservative ascetic ideal of Stoic moralists as well (cf. 2.23.141–3, 145).[75] Against Carpocratian promiscuity and Tatian's interpretation of Paul,[76] he writes, "We too confess that incontinence and fornication are diabolical passions, but the agreement of a controlled marriage occupies a middle position" (3.12.81). Clement sees in the Encratic condemnation of marriage what Paul saw in the Corinthian "ascetics": spiritual pride in human flesh; they "live for the body, not for the spirit" (3.6.46). There is nothing meritorious about celibacy unless it arises from love of God (3.6.51); rather, inhibitions of and hatred toward sex and marriage are a blasphemy against God's creation and his command to "increase and multiply" (3.4.37). Thus, using the Pastorals, Clement argues that the "blessed Paul" attributes to "those who revile marriage" the "spirits of error and doctrines inspired by demons" (3.5.51; 1 Tim. 4.1–3) and affirms marriage as part of God's good creation that is to be received with gratitude, for "it is sanctified by the Word of God and by prayer" (3.12.85; 1 Tim. 4.4–5). Then, "if the married couple agree to be continent, it helps them to pray; if they agree with reverence to have sexual relations, it leads them to beget children" (3.12.81; cf. 1 Cor. 7.5).

Echoing the ancient and Stoic sages' dictum, Clement presents three reasons for the necessity of marriage: for one's fatherland (πατρίδος), for the succession of children, and for the fulfillment (συντελειώσεως) of the universe insofar as it depends on people (2.140.1). Furthermore, Clement argues that it is Jesus himself who taught monogamy "for the sake of begetting children and looking after domestic affairs" (3.12.82). Therefore, marriage in accordance with reason (i.e. marriage for procreation) is not sin, and "marriage and fornication are therefore different things, as far apart as God is from the devil" (3.12.84). Self-control is the key to the chaste marriage (σώφρων γάμος)[77] in which the husband should not feel sexual desire for his wife but show her Christian love; he ought to produce children by a chaste and controlled will apart from desire (ἀπάθεια) and in service of God (3.7.58). This Christian marriage leads to mutual support and self-control and concord with the Logos, reflecting a harmonious order of Christian life (2.23.143). Indeed, "who are the two or three who gather in the name of Christ with the Lord in their midst?" asks Clement (3.10.68). "By three does he not mean husband, wife, and child? A wife is united with her husband by God" (3.10.68; translation from J. Ferguson; Matt. 18.20). Hence, it is according to God's will for a couple to please each other and to care for the Lord's business together (3.12.88;

cf. 1 Cor. 7.32–3). Here, Clement transforms Paul's concern for distraction in marriage in 1 Corinthians 7.32–3 into the basis for divine approval of marriage.

Virginity and continence: not a norm but a virtue

Going beyond this common ideal on the chaste and harmonious marriage and the preservation of social order through marriage, the Apologists build their claim for the higher sexual standard of Christians: virginity and continence. A life of sexual purity and continence draws unanimous praise from the Apologists. *Some* Christians, in hope of becoming closer to God, live as virgins practicing lifelong continence.[78] Quoting Jesus' saying about the eunuchs for God's kingdom, Justin boasts about those men *and* women who have remained pure even for sixty or seventy years[79] and offers the most telling example of abstinence in the story of "the would-be eunuch of Alexandria."[80] A youth from Alexandria, in an attempt to prove Christian continence against the false pagan charge of Christian licentiousness, asked the prefect for permission to be made a eunuch; though the prefect rejected his petition, he still remained continent. Minucius Felix, who preserved Fronto's disturbing accusations about alleged Christian promiscuity through the words of Caecilius, highlights the fact that many Christians "find in perpetual virginity food for satisfaction rather than for boasting; in a word, so far removed is the desire for unchastity, that to some even chaste connexion raises a blush."[81] According to Tertullian, *some* indeed, the young and the old alike, keep virginity for self-protection against sexual sins and as a way to attain eternity.[82] For Tertullian, what stands at the top in various "degrees of perfection" is a lifelong virginity, which is followed by a life of virginity since baptism, that is, continent marriage by a couple or continence by a widow or widower.[83]

In truth, even for the married, Clement speaks of the "true gnostics" who have reached spiritual perfection as the ones who live with their wives as with their sisters: without any sexual relations.[84] Whereas the human ideal of continence, set forth by Greek philosophers, "teaches that one should fight desire and not be subservient to it so as to bring it to practical effect," the Christian ideal is "not to experience [sexual] desire at all";[85] and this Christian continence cannot be attained except by God's grace.[86] The "true gnostics" have risen above passion and desire and show love for the Creator of all things and his creation;[87] they live a gnostic life, becoming like the Savior and having attained a state of continence no longer maintained with difficulty.[88] Here, the Christian gnostic wife separates herself from the bondage of the flesh and attains perfection in the same way as her husband:[89]

> For souls . . . are equal. Souls are neither male nor female (οὔτε ἄρρενες οὔτε θήλειαι), when they no longer marry nor are given in marriage. And is not woman translated into man, when she is become equally unfeminine, and manly, and perfect (καὶ μή τι οὕτως μετατίθεται εἰς τὸν ἄνδρα ἡ γυνή, ἀθήλυντος ἐπ᾽ ἴσης καὶ ἀνδρικὴ καὶ τελεία γενομένη)?[90]

By reaching the state of continence and thus perfection (an essentially male virtue[91]), the gnostic couple has united knowledge, faith, and love[92] and realized the resurrection state on earth.[93] Indeed, this kind of strict asceticism impressed the distinguished court physician of the day, Galen, who gave Christianity significant merit on that account.[94] The Apologists do not fail to emphasize that this life of complete continence, the kind of life matched only by the philosophers, is lived by Christians from ordinary stock – men and women who may have been regarded by their pagan critics as simple but whose lives are devoted to God.[95] Therefore, in short, in Christian praxis and life:

> temperance is present, continence is exercised, monogamy is preserved, purity is guarded; injustice is driven out, sin is uprooted, righteousness is practiced, law is the guiding principle, piety is performed, God is acknowledged; truth controls, grace preserves, peace protects; holy Logos leads, Sophia teaches, Life controls, God reigns.[96]

Christian morality for the established social order

The Apologists, as the other second- and third-century Christians generally did, certainly encouraged, honored, and took pride in Christian celibacy and complete sexual continence as a superior way to follow Christ. However, they (except Tatian) did not make this a norm for Christian life or a requirement for salvation. They never renounced sexual relations per se; marriage was a divinely ordained institution for procreation and partnership, which fulfilled God's design for creation. They saw marriage and celibacy as equally valid options, in fact, as distinct gifts from God for Christians, on the principle of disciplined sexuality and also for practical purposes. According to the apostolic teachings, the distinction between celibacy and marriage was not between "the good" and "the bad" but between "the good" and "the better."[97] Thus, their *via media* stance, they understood, was based on the "fact" that "in general all the epistles of the apostle [Paul] teach self-control and continence and contain numerous instructions about marriage, begetting children, and domestic life . . . they nowhere rule out self-controlled marriage."[98] As Clement emphasizes, these apostolic teachings, rather,

> preserve the harmony of the law and the gospel and approve both the man who with thanks to God enters upon marriage with sobriety and the man who in accordance with the Lord's will lives as a celibate, even as each individual is called, making his choice without blemish and in perfection.[99]

In utter contrast to the Apocryphal Acts, as we shall see, the Apologists painstakingly pointed out the acceptability of Christian ascetic morality (i.e. chaste marriage) to the pagan (Stoic) intellectuals and aristocrats. They honored celibacy (i.e. rejection of marriage and thus procreation) as an ethical ideal only in a way that would not violate the conservative social norms and moral values.[100] Even Tertullian, who was notorious for his puritanical position on sexuality and marriage, was a passionate conservative as far as upholding the basic household structure and social conventions was concerned.[101] Whereas the Apologists denounced both vulgar immorality and radical asceticism as threatening the traditional norms, they presented Christian sexual asceticism as in accordance with the preservation of the Greco-Roman social structure in which Christianity should take its root.

Tatian and encratism

Among the Apologists, however, there was one who broke with this conservative representation of Christianity by advocating rigorous asceticism for *all* Christians. Tatian's violent criticism of classical Greek culture and philosophy has already been noted in the previous chapter; there, however, he still acknowledged that he was part of the Greek *paideia* as a herald of the superior truth – Christian philosophy. Nonetheless, in the realm of sexuality and social ethos, he placed himself completely outside the Greco-Roman mores and rejected sexual intercourse and marriage per se in direct contrast to the rest of the Apologists.

In *Oratio*, we see a trace of Tatian's radical asceticism: he links marriage with pederasty and adultery,[102] and renounces Greek "fornication" and "madness" in contrast to Christian women's chastity.[103] According to Clement (in his criticism of Tatian), Tatian regarded physical intercourse as destructive to prayer and marriage and also as fornication and invention of evil;[104] true disciples should imitate the example of the Lord himself who never married.[105] "A certain man who disparages birth," cited by Clement, might also be Tatian, who interprets laying up treasure on earth where moth and rust corrupt as procreation[106] – the very purpose of marriage and foundation of society according to the Greco-Roman moralists and the Apologists. Tatian's contrast of "the old man" with the "new," as the metaphor of radical dichotomy between law and gospel used by Paul, takes a rather remarkable turn: "Adam, born from earth, remained under the law that ordered procreation, marriage, and divorce; Christ, the 'new man from heaven,' liberates his own from all these constraints."[107] Then, to Tatian, there exists an unmistakable "antithesis between the sexual union exemplified in Adam and Eve and the believers' spiritual union with Christ."[108] Therefore, sexuality was not there for discipline or control: "it was there only to be renounced."[109]

Irenaeus and Eusebius (following Irenaeus) also asserted that on account of Tatian's sexual rigorism he separated himself from the "Great Church" and founded the encratic "heresy" in Eastern Syria.[110] However, their condemnation of Tatian as the heresiarch of encratism should be balanced with the "normative" nature of encratism in Eastern Syrian Christianity.[111] What seemed extreme and heretical in the West in terms of asceticism was integral and "orthodox" in the East Syria. Tatian's encratism certainly influenced subsequent Syrian Christianity and the social world of the *Acts of Thomas*.[112] In fact, encratism was more than a geographical phenomenon. By rejecting the fundamental institution of society (i.e. marriage and reproduction), his Christianity shared its radical representation with the Apocryphal Acts (of different provenance) and challenged the whole Greco-Roman social order and the continuation of civilization.

124

Apocryphal Acts: antithesis of the social ideal and resistance to the social order

As we enter the conceptual world of the Apocryphal Acts, the word *enkrateia* or encratism becomes central, denoting a "radical" form of asceticism that completely rejects sexual acts regardless of marital status. If the word "chastity" in the Stoic moralists and the Apologists indicates sexual fidelity within marriage, the word "continence" in these Acts denotes sexual abstinence in the encratic sense. In the encratic world, "the rhetorics of gender, sexuality and salvation [are] combined into a powerful discourse aimed at creating an alternative sphere of reality" as opposed to this present corrupt world.[113] Here we also see a connection between sexual renunciation and human freedom, with resulting social implications. These Acts portray the "superiority" of Christian sexual morality and ethos with the exaltation of virginity and radical sexual continence on the one hand and with the condemnation of marriage and sexual intercourse on the other. Both threaten the traditional social norms and disrupt the established order of Greco-Roman society.

An encratic gospel: exaltation of virginity and radical sexual continence

The message of salvation in the Apocryphal Acts is primarily "the word of God about abstinence (ἐγκράτεια) and resurrection."[114] In a series of beatitudes in the *Acts of Paul and Thecla*, virginity is directly juxtaposed with a blessed life with God and is seen as a prerequisite for the future glory of resurrection and the reward of heavenly bliss:

> Blessed are the pure in heart, for they shall see God; blessed are those who have kept the flesh chaste, for they shall become a temple of God; blessed are the continent (οἱ ἐγκράτεῖς) for God shall speak with them. . . . Blessed are the bodies of the virgins, for they shall be well pleasing to God and shall not lose the reward of their chastity. For the word of the Father shall become to them a work of salvation in the day of the Son, and they shall have rest for ever and ever.
>
> (5–6)

Here the encratic ideal is joined with the eschatological motif. The virgin body ensures the work of salvation, intimate communion

125

with God, and an eternal rest; "the pure in heart," who are promised to "see God," are none other than "the pure in body" whom God will surely reward for their continence.

These "revised" beatitudes reveal the author's apparent attempt to offer the "correct" interpretation of 1 Corinthian 7 in a familiar Dominican aphorism: "blessed are those who have wives as not having them, for they shall experience God (1 Cor. 7.29) . . . blessed are those who through love of God have left the form of this world (cf. 1 Cor. 7.31), for they shall judge angels." Whereas Paul in 1 Corinthians 7 prefers celibacy for the eschatological reason and single-minded devotion to Christ, but at the same time relativizes both celibacy and marriage in view of the impending eschaton, "Paul" in the *Acts of Paul and Thecla* prescribes celibacy as an essential condition for the coming of the eschaton; likewise, the other-worldly resurrection is reserved only for the continent. Indeed, Paul's "heretical" opponents in this *Acts*, Demas (see 2 Tim. 4.10) and Hermogenes (see 2 Tim. 2.17), accuse him of teaching that "there is for you no resurrection unless you remain chaste and do not pollute the flesh" (12). According to them, resurrection "has already taken place in the children whom we have," i.e. through marriage and procreation (14). This is the exact opposite of the "Pauline" doctrine of this *Acts* but a familiar echo of Plato's and Clement's view of marriage and procreation as a means of communal immortality. As a requirement for future resurrection, celibacy, which is regarded as a commendable and exceptional option by the Apologists, here becomes a demand incumbent upon all Christians who believe and hope in the true God.

It is the proclamation of this gospel of celibacy and continence that draws many (mostly young women) to conversion, as in the case of Thecla, an Iconian aristocratic virgin. However, it is also the same gospel that creates havoc with familial bonds and thus engenders major persecutions by family members (Thecla's mother) or by men of authority such as Thecla's betrothed Thamyris, her "would-be suitor" Alexander, and the proconsuls (8–9, 15–21). However, this virginity must be preserved from "corruption and uncleanness" at all costs. Indeed, as the beatitudes suggest, Thecla will ultimately overcome all the dangers and forces that threaten her virginity and will also experience God's empowerment and blessings along the way. Thecla, spellbound by Paul's encratic gospel, refuses to marry Thamyris; and as a result, she is condemned to be burned to death by her own mother and the governor. Nonetheless, God's miraculous intervention by a cloud of water and hail delivers her from fire and protects her purity. In Antioch, Thecla's virginity is threatened again by a sexual advance from Alexander, the first one (πρότερος) of the Antiochenes, and, upon her public refusal and humiliation of Alexander, she is condemned to the wild beasts. Interestingly, the virgin's physical beauty and her nudity at the scene of her virtual martyrdom attract men's special attention. However, significantly, Thecla is supported by female characters such as Queen Tryphaena, the female crowd, and even a lioness in the arena; and God comes again to rescue her with lightning and fire at the fateful moment of her self-baptism, not only to save her life but to preserve her virginity intact.

Two miracle stories in the *Acts of Peter* portray the preservation of virginity in the most drastic of ways. One preserved in Coptic fragments relates to Peter's daughter:[115] Peter, criticized for apparently neglecting his own paralyzed daughter while performing many healings for others, raises her up to prove God's curative power. However, he immediately reverses the miracle by having her return to her former state to conform to God's will. For her beauty had been a stumbling block to many, including a rich man named Ptolemy. He took her to be his wife but brought her back to Peter after finding her paralyzed from head to foot. Peter then praised God for keeping her from "defilement and violation" and explains to the crowd, "This is the reason why the girl remains thus to this day." Meanwhile, Ptolemy also went through a transformation: he repented and was delivered by God "from corruption and shame," and eventually became a benefactor of the Christian community. This is a "happy ending," which demonstrates that outward suffering, i.e. paralysis of Peter's daughter, is God's blessing in disguise, for it has the effect of preserving virginity and even of saving a soul.

The other episode of the gardener's daughter seems even more extreme. There a gardener beseeches Peter to pray for his virgin daughter; and when Peter asks God to give her what is most expedient for her soul, she immediately falls dead. Then, Peter exalts God for this "reward worthy and ever pleasing to God, to escape the shamelessness of the flesh and to destroy the pride of the blood." The distraught father, however, pleads with Peter to resurrect her, and Peter complies with his demand; but the revived virgin daughter ends up being seduced and disappears. This "tragedy," with the previous happy ending story, underscores a clear message: virginity is what guarantees the divine blessing and miracle and is thus preferred to health and even life; in contrast, sexuality embodies evil and death. Hence, both apostles John and Thomas offer praises to God for protecting and preserving their virginity from "the foul madness of the flesh" (σαρκὶ ῥυπαρᾶς μανίας) and "pollution" (i.e. marriage) and regard it as the essential condition for their ministries.[116] Sexual continence and its preservation from the corruption that is characteristic of the entire society constitute the central message of the encratic gospel.

Renunciation of marriage and family and social deviancy

On the flip side of the exaltation of virginity, in contrast to the Apologies, condemnation of marriage and sexual intercourse fills each of the five Apocryphal Acts. The Latin version of the *Acts of John* presents the nature of marriage thus:

> Know therefore more fully the mystery of the nuptial union: it is the experiment of the serpent, the ignorance of teaching, injury of the seed, the gift of death, . . . [a work of destruction . . . an ambush of Satan . . . an unclean fruit of parturition . . .] the impediment which separates from the Lord, the beginning of disobedience, the end of life, and death.[117]

The origin of marriage is neither the divine sanction at the creation (Gen. 2.24) upheld by the biblical tradition and most Apologists, nor is it the divinely inspired prophecy of Adam put forth by Theophilus. Instead, in this *Acts*, marriage has originated from Satan as his destructive device to separate humanity from the Pure God; and as the first sin of humanity (Adam and Eve), it represents the beginning of the Fall and death itself.

Indeed, in the *Acts of Andrew*, Andrew, while exhorting Maximilla to resist her husband Aegeates' threat of sexual union, describes the marital union as the primal sin of Adam and Eve in their imperfection (37). Their fateful sin must be corrected by the absolute renunciation of sex by Andrew and Maximilla, which plays the salvific role of reversing the effect of the Fall (37).[118] Then, Andrew declares to Maximilla:

> I rightly see in you Eve repenting and in me Adam converting. . . . You healed her deficiency by not experiencing the same passions, and I have perfected Adam's imperfection by fleeing to God for refuge. Where Eve

disobeyed, you obeyed; what Adam agreed to, I flee from; the things that tripped them up [i.e. sexuality], we have recognized.

(37)

Sexual intercourse and marriage are not just the consequence of the Fall, but they constitute the Fall itself as the first act of disobedience. Therefore, "Adam died in Eve through his complicity with her," i.e. by his sexual union with her. However, Andrew continues to say, "I now live in you [Maximilla] through your observing the commandment of the Lord [i.e. continence] and through your transporting yourself to a state worthy of your being" (39). Only celibacy, the renunciation of the very sin that caused the Fall, can restore the prelapsarian integrity; and with the divine gift of free will, "each person should correct his or her own fall" here and now (37).

This protological view that sees sexuality as the primordial sin and the cause of death and its renunciation as the prelapsarian restoration receives a more advanced treatment in the *Acts of Thomas*, where marriage is "treated as the linchpin of the towering structure of the 'present age.'"[119] In the present age, marriage is a symbol of human bondage first suffered by Adam and Eve with their wrong choice and is inevitably bound up with death. Since original human nature according to God's will is incorruptible, immortal, and thus asexual (12, 15, 43), marriage and procreation, on which the stability of the present society depends, keeps perpetuating the cycle of death and the sin of propagating the pride and violence of fallen humanity against God.[120] Therefore, it is the act of *enkrateia* that will "undo the Fall" and restore humanity to the original state of asexual immortality, and here again the act of continence epitomizes human freedom and perfection.[121]

The *Acts of Thomas* characterizes sexual continence especially as a heavenly marriage, which is a spiritual union with Christ, "the true bridegroom" and "the true husband" (124, 14, respectively), as opposed to an earthly marriage. The essential contrast between the earthly and the heavenly marriage is unmistakable: the former is temporary and passes away, but the latter remains in eternity; the former union is of destruction, but the latter union is of eternal life; the earthly bridegroom is mortal and passes away, but the heavenly bridegroom, Jesus the Lord, stays immortal in eternity (124).[122] The heroine of this *Acts*, Mygdonia, rejects her earthly husband Charisius for her heavenly bridegroom, the Lord Jesus; and to Charisius' tearful plea to return to him in conjugal union, she says: "He whom

129

I love is better than you and your possessions . . . he whom I love is heavenly. . . . Jesus alone remains forever, and the souls which trust in him. Jesus himself shall free me from the shameful deeds which I did before with you" (117). Earlier in this *Acts*, at the royal bridal chamber, Jesus in the form of Thomas appears to the newlywed couple as they are about to consummate their marriage. As Jesus warns them of the trials of earthly marriage and nurturing children and dissuades them from "this filthy intercourse" (τῆς ῥυπαρᾶς κοινωνίας ταύτης), he promises that they will "receive that incorruptible and true marriage" (τὸν γάμον τὸν ἄφθορον καὶ ἀληθινόν) and enter into that "bridal chamber full of immortality and light" (12). After being converted to "the gospel of continence," the bride confesses:

> I am in great love, and I pray to my Lord that the love which I have experienced this night may remain, and that I obtain that man whom I have experienced today. . . . And that I have set at naught this husband and these nuptials which have passed away from before my eyes is because I have been joined in a different marriage. And that I had no conjugal intercourse with a temporary husband, whose end is repentance and bitterness of soul, is because I have been united to the true husband.
>
> (14)

The bridegroom also declares, "I thank you, Lord, who have redeemed me from falling, and have led me to something better, . . . whom I have experienced and am not able to forget; whose love is fervent in me and of whom I cannot speak as I ought" (15). All of these responses are charged with erotic expressions and marital imageries. Here exists a paradox in the portrayal of the encratic ideal: this *Acts* employs "erotic language and marital imagery to describe ascetic experience – imagery derived from the very institutions and obligations that the ascetic practitioner forgoes."[123]

In fact, other Acts draw on erotic imageries and elements as well, especially in describing the relation between the ascetic apostles and their women converts. For instance, in the *Acts of Paul and Thecla*, the betrothed virgin Thecla's unabashed desire for Paul and captivation by his encratic gospel results in her desperate yet dangerous search for the apostle. Paul was thrown into prison by her fiancé on account of his teaching and Thamyris' jealousy (13, 18–19); there, "chained to him by affection," she kisses Paul's bonds (18) and throws herself on the place where he had been sitting (20). Even after her condemnation by the proconsul for rejecting marriage, Thecla is restless in search for Paul "as a lamb in the wilderness looks around for the shepherd" (21); and she regards a vision of the Lord in the form of Paul as a sign of Paul's care for her.

In the *Acts of Andrew*, the erotic motif is more pervasive. Just like Thecla, the heroine Maximilla's devotion and attachment to Andrew, who acts as "the erotic stand-in for the divine lover," is quite extraordinary.[124] This honorable matron of the proconsul takes "the stranger" Andrew into her bedroom where the "spiritual intercourse and childbirth" will take place (6–13). Maximilla, even employing a slave girl as her substitute for Aegeates' sexual demand, "spends her nights resting with Andrew" along with other converts (19). She "has so given way to desire for him that she loves no one more than him" and "has become intimately involved with the man," reports the servant of Aegeates (25). Finally, renouncing "Aegeates' filthy intercourse," Maximilla describes her newfound love in this way:

> I am in love, Aegeates. I am in love, and the object of my love is not of this world and therefore is imperceptible to you. Night and day it kindles me and enflames me with love for it. . . . Let me have intercourse with it and take my rest with it alone.
>
> (23)

In the *Acts of Thomas*, where the erotic theme is mainly directed to the converts' relationship with the heavenly bridegroom Jesus, Mygdonia's affection for and dedication to Thomas, who is seen as the Twin of the Lord Jesus, is still unambiguous. She, too, incurring the jealousy and anxiety of her husband, leaves home and listens to the apostle day and night (95). Her fidelity to Thomas is such that Charisius, her husband, laments that she is snatched by the "evil eye" (βάσκανος ὀφθαλμός) of the apostle (100) and restless in her search for him; for "nothing seems lovable to her except that man and his words" (99).

Obviously, the erotic elements in the Apocryphal Acts point to a spiritual bonding between the apostles and the women converts, not an earthly consummation of "their love." This "spiritualized" erotic motif appears to be an inversion of "the ideology of *erōs*" in Greek romance.[125] As noted by a number of scholars, marriage as a conventional "happy ending" is a central theme of Greek romance, with the erotic love between the young beautiful aristocratic lovers as the chief drive for that union.[126] Their heroic chastity through many incredible crises and misfortunes ultimately functions to foil the climactic consummation of their passionate love in marriage at the end, a marriage which stands for a civic duty and stable social order, and thus satisfies the shared expectation of the readers.[127] Therefore, these erotic elements of sexual renunciation in the Acts challenge and counteract the ultimate goal of the romance. At the same time, those erotic gestures of the heroines of the Acts toward the apostles (however spiritualized) depict the most shameful and disturbing actions of women (especially those of the upper class), which the Greco-Roman moralists vigorously denounced and simultaneously feared. Their scandalous pursuit of the "strangers" and their refusal of conjugal chastity and procreation suggest a dissolution of family life and present a direct threat and rebellion to the traditional social ideals and stability that both the pagan elites and the Christian elites (such as the Apologists) heartily embraced and endorsed. Thus, in the Apocryphal Acts, "we move from a celebration of sexuality in the service of social continuity to a denigration of sexuality in the service of a challenge to the establishment."[128]

Indeed, this "apostolic love triangle" among a woman, her husband (or fiancé), and the apostle whose encratic gospel she embraces, wreaks devastation on her marriage and family.[129] Kate Cooper sees "the rivalry between two men over the allegiance of a woman" as the crucial narrative outline[130] and the theme of continence against marriage and sexual intercourse as merely a proxy or façade for the real conflict between two men.[131] Although I do not agree with her on the role of the continence theme, there is no doubt that the disruption in marriage and the clash between the apostle and the husband usually result not only from the apostle's preaching of abstinence but also from the husband's suspicion of erotic love between his wife (fiancée) and the apostle, who takes over the role of romantic hero in place of the husband.[132] The apostle's contact with the female convert invariably brings about the breakdown of marriage and the ensuing persecution from her husband, usually a man of superior political status, who would not accept the same kind of continence preached by his morally superior "rival" – the apostle. In this dynamic, the only way to regain his lost honor as a husband and man is to win his wife's love back and/or remove his rival by force, which leads to the martyrdom of the apostle.[133] In this sense, the "rivalry" between the ascetic apostle and the socially and politically powerful husband signifies the larger social, ideological, and rhetorical clash between the "new" radical Christianity and the ancient tradition and social conservatism of Greco-Roman society supported by politics, law, and philosophy.

However, as important as the "rivalry" between the apostle and husband may be, more crucial and significant to the narrative structure is the theme of continence as a cause of male rivalry and domestic conflict. From the perspective of the Apocryphal Acts, Christian identity is bound up with the superior morality of Christians, which is chiefly exhibited in sexual continence. The apostles' gospel of continence affects not only women but also men and estranges entire households and cities as well as husbands. The repeated accusations of the husbands, family members, and the crowd against the apostles as "sorcerers," "corrupters," "deceivers," and "destroyers and enem[ies] of the household" for leading both men and women astray resonate with the angry cry of the conservative pagan critic Celsus against the alarming disruption of family by Christianity.[134] The apostle is portrayed in the Acts as a social deviant whose "chastity, endurance, and freedom from structured social obligations" proves him an "asocial" being.[135] His gospel of continence breaches the relationships between parents and children,[136] between brothers,[137] as well as between husbands and wives (see below). The *Acts of Peter* summarizes the effect of the apostolic preaching of continence as follows:

> many other women delighted in the preaching concerning chastity and separated from their husbands, and men too ceased to sleep with their wives, because they wished to serve God in chastity and purity. And there was a great commotion in Rome.
>
> (34)

The apostle "deprives [both] the husbands of wives and maidens of husbands."[138] The encratic gospel has far greater disruptive repercussions than mere male competition for woman's allegiance; it disturbs not just marriages but also families and the larger sociopolitical structures.

In this theme of continence, the women converts' choice of and persistence in sexual renunciation do stand out and are critical to the narrative effect and development. The conflict takes place not only between the apostles and the husbands but also between the husbands and their continent wives. For the latter reject not merely immoral or evil suitors but especially loving and devoted husbands who would otherwise well deserve the contemporary moralists' acclaim.[139] Thus, Thecla's fiancé Thamyris weeps bitterly for the loss of his would-be bride; Maximilla's husband Aegeates falls at her feet with tears, hoping to persuade her to continue their conjugal union; Mygdonia's husband Charisius mourns with sorrow for loss of her love. Aegeates' entreaty to Maximilla expresses genuine affection and a deep sense of grief:

> I cling to your feet, I who have been your husband now for twelve years, who always revered you as a goddess and still do because of your chastity (σωφροσύνη) and your refined character, even though it might have been tarnished[140] . . . your parents thought me worthy to be your husband. . . . If you would be the woman you once were, living together with me as we are accustomed to – sleeping with me, having sexual relations with me, bearing my children – I would treat you well in every way . . . I will do you no harm – I am unable to do – but I will torment you indirectly through the one you love more than me.[141]

The conjugal bond expressed in this plea recalls the ideal marriage extolled by the Stoic moralists and the Apologists. The elements of chastity, mutual love, harmonious partnership, and procreation are all representative of the model marriage and family that are the fundamental foundation of Greco-Roman society.[142] The fact that conjugal union is an accepted social norm and sacred custom is further confirmed by Charisius' appeal to Mygdonia against Thomas' teaching:

> Why will you not eat with me? And will you not also have intercourse with me according to custom . . . this sorcerer and deceiver teaches that no man should cohabit with his wife, and he reverses what nature demands and the deity has ordered (96). . . . I am your husband since the time of your virginity, and the gods as well as the laws give me the right to rule over you.[143]

In this sense, the Christianity of the apostles and these upper-class women, whose conversions to continence alienate their husbands, repudiates the social establishment and mores of this (Greco-Roman) world. Whereas "the rhetoric of chastity" (sexual fidelity) is intended to maintain the social order, "the rhetoric of continence" (abstinence

134

from sex) is meant to disrupt it.[144] This conjugal and sexual renunciation demonstrates "Christian rejection of contemporary social structure and the outrage this engendered."[145]

This profoundly anti-familial and anti-social tendency of the encratic gospel also manifests itself in depreciation of children. As mentioned earlier, in the *Acts of Paul and Thecla*, the apostle's teaching of resurrection as a goal and reward for those keeping their virginity is contrasted with the "heretical" view that the resurrection is the present reality in the process of begetting children (14). In the *Acts of Thomas*, the Lord's revelation of the nature of earthly and heavenly marriage to the new couple highlights the afflictions of having children, "whose end is destruction" (12). This view categorically renounces procreation as an acceptable ground for marriage against those who might argue for it (e.g. Greco-Roman tradition, Stoics, and the Apologists). Children are portrayed as the "most grievous punishments" of the earthly marriage because they become "unprofitable, being possessed by demons" (12); they are distractive to parents and "good-for-nothing, doing unprofitable and abominable works" (12). In the *Acts of John*, children are mentioned as one of "many obstacles which cause unrest to human reasoning" (68). In the contemporary Greco-Roman society, there was a tremendous social need and legal pressure for procreation, and children were prized as an important investment for the future. Every female who lived to childbearing age would have had to produce an average of five children simply to keep the population steady.[146] Therefore, this kind of extreme renunciation and devaluation of children was decidedly antagonistic and menacing to the stability and continuation of the Greco-Roman society.

Finally, the "rhetoric of continence" in these Acts destroys the existing family relations by sex (marriage) and blood and establishes a new family relation and loyalty whose members exhibit "superior" morality of continence.[147] Conversions of both husband and wife result in a new relationship of brother and sister in Christ, as Drusiana in the *Acts of John* testifies in her prayer: "Jesus Christ, . . . you protected me when my former husband, Andronicus, did violence to me, and gave me your servant Andronicus as a brother" (82). In the *Acts of Andrew*, Maximilla and Stratocles join the new Christian kinship as brother and sister, casting off their former relation of sister and brother-in-law (10). In the *Acts of Thomas*, conversions in the royal family reconfigure the existing family relation: Mygdonia, wife of Charisius (a relative of King Misdaeus), Queen Tertia, Prince Vazan, and his wife Mnesara are reunited as brother and sisters in the Lord and join the family of converts (155–6). These Acts portray the new "superior" Christian kinship particularly as a sibling relationship based on the converts' Christian commitment through their sexual continence.[148] Therefore, the new Christian surrogate family created by the heavenly marriage and sibling relations necessitates a disintegration of the earthly marriage and blood relations.[149]

Continence as autonomy and authority: portrayal of female converts

The socially disruptive and subversive impact of continence in these Acts is most visible in the portrayal of the female converts who exercise considerable "autonomy and authority" through their sexual and marital renunciation. As indicated earlier, most of the female converts are upper-class women, whose prominent and powerful husbands (or fiancés) embody the conventional socio-political authority and established patriarchy. They are women of intelligence and wealth, and some are even described as superior to their husbands in those very aspects.[150] The attraction of women of high social status to Christianity is in fact well attested in the early Christian documents, including the New Testament.[151] In contrast to Kate Cooper's claim of "the continent heroine as an idealized listener" whose role is passive and ambiguous between the male contestants for power,[152] these women in the Apocryphal Acts act as the female counterpart of the charismatic ascetic apostles and display superior moral virtues and spiritual power over their husbands. They do not function as "the conduits, or the channels, of the power struggle between the men,"[153] but as the active partners of the apostles in the struggle against the established social order; the power struggle is not only between the apostles and the male householders but also between these women and their husbands/powerful males.

The heroines' embrace of the encratic gospel brings about fierce opposition and persecution by their husbands and other male authorities. Yet it also leads (through those crises) to their transformation from the model of traditional female virtues as daughters and wives to the model of independence and empowerment (shame and rebellion by the traditional standard). They even embody the "model of Christian perfection,"[154] who steadfastly acts upon the divine will. Thecla (*Acts Paul Thec.*), Maximilla (*Acts Andr.*), Mygdonia and Tertia (*Acts Thom.*), Drusiana (*Acts John*), and the four concubines of

136

proconsul and Xanthippe (*Acts Pet.*) – their sexual renunciation and determination to preserve their continence represent fundamental rejection of and resistance to the established construct of female body and role as well as to the culturally entitled male ownership of the female body. Their abstinence puts an end to the primary role of the female body as a site for reproduction and also to the social hierarchy derived from the sexual hierarchy of male dominance and female passivity. "In a society in which the woman's body was both indispensable and dangerous, object of desire and fear"[155] and thus was in need of male control, their bodies, from the moment of their conversion, do not belong to men (their husbands) but to God (or the Lord Jesus, the heavenly bridegroom). God, who called those heroines to continence, is on their side empowering them (through the apostles) not only to endure through but also to triumph over those hostile threats of punishment on the one hand, and the emotional appeals of love on the other. Thus, their continence ultimately represents the "indestructible power of Christ."[156] Thus, in all the Acts, the male opponents' frustrated attempts to force those heroines to accept marriage and family life as the social norm (as indeed expected in the current social framework) only amount to acts of absurd "anomaly" and "madness," deviant from the Christian worldview set forth by the encratic gospel – the complete reversal of social values.

Here we also observe an inversion of the traditional gender attributes on the one hand and a blurring of gender differentiation on the other. The ancient rhetoric and physiognomy of gender polarized the qualities and virtues of male and female and at the same time used the category of "male" to express the ideal human body and character in a range of a continuum with the male and female at opposite ends.[157] The firmly polarized male and female distinctions pointed to the impenetrable gulf between men and women. Conversely, the model of a continuum running between opposite poles of masculinity and femininity, according to one's level of metaphysical perfection (independent from biological sex), indicated a certain fluidity and blurring between the two. In both models, however, the "woman" and "female" nature were always inferior to the "man" and "male" nature, which embodied the ideal human nature. In terms of gender distinction, maleness was associated with reason, speech, self-control, courage, independence, ideas, spirit, and pursuit of honor; but femaleness was equated with passion, emotion, (bodily) senses, weakness, dependence, and preservation of shame.[158] Whereas the man operated in public, the woman was confined to a private and domestic space. In truth, maleness corresponded to the ideal Greco-Roman values, virtues and honor, whereas femaleness expressed just the opposite. In the continuum theory, the female was conceived as an imperfect or incomplete male;[159] but she could "become male," i.e. transcend the gender distinction and ascend to a higher stage of moral and spiritual perfection, by acquiring masculine virtues and qualities.[160] Conversely, a man was also in danger of "becoming female" i.e. having his masculinity diminished or weakened, by disclosing feminine traits and characters.

In a soteriological sense, maleness or manliness represented nearness to God, salvation, and perfection,[161] and thus could also point to the restoration of the prelapsarian asexual state.[162] Therefore, the famous exhortation in the gnostic Nag Hammadi text was in reality representative of the common cultural and Christian view: "Flee from the bondage of femininity, and choose for yourselves the salvation of masculinity."[163] Jesus' words regarding Mary Magdalene in the famous Logion 114 of *The Gospel of Thomas* expresses the similar idea: "'See, I shall lead her, so that I will make her male, that she too may become a living spirit, resembling you males. For every woman who makes herself male will enter the Kingdom of Heaven.'" Woman must "become male or manly" in order to attain salvation and spiritual perfection, and man must also develop his masculinity as far as possible.[164] In this kind of gender polarization and fluidity, framed in an androcentric worldview and culture, the way for women to "escape from bondage of femininity and become male" was sexual asceticism (*askesis*) – the male virtue par excellence.[165] The continent life rejected "all that defined women as female, particularly their association with the physical and corporeal," chiefly in their reproductive function.[166] As such, ascetic renunciation functioned as a means to negate gender differentiation and granted women power both by denying female weakness and shame, and by presenting a potential threat to men and the sociosexual standards of gender.[167] Thus, virginity or continence for women provided them a paradoxical but powerful alternative in which women could compete with and even outdo men. Celibate women could also exercise their "autonomy" and "authority" beyond the conventional sphere of their confinement – marriage and motherhood.

In the Apocryphal Acts, the men of position and authority are described as exhibiting increasingly "womanish" or "female" attributes, while the continent heroines display increasingly "manly" or "male" qualities. In the *Acts of John*, Lycomedes, the wealthy *strategos* of Ephesus, falls down before John and pleads with him to restore his wife, Cleopatra, who has been paralyzed for a week and now lies lifeless. Despite a vision that assures Cleopatra's resurrection through John, Lycomedes begins to blame and lament his fate with bitter cries. Although the apostle rebukes him for his unbelief and admonishes him to control himself, he falls to the ground and dies. When John raises up Cleopatra and leads her to faith, John informs her about Lycomedes' death but assures her that God will restore his life. Cleopatra, in contrast to Lycomedes, becomes "neither distraught nor excited" in her silent grief (24); moved by her self-control (συνέχον), restraint (ἀνάγκην), and faith, John prays for her, and she resurrects her husband with John's help (24).

In another episode (62–86), Drusiana, after embracing the gospel, renounces marital relations with her husband Andronicus; and, having endured his persecution and violence, she persuades him to faith and to live in continence. However, after finding out that "the *protos* of the Ephesians" Callimachus has fallen in love with her, Drusiana is so distressed that she becomes ill and dies. Andronicus in bitterness grieves over her death so much that John has to silence him. Callimachus, nonetheless, steals the body of Drusiana with his steward Fortunatus' help in order to commit necrophilia, but both he and Fortunatus are killed by a snake. John raises up Callimachus and leads him to faith and also raises Drusiana to life. Then, Drusiana, appointed by John, gladly raises Fortunatus to life, invoking Christ in his polymorphy. Out of John's disciples, it is Drusiana who exhibits superior spirituality and morality; she is resolute in her continence, persuades her husband to faith, understands Christ's polymorphy, forgives her offenders, and performs a miracle of resurrection, while Andronicus and Callimachus are still tied to their passions of sorrow and unforgiveness even after their conversion.

Those "loving husbands" (Thamyris, Aegeates, and Charisius), who mourn for their lost conjugal union, also betray the female nature by their lack of self-control (*enkrateia*) over their emotions and judgments and become increasingly hysterical, controlled by their jealousy and anger. On the contrary, Thecla, Maximilla, and Mygdonia undergo a "manly" or "male" transformation and are explicitly addressed as men; in this paradoxical "metamorphosis," they break out of their traditional roles and relationships, gain significant autonomy and independence from the world of male domination, and even exercise their ministerial authority.

The "masculinization" of Thecla, the most outstanding example of "the liberated female ascetics,"[168] is an important narrative *topos* in the *Acts of Paul and Thecla*, which involves several related aspects. Thecla's conversion transforms her relationship with men, in which she resists male dominance and increasingly gains and exerts considerable independence. She not only rejects her fiancé Thamyris in Iconium but, in her journey to Antioch in search for Paul, publicly confronts the sexual aggression of the prominent Antiochene Alexander. She tears Alexander's cloak and pulls off his imperial crown, which results in her condemnation to the wild animals. Here Thecla not only rejects male ownership of her body but also inflicts shame on men by her rejection (whether he is her fiancé or an illegitimate suitor). However, both in the previous trial by the governor in Iconium and at this definitive moment in Antioch, Paul shows his "feminine" features by his "cowardly" retreat and failure to defend Thecla, and he vanishes from the scene.

Although the inverted version of the erotic *topos* between Paul and Thecla exists, the narrative from then on shifts from her relationship with Paul to her independence from Paul. As Thecla (who now identifies herself as a "servant of God") faces her second martyrdom, she does not turn to Paul but to God and baptizes herself in the arena (34). After her miraculous deliverance, Thecla becomes a successful itinerant evangelist who not only converts the extended household of Queen Tryphaena but also gains a reputation as a teacher who "enlightened many by the word of God" and is confirmed by Paul at the end (37–43). In this narrative, it is noteworthy that Thecla moves from the conventional female space of household into the public (male) space, where she challenges man's honor and engages in male activities, including the gladiatorial games (27–36).[169] Finally, her masculinization reaches a climax in her gestures of "shedding her femininity": cutting off her hair (25) and donning of a man's cloak (40).[170] With these physical gestures, Thecla incorporates the bodily dimension of maleness as well as the social and spatial spheres of maleness.[171] Thus, the virgin Thecla's gradual masculinization brings about a new identity of "a servant of God" and corresponds to and demonstrates her increasing autonomy and authority.[172]

In the *Acts of Andrew*, Maximilla's masculine identity is again bound up with her continence. In Andrew's exhortation to Maximilla to resist Aegeates' threat and to remain continent, Andrew likens himself and Maximilla as a redemptive couple who would undo the sin of Adam and Eve through their sexual renunciation.

140

There he appeals to her inner "man" (40). Andrew recognizes and addresses her as a "man" with the characteristic qualities of the male:

> You have done well, O man (ἄνθρωπε), . . . O man (ἄνθ-
> ρωπε), if you understand . . . that you are immaterial, holy,
> light, akin to the unbegotten, intellectual, heavenly, trans-
> lucent, pure, superior to the flesh, superior to the world
> (38). . . . I beg you, wise man (ἀνδρός), that your clear-
> sighted mind stand firm. . . . Do not be overcome by the
> inferior. You whom I entreat as a man (ἄνθρωπον), assist
> me in my becoming perfect.[173]
>
> (40)

Here these typical male virtues represent the ideal human character in spiritual perfection, the prelapsarian state of humanity. They are contrasted with what is "inferior" (i.e. feminine nature) and threatens to overcome them, which is symbolized by the sexual and marital union urged by Aegeates. Maximilla is profoundly affected and empowered by this revelation of her new male identity by the apostle, and "she became what the words themselves had signified" (46).[174] Then, she "deliberately and resolutely . . . rebuffed him [Aegeates]" (46). Her self-realization of masculine identity confers upon her independence and empowerment and strengthens her resolution to stay continent. Thus, while Aegeates pleads with her to be "the woman you once were" (36), Andrew entreats her to be a man "superior to the flesh" (38). As noted by Rosamond Rodman, "Andrew's use of the masculine in his exhortation to Maximilla (in AA, 38–41) contrasts with the feminine ways in which Aegeates refers to her, as wife, lady, and goddess (AA, 14, 23)."[175]

Finally, Mygdonia's manly transformation in the Acts of Thomas involves, like Thecla, both physical and spiritual aspects. Upon her conversion, she renounces her beauty and fine clothing and adorn-ment, the characteristic symbols of femininity. She cuts her hair and tears her clothes (114) – a measure that destroys any feminine and thus sexual attractiveness for the sake of her continence. Also, as in the case of Maximilla, her steadfastness in her ascetic conviction is contrasted with Charisius' erratic and emotional nature and "shame-lessness" (cf. 116–17). She not only exercises superior self-control but also exhibits superior intelligence to her husband, both of which are typical male virtues (95). In her commitment to contin-ence, she even confronts Thomas, who under threat advises her to obey Charisius:

If you [Thomas] could not express the thing by a word, how will you force me to suffer the deed? . . . And now you say this because you are afraid. Who changes a work which he has executed and in which he has been praised?

(130)

As in the case of Thecla and Paul, here the "manly" heroine's authority and autonomy is highlighted even at the expense of the apostle's manly virtue. Then, with the seal of baptism, Mygdonia, now identified as a servant of Christ (121), converts her mother and nurse, Marcia, and Tertia, the wife of king Misdaeus (136–7), and anoints them after their baptism (157). Thus, Mygdonia, in her "male" transformation, demonstrates her control of her own body, independence, and ministerial authority.

These heroines in the Acts are the "male women,"[176] who have overcome the vulnerability of female body and the inferiority of female nature with their resilient *enkrateia*, and thus they serve as the "liberated" models of female piety and authority.[177] They represent the contrasting example to the Christian women in the Pastorals, whose virtue primarily consists of wifely submission to their husbands and their chastity in marriage.[178] Although it is true that the ancient construction of gender ideology is essentially androcentric, there is no doubt that, given that cultural mold, this kind of gender reversal and transformation was perceived both as an impressive triumph and even more as a threat and resistance to the proper order of nature and society.[179]

Christian critique of and alternative to the established social order

This type of Christian self-representation confirms the charges of the pagan intellectuals that Christians destroy societal equilibrium and traditional values. It is undeniable that both the conservative and the radical Christian ascetics recognized "sexual renunciation as a privileged emblem of human freedom."[180] However, it is the radical ascetics who capitalized on this ascetic freedom, especially that of the upper-class women, to critique the traditional Greco-Roman values of the hierarchical household and society and to offer an alternative worldview and social order. The sexual renunciation of the Apocryphal Acts is the epitome of Christian perfectionism. As such, it is deeply critical of the contemporary moral and social status quo on the one hand and brings a divine principle of autonomy, "equality," and power on the other hand – as a symbol of the recovery of the lost paradise.[181] The Acts' radical "asceticism breaks down the dominant culture through performances that aim toward establishing a counter-cultural or alternative cultural milieu" and creates and articulates a new individual and social identity.[182] The "Christian" rejection of sexuality, marriage, and family in these Acts stands at the core of the "Christian" identity; and, independent from and transcending the existing social and cultural ties and responsibilities, it re-creates the family of the continent who will hasten both the end of this world and the inauguration of the other world by living like angels (cf. Luke 20.34–6). Labeled as "deviant" by the pagan and Christian elites alike, the Apocryphal Acts are unapologetic for their "deviancy" and completely "normalize" it in their inversion of gender and social conventions.

Martyr Acts: renunciation of social mores

As in the cases of the Apologists and the Apocryphal Acts, Christian identity, confession of faith, and claims of moral (sexual) superiority go hand in hand in the Martyr Acts. Martyrs, by their heroic endurance and steadfast commitment to their God in the face of horrendous tortures and death, already exhibit the superior moral strength and ascetic ideals of the philosophers. While the claim of sexual purity forms a relatively small part of the martyrs' defense of Christian moral integrity, the issues of sexuality, gender, and family feature prominently in the treatment of the women martyrs. As in the case of the Apocryphal Acts, the socially disruptive and subversive forces of Christianity are most evident in the portrayal of female converts – women martyrs. The Martyr Acts present the gender inversion and renunciation and redefinition of the conventional family relation and social establishment.

Continence and sexuality

While one of the most serious accusations of the pagans against Christians was sexual immorality, the martyrs' claims of sexual renunciation or continence, or the examples of virgin martyrs, are surprisingly few in the Martyr Acts. The ascetic defense of the martyr is most explicit in Apollonius' apology: "The disciples of the Logos who has come amongst us die daily to pleasure, curbing their desires by continence (ἀποθνήσκουσι ταῖς ἡδοναῖς, κολάζοντες τὰς ἐπιθυμίας δι᾿ ἐγκρατείας) in their wish to live according to the divine commandments."[183] The divine mandate for Christians demands a life of continence, which involves shunning every form of "undisciplined pleasure" and "every evil glance from [their] flattering eyes" so that their hearts may remain inviolate.[184] It is striking that this refined martyr relates continence specifically to the purity of the eyes and shares the Apologists' concern in observing Jesus' teaching on lustful glances in Matthew 5.28 (cf. 18.9).

In a longer literary version (Recension C in Musurillo's edition) of the *Acts of Justin and Companions*, Charito, the only female martyr, declares to the prefect, "I have become God's servant and a Christian, and by his power I have kept myself pure and unstained by the taints of the flesh (καθαρὰν ἐμαυτὴν τηρῶ τῇ δυναμει τούτου καὶ ἄσπιλον τῶν τῆς σαρκὸς μολυσμῶν)" (C.3.3). Her ascetic declaration is a reply to the prefect's accusation of her ill reputation, the charge tinged with sexual innuendo. This response, which implies her virginity, is certainly a significant addition to the other shorter versions, where she simply states she is a Christian.[185]

The other virgin martyr mentioned is Potamiaena, who, outstanding in "her bodily purity and chastity" (τῆς τοῦ σώματος ἁγνείας τε καὶ παρθενίας), was defending her virginity even in her martyrdom for "the perfection of her body as well as her soul."[186] Remarkable in this account is the explicit threat of sexual violence upon the female virgin martyr: the prefect not only tortured her but also "threatened to hand her over to his gladiators to assault her physically" – most likely a sexual assault.[187] Furthermore, she was subject to the crowd's insults and "vulgar remarks."[188] Like Thecla, Potamiaena's struggle consists of the preservation of both her faith and her virginity, but, unlike Thecla, her deliverance does not come in this world but in the next world through a martyr's death. As observed by Francine Cardman, the chastity and continence of the women, highly praised by Christian authors of all spectra, were "a point of extreme vulnerability before their persecutors,"[189] who could exploit the women for further degradation perhaps in deliberate mockery of the Christian claim of chastity and continence.[190]

Indeed, while the issue of virginity and continence per se does not develop further in the Martyr Acts, the issue of sexuality and gender in connection with the female body stands out. The high proportion and prominence of women among early Christian martyrs is a recognized fact.[191] Female martyrs go through the same degrees of torture and suffering and the same types of sentence and execution that their male counterparts do (e.g. decapitation, condemnation to beasts, and burning).[192] Nonetheless, their experience of martyrdom does differ from that of male martyrs due to their sex and gender.[193] The main difference has to do with the sexual dimensions of their punishment,[194] which highlight the exposure and display of their bodies and the ensuing reactions of the spectators.

For example, one of the earliest known female martyrs, Agathonicê, is stripped of her clothes before being led to the stake, and the crowd grieves for her physical beauty about to be lost.[195] Perpetua and Felicitas, faced with a cow (instead of the usual bull) so that "their sex might be matched with that of the beast," are first thrown naked into the arena, but "the crowd was horrified when they saw that one was a delicate young girl and the other was a woman fresh from childbirth, with milk still dripping from her breasts."[196] They were brought back in tunics, but Perpetua's thighs were again exposed. The editor of their martyrdom account points out her effort to guard feminine modesty even in the midst of pain.[197] Potamiaena in her martyrdom endures the pouring of boiling water on her naked body and is finally burned at the stake.[198] The slave Blandina in the company of Gallic martyrs, after being scourged and burned on hot irons, was stripped and tossed into a net for the attack of a bull; the mob marveled at her unspeakable suffering.[199] The women martyrs' "public denuding" represented the authorities' attempt to impose sexual dishonor on the condemned women.[200] As Brent Shaw points out, "These two aspects, sexual shaming and physical punishment, were integrally interrelated" for women martyrs.[201]

However, it is in the very context of physical and sexual violence that the female martyrs achieve the greatest victory over the established order by "overcoming" the traditional gender construction. The paradox of female martyrs shows that, at the point of their greatest vulnerability and humiliation, i.e. exposure of their female bodies to violence, they display and embody the most powerful and prominent "male" virtues and strengths. Despite the highly gendered features of female martyrs, including sexual innuendos, the Martyr Acts paradoxically accord these very women the highest manly virtues of self-mastery (*enkrateia*) over their pathos and bodies, even to death.

In the previous chapter, I have already mentioned the heroism of martyrs in physical endurance and spiritual power. As the imitators of Christ, the Invincible Athlete, they are the triumphant athletes and gladiators for Christ, revealing God's presence and power in their contests and sufferings. In that matter, they embody resistance to and subversion of the values of the dominant society. Since the athletic and gladiatorial games are the archetypal male activities of the time, the male martyrs act "inappropriately" toward the dominant culture "not by being 'unmanly,' but by using their courage to defy the political and social order. The male martyr takes on the role of the hero in combat, a role appropriate to men."[202] However, female martyrs, whose courage is particularly highlighted in the Martyr Acts (e.g. Blandina, Perpetua, Felicitas, and Potami-aena), are "doubly transgressive."[203] For "the female martyr is in a sphere not appropriate to her, thrust into combat that requires a male virtue – courage."[204]

The Martyr Acts' portrayal of female martyrs as athletes and gladiators and the Acts' particular attention to the "masculine" virtues of the female martyrs especially before the "double" violence – not only physical but also sexual – imply both the empowerment of women martyrs and their radical challenge to the dominant social value and order, more radical than that of their male counterparts. To the amazement of the crowd and the dismay of the governors, the female martyrs refuse to break under the extreme conditions; by their perseverance and courage, they defeat and inflict shame on the male authorities. These heroines transcend the socially constructed limits of their gender and both exemplify and embrace the "perfect masculinity" of martyrdom.[205] After all, it is the slave girl Blandina who represents "the crucified one," Christ the Perfect Martyr, who in turn appears to the Christian witnesses in the very person of Blandina.[206] Though "tiny, weak, and insignificant as she was," Blandina defeated the condemnation of Devil in the form of the (male) authorities and inspired "her brothers."[207] In this sense, these female martyrs are also "male women" who exercise their autonomy over their own bodies, exert their influence over other (male) martyrs, and achieve their Christian victory against the socio-political (male) authorities.[208]

Rejection of traditional family identity and loyalty

Like the Apocryphal Acts, the Martyr Acts stress the disruptive effect of Christian commitment on traditional Greco-Roman fami-lial identity and bonding. Martyrs are portrayed as renouncing their natural family ties in favor of their commitment to martyrdom and their new Christian identity and kinship. For instance, Sanctus, one of the martyrs of Lyons, when asked by the governor about his identity, refuses to recognize any other identity but a Christian one: "instead of giving his name, birthplace, nationality, or anything else," he keeps on repeating, "I am a Christian!"[209] Similarly, one of Justin Martyr's companions, Hierax, when asked about his parents, answers, "'Christ is my true father,' . . . and our faith in him is our mother. My earthly parents have passed away."[210] Also, Papylus (Pamfilus), when asked about his children, replies, "I have children in the Lord in every province and city."[211] The martyrs deny any earthly or natural ties and acknowledge only their spiritual identity and kinship. They are simply following the teaching of Jesus who redefined family relations: his kin group is not to be defined by blood relation, but whoever does the will of the heavenly Father constitutes the new family born of the Father.[212] In light of the newfound eternal family, the transient and earthly family identity and loyalty are meaningless and discarded.

However, in the Martyr Acts, as in the case of the Apocryphal Acts, this kind of denial of and break from conventional familial relationships is most visible in the examples of the female martyrs. In this case, the heroines are not identified as virgins or those insisting on continence within marriage but as married women with children. Obviously, motherhood was the quintessential responsibility of women who were to continue the family line through childbearing and to preserve and transmit the traditional culture and values to the next generation.[213] Agathonicê, Perpetua, and Felicitas were mothers – but mothers who let go of their maternal roles for the sake of martyrdom. They dismissed what was traditionally a woman's most sacred duty for their faith. When Agathonicê refused to sacrifice to the gods and chose martyrdom, the crowd shouted, "Have pity on yourself and on your children," an appeal to be repeated by the proconsul.[214] Nonetheless, she responded to them, "My children have God, who watches over them," and, unaffected, she "threw herself joyfully upon the stake."[215]

In the *Martyrdom of Perpetua and Felicitas*, Perpetua, a young mother from a noble African-Roman family, was distressed over the welfare of her infant son while in prison. Initially anxious to nurse her son, she received permission to keep him with her in prison while waiting for trial (3.6–9). However, after the first vision, which confirmed her martyrdom, Perpetua realized she would have to suffer and "no longer have any hope in this life" (4.10). Then, her father appeared at the trial with her son to coerce her to recant, as her break with her embittered father was culminating (see p. 150). Nonetheless, Perpetua refused to offer sacrifice and was condemned to the beasts. As a result, he took her son away from her in prison. Perpetua took this separation from her baby as God's will: "But as God willed, the baby had no further desire for the breast, nor did I suffer any inflammation; and so I was relieved of any anxiety for my child and of any discomfort in my breasts" (6.7). For Perpetua, this relief from the demands of mothering indicated divine approval of her martyrdom.

In the case of Felicitas, pregnant in her eighth month at the time of imprisonment, the main anxiety seemed that her pregnancy might delay or deter her from fulfilling martyrdom (15.1–2). So, her fellow confessors earnestly prayed for her, and, two days before the "contest," Felicitas delivered a premature baby girl – once again, a clear sign of God's favor and intervention for her martyrdom. Felicitas then contrasted suffering for herself (labor and delivery) with suffering for Christ (martyrdom) (15.6). Thus, Felicitas is described as being "glad that she had safely given birth so that now she could fight the beasts, . . . from the midwife to the gladiator, ready to wash after childbirth in a second baptism" (18.3). "Just as God relieved Perpetua's maternal responsibilities so she could focus on her martyrdom, he freed Felicit[a]'s burden of motherhood" for the same purpose.[216] Physical motherhood must be foregone in the face of martyrdom; natural familial ties should be renounced to seek and fulfill God's will.

For Perpetua, equally distressing, if not more so, was her renunciation of her father and filial piety. The record of Perpetua's conflict with her father, alternating with her visions, dominates her own prison account. From the outset, she acknowledges her father's relentless effort to dissuade her from Christian faith as the expression of his love; she also knows what is expected from her as a noble matron and daughter.

In the Roman household, the father (*pater familias*, usually the oldest male) occupied a central position with religious and legal authority; he also exercised sovereign power and authority (*patria potestas*), at least in theory, over his children (regardless of their ages) and other members of the household as long as he lived. *Patria potestas* symbolized a "paradigm of patriarchal power" and defined both the role and the social expectations of the *pater familias*.[217] Between father and his children existed the virtue of *pietas* (dutiful respect) as the ideal of family relations.[218]

Based on this filial piety, a close and affectionate father–daughter bond was possible and significant especially in the upper-class families.[219] As noted by Lisa Sullivan:

Roman elite fathers expected their daughters to depend upon them for protection and support, and as a biological extension of her father, a daughter's presumed potential for sustaining the public identity, and reputation of her father and blood kin was immense.[220]

This expectation certainly held true even after the daughter was married; except in the case of a *manus* marriage where a woman was placed under her husband's control (which was rare in the late Republic and imperial period), married women remained in their father's power. All of this provided an immediate pressure for Perpetua to acquiesce; she was all too well aware of the value of conformity to society's expectations.

For Perpetua, however, her Christian identity defines her onto-logical nature, and thus she has no other identity or name (3.1–2).[221] This claim asserts her independent (Christian) identity, which supersedes and even negates her traditional (social) identity as daughter, wife, and mother; her loyalty and subordination shift from her earthly father to her heavenly Father. With this claim, Perpetua renounces her familial identity and all of the attendant ties and thus provokes a violent reaction from her father. After her father's departure with "diabolical arguments" (3.3), she reports: "I gave thanks to the Lord that I was separated from my father, and I was comforted by his absence" (3.4).

In the second confrontation following her first vision of Paradise and the welcoming shepherd (an alternative father figure), her father emotionally appeals to her with persuasions about his "gray hair," fatherly affection, filial piety, and family reputation and welfare. He kissed her hands and threw himself down before her, and even "[w]ith tears in his eyes he no longer addressed me as his daughter but as a lady/mistress (*non filiam nominabat sed dominam*)" (5.5). This scene is particularly significant and astonishing, for, as Jan den Boeft and Jan Bremmer have shown, the wording of the petition, the gestures of humiliation, and the address of *domina* point to the language and behaviors common in Greco-Roman prayers to gods/goddesses.[222] The father's words and acts of self-humiliation in a posture of a supplicant before his daughter are indeed unthinkable in any reasonable circumstances and are thus profoundly subversive to the established social norm and sensibility. Nevertheless, Perpetua stands defiantly unmoved in her conviction and resists all of his deeply moving pleas.

The third encounter takes place at the trial, where her father brings her infant son to appeal to her maternal responsibility. Here, he conjoins Perpetua's duty to offer sacrifice with her maternal duty for her baby; this wedding of traditional religious ritual and social/ familial mores forms the core of paganism, which is heartily embraced by the Governor Hilarianus. Perpetua, however, rejects both religious and motherly duties: "I will not," she retorts and again confesses, "*Christiana sum*" (6.4). At her father's further attempt to persuade her, the governor orders him to be thrown to the ground and beaten; he then closes the case with the sentence of her condemnation to the beasts. Here, one cannot help but notice the dramatic contrast of Perpetua's reactions: although she "felt sorry for [her father's] pathetic old age," she "returned to prison in high spirits" for her ordeal (6.5–6).

During the final confrontation, her father, "overwhelmed with sorrow," plucks the hairs from his beard and throws them on the ground; then, he again throws himself on the ground and curses his old age (9.2). In response, Perpetua simply feels "sorry for his unhappy old age" (9.3). Her account of her father's reactions discloses the intimate tie once most likely enjoyed between them. At the same time, it reveals the deeply anti-familial and anti-social force of Christian faith. Throughout the confrontations with her father, Perpetua's emotional detachment and independence from that filial bond and the *patria potestas* are remarkable, if not scandalous. In these accounts, Perpetua overcomes this socially vested authority and overturns the traditional patriarchy – the fundamental hierarchy of the society.

Following the gender inversion,[223] the role reversal occurs between Perpetua and her father: a powerful but helpless father at a weak yet "unruly" daughter's feet, begging for her to change her mind.[224] This scene recalls the desperate yet frustrated pleas of the loving husbands to their continent wives in the Apocryphal Acts. Like the heroines of those Acts, Perpetua takes charge of the situation, and her father, like the pathetic husbands, stands at the mercy of her will. Perpetua's father and those husbands, the representatives of the Greco-Roman *mos maiorum* and "family values," are portrayed as antithetical to and utterly impotent before Christian moral authority. This elite African-Roman woman's new Christian identity and obdurate disobedience to her father's authority make "a statement *against* the Roman social order, deliberately stepping outside prescribed social boundaries and by doing so neutralizing established family metaphor."[225]

Redefinition of familial relations

As the martyrs reject and experience separation from physical family ties, they join the new Christian kinship relations. When the "mother-martyrs" withdrew from their maternal responsibilities for martyrdom, their children were placed in Christian parental care. In this sense, the Martyr Acts do not share the Apocryphal Acts' categorical depreciation of children. Agathonicê was confident that God the heavenly Father would take care of her children. Though Perpetua's son remained in the care of her earthly father, Felicitas' newborn girl was taken up by a Christian woman who brought up the baby as her own daughter.

Whereas physical motherhood is suggested as a hindrance to martyrdom, spiritual motherhood is portrayed as beneficial and critical to martyrdom. The author of the *Martyrs of Lyons* compares Blandina to the Maccabean mother who encouraged all her children to martyrdom and "sent them before her in triumph to the King."[226] As a spiritual mother of fellow confessors and martyrs, she inspired them and replicated in her body "all her children's sufferings" and "hastened to rejoin them."[227] In fact, the maternal language and metaphor for martyrs are striking in the *Martyrs of Lyons*. In the tribunal, Alexander, a Phrygian physician and future martyr, urged tortured Christians to make their confession by acting out the behavior of a mother giving birth (1.49). As indeed "those who had previously denied the faith were now confessing it once more," the crowd got angry and identified Alexander as the cause of that change (1.50). Thus, "the virgin Mother [the church] experienced much joy in recovering alive those whom she had cast forth stillborn [i.e. the Christians denying their faith]" (1.45); through the martyrs, they "were conceived and quickened again in the womb and learned to confess Christ" (1.46). Martyrdom is a new birth, which necessarily involves painful labor and perseverance. Martyrs served as mothers especially for those weaker brothers and sisters who needed that extra push for their new birth; the martyrs showed them "a maternal love, shedding many tears on their behalf before the Father" (2.6). Ultimately, the Church is identified as the Mother who would take the maternal role for all Christians, including her martyrs (1.45).

Similar to the case of motherhood, spiritual fatherhood or the father figure is contrasted with and replaces the physical father. In the *Martyrdom of Perpetua*, as Perpetua rejects her earthly father, she gains her heavenly Father. There is an inverted parallel between her physical father and the old shepherd in her first vision. The gray-haired shepherd surrounded by a multitude in white robes points to the fatherly image of God and resembles her father's physical description (4.8–9; 5.2). This heavenly Father welcomes Perpetua, calling her his child (τέκνον), and nurtures her with a mouthful of cheese (4.9). In her fourth vision, after Perpetua defeats the Devil in the form of an Egyptian, the *lanista* of marvelous stature rewards her with golden apples and a kiss, saying: "Peace be with you, my daughter (*filia, pax tecum*)!" (10.13). Whereas Perpetua's physical father is ashamed of her choice, this new spiritual father figure is proud of her commitment and victory.[228] He affirms the new kind of father–daughter relationship. In contrast to the disturbing appearances of her father in real life, "it is a serene father-figure – not tormented and tormenting, but solacing – who appears to Perpetua in her first and last visions."[229] Thus, her heavenly Father replaces her natural father whom she has rejected and honors her with paternal welcome and recognition of her choice.

In fact, God is the only Father explicitly identified in the Martyr Acts.[230] While the prominent female martyrs are mothers and/or take maternal roles for fellow Christians, no male martyrs are identified as fathers or take the paternal role.[231] The genuine father figure and paternal role is reserved only for God; Perpetua's father (the only human father identified) is portrayed as a menace to Christians' loyalty to their heavenly Father. This again may have been a literal interpretation of Jesus' command, "call no man Father," in Matthew 23.9.[232] Then, it confirms afresh Celsus' fear of the subversive effect of Christianity in households.[233]

As the new Christian kinship defies natural blood relations and is redefined by the relation to God the Father as siblings and mothers, it also crosses social barriers and embraces people from radically different socio-economic statuses. Martyrdom is a great social equalizer: slaves, mistresses, noble matrons, senators, physicians, aged bishops, and youths all belong to the same family of God as brothers and sisters and share the same honor of martyrdom. Especially, the portrayals of the heroism of the weak and the lowly (e.g. women and slaves) strongly indicate the social reversal: "Christ proved that the things that men think cheap, ugly, and contemptuous are deemed worthy of glory before God," because of their love for him.[234] This kind of alternative relationship and perspective counteracts the established social boundaries and challenges the hierarchical structure and power relations of Greco-Roman society.

Resistance to and reconfiguration of the established social order

Indeed, as Everett Ferguson has mentioned, persecutions provided an "equal opportunity" of martyrdom for both men and women,[235] and, for female martyrs, martyrdom meant "gaining of personhood" and authority.[236] Along with the ascetic call to virginity and continence, the call to martyrdom offered women empowerment and "liberation" from the traditional female gender roles.[237] Like the heroines of the Apocryphal Acts, the women martyrs experience transformation of their gender stereotypes and empowerment on the way to martyrdom. As previously noted, through the "liberating" portrayal of the female martyrs, the Martyr Acts highlight the superiority and subversive force of Christian asceticism. Here we will revisit the issue of gender inversion and its relationship with women's empowerment and social resistance through the particular example of Perpetua in her *Martyrdom*.

As a number of scholars have observed, Perpetua's account of imprisonment, visions, and conflicts expresses her progressive empowerment and "a movement of resistance against the dominant cultural narratives of relationship, paternal authority, and femininity."[238] After the initial encounter with her father, her first vision comes as a result of her brother's request that she seek a vision about whether she will be condemned or freed (4.1).[239] In that vision, she saw a ladder reaching all the way to heaven. The ladder was flanked with weapons of torture, and at its bottom lay an enormous serpent/dragon, the symbol of Satan (cf. Rev. 12.3). Confessing the name of Christ, Perpetua then trod on its head (cf. Gen. 3.15) and ascended to Paradise, where she was welcomed by a gray-haired shepherd. This vision confirmed her martyrdom and was followed by her father's distressing second visit. After her third confrontation with her father and the final separation from her baby at the trial, Perpetua had the second vision in which her deceased brother Dinocrates was suffering in darkness. Realizing her power, she prayed for him; and, in the third vision, he was refreshed with the water of life in heaven and delivered from his suffering. In the final vision following the last confrontation with her father, Perpetua was led into the arena for a gladiatorial combat. Her opponent, a foul Egyptian, later identified as the Devil, was rolling in the dust. As Perpetua was stripped naked, she found herself to be a man. The game was presided over by a *lanista* of superhuman size, dressed in purple tunic and golden sandals. In their fight, the Egyptian tried

153

to get hold of Perpetua's feet, but she kept striking his face with her feet. As Perpetua got hold of his head, he fell flat on the ground, and Perpetua stepped on his head. As the victor of the combat, Perpetua received a branch with golden apples, a kiss, and a paternal greeting from the *lanista*.

In these visions, the first and fourth visions form a kind of *inclusio* in two ways: first, in terms of a substitution of her father with the new father figures, the gray-haired shepherd and the *lanista* (as already discussed); and, second, in terms of the way in which Perpetua defeats the Devil – by treading on the head of the dragon/ Egyptian with her feet.

The second *inclusio* has several interesting aspects to be uncovered. First, the "metaphor of trampling"[240] unites Perpetua's account and conveys the social "subversion of the top by the bottom."[241] There is a suggestive connection among the dragon, Egyptian, and Perpetua's father in this imagery. In Perpetua's three confrontations with her father that occur within this *inclusio* (second through fourth), her father is repeatedly portrayed as throwing himself to the ground, or being thrown to the ground and beaten before Perpetua. Her father's position on the ground resembles the Egyptian who rolls in the dust and falls flat on the ground; it also symbolically corresponds to the position of the dragon at the foot of the ladder.[242] In addition, while both the dragon and the Egyptian represent the Devil, the dragon can also be seen in light of the contemporary handbook for the interpretation of dreams by Artemidorus.[243] According to him, venomous animals stand for powerful men, and the head symbolizes parents.[244] Thus, the dragon may signify both the Devil and paternal authority, as her father is also described as "diabolical" by Perpetua. If so, on the one hand, her father's authority, pleas, and behaviors may be regarded as the particular examples of the Devil's scheme to prevent Perpetua from martyrdom. On the other hand, Perpetua's defiant rejection of and detachment from her father may signify the concrete expression of her trampling the dragon and Egyptian. Perpetua achieves her victory (martyrdom) and gains life through the power of the feet over the head. This metaphor, pervasive in the account, reveals inherent evil in the traditional social hierarchy and overturns its power structure.

Second, gender inversion takes place in this *inclusio*. As we have observed in the Apocryphal Acts, while the heroine goes through "masculinization," her male familial opponent undergoes "feminization" in character. Like Thecla, Perpetua's masculinization involves social, spatial, and physical dimensions. Perpetua moves away from the conventional feminine identity and role and increasingly displays male qualities; she separates herself from physical maternity as well as obedient daughterhood and emerges as an independent and autonomous decision-maker over her body and fate. With independence and autonomy comes spiritual empowerment, which manifests itself in her intervention for her deceased brother Dinocrates and his subsequent deliverance, as well as the adjutant Puden's recognition of her spiritual power (9.1). In contrast, her father becomes increasingly "womanish," as he loses control over his emotions and exhibits self-abasing actions. He cries and becomes overwhelmingly emotional and hysterical, and desperately dependent upon his daughter's will. Finally, he even tears his beard; and this loss of the beard indicates the further feminization of the father.[245]

The physical dimension of gender transformation occurs most famously in the fourth vision of Perpetua, where she is transformed into a man for the fight with the Egyptian. As a man, she is rubbed with oil by her male seconds, takes the role of a gladiator, and conquers the Egyptian. The bodily transformation ends there, for the *lanista* addresses her as his daughter after the victory. Indeed, as Perpetua marches into the arena with joy and serenity on the day of her martyrdom, she is identified as "the beloved of God (*Dei delicata*), as a wife of Christ (*matrona Christi*)" (18.2). Perpetua retains her biological sex, but her identity is not the wife of an earthly husband[246] but the wife of Christ, who is in fact the heavenly husband of both Christian men and women.

Nevertheless, her social and spatial masculinization continues, as she takes an undisputed authority and leadership in Saturus' vision and in life.[247] In Saturus' vision, the bishop and the presbyter prostrate themselves before Perpetua and Saturus and plead with them to settle the ecclesiastical dispute (13.1–3). In prison, she asserts the "human rights" of prisoners to the military tribune; in the arena, she claims martyr's free will and resists being dressed as a pagan priest/priestess (18.4–6). She puts down the crowd's stare by her own intense gaze (18.2) and pronounces God's judgment upon them (18.8). She exhorts her brother and catechumens to "stand fast in the faith and love one another, and . . . not be weakened by what we have gone through" (20.10), and finally she faces death with her own act of will (21.9). To the end, Perpetua asserts her independence and exercises her authority in contrast to the cultural construction of her gender. Thus, the *Martyrdom of Perpetua* is illustrative of the "rhetoric of resistance,"[248] which critiques not only political order but also social ideology, relationships, and structures, and is therefore representative of the other Martyr Acts in their subversive thrust.

Summary and conclusion

Asceticism is essentially this-worldly and social, for it is primarily concerned about the lifestyle in this world (in light of the other world), and it always involves a dichotomy of social values in terms of what it rejects and what it embraces. In Christian sexual morality, which was the hallmark of Christian asceticism and Christians' moral and social self-definition, this dichotomy is most pronounced. Adopting the philosophical language of Stoic-Cynic moral disciplines, all Christians, whether conservative or radical, condemned and rejected the popular sexual and social practices of the dominant society: fornication, homosexuality, adultery, divorce, remarriage, incest, contraception, abortion, and exposure of infants. Both Jesus (in the Synoptics) and Paul affirmed and redefined "Christian" marriage and family in light of and vis-à-vis the dominant social values and norms, but also introduced an extraordinary option of lifelong virginity for single-minded pursuit of God and the eschatological reality. Whereas Jesus appeared ambiguous about his preference, Paul clearly preferred celibacy to marriage, while recommending marriage for those who were not given the gift of celibacy for practical reasons of ministry.

While asserting the superiority of Christian sexual morality as a defense against pagan accusations, the Apologies, Apocryphal Acts, and Martyr Acts attested to the bifurcating development of the Dominical and Pauline tradition in close interaction with the Stoic-Cynic asceticism in the subsequent century. All of them saw sexual purity as the distinctive Christian value and categorically dissociated sexual sins from Christian practice. However, in terms of what constitutes sexual purity and sins, they disagreed. Embracing the disciplined sexual ethics of Stoicism and the conservative "family values" of the Empire, the Apologists (except Tatian) highlighted Christian sexual asceticism in a way that could gain acceptance and respect from the pagan elites. Corresponding to the Stoic ideal, they confined sexual intercourse to the marriage bed for procreation alone. Following the Gospel and deutero-Pauline tradition, they upheld the sanctity of marriage as a divine institution, with the principle of conjugal partnership comparable to the philosophized ideal of the Stoics. They certainly redefined the existing sexual codes and marriage (e.g. condemnation of divorce and remarriage). However, by defending marriage and procreation, they affirmed the Christian social duty in this world and accommodated the established Greco-Roman social order and structure (however christianized).

The Apologists surely honored and took pride in Christian virginity, which was indeed an admirable but "asocial" (and thus potentially subversive) choice in the ancient world, where it "was there to be lost" in the "natural" social role of marriage and procreation.[249] However, they did not deny its exceptional character and praised it as a virtue, not as a norm. Here, they followed Paul in distinguishing "good" and "better" but tempered Paul's "ascetic" stance and limited it to the few "elites." While recognizing celibacy as a "gift," they ironically set up a two-tier spirituality, which Paul never intended to create. Virginity became a "gift" less of divine grace than of human will and was thus reserved for the few perfectionists "who would draw closer to God"; the paradigm of chaste marriage was set for the rest. For them, the principle of (physical) creation demanded the continuation of God's creation through marriage, family, and social order.

For Tatian and the authors of the Apocryphal Acts, a life of virginity and continence marked the standard by which every Christian was called to live by virtue of their conversion. Here they transformed Paul's practical preference for celibacy into an absolute mandate. Being Christian meant a radical separation from the present corrupt world, which was perpetuating itself by sexuality and marriage. The Christian call was to restore the pristine purity before the Fall by rejecting the very cause and effect of the Fall – sexuality and marriage – and thus to put a stop to this vicious cycle in anticipation of entering the celestial world. Thus, celibacy and continent life were required for every Christian, and every Christian was to be a perfectionist; in this sense, the Apocryphal Acts truly "democratized" the ascetic call. Converts were to achieve this perfection precisely in their body, which "had become a tangible *locus* on which the freedom of the will could be exercised, in choices that intimately affected the conventional fabric of society."[250]

Therefore, by their freedom and action, the continent disrupted and resisted the present structures of society built on sexuality, marriage, and family. They subverted the inherent traditional values and became social deviants whose ascetic power threatened the social status quo. This kind of social rebellion and subversion is best illustrated in the portrayal of the women converts in the Apocryphal Acts. By their ascetic power and authority, they embody traditional male virtues, defy the social hierarchy, and experience "liberation" from the conventional female social duties. Their anti-familial and anti-social stance toward the dominant world points to the alternative kinship group defined by Christian identity and continence.

The socially subversive thrust of Christianity manifests itself in the Martyr Acts as well, especially in the representation of the women martyrs. While female martyrs were subject to the gender-specific punishment (besides the common tortures and sufferings) that underlined female nudity and sexuality, they overturned the dominant power and social sensibility by exhibiting male strength and heroism under extreme conditions. As in the Apocryphal Acts, the gender inversion not only brought liberation and empowerment for women but also posed threats to the traditional patriarchy and social structure. Female martyrs rejected their conventional gender roles as mothers, daughters, and wives and exercised their authority as spiritual leaders of the Christian community. This Christian renunciation of family by marriage and blood led to the redefinition and reconfiguration of family by Christian confession and identity.

Thus, the sexual asceticism in these bodies of literature defined the Christian social identity vis-à-vis the dominant society and tradition, which could be characterized as an "accommodation" for the Apologists and a "resistance" for the Apocryphal and Martyr Acts. With the dawn of the Constantine era, the encratism of the Apocryphal Acts found its "orthodox" accommodation in the institutionalized form but lost its socially subversive thrust. By then, the virgin life had become a badge of the ecclesiastical hierarchy with an elitist premium. In this way, the Apologists' distinction between "good" (marriage) and "better" (celibacy) would inadvertently govern the moral and ecclesiastical hierarchy of the subsequent orthodox Church. However, in the late second and early third centuries, the dichotomy still reflected the divergent self-definitions of the Christian groups. This dichotomy of accommodation and resistance (and transcendence) will continue as we deal with the political realm of Christian self-definition in the next chapter.

4

CHRISTIAN LOYALTY TO
THE EMPIRE

The political self-definition of Christians came out of the pressing
issue of their loyalty to the Empire in light of their ultimate
allegiance to Christ. With charges of atheism and social subversiveness, the allegation of treason loomed large for Christians of this
period, which especially threatened their survival.[1] Given the close
link between religion and politics in the Greco-Roman world, religion and patriotism went hand in hand, and the charge of political
subversiveness was a logical extension of the charge of atheism.
Christians' divergent and ambivalent stances toward the Empire
reflected in the Apologies, Apocryphal Acts, and Martyr Acts in turn
reveal their responses to that intricate religio-political relationship.
Their reactions present a common concern but also exhibit contrasting "solutions" to the pagan accusations. Whereas the Apologists
adopt accommodation and accentuate the allegiance of Christians to
the Empire, the Apocryphal and Martyr Acts confirm the Christian
threat and resistance to the Empire. The Apocryphal Acts highlight
the revolutionary character of Christian loyalty to the heavenly
kingdom, and the Martyr Acts, as inherent in the genre, stress non-
violent resistance in the inevitable conflict between the Lord Christ
and the Lord Caesar. Before we engage this topic, we will review
briefly the contemporary prevalent phenomenon with which all
Christians wrestled in one way or another – the imperial cult.[2]

Imperial cult: unity of religion and politics

Characteristic of the ancient world, including that of Greco-Roman
society, was a fundamental unity in religion, society, and politics.
The *pax deorum*, *mos maiorum*, and *pax Romana* were systemically
intertwined and provided the essential foundation of the socio-
political and religious order. Since the time of Augustus, the

159

imperial cult based on the "imperial theology of power"[3] had become the crux of that unity. As the Romans transitioned from the Republic to the Empire, between them and their gods stood a new mediator who appeared in the figure of the divinely sanctioned emperor.[4] Inheriting the Hellenistic conception of deity, kingship, and power, Romans reorganized and systemized the Hellenistic ruler cult by focusing on the figure of the emperor as the integrative center of the newly built Empire. With an ideological underpinning, the imperial cult, i.e. "the public association of emperors with gods, divine forces, sacred rites, altars and temples,"[5] was a political act of loyalty and a response to power in religious terms. Throughout the Empire it was the imperial power that evoked homage and "worship" from the subjects; cities and provinces competed against one another to establish the cult of the emperors and recognize them, both the living and dead, as divine. Thus, the imperial cult exemplified the essential "alliance of throne and altar"[6] of Greco-Roman society and functioned as the unifying principle for the vast and diverse Empire. Whereas Christianity consciously separated the mortal from the divine, in the cult of the emperor, people from all social strata came to bridge the very unbridgeable gap, with metaphors, legends, art forms, and sacred rites.

The cultic development of emperor worship began with Julius Caesar, but it was Augustus who institutionalized and established its pattern for subsequent emperors. His reign, marked by religious and social conservatism, sought to rebuild "national faith and faith in the nation."[7] Through massive religious reforms and restorations, he conveyed the message that the *pax deorum* for the Empire now meant the *pax deorum* for the emperor and vice versa. By assuming the office of *pontifex maximus* (13 BCE), Augustus officially symbolized the unity of the Empire and faith in his person, and by turning his house into a public shrine, he made his household worship an official cult of the Empire.

While reticent in receiving direct worship of himself, Augustus, with exceptional political flair, redirected the loyalty (*pietas*) of his subjects from himself to the worship of the personified divine virtues, which in fact provided safe ground to expect devotion and *pietas* from them. Thus, he was portrayed as manifesting and embodying the divine virtues of "success and good fortune (*felicitas* and *fortuna*), of victory and peace (*victoria* and *pax*), of liberty and justice (*libertas* and *iustitia*) and of humaneness towards men and piety towards both gods and men (*clementia* and *pietas*)."[8] Based on these virtues, Augustus (then Octavian) received extraordinary and unprecedented divine honors:[9] from 30 BCE onward, his birthday was celebrated as a public holiday; in 29 BCE, his name was included in hymns with the gods, and the day of his entry into the city was honored with sacrifices; in 28 BCE, quinquennial vows were made in his name; in 27 BCE he was given the title of Augustus, which had a numinous quality of ancient *augere* and *augurium*. Moreover, Rome instituted a festival and games in honor of his fortune (the *Augustalia*); a month, temples, altars, and the Shield of Virtue were dedicated to him; he was given the title, "Father of the Fatherland" (*pater patriae*), and his statue was placed in the temple of Apollo; and the senate passed a decree that at every banquet a libation should be poured out to his *Genius*. All of these meant the integration of the imperial cult into a broader spectrum of traditional cults with the consequence that the emperors became the object of the same cult-acts as the gods.[10]

Along with cultic development, formulation of divine titles based on their power and virtues provided the conceptual framework of the emperors' divinity. The following titles in particular betray the divine claims of the emperors with serious implications and parallels with the titles applied to Christ in early Christian literature, including the New Testament: god (θεός, *divus/deus*), son of god (υἰὸς θεοῦ, *divi filius*), lord (κύριος, *dominus*), and savior (σωτήρ). Concerning the first title, in the first year of Augustus (27 BCE), an oath formula, "by Caesar, god of gods" was introduced.[11] According to Suetonius,[12] Domitian officially claimed the title *dominus et deus* (cf. John 20.28), and, according to Martial, libations were poured out to him as a god.[13] The title "son of god (*divi filius*)" was notably common in inscriptions and coins. By deifying his adopted father, Julius Caesar, Augustus safely assumed the title *divi filius*. Following this example, by virtue of deifying the predecessor, the successor took the title *divi filius*. Thus, Tiberius was accepted as the son of *divus* Augustus, Hadrian, the son of *divus* Trajan, Marcus Aurelius, the son of *divus* Antoninus Pius, and so on. Moreover, emperors called themselves and posed as the sons of their favorite traditional gods. Hence, Augustus was proclaimed as the son of Apollo, and the Antonines (Trajan, Hadrian, Antoninus Pius, and Marcus Aurelius) as the sons of Jupiter. The most pervasive and prominent title was κύριος. It was first applied to Augustus in 12 BCE; under Nero the title "Νέρων ὁ κύριος" was used almost as a stock formula.[14] This title provided the most conspicuous parallel with the Christian claim of "Jesus Christ the Lord" (e.g. 2 Cor. 1.2; Phil. 2.11) and Christ as "the Lord of Lords." (e.g. Rev. 17.14; 19.16).

161

Finally, the title "savior" (σωτήρ) was integral to the propaganda of the "imperial soteriology."[15] Throughout the imperial period, the title σωτήρ τοῦ κόσμου, the significant designation of Jesus in the Johannine corpus, was conferred on Augustus, Claudius, Nero, Vespesian, Titus, Trajan, and Hadrian.[16] When Augustus brought *pax Romana* and restored *pax deorum*, he was hailed conclusively as a "god the son of the god Caesar, Savior who brings liberty," who brought salvation and peace, new order, and victory.[17] Quite literally, the emperor was a "savior" who had brought an earthly paradise to humanity; his kingdom and its salvation and benefits were of this world.[18] Like the Christian Gospels, imperial propaganda promulgated the "good news" (εὐαγγέλιον) of "the dawning of a new age of peace on earth and goodwill towards men brought by the advent of a divinely sent saviour."[19] During the Antonine age, this imperial gospel saw its culmination with the representations of the emperors as the divinely elected vicegerent of Jupiter on earth.[20]

This imperial "theology" and ideology exhibited its concrete manifestation and materialization in the imperial rituals and art forms. Festivals, games, sacrifices, oaths, and other imperial ceremonial acts on the one hand, and the emperor's priests, temples, images, and statues on the other brought a virtual and tangible reality of and an access to the emperor's presence. This phenomenon was even more conspicuous in the provinces. According to Simon Price, the imperial festivals, which celebrated imperial birthdays and anniversaries in regular cycles and other special occasions in conjunction with traditional deities, formed the "essential framework" of the imperial cult and as such constituted an integral part of the social, political, and cultural life in Roman Asia.[21] All the major civic centers provided settings of the festivals. With incense and special libation bowls bearing imperial images, imperial sacrifices were offered at prominent locations of the civic square: council houses, imperial temples, sanctuaries of local deities, theaters, and gymnasiums. Competitions in art and athletics in honor of the emperors were held in theaters, stadiums, and gymnasiums. These political, religious, and public centers, which housed imperial statues and special rooms for the imperial cult, were linked together by processions in which the whole city participated.[22]

Indeed, the imperial cult permeated not only public life but also the whole public space, with imperial statues and portraits "in public buildings, on the streets, on fountains, and on city gates" as a constant reminder of the sovereign.[23] The imperial statues represented the divine features of the emperor, depicting him in military and priestly garb, and also as naked, just like the Olympian gods. As representations of the emperors' divine power, they functioned as a place of asylum, served as a medium for divine portents and even solicited worship in association with imperial rituals and mysteries (cf. Rev. 13.15). Besides statues, the imperial coinage constituted the most common visual means of imperial propaganda. Bearing the image of the emperor with his title (e.g. DIVI FILIVS, CAESAR AVGVSTVS), it celebrated ever-increasing imperial virtues and benefactions: *Victoria, Concord, Salus, Aeternitas,* and *Spes.*[24] Therefore, by watching the emperor's image, "by joining in sacrifice, and by enjoying the imperial games, a citizen of the Roman Empire was reminded of who ruled the world."[25]

The chief sponsors of the imperial cult were the aristocrats and provincial elites, who were in turn imperial clients. The priests of Augustus (*flamines Augustalis*), from the imperial family, supervised the annual sacrifices of vows on behalf of or to the emperors, and the priestly colleges (*sodales Augustales*), composed of twenty-one senators with imperial members, ran the games in honor of the emperor.[26] Both offices were given considerable privileges and honors. In Asia Minor, the members of the prestigious Provincial League of Asia (Κοινόν Ἀσίας, *Commune Asiae*) functioned as the imperial priests and supervisors of the collective cult of currently reigning and deified past emperors – including building temples, organizing annual festivals and games, and composing hymns in honor of the emperor. Thus, "the political-religious institutions in which power relations were constituted were virtually inseparable from the local social-economic networks of imperial society."[27]

Not only the "rich and powerful" stood at the center of the propagation of the imperial cult, but the intellectuals also accepted it, including its power relations; men such as Plutarch, Pliny, Aristides, and Dio of Prusa simply took it for granted and were rather silent about it.[28] Regardless of what they believed about the divinity of the emperor, they were part of the culture, which valued the customs and ritualized and mythologized imperial power and ideology. Hence, Pliny, when examining Christians in Bithynia, did not hesitate to conjoin the image of Trajan with the statues of traditional gods for the sacrifice test.[29] He used the imperial cult along with the traditional cult as a means to compel the submission and loyalty or to justify the punishment and condemnation of Christians.[30]

Apologies: Christian loyalty to the Empire

Given the pervasive reality of the imperial cult and the perilous predicament of Christians, the Apologists found themselves in a delicate position. They carefully weighed the balance between Christian denial of the imperial cult and their expression of loyalty to the Empire. Just as they denied the accusation of atheism and redefined it, they also disavowed the charge of political subversion and treason, and redefined true loyalty from the Christian perspective. They attempted to break the complex web of *pax deorum*, *mos maiorum*, *pax Romana*, and imperial cult and tried to reconfigure the web with the Christian God, Christian loyalty, and *pax Romana*. Their approach reveals one of ambivalence but eventual unity between Church and Empire.

Christian loyalty and the imperial cult

The Apologists' profession of Christian loyalty "rightly" starts with the praise of the emperor(s). Their remarks on and addresses to the emperors appear to be patterned after the rhetorical convention of the day, illustrated by Menander's handbook on panegyrics in the third century.[31] Menander's advice includes the following: statement about the king being sent from god and heaven and acknowledgment of his greatness (370.21–6; 422.26–9); praise of the king's "love of learning," intelligence, and eagerness for studies; exploitation of his philosophical bent and recognition of his surpassing excellence in *paideia* (371.14–372.2); praise of the achievements of the king in peace, such as the king's mildness, humaneness, accessibility, and his establishment of justice (374.25–375.4, 8–10); and a closing prayer that god would grant him a long and successful reign and that he be succeeded by his sons (377.19–30).[32] Interesting parallels emerge in the works of Justin, Melito, and Athenagoras, who directed their apologies to Marcus Aurelius. They highlight the fact that the emperor is a philosopher and also make use of the Platonic ideal of the "philosopher-king" as a basis of their petition for justice to the emperor(s).[33] Justin identifies Antoninus, Marcus and Lucius as "truly pious and philosophers," "lover[s] of truth" and "guardians of justice and lovers of culture," who judge and rule by reason and divine wisdom.[34] Melito portrays Marcus Aurelius, along with Hadrian and Antoninus Pius, as the "pious and good emperor," who excels in humanity and philosophy (πολύ γε φιλανθρωποτέρος καὶ φιλοσοφωτέρος). Therefore, the philosopher-emperor should protect Christian "philosophy" from pagan violence.[35]

As examined by William Schoedel, Athenagoras' idealization of the emperor in the Menanderian model is particularly striking.[36] Like Justin and Melito, Athenagoras, in his *Legatio*, fully "exploits" the philosophical emperors' (Marcus Aurelius' and Commodus') "nature and learning (φύσις καὶ παιδεῖά)" (37.1). He praises them for their accomplishments and superiority to all people in the whole range of *paideia* and for their excellence in "the wisdom and power" of their rule (6.2). As good (χρηστοί), moderate (μέτριοι), humane (φιλάντρωποι), and learned (φιλομαθεστάτων) kings (37.1; 2.1), their actions are grounded in their "philosophy and profound *paideia*" (2.3). "For that reason," Athenagoras acclaims,

> individual men, admiring your gentle and mild natures, your peaceableness and humanity toward all, enjoy equality before the law; the cities have an equal share in honour according to their merit; and the whole empire enjoys a profound peace through your wisdom.
>
> (1.2)

Later, he closes his work with a prayer for their reign "that the succession to the kingdom may proceed from father to son, as is most just, and that [their] reign may grow and increase as all men become subject to [them]" (37.2).

On this basis of their virtues, Athenagoras pleads with them to extend their reason, justice, and humanity to the Christians and appeals to them to consider Christian philosophy. Inviting them to examine "the heavenly kingdom," he compares the reign of Marcus Aurelius and Commodus with that of Father God and Logos the Son:

> [A]s all things have been subjected to you, a father and a son, who have received your kingdom from above (ἄνωθεν) ("for the king's life is in God's hand", as the prophetic [S]pirit says), so all things are subordinated to the one God and the Word that issues him whom we consider his inseparable Son.
>
> (18.2)

Here Athenagoras not only employs rhetoric but also brings theology with it. While recognizing the divine origin of their kingship as part of the conventional panegyric rhetoric, he "christianizes" the imperial power. He traces its origin not to Jupiter/Zeus but to "the one God and the Logos" with biblical allusions. Robert Grant points out that this analogy should be seen in light of 1 Corinthians 15.25–8, which speaks of the eschatological subordination of all things to the Son and the Father, and Matthew 28.18, where the risen Christ declares that all power in heaven and on earth has been granted to him.[37] Moreover, the divine origin of the emperor's power is clearly seen in Romans 13.1–6 and John 19.11, which mention the earthly authority given by God and "from above" (ἄνωθεν), respectively. Thus, Athenagoras, while adopting the prevalent imperial ideology in praise of the emperors, sets it in a Christian context (just like Paul) and thus subordinates imperial power to the one God and the Logos-Son. In fact, other Apologists take the same strategy, and this will prove to be a pattern for the later Christian writers as well. Athenagoras' use of "Christological" analogy in reference to the imperial father and son anticipates the binatarian political theology of Eusebius in the fourth century.[38]

With respect to the imperial cult, the Apologists draw a critical distinction between worship of the emperor and honor paid to him, as they continue to underscore the Christians' political loyalty to the emperor. Quoting Jesus' teaching in Matthew 22.17ff., "Give therefore to Caesar the things that are Caesar's and to God the things that are God's (NRSV)," Justin declares, "we worship God only, but in other things we gladly serve you, acknowledging you as emperors and rulers of men and women, and praying that with your imperial power you may also be found to possess sound judgment."[39] He distinguishes here the spiritual realm of worship due to God from the political realm of honor and power due to the emperor, the distinction that might have not been intended by the Evangelist.[40]

Theophilus also separates religious from political loyalty. Christians worship the real and true God the Creator alone; however, the emperor is God's creature and worthy of not worship but legitimate honor as a man appointed by God to judge justly (cf. Rom. 13.1).[41] Again drawing from the Scriptures, he states that honoring the emperor (1 Pet. 2.17) "by wishing him well, by obeying him, by praying for him [cf. 1 Tim. 2.2]" is performing the will of God (1 Pet. 2.15) and obeying God's law (Prov. 24.21).[42] This distinction is made by Minucius as well: "Princes and kings may rightly be hailed as great and elect among men, but homage to them as gods is base and lying flattery; honour is the truer tribute to distinction, affection the more acceptable reward to worth."[43] Likewise, Tatian distinguishes the appropriate honor entitled to man (i.e. the emperor) from the fear belonging to God alone, and yet he still confirms his loyalty and civil duty to the emperor.[44]

In his *Apology*, Tertullian similarly applies the Creator–creature dualism to the issue of emperor worship. The emperor cannot be God, for if he were, he could not be an emperor; as a human being, he is subordinate to God in majesty and power (33.3–4; 34.3). Thus, for Tertullian, his "Lord is One, God omnipotent, eternal, who is also the Emperor's Lord" (34.1). However, he reserves an extraordinary praise for the emperor. Christians should respect the emperor as "the chosen of our Lord (33.1)," subject to no one but God (32.2), greater than and above all pagan gods (29.3; 30.1), whom the Romans fear more than their gods (28.2). As a matter of fact, the emperor belongs more to the Christians than to the Romans, for it is the Christian God who appointed him (33.2; cf. Rom. 13.1). Even the emperors acknowledge "who has given them the empire" (30.1). In this way, while denying worship of the emperor, all of the Apologists articulate that the basis of their loyalty and thus Christians' loyalty to the emperor is the divine approval and delegated authority from God.

Interestingly, in light of the significance of the imperial cult in the Martyr Acts (see p. 180), the Apologists' critique of the imperial cult is almost absent or only minor. As Bowersock indicates, their silence is similar to that of the contemporary pagan intellectuals.[45] Justin scorns Antinous, who was Hadrian's male lover and deified by him upon drowning, but Justin's remark appears only in passing without mentioning Hadrian.[46] Tertullian opposes taking oaths by "the genius of the Caesar" (*per genios Caesarum*) but approves taking oaths "by his health" (*per salutem eorum*) and once again affirms the divine election of the emperors.[47] The Apologists' apparent neglect of and silence on the "evil" of the imperial cult[48] reveal that it "appears paradoxically to have been an institution which Christians could tolerate around them."[49] Yes, they warn the emperors of the inescapable judgment of God[50] and complain about injustices to Christians who are in harsh predicaments.[51] Nonetheless, the Apologists are in conformity with the Pauline and Lucan attitude toward the earthly authority over against the Revelation, an attitude which would continue to govern the Church–Empire dynamic to the post-Constantine era.

Christian support for the Empire

As a sign of Christians' loyalty, the Apologists stress the active and practical Christian support for the Empire. The Apologists insist that, just as Christian teachings promote moral excellence, they also teach loyal citizenship and civil obedience. Justin affirms that Christians are good citizens who, following Christ's command, promote peace, acknowledge the emperors as the rulers, and gladly pray for them.[52] Indeed, every element of these "signs" of loyalty and support is repeated by the subsequent Apologists.[53]

Of all the Apologists, Tertullian underlines even more the Christians' active participation in the welfare of the Empire. With the exception of the temples, Christians are everywhere in the Empire, including palace, senate, forum, and military forts and camps;[54] they live, sail, and fight along with the Romans, bearing the responsibility of military service (42.2–3).[55] Moreover, Christians, following the apostolic precept (1 Tim. 2.2) (31.3), and "from the heart" without blush,

> are ever making intercession for all the Emperors. [Christians] pray for them long life, a secure rule, a safe home, brave armies, a faithful senate, an honest people, a quiet world – and everything for which a man and a Caesar can pray.
>
> (30.4)

The dual theme of Christian service in the army and effectual prayers for the emperor climaxes in the story of the so-called "Thundering Legion" (*Legio XII Fulminata*): "the great drought in Germany was broken by rain obtained through the prayers of Christians, who, as it chanced, were among his [Marcus Aurelius'] soldiers" (5.6). This story is confirmed by Eusebius in greater detail.[56] According to him, bishop Apollinaris, who wrote an apology to Marcus Aurelius, testifies that, in the battle of Marcus Aurelius against Germans and Samaritans, the Christian soldiers of the Militene Legion prayed for the emperor, and a miraculous rainstorm came on the Danube, gave water to Roman troops, and struck the enemy with lightning (173 CE).[57] It is in fact Apollinaris who proudly (but incorrectly) attributes the origin of the name *Fulminata* to the emperor's reward for Christians for that miracle.[58] To these Apologists, this incident is apparently significant proof of Christian loyalty; their attestation of Christians in the Roman army is their apologetic means by which they could refute the pagan critics' charge of Christian disloyalty and rejection of military service for the emperor.[59] In this way, Apollinaris and Tertullian inadvertently provide the first literary evidence of Christian soldiers since the time of canonical Gospels and Acts (cf. Luke 7.1–10; Matt. 8.5–13;

Acts 10.1–48).[60] Thus, "more than all other people we are your helpers and allies in the cause of peace," confidently claims Justin.[61] Surely, according to the Apologists, Christians' prayer and civil and military conducts are more efficacious means of supporting and protecting the Empire than those of pagans.[62]

Unity between Church and Empire

In this context, it only takes one little step for the Apologists to join Christianity with the prosperity of the Roman Empire. Melito, bishop of Sardis, whose apology is preserved only in a few fragments by Eusebius, champions this extraordinary thesis.[63] He appeals to Marcus Aurelius for toleration of Christians "on the grounds of common interest" between the Christian philosophy and the universal empire founded by Augustus, in which Christ himself had been raised.[64] Since Roman power grew in glory and splendor concomitant with the growth of Christian philosophy, Christianity has been not only responsible for the success of the Empire but also beneficial to its welfare.[65] Indeed, the surest proof of this is the fact that only "bad emperors," namely, Nero and Domitian, persecuted Christians, but all the "good and pious emperors," including Hadrian and Antoninus, showed a favorable disposition to Christians, even correcting the harms done by the bad ones.[66] Thus, Hadrian wrote to Fundanus, the proconsul of Asia, and Antoninus wrote to Larissans, Thessalonians, and Athenians that "no violence should be used in connection with [Christians]."[67]

Tertullian in his *Apology* readily joins the thesis of Melito.[68] Christians' prayers for the emperors and the Empire have to do with "the whole estate of the empire and the interests of Rome" (32.1). Rome is not the great whore whose destruction is certain and imminent (Rev. 18) but the great Empire, which will last as long as the world (32.1; cf. 2 Thess. 2.6–8).[69] Fearing the end of the age by suffering and destruction, Christians, who enjoy the benefit of the Empire, pray that the end of the world be delayed, and, by doing so, they help the continuance of Rome (32.1). Knowing this, the "good and wise emperors," such as Marcus Aurelius, have been protectors of Christians (5.6). In fact, Tiberius, whose reign saw the rise of Christianity, even recognized the truth of Christ's divinity (5.2). Persecution began with Nero and was repeated only by Domitian, both "unjust, impious, foul" men whom all the pagans also abhor and condemn (5.3–4). Their wicked "laws" of persecution were in part frustrated by Trajan with his prohibition of

"Christian hunting" and were never enforced by Hadrian, Vespasian, Antoninus Pius, and Lucius Verus – the models of the "good and wise emperors" (5.7). Therefore, on this, "consult your histories," urges Tertullian (5.3).

According to Tertullian, Roman history supports his claim of Christian loyalty and benefit to the Empire and reveals the error of attributing Roman success to Roman piety. Ascribing Roman power and grandeur to Roman piety (*pieta* and *religio*) had been a common view upheld by the imperial ideology and shared by the cultivated such as Plutarch and Pliny as well as Posidonius, Polybius, Livy, Cicero, and the Augustan poets (cf. 25.2–3).[70] It reflected a sense of "Manifest Destiny" for them, in which gods willed and destined the success and empire for Romans for their religious *devotio* and *pieta*.[71] Tertullian directly counters this "sacred" view by pointing out that the greatness and victories of Rome came rather from Roman irreligion and sacrilege – wars, destruction of cities and temples, and plunders – and that their gods were completely power-less (25.12–17).[72] He then points to the one true God who dispenses the kingdoms and to whom belong "the world that is ruled and the man who rules it" (26.1). It is the invisible but sovereign God of Christians who "has ordained the progression of empires each at its time in the world's story" (26.1). Thus, the success of Rome, in its ever-increasing expansion and reign, is in reality the gift of God in his providence (26.2)[73] for the rise of the Church; the credit rightly belongs to the true God for the piety of Christians. In their essentially historical arguments, Tertullian and Melito now claim for Christianity what pagans have claimed for their religions.[74] Thus, the "proven" advantage of Christianity to the Empire more than compensates for its "barbarian" origin.

Therefore, the destinies of the Church and the Empire are to be joined together in God's providence. In fact, we can witness this welding of the two already in Justin's apologies. It is part of the providential plan that the incarnation should take place in Judaea during the time of Roman rule and that Christianity should grow under the Roman government.[75] In 70 CE, Jerusalem should be destroyed by Roman legions, which acted as the instruments of God's justice for the murder of Christ and as a radical intervention to stop the "Old Testament" rites and sacrifices.[76] The new dispensa-tion of Christ has made them obsolete. Even the banners and trophies of the Roman army anticipated the shape of the cross.[77] The Apologists presuppose the Church as belonging to the gentile world, particularly to the Roman Empire, and "christianize" the Roman imperial policy of "alliance of throne and altar."[78] This again looks back to the Lucan perspective and looks ahead to the arguments of Origen and Eusebius that the Church and Empire should collaborate as congenial partners in service of the one true God. The unity of Church and Empire is not only the goal but also the imperative. In Henry Chadwick's words, this

> reminds us how near we stand to Constantine's labarum and how many of the presuppositions of the Christian empire existed long before when the Church was being harried by the empire and as far from being established as anything could be.[79]

Here exists an interesting paradox in the Apologists' arguments for the alliance of Christianity and the Empire. Surely, they distinguished between worship of the emperor and honor given to the emperor and thus separated the religious and political realms in a society where both were always interlinked. Following this logic, they demanded religious freedom and thus the "separation of Church and State" from the Roman government, where no such separation existed – a brilliant and radical innovation in the ancient world.[80] Nonetheless, they ended up espousing and envisaging the eventual union of the two with a "christianized" version. The Apologists' defense of Christianity establishes a Christian's existence no longer as a sojourner but as a loyal dutiful citizen of the Empire. The nascent political theory of the Christian empire, the union of the heavenly kingdom and the earthly one, looks forward to its full realization on earth.

Apocryphal Acts: Christian subversiveness to the Empire

In contrast to the Apologists' appeal to the Christian allegiance to and alliance with the Empire, the Apocryphal Acts present the Christian threat to and judgment over the Empire. Just like the Acts' religious and moral/social stances, their basic attitude toward the Empire is confrontational with a dualistic value system.[81] With apocalyptic imageries, these Acts project a political enmity between Christianity and the earthly kingdom, particularly the Roman Empire.[82]

Apostles vs. political authorities

The antithesis between Christianity and the Empire is mainly dis-played by the conflicting encounters between the primary charac-ters (mostly apostles) and the political authorities, such as the governors (proconsuls), king, and emperor. In the *Acts of Paul and Thecla*, Paul's "wicked" companions Demas and Hermogenes advise enraged Thamyris to take Paul before the governor and "say that he is a Christian" (16); for "he will die at once" (16), and then Thamyris will have Thecla as his wife (14). This suggestion reflects the current historical reality that Christian identity itself made one liable to death. The Apologies and Martyr Acts both protest and testify to the condemnation by the local authorities based on the Christian Name alone. After the governor imprisons Paul and casts him out of the city, he also condemns the new convert Thecla to death for breaking the "law of the Iconians" by refusing to marry Thamyris (20). Once again, this attests to the fundamental unity in religion, politics, and social order; Paul's Christian identity and preaching and Thecla's refusal to marry her fiancé all amount to violation of law and invite judicial condemnation by the imperial authority.

Thecla is rescued from martyrdom by miraculous intervention, but in Antioch she is again brought before a governor only to be later condemned to the wild beasts. She had shamed Alexander by publicly refusing his sexual advances and pulling off his crown with the imperial insignia (26). It is significant that she is explicitly charged with "sacrilege" (ἱερόσυλος) (28), which suggests the con-text of the imperial cult. Judging from his socio-political status ("the first of Antioch") and his attire (priestly crown), Alexander may well have been a priest of the imperial cult.[83] Thus, Thecla's acts of tearing his cloak and pulling off his crown not only indi-cate personal insult to Alexander but also signify her offense to the imperial symbol and her defiant challenge to the existing imperial authority. Indeed, the deeds deserve the charge of "sacrilege" from the authorities' point of view. However, divine intervention once again saves Thecla from the fierce beasts, and the governor, over-whelmed by her power, releases "the pious Thecla, the servant of God" (38). These instances unabashedly portray Christians as law-breakers and rebels against the present political establishment, which is part of the oppressive forces against them. Yet their God repeatedly overpowers the earthly authorities that stand opposed to God's servants. Therefore, Thecla extols God, "my helper in prison, my help before the governors, my helper in the fire, my helper among the beasts" (42).

The conflict theme continues in the rest of the *Acts of Paul* and other Acts in conjunction with the theme of male rivalry and encratic disruption in marriage. As mentioned in the previous chapter, the apostle's encratic message causes the breakdown of marriage and social custom and also causes the ensuing persecution from the woman convert's husband. The husband is typically a man of political power (e.g. proconsul, prefect, and king), who upholds the traditional cult, "family values," and social order. The domestic and social conflict naturally becomes political as the apostle denies and opposes the husband's political authority and judicial pressure brought to bear, and acts as a deviant and lawbreaker. The men in control incarcerate, scourge, and finally execute the apostles through their invested political power. However, the apostles not only stand firm in their Christian truths but also defy the very political coercion and force with their charismatic power and ultimately with their martyrdom.

In the *Acts of Paul*, Paul's preaching of Christian monotheism and denunciation of pagan idols and images in Ephesus (7) incite a great uproar from the goldsmiths (cf. Acts 19.23–40), and he is condemned to the beasts by the proconsul Hieronymus. While in prison, Paul converts both Artemilla (wife of Hieronymus) and Eubula (wife of Diophantes, Hieronymus' freedman) to the encratic gospel. When Hieronymus hears that "the women sat night and day with Paul," he becomes personally involved in the execution of Paul by hastening the day of fight and ordering "a very fierce lion." The author contrasts Paul's "dignified bearing" with Hieronymus' grief over his wife and fury over Paul, joined by the crowd, who cries, "Away with the sorcerer! Away with the prisoner!" In a fable-like surprise, however, the animal set loose against Paul turns out to be the very lion baptized by Paul. Then, a violent hailstorm hits the crowd and Hieronymus' ear, delivering Paul and the lion from them.

The hailstorm miracle demonstrates the power of the one true Christian God and signifies not only Paul's victory over Hieronymus on a personal level but also God's judgment over the earthly authorities represented by Hieronymus. God's judgment always neutralizes and humiliates the earthly reign (i.e. Roman Empire) that does not acknowledge his universal kingship. Thus, this event anticipates the fulfillment of Paul's previous warning to Artemilla and Eubula that "the world will be destroyed . . . because of the lawlessness of men. God alone abides." Lawlessness is defined from a Christian apocalyptic perspective; Paul is the one who abides in the law of God, whereas the Roman Governor Hieronymus becomes the lawless one who rebels against the sovereign rule of God. The subsequent healing of Hieronymus' ear by a youth (possibly Christ's polymorphy) only magnifies the utter powerlessness of the governor before God's reign and power.

In the *Acts of Andrew*, an intense conflict takes place between Aegeates, the proconsul of Achaea, and Andrew, who scorns Aegeates' character and confronts his authority. The erotic rivalry between Andrew and Aegeates over Maximilla is only part of the greater power struggle between them. Maximilla's conversion to the encratic gospel by Andrew sets off a series of losses and defeats for Aegeates. Aegeates loses not only the conjugal love of Maximilla and filial piety of Stratocles but also his "rightful" authority over them, his household, and the "entire crowd" of Patras (cf. 26). All of them turn their affections, loyalty and submission to Andrew, whose supernatural power and authority prove superior to the cruel military power of Aegeates. Aegeates' exercise of brute force upon Andrew alienates and outrages them even more as their sympathy and reverence for Andrew grows greater.

In the martyrdom scene, the apostle's attitude toward death reveals contempt for the earthly transient authority of the Empire. Death is not a defeat but a final triumph; he rejoices for death as a means of achieving "perfection" for the next life (cf. 54, 61, 63). Thus, Andrew's crucifixion highlights his disdain over Aegeates' earthly power and his transcendent authority given by God. In his incredibly lengthy speech on the cross, Andrew castigates Aegeates and makes clear who is in charge:

> Even if you really did change your mind, Aegeates, I would never accede to you. . . . Were you to say you yourself were mine, I would not trust you. . . . Would you untie the one recognized by his kindred, the one who received mercy, the one loved by him, the one alien to you, the stranger who appeared so only to you? . . . I possess the one with whom I will be a compatriot for countless ages. It is to him that I go. It is to him that I speed on, to the one who made me recognize even you by saying to me: "Mark Aegeates and his gifts. Do not let that rogue frighten you, and let him not suppose that he can seize you, for you are mine. He is your enemy. He is a corrupter, a cheat, a destroyer, a slanderer, merciless, a maniac, a plotter, a murderer, an insolent egotist, a flatterer, a magician, terrible, petulant,

insensitive, and decorated on all sides by his material veneer."

(62)

Then, Andrew pronounces a prophetic judgment upon Aegeates, foreshadowing his total demise:

You will weep, beat your breast, gnash your teeth, grieve, despair, lament, anguish, and behave like your relative the sea, which you now see furiously troubled by waves because I am leaving all of you. . . . Aegeates, enemy of us all, . . . [you] stand there quiet and calm, unable to do anything you dare. My kindred and I speed on to things our own, leaving you to be what you are and what you fail to understand about yourself.

(62)

Finally, Aegeates' tragic suicide, which follows Andrew's triumphant martyrdom, intensifies the defeat of the earthly force and symbolizes the ultimate Christian victory over the political power of the earthly kingdoms.

This kind of pattern continues in the *Martyrdom of Peter*, where the prefect Agrippa takes the role of chief antagonist against Peter. Agrippa and Albinus, a friend of the emperor, plan to execute Peter because the prefect's four concubines and Albinus' wife heard Peter's encratic message and "repented and agreed among themselves to abstain from cohabitation with Agrippa" and Albinus, respectively (33, 34). Agrippa orders Peter's crucifixion with the charge of "irreligion" (ἀθεότητος) (36). However, Peter gladly accepts the crucifixion according to the Lord's directives in the famous Quo Vadis vision and labels Agrippa as the Devil's servant. Peter's martyrdom achieves victory over Agrippa, who is in fact reprimanded by Nero for having Peter killed without his knowledge (41).

In the *Acts of Thomas*, Thomas also faces opposition by the powerful husband-team of king Misdaeus and his relative Charisius, whose wives embrace the apostle's teaching of abstinence. Just as in the case of the other Acts, the erotic rivalry turns into a political struggle between the alienated husband and the seditious apostle, which leads to the latter's martyrdom. The contest of power is between that of this world and that of the other world; and the contrast between the "earthly-physical (military)-inferior-power and defeat" and the "heavenly-spiritual-superior-power and victory" becomes unmistakable. The husband-king's wife, son, daughter-in-law, captain, and the whole multitude transfer their loyalty and obedience from the king to the foreign apostle of the "new God" (cf. 164). Though incarcerated, Thomas is not confined by the earthly authority. In his interrogation by Misdaeus, Thomas also spells out who is in control: "'I am the bondsman of one only, over whom you have no authority.' . . . 'My Lord is your master, and he is Lord of heaven and earth'" (163). Thomas subjugates the king under the universal Lordship of Jesus Christ, for "Jesus is more powerful than all powers and kings and princes" (119).

As in the case of the other apostles' martyrdom,[84] the events surrounding Thomas' martyrdom also accentuate the paradoxical victory of the heavenly power. At his martyrdom, Thomas prays to Christ, "Let not the powers and the officers perceive me, . . . when I am borne upward let them not rise up to stand before me, by your power, . . . for they flee and hide themselves" (148). After his death by spears, Thomas appears to his enemy, King Misdaeus, whose other son (besides Vazan) needs deliverance from demons. After his son becomes whole through the power that emanates from the place where the bones of the apostle have lain, Misdaeus finally converts (170). The king's desperate dependence even on the remains of Thomas and his subsequent conversion show the ultimate triumph of Christ and his apostle. Indeed, this proves that the king is at the mercy of Jesus Christ, "the King of Kings and Lord of Lords," and the priest's prayer for the king is that "[Christ] may no more remember evil against him" (170). It is the Lord Jesus who wields his compassion, power, and judgment over the earthly king whose allegiance is now transferred to the heavenly king.

Christian threat and challenge to the Empire

As foreshadowed in the conflicts between the apostles and the (Roman) political figures, the Apocryphal Acts' antagonistic political stance culminates in the antithesis between Christ and the emperor. The *Acts of Peter*, which reflects the contemporary social and political patronage network of the Empire, redefines patronage from a Christian perspective and challenges the prevailing establishment.[85] The patronage system was a principal form of power relations in the Empire, in which the patron of superior status and power provided benefaction such as material support, protection, and socio-political influence and prestige; and in return the client of inferior status shows gratitude in the form of loyalty, honor, praise, gifts, or other favors the patron might demand.[86] The system worked in multiple socio-political strata and reinforced the existing order and hierarchy. The imperial cult in particular capitalized on this patronage system by propagating the cultic response and homage to the emperor as the greatest patron and benefactor of the Empire with his ever-increasing virtues.

The *Acts of Peter* presents Christ as the superior and thus true patron of believers, superior to the human patrons, including the emperor. Robert Stoops has shown how this *Acts* attempts to limit the function and influence of human patronage in light of the sole and complete patronage of Christ.[87] The apostate-but-restored senator Marcellus (8), the convert Eubola (17), the resurrected senator and his widowed mother (29), and even rich but adulterous matron Chryse (30) all function as patrons by offering their gifts to the Christian community, but they do not gain reciprocal honor, loyalty, and power. They are instead redirected to Christ alone, while human patrons are relegated. Moreover, none of these wealthy and powerful people serves as a paradigm of faith.

The *Acts of Peter*'s redefinition of the patronage system is particularly conveyed in Marcellus' diversion of imperial patronage to the Christians to the extent that the Emperor Nero complains that he is deprived of the resources for his own supposed role of patron (8). This *Acts* apparently depicts the greatest patron of the Empire to be bankrupt and powerless in contrast to the historical image and reality. Instead, Christ replaces the emperor as the superior and sole patron, and the "universal and unmediated character of Christ's benefactions," through his apostle's miracles and power, transcends and undermines the imperial patronage in every way.[88]

The same *Acts* continues to counteract the imperial power and cult.[89] There is a scene where a marble statue of Caesar is kicked into pieces by a demon exorcised by Peter (11). Marcellus, the senator and owner of the imperial statue, is frightened at this "great crime" and the subsequent punishment. As mentioned earlier, the imperial cult constituted an integral part of the social, political, and cultural reality in Greek Asia, and numerous imperial statues represented the visible image of the emperor's omnipotent presence.[90] According to Philostratus, during the reign of Tiberius, the imperial statue "was more feared and venerated than the statue of Zeus at Olympia."[91] In this *Acts*, Peter tells Marcellus that if he believes in Christ wholeheartedly, he can restore the statue by sprinkling it with water. With the confession of his complete faith in Christ,

177

Marcellus sprays water on the broken "stones." The statue is made whole, and this saves Marcellus from harm. This whole scene "deflates the constitutive power surrounding the cult" and betrays the real nature of the imperial statue as mere "stones."[92] By doing so, it demythologizes imperial power and challenges the authority of the imperial cult and the emperor himself.

The attitude of animosity to and denunciation of the emperor and the Empire reverberates in the *Martyrdom of Peter*. Following history and Christian tradition, the author's portrayal of Nero is thoroughly negative. His "wicked and bad" nature is fully exposed after Peter's martyrdom; he gets angry because he has "intended to punish [Peter] the more cruelly and severely" for Peter's missionary activities among his servants (12). Furthermore, Nero "sought how to destroy all those brethren whom Peter had instructed" (12). However, the apostle appears to him in a vision, strikes him and says, "Nero, you cannot now persecute or destroy the servants of Christ. Keep your hands from them" (12). This vision "embodies a powerfully subversive image – the emperor enduring a servile punishment" from a Christian preacher and "an inversion of reality" of the Christian martyrs, who were at times tortured and killed at imperial festivals.[93] Because of this vision, "Nero became greatly afraid and left the disciples alone from that time" (12), and in this way Peter "decisively removes Nero as a threat to his community."[94] The apostle does what is conventionally unthinkable: he confronts the Caesar, triumphs over him, and curtails his power with God's power. The *Acts of Peter* clearly locates in Christianity the superior power and authority that overcome the most powerful figure in the world.

The radical enmity between Christianity and the Roman Empire climaxes in the *Martyrdom of Paul*. This enmity is expressed through the apocalyptic language of Christ's universal kingship.[95] Patroclus, a revived cupbearer of the emperor, confesses before Nero that Jesus Christ is "the king of the ages," who "destroys all kingdoms under heaven" and who alone will remain "in all eternity" (2; cf. Rev. 19.11–21; 16.12–16). With three other "chief men of Nero," he pledges his allegiance to fight for Christ as his soldier (2). On account of this alarming statement, Nero carries out his savage persecution against Christians, executing many of them without trial. Paul is brought to Nero as a ringleader, and he declares that the soldiers of Christ are enlisted all over the earth and predicts his resurrection. He identifies himself as "a faithful soldier of the living

God" and warns of a death of fire for those who do not worship the eternal king Christ (4). Then, after prophesying his appearance to Nero after death, Paul is executed. However, when the executioner decapitates Paul, milk spurts out on to the soldier, and witnesses glorify God. This news bewilders the emperor, philosophers, and a centurion. Paul, "the soldier of God," appears to them and pronounces a judgment upon Nero for unjustly shedding "the blood of the righteous"; then Nero releases the prisoners, including Patroclus, in great perplexity and fear (5–6).

The anti-imperial and subversive sentiment is more than clear. In this martyrdom narrative, the term "soldier" and its cognate words occur fourteen times, and the terms "king," "great king," and "eternal king" occur twelve times.[96] This military language, coupled with the concept of the universal destruction of the world and the anti-Roman stance with the ascetic demands, strikingly resembles the apocalyptic New Prophecy, concurrent with the date of the *Martyrdom of Paul*. Christians are the loyal soldiers not of the emperor but of Christ; they serve Christ the eternal king as opposed to the temporal ruler. Harmony with the Empire is impossible, for they cannot serve two masters. This is a radical transformation of attitude from that of the Lucan Acts and the Pauline Epistles; it surely resonates with the sentiment of the Revelation. The Paul of the Apocryphal Acts is "a challenger to State authority, an enemy of the Emperor and a seeker after martyrdom";[97] in fact, all the apostles with the exception of John fit this description. The antithesis between the Church and the Empire is definite and absolute; the Christianity of the Apocryphal Acts is the "living embodiment of the revolutionary forces which at the very moment Celsus was attempting to thwart."[98]

Martyr Acts: Christian resistance to the Empire

Intrinsic to the genre of the Martyr Acts is the inevitable clash between the allegiance to Christ and the absolute loyalty to the Empire. Just as the martyrdom narratives of the apostles in the Apocryphal Acts heighten the disparity between Christianity and the Empire, the Martyr Acts feature the fundamental conflict between the Lord Christ and the Lord Caesar. In the context of the ever-persistent reality of the imperial cult and ideology, the Martyr Acts intensify the political implications of martyrdom and demonstrate its paradoxical victory over the Empire.

Christ vs. Caesar

The precedent set by Pliny in trials of Christians was repeated again and again in the subsequent trials of Christians by Roman authorities. In the Martyr Acts, the Roman magistrates consistently demand that Christians offer sacrifice to the gods and/or the emperors or take an oath by the gods and/or the emperors' genius. Along with the traditional cults, the imperial cult provides the litmus test for Christian loyalty to the Empire. The Christian confession of the one true God precludes not only the worship of the traditional gods but also the cult of the emperors; thus, the martyr's confession is a political act as well as a religious one. Christian "atheism" always results in Christian subversiveness to the Empire, since the enemy of the gods is the enemy of the Empire and vice versa.

Since "Caesar and Christ are . . . the archetypical heroes of two antithetical cosmologies,"[99] the contest of power between the Lord Christ and the Lord Caesar becomes significant in several Acts. In the earliest Acts, the *Martyrdom of Polycarp*, the two confrontations of Polycarp with the government focus on this issue. First, the police captain Herod tries to persuade Polycarp, saying: "Now what harm is there for you to say 'Caesar is lord (Κύριος Καῖσαρ),' to perform the sacrifices and so forth, and thus save your life." (8.2) Then, at the trial, the governor demands that Polycarp "swear by the Genius of the emperor (ὄμοσον τὴν Καίσαρος τύχην)," "recant" (9.2), and "curse Christ" (9.3). Both the captain and governor represent the deeply ingrained imperial ideology that religiously legitimated the (supposedly) absolute power of the emperor. Thus, in the *Acts of the Scillitan Martyrs*, the proconsul Saturninus defines the *mos Romanorum* in that manner: "our religion is a simple one: we swear by the genius of our lord the emperor and we offer prayers for his health" (3).[100] He then commands the Christians to take oaths by the genius of the emperor (5).

In the *Martyrdom of Apollonius*, after Apollonius' confession of his Christian identity, the proconsul Perennis issues Apollonius the same command: "swear by the Genius of our lord the emperor Commodus" (ὄμοσον τὴν τύχην τοῦ κυρίου ἡμῶν Κομόδου τοῦ αὐτοκράτορος) (3). Later, he repeats, "do what I tell you: offer sacrifice to the gods and to the image of the emperor Commodus" (7). In another example, Hilarianus the procurator in the *Martyrdom of Perpetua and Felicitas* orders Perpetua to "offer the sacrifice for the welfare of the emperor" (*fac sacrum pro salute imperatorum*) (6.3).

Whether one is to sacrifice to or for the emperor, or to swear by his genius, the underlying command comes from the emperor,[101] which requires a cultic enactment of the subjects' political loyalty and the acknowledgment of the "imperial soteriology."

Under this pressure, the martyrs, like the Apologists, distinguish the worship of the emperor from the proper honor and obedience due to the emperor. Polycarp does recognize the Christian teaching "to pay respect to the authorities and power that God has assigned us [Christians]"[102] but rejects the command: "I do not intend to do what you advise."[103] Speratus, one of the Scillitan martyrs, stresses Christian civil obedience, "I have not stolen; and on any purchase I pay the tax," but articulates who his Lord is: "I serve that God whom no man has seen, nor can see, with these eyes."[104] According to a fellow woman martyr Donata, Christians "pay honour to Caesar as Caesar; but it is God [they] fear."[105] Apollonius states that Christians "obey any law passed by the emperor" and "respect him" but "worship the immortal God alone."[106] He explains the evil of taking an imperial oath with Christ's teaching "never to swear and in all things to tell the truth" (cf. Matt. 5.37; Jas. 5.12).[107] He says that he would swear that Christians pay honor to the emperor and pray for his authority only by "the one, true God, the One existing before all the ages," for it is by God's will that the emperor rules over the earth.[108]

The martyrs' distinction and persistent refusal to conform to the authorities' orders amount to blaspheming the "august emperors"[109] and instantly make them outlaws, traitors, and threats to the Empire; for they desacralize and destabilize the imperial myths and ideology, which sustain the whole system of power in the Empire. Polycarp's famous retort comes in response to the governor's demand: "For eighty-six years I have been his servant and he has done me no wrong. How can I blaspheme against my king and saviour (τὸν βασιλέα μου τὸν σώσαντά με)?"[110] It is impossible for a Christian to accept the imperial cult and to render to the emperor what he demands especially because "Jesus Christ [is] reigning eternally."[111] Speratus replies to the proconsul, "I do not recognize the empire of this world. Rather, . . . I acknowledge my lord who is the emperor of kings and of all nations."[112] The first recorded military martyr Basilides also refuses to take an oath on account of his Christian faith.[113] Contrary to the Roman authorities, Christians do not live by the imperial ideology. They rather strike at the core of the Roman political theology and unmask its hollow reality and the unseen kingdom beyond what is seen.

The depiction of Christ or God as "king" and "emperor of kings" carries an apocalyptic imagery set above and against the emperor and his earthly empire.[114] The portrayal of God/Christ as the heavenly monarch who is the final Judge accentuates the contrast and antagonism between God's eternal and universal kingship and the temporal reign and limited authority of Caesar. Therefore, the extent of the Christians' loyalty to the emperor/Empire is determined not by what Caesar requires but by what their God requires. Hence, Apollonius declares that sacrifices and oaths (the typical signs of loyalty) only belong to the "almighty God, the lord of heaven and earth and of all that breathes";[115] he is "the invincible God who comprehends all things."[116] After all, "a divine decree cannot be quelled by a decree of man."[117]

Martyrs vs. political authorities

In these unavoidable confrontations, the contest of power between the Lord Christ and the Lord Caesar is mirrored in the power struggle between the martyrs and the Roman magistrates in a way similar to the Apocryphal Acts. Public trials and executions were designed to provide the greatest display of the all-powerful Roman rule and justice before the very eyes of the subjects. In trials, officials were expected to successfully force the accused to confess their guilt and submit to the norms and authority of the Empire.[118] Nevertheless, there was room for a "contest about truth" and thus a contest of power between the inquisitors and the accused; when the magistrates failed to exact an admission of guilt and submission to the law from the defendants, the trials could undermine the authority of the government.[119]

For the convicted and condemned, the Roman penal system had among its aims retribution, humiliation, and deterrence with ruthless infliction of pain and suffering to the effect that the spectators would endorse the course of justice enforced by the government and the (supposedly) deserved fate of the criminals.[120] The spectacle of death in the arena was

> a ceremony which served to reinforce the existing power structure by reducing the condemned to the level of an object. The body of the condemned became a vehicle for the reaffirmation of the public order, indeed, for a reaffirmation of the power of the central government. . . . A person sentenced to die in the arena lost human dignity, lost control of his or her body, became a slave.[121]

Both the government and spectators expected

> to see penitence and terror in the condemned, they expected
> to hear them scream, and they expected to see the terror in
> their faces as they confronted the beasts or the other savage
> forms of execution which were employed in the arena.[122]

Nonetheless, once again, if the punishments and executions failed
to produce the expected results, that could also upset the established
authority and the existing socio-political order. Thus, the public
trials and spectacles of martyrdom, though with enormous inequal-
ity of power, offered the critical moments of a public contest of
power between Christians and the magistrates.

Given this context, the Martyr Acts' portrayals of the Christian
martyrs' attitudes and behaviors in both trial and arena directly
challenge the sovereign power of Rome as well as the societal
expectations, and overpower the imperial representatives. What is
supposed to happen does not occur; the reverse takes place. For one
thing, the accused do not deny their identity and throw themselves
at the mercy of the authorities; it is the magistrates who are desperately attempting to deliver the accused from official condemnation.
As seen, both the captain and governor are anxious to dissuade Polycarp from his defiance and are hesitant to pass sentence despite his
repeated refusal to comply: "Save your life" (8.2);[123] "Have respect
for your age" (9.2); "Recant" (9.2); "Swear and I will let you go"
(9.3); and "Try to move the people" (10.2). To the group of Scillitan
Christians, the proconsul says, "If you return to your senses, you can
obtain the pardon of our lord the emperor" (2).[124] After Speratus'
confession of his loyalty to God and rejection of the imperial oath,
the proconsul exhorts others, "Cease to be of this persuasion" (7),
and "Have no part in this folly of his!" (8). The rest all persist in
their Christian identity, and finally the sentence reads: "whereas
though given the opportunity to return to the usage of the Romans
they have persevered in their obstinacy, they are hereby condemned
to be executed" (14). In the *Martyrdom of Apollonius*, Perennis the
proconsul even grants Apollonius three days to consider his refusal
to obey – to no avail, however (10). Perennis' repeated and urgent
plea for Apollonius to change his mind rather provides Apollonius
opportunities to articulate his faith and foil the proconsul's determination with a resolute choice for martyrdom. At the end, Perennis
pronounces the sentence only reluctantly as if he is trapped by the
imperial decree.

Certainly, what the officials want is not martyrdom but apostasy. Yet the accused or arrested Christians do not submit to the law or the command of the governors; they persist in their denial and refusal. In other words, the magistrates can bring in no desirable outcome – recantation and submission to the imperial law. Rather, Christians' defiance of authority dominates the trials; they successfully confront and overcome the "helpless" officials in terms of the results – the undaunted confession of the Christian Name and their condemnation to a glorified death.

Even the authorities' use of gruesome tortures cannot break the martyrs' will and conviction; instead, it is the martyrs' heroic endurance and supernatural strength that break the magistrates' will to coerce apostasy. In the *Martyrdom of Carpus, Papylus, and Agathonicê*, upon his refusal to sacrifice to the gods, Papylus (Pamfilus in Latin recension), following Carpus, "was [also] hung up and scraped and endured three pairs [of torturers], but did not utter a sound" (35). In the Latin recension, Pamfilus tells the proconsul, "These torments are nothing. I feel no pain because I have someone to comfort me" (3.6). "When the proconsul observed their extraordinary patience," he finally sentenced them to be burnt alive (36; 4.1 [Latin]).

In the *Martyrs of Lyons*, Blandina embodies the dramatic reversal of the power struggle at the trial. With her entire body broken and torn, her physical perseverance was such that her torturers became weary and exhausted. "They themselves admitted that they were beaten, that there was nothing further they could do to her" (18). Blandina thus wins the struggle and receives an acclaim of a "noble athlete" (19). Her fellow martyr, Sanctus, also "withstood all the indignities that men heaped on him with extraordinary, superhuman strength" to the point that "he resisted them with such determination" (20). To the tormenters' utter amazement, Sanctus' disfigured body straightened out and recovered its former appearance despite their repeated assaults (24). In this sense, the martyrs' bodies become the sites of the contest of power, and their bodily endurance displays the most tangible demonstration of their resistance.[125] Hence, the "tyrant's instruments of torture [have] been utterly overcome by Christ through the perseverance of the saints," concludes the *Martyrs of Lyons* (1.27). Then, the martyrs rejoice over their sentence as a way to earn the "crown of immortality" and triumphantly disparage the authorities' painstaking efforts toward defection.[126] The condemned shout in high spirit: "Thanks be to

God (*deo gratias*)!"[127] This is hardly a scene of defeat; the martyrs prevail in the contest of power.

Christian victory over the Empire

As we move to the spectacles of martyrdom themselves, the martyrs' victory in the arena becomes even more significant. As mentioned, the public executions in the amphitheater or arena symbolize and graphically exhibit the unqualified dominance of the ruling power of Rome over the social outcasts, deviants, and criminals who dared to challenge that political establishment. The executions form the important part of the public spectacles, which in turn were part of the political machinery of the imperial system. Undoubtedly, the chief sponsor of those public spectacles is none other than the emperor himself, patron *par excellence*.[128] The public executions maximize the horror of violence, inspiration of fear, and degradation of the condemned individuals to the point of aversion and deterrence, but also cause exhilarating sensations in the crowds.[129] Through the murderous games performed by and excruciating pains inflicted on the condemned, the crowds experience the satisfaction of "righteous" vengeance and the superior power of the government. The martyrs' mutilation, denuding (especially that of female martyrs), mauling by animals, and brutal death correspond to that aim of the public executions.

However, the martyrs' tantalizing victory takes place in this context where it is least expected. As in the trials, the martyrs completely destroy the vengeful expectations of the authorities and spectators and turn them upside-down. The Martyr Acts emphasize that the martyrs exercise their conscious freedom in choosing to die for their faith. "We came to this of our own free will," insists Perpetua on behalf of her fellow martyrs.[130] By their voluntary act, the martyrs refuse to be perceived as humiliated and avoid "a coward's death."[131] This assertion of their free will is then an ultimate protest against the unjust and oppressive regime that does not acknowledge the "Father and the King of the heavens."[132] Therefore, they do not behave like the typical criminals in the amphitheater: no anxiety, no signs of fear or shame, no shuffling, no expressions of guilt or repentance, and no feelings of sorrow or regrets.[133] In contrast, they march into the arena with joy and readiness, with calm faces and shining countenance.[134] They overwhelm their persecutors with their "intense gaze" and jubilant songs.[135] They rejoice as their bodies are scourged, torn apart, and roasted in hot iron seats.[136] Even at the very moments of their violent deaths whether by burning, beheading, or wild beasts, they smile, glorify God, and take control of their lives for the victor's crown.[137] The martyrs' bodily expressions, gestures, and movements represent a confident affirmation of their faith and a compelling demonstration of their contempt for and renunciation of the entire Roman system of power.[138]

The martyrs not only resist the Roman temporal power but also place themselves in a higher tribunal than their earthly persecutors by pronouncing God's eschatological judgment upon the persecutors. Condemned to burning, Polycarp warns the governor about "the fire of everlasting punishment" and the coming judgment for the impious.[139] Pamfilus, nailed at the stake, declares, "looking forward to God's true judgment we prefer to endure this and to despise the commands of the perishable judges."[140] In God's eternal judgment, where there will be no mercy, eternal fire will burn, and "God will destroy everything with it, judging every soul."[141] In the amphitheater, Perpetua and her company of martyrs signal this message to Hilarianus: "You have condemned us, but God will condemn you" (*Tu nos, inquiunt, te autem Deus*).[142] Finally, Apollonius admonishes Perennis about the same death for all humankind – emperors, the great and the insignificant, and the rich and the poor – and God's universal judgment after death.[143] The martyrs' open defiance and challenge come from knowing who is really in charge; their God is the ultimate Judge of all things, including the Roman Empire. Therefore, there is no ambiguity in their allegiance. "As the disciples and imitators of the Lord," the martyrs, by their death, cement "their unsurpassed loyalty towards their king and master."[144]

The Martyr Acts highlight this triumphal aspect of martyrdom. It is "a dramatic public act of defiance in the very place where Roman society had chosen to put itself on display and to assert its own superiority."[145] Martyrs indeed "exploit the ritual of execution to demonstrate the superiority of their faith over the temporal powers," which personify the Devil the Adversary.[146] They are the paradigm of the great reversal. This is the paradoxical power and victory of Christianity.

Summary and conclusion

The political self-definitions of Christians took shape in a period where they were considered and treated as public enemies or threats to the well-being of the Empire. In a culture where traditional

polytheism and the imperial cult formed the bedrock of religious, social, and political order, Christian monotheism disturbed
every aspect of the society, and Christian identity was a capital
crime punishable by death. For the Apologies, Apocryphal Acts,
and Martyr Acts, there was no question that Christian loyalty to
God and Christ took precedence over loyalty to the emperors, who
claimed to offer earthly "salvation" and demanded cultic "worship"
of their power. They shared the conviction in the limited and
delegated authority of imperial power in light of the universal
Kingship and Judgment of their one true God. Nonetheless, there
was a "parting of ways" in further articulations of the political
implications of Christian faith.

The Apologists emphasized Christians' allegiance to the emperor/
Empire while drawing a fundamental distinction between religious
and political loyalty. On one hand, with this distinction, they separated religious and political obligations and thus attempted to
"secularize" the imperial theology of power. On the other hand, with
the aid of the current culture of panegyrics, they "christianized" the
imperial power by endorsing its divine appointment and approval
and by developing the view of divine providence in the destinies of
Christianity and the Empire. Thus, they ended up leaving conflicting legacies in Christian political thought: "separation of Church
and State" based on the principle of religious freedom and "alliance
of Church and State" based on the Christian theology of divine
monarchy.

For the writers of the Apocryphal Acts, there seems to be no
common ground between Christianity and the Empire. As in the
cases of religious and social encounters, Christianity and the pagan
Empire are radically opposed to each other. The apostles' encounters with the (Roman) authorities cause or result in conflicts and
persecutions due to their message of monotheism and encratism.
Apostles are seen as lawbreakers, deviants, and a threat to the establishment whose power is of this wicked world, and their political
conflicts invariably lead to their martyrdom. However, they are
the winners of the power struggle, in judgment of the earthly
authorities. They despise and overpower their enemies, and their
happy ending (i.e. martyrdom) is contrasted with the tragic end or
defeat of their political opponents. With apocalyptic dualism, the
Apocryphal Acts portray the drastic "antithesis of Church and State."

Finally, authors of the Martyr Acts demonstrate Christian resistance to the Empire. Like the Apologists, they distinguish between
religious and political loyalty, but, unlike the Apologists, they do

CONCLUSION

Christianity in the late second and early third centuries was in the process of "coming out" into the dominant Greco-Roman culture in a volatile situation. The Apologies, Apocryphal Acts, and Martyr Acts – the "unique" Christian literary bodies in the contemporary historical scene – seriously engaged with both the outer world and the inner Christian community on behalf of the latter. Each of the corpora presented the distinct Christian message, ethos, and worldview in the current language of the culture and at the same time developed and reshaped Christian tradition in relation to the dominant society, which was unsympathetic, if not hostile. With propagandistic, apologetic, and didactic/edificatory purposes in mind, each body constructed and defined Christian self-identities and boundaries vis-à-vis Greco-Roman society. The result does not form a unilateral line but a triangle that draws the common outer boundary from the larger world but with three individual sides; the making of the Christian self-definitions and boundaries occurred in view of "others" both without and within, with an indelible impact on the subsequent course of Christian relations to the world.

The "fundamentals" of Christianity put forth by each body of literature in the three descriptive categories covered in Chapters 2, 3, and 4 reveal and communicate the Christian ideals with the boundaries of the negotiable and the non-negotiable from the perspective of each corpus. The essentials here project the ideals more than the realities themselves; the assertion of what Christians believe and practice delineates what they should believe and practice. Furthermore, the fundamentals of "what it means to be a Christian" answer the question, "what difference did Christianity make?"[1] Christianity for the Apologists brings about theological and moral reformation of individuals according to the socially approved structure and norms and fulfills the ideal of the established order and civilization.[2] For the authors of the Apocryphal Acts and Martyr Acts, Christianity results in one's radical renunciation of the larger society's norms and "a counter-cultural formation of 'the new human.'"[3]

The Apologists did not draw a clear-cut distinction between the Greco-Roman world and Christianity. Rather, they saw more than a glimpse of hope in the redemption of this world through the activity of the Divine Logos who has come as the Christ. Conversion to Christian philosophy as the fulfillment of Greco-Roman civilization meant a paradigm shift, a radical one from traditional polytheism to Christian monotheism, but not a drastic rejection of the existing society and culture. Despite their criticism of popular culture, the Apologists were optimists in their approach to the dominant society and in the human ability to respond to divine revelation. Christian philosophy makes one a worshipper of the true God and thus a better citizen in the Empire. Just as the Christian philosophy is comparable to and eventually supersedes the best of the Greco-Roman philosophies, Christian sexual morality is also compatible with and ultimately supplants the best of Stoic sexual ethics, faithfully teaching social responsibilities of marriage and family and even virginity according to the traditional values of the Empire.

Finally, while distinguishing religious from political loyalty, Christians fulfill all political responsibilities, including bearing arms for the emperors, and eagerly pray for the prosperity of the Empire. The Christian philosophy and the Empire share the "manifest destiny" in God's providence. The Apologists affirm the place of Greco-Roman world and society in God's salvific plan and the role of Christianity within and with the Empire. By doing so, they, representing Christian elites, ironically develop the inclusive two-tier standards that can both differentiate and cater to the elites and the masses, the powerful, and the powerless. While respecting and maintaining "the place of martyr's struggle in the forefront of the church's relationship with the world,"[4] the new race of Christians is to live as the loyal citizens under the divinely appointed rulers of the earthly kingdom.

In contrast, the Apocryphal Acts takes an entirely different outlook toward the dominant society. Christian monotheism is displayed in its superior power and message, which stand in diametrical opposition to the Greco-Roman world – the epitome of the fallen and corrupt world dominated by demonic powers. The truth of Christianity manifests itself in its triumphal miracles and exorcisms in judgment over the traditional religious, social, and political system. The Acts are pessimistic with respect to the world; there is no hope of redemption of this wicked world, and therefore Christians should renounce and separate themselves from it. Christianity overcomes the evil powers, suspends the continuation of the present society, and threatens the order and prosperity of the Empire.

Conversion to the true God calls for the absolute rejection of the world, most notably, sexual relations; sexual continence functions as the weapon of resistance to the established structure, mores, and values. Thus, Christians, especially women, restore pristine purity prior to the Fall by their sexual renunciation and are thus bound to be counter-cultural and subversive. Despite the androcentric context, female converts to the encratic gospel in the Acts are not victims but victors who transcend the traditional gendered limitation often at the expense of their male counterparts. In this sense, their pessimism toward this world notwithstanding, the Acts are paradoxically optimistic concerning the human will to achieve pre-lapsarian perfection, regardless of one's gender. In fact, this optimism in human capacity "democratizes" the call to the encratic "elitism," implicitly censuring the "double standard" of the other Christian camps (e.g. the Apologists). The new race of Christians is to create an alternative world of perfection, which is antithetical to the present society and governed by the pure Divine Monarch.

The Martyr Acts also dichotomize Christianity and Greco-Roman society. The issue comes down to the conflict between the two opposing ways of worship. They depict the essential problem faced by the Christians: sacrifice to the idols/demons or to the true God? If Christian identity in the Apocryphal Acts necessitates sexual abstinence, Christian identity in the Martyr Acts requires the most absolute and efficacious sacrifice to the true God: martyrdom. Hence, the martyr's confession, "I am Christian," is always juxtaposed with the martyr's rejection of pagan sacrifice. Martyrs' sacrifice takes after the sacrifice of Jesus Christ, the first or proto-martyr, who, as such, is the Invincible Athlete and the Supreme Sacrifice. The Martyr Acts exploit the Greco-Roman culture of violence to showcase the heroic valor of the martyrs; as the "athletes of piety" and the "gladiators of Christ," they fight the contest against the Devil embodied in the Roman Empire. On the one hand, the martyrs are God's chosen ones for the contest; on the other hand, they are depicted as having chosen martyrdom as the champions of human capacity and free will. Therefore, martyrdom is the other

191

"democratized" ideal for anyone who would imitate Christ but who must demonstrate his or her spiritual superiority in extraordinary death. The Acts especially highlight the heroism of women martyrs whose mastery of will and endurance of the gendered punishments and torture overshadow their male counterparts. As in the Apocryphal Acts, Christian conversion simultaneously brings about a disruption in family and social norms and a formation of Christian kinship. The martyrs defy and ultimately "defeat" the Roman authorities in the power struggles of trials and executions, and their paradoxical "victory" undermines the traditional system and hierarchy of power.

Each literary corpus presents a paradigm of Christian perfection or ideal: the Apologies present a noble philosopher; the Apocryphal Acts present a wonder-working ascetic (divine man); and the Martyr Acts present a heroic martyr. This portrait of an ideal Christian actually corresponds to the portrait of an ideal human being in the Greco-Roman world: philosopher and/or divine man. The Christian hero is the Greco-Roman hero christianized. The Christian self-identity may be "of the culture," "above the culture," and "against the culture" in their selective approach to certain aspects of culture,[5] but it is never apart from the given culture. Despite their differing portrayals, the Apologies, Apocryphal Acts, and Martyr Acts all define the Christian self by the accepted categories of Greco-Roman culture and values. Philosophers, ascetics, and martyrs are not necessarily exclusive categories; a philosopher usually embraced an ascetic lifestyle and at times assumed a heroic "martyrdom" for the sake of his/her philosophy, as in the case of Socrates. All of them represented the cultural icon of the cultivated elite, at least in theory: the quintessential types of the Greco-Roman human ideal. A Christian was ultimately called to embody all three types of virtues. Nonetheless, each corpus still highlights one type over the others according to each model of Christian perfection. For the Apocryphal Acts and Martyr Acts, ascetics and martyrs, always minority in number, respectively epitomized "spirituality on the edge" in resistance to the spiritual status quo of the majority.

In the course of defending and presenting Christian truths and in light of the growing "orthodox consciousness," the Apologists were to become the major force of the Church in formulating doctrines, creeds, and canons of belief and practice. Their rational and philosophical presentation of the Christian message would become "the mother of Christian theology"[6] and would eventually come under the covering of "the one holy catholic Church."

However, the Apocryphal Acts and the Martyr Acts represented the radical position which understood Christianity as counter-cultural power and which propelled spiritual overachievers and perfectionists who would demonstrate their piety through "democratic" spiritual elitism. Already in the late second and the early third century, the ascetics and martyrs were the two types of overachievers whose charismatic power needed to be contained and delimited within the Church. The Apocryphal Acts were rejected by the Great Church, which was at pains to establish her solid ground in the Empire. The Martyr Acts, while projecting a similar attitude, were embraced by the Church and were contained within her own rhetoric and liturgy. The Martyr Acts became the vehicle through which the Great Church sought historical continuity with the persecuted past.[7]

This work challenges to an extent the traditional premise that the post-Constantinian ascetics were the heirs of the spirituality of the martyrs.[8] The development of a distinct "Christian" sexual morality and asceticism is more of a late second- and third-century phenomenon. The surge of asceticism in the fourth and fifth centuries succeeds not just the spirituality of the martyrs (from the Great Persecution in the fourth century) but also and primarily the radical ascetics in the second and third centuries. The later ecclesiastical ascetics and monastic communities "domesticated" the "radical" encratism of the Apocryphal Acts within the already established double standard of the Church for the ordinary and the extraordinary.

This study demonstrates the complexity of the issues in constructing early Christian self-definitions from the margins of Greco-Roman society. This complexity was played out in the interrelations and interactions among the Christian groups on the one hand, and in the interactions with the larger society and culture on the other hand. The formation and development of the Christian self-identities did not involve a monolithic process but a multi-faceted, dynamic, and flexible course molded by external and internal affairs. It is to the credit of these three pioneering bodies of literature that the Christians seriously and intelligently articulated their place in the Greco-Roman soil. The religious, social, and political minority claimed the universal truth, ethos, and rule that would eventually "take control" of the world empire. Ironically, many of the triumphs and dangers of the later "Christian Empire" were already foreshadowed in these earlier self-representations.

The complexity in defining Christian self-identity is still witnessed in the post-modern world as well. After a full circle of

NOTES

INTRODUCTION

1 The other extant Greek works, the *Epistle to Diognetus* and *Apology* of Aristides, are excluded from this study because of their earlier time frame.
2 *Hist. eccl.* 4.26.5–11.
3 *Hist. eccl.* 4.27; 5.5.1–4.
4 There have been extensive scholarly debates on the chronological sequence of and intertextual relationships among the Apocryphal Acts. See for example MacDonald 1997: 11–41; Pervo 1997a: 43–56; Stoops 1997: 57–86. Bremmer (2001a: 152–4) places the Apocryphal Acts in the order of *Acts John*, *Acts Paul*, *Acts Pet.*, *Acts Andr.*, and *Acts Thom.* in the period of 150–230 CE.
5 *De baptismo* 17.5.
6 Cf. Bremmer (2001a: 157–9), who sees the origin of the Acts except *Acts Thom.* all in Western Asia Minor, particularly *Acts John* and *Acts Paul* in the region of Northern Lycia and Iconium and *Acts Pet.* and *Acts of Andr.* in Bythinia.
7 Cf. Goodspeed 1966: 25.
8 Musurillo 1972: xii. For the similar "canon" of the pre-Decian Martyr Acts, see Barnes 1968b: 509–31.
9 *Hist. eccl.* 4.15.1–44.
10 *Hist. eccl.* 4.15.48.
11 *Hist. eccl.* 6.5.
12 *Hist. eccl.* 5.21.
13 *Hist. eccl.* 5.1.
14 *Hist. eccl.* 4.17.
15 See the section, "Literature of the second century: Apologies," in Chapter 1, pp. 28–9.
16 See the section, "Literature of the second century: Apocryphal Acts," in Chapter 1, pp. 29–39.
17 See the section, "Literature of the second century: Martyr Acts," in Chapter 1, pp. 39–47.
18 See Niebuhr 1951: 45–82.
19 See Niebuhr 1951: 83–115.
20 See Niebuhr 1951: 116–48.
21 Stassen *et al.* 1996.

22 Pervo 1987; Tatum 1994; Hock *et al.* 1998.
23 Musurillo 1972: xii.
24 Musurillo 1972: lvii.
25 Cf. Lieu 2002: 302.
26 Lieu 2002: 311.

1 SECOND-CENTURY CHRISTIAN LITERATURE IN ITS HISTORICAL-CULTURAL CONTEXT

1 See Eusebius, *Hist. eccl.* 4.23.
2 Baus 1980: 208; see also Bauer 1934.
3 On Syrian Christianity, see Drijvers 1984.
4 *Hist. eccl.* 5.1; *Mart. Lyons.*
5 *Haer.* 1.10.2.
6 Cyprian, *Ep.* 71.4.
7 Baus 1980: 210.
8 These figures are based on a projected growth rate of 40 percent per decade until 350 CE in Stark 1996: 5–7; Hopkins 1998: 192–5.
9 Origen, *Cels.* 3.44, 55.
10 On this topic see further Bremmer 1989: 37–48. Cf. Harnack 1908: 217–39.
11 Cf. Hopkins 1998: 207–9; Gamble 1995: 1–41, especially 4, 10.
12 Frend 1997: 303.
13 Markus 1980: 7.
14 Siker 2000: 253.
15 Cf. Dunn 1977: 378–9.
16 Wilken 1980: 124.
17 *Ep.* 10.96
18 *Annals* 15.44
19 *Nero* 16.2
20 On the topic of superstition in Greco-Roman world in general and its relationship with the persecution of the Christians, see further Janssen 1979: 131–59.
21 Wilken 1980: 105–6.
22 On the persecution of Christians as a result of the ideological clash between *Romanitas* and Christianity, see Plescia 1971: 120–32.
23 On the idea of *pax deorum*, see Fowler 1911: especially 184–6.
24 Simon 1973: 387.
25 Wilken 1984: 53, 56.
26 Eusebius, *Hist. eccl.* 4.13; cf. Frend 1965: 239–40.
27 *Apol.* 40.2.
28 Walsh (1991: 255–77) attributes the significance of this charge to the second half of the second century and the third century, especially from the reign of Marcus Aurelius on.
29 *1 Apol.* 6; *2 Apol.* 3; *contra* Walsh 1991: 262.
30 For the account of Polycarp's martyrdom and the circumstance that led to it, see *Hist. eccl.* 4.15 and *Mart. Pol.*
31 *Hist. eccl.* 4.15.26; *Mart. Pol.* 12.2.
32 Tertullian, *Apol.* 6.10.
33 *Oct.* 9.6; 31.1–2.

34 de Vos 2000: 878; cf. Benko 1984: 103–31.
35 For a succinct survey of pagan criticism of Christianity during this period, see Benko 1980: 1055–118.
36 Frend 1965: 274.
37 Lucian, *De morte Peregrini* 12–13.
38 For Galen's references to Christianity, see the edited and translated text in Walzer 1949: 10–16.
39 Aurelius, *Meditations* 11.3.
40 Cf. Frend 1965: 268–9. For Marcus Aurelius' social conservatism and Stoic asceticism, see Francis 1995: 21–52.
41 See Andresen 1952: 157–95; Andresen 1955: 312–44.
42 The standard English translation is one by Chadwick (1953), which will be used throughout this study.
43 Simmons 2000: 841.
44 Cf. Wilken 1984: 117.
45 *Hist. eccl.* 4.15.1.
46 *Leg.* 1.4.
47 *Hist. eccl.* 4.26.3.
48 *Acts Just.*; cf. *Hist. eccl.* 4.16.
49 *Hist. eccl.* 5.1; *Mart. Lyons.*
50 On the New Prophecy, commonly known as Montanism, see further the excellent recent treatment: Trevett 1996; Tabbernee 1997.
51 Frend 1965: 293.
52 *Hist. eccl.* 5.16.18.
53 Frend 1965: 291.
54 Frend 1965: 291.
55 On this issue, see Frend 1974: 334–43.
56 *Hist. eccl.* 6.5.
57 *Strom.* 2.20.125.
58 *Hist. eccl.* 6.1, 4–5.
59 *Apol.* 40.12–13.
60 See *Mart. Perp.*
61 *Commentary on Daniel* 4.51 (cited by Frend 1965: 323).
62 Kennedy 1982: 5.
63 Cf. Fitzgerald (1969: 481–520) sees conversion as the primary aim of the Apologists and missionary intention shaping their apologetic purpose.
64 See Dihle 1994: 285–303.
65 Grant 1988b: 53–4.
66 Grant 1988b: 79–80; also, see Grant 1988a: 1–10.
67 Barnard 1968: 1–3.
68 Grant 1953: 99–101; cf. Grant 1988b: 112–15; Grant 1988a: 10–11. Grant even suggests that Tatian wrote after the violent martyrdoms in Lyons and Vienne in 177, as he argued for resurrection even after the burning of flesh and consumption by beasts and burial in rivers (6.2; 6.31–7.2). For a critique of Grant's view, see Clarke 1967a: 122–6.
69 Grant 1988b: 186–7.
70 Cf. Keresztes 1990: 213–22
71 *1 Apol.* 1; 68.3.
72 See Russell and Wilson 1981.
73 Millar 1977: 564–5; cf. Grant 1986a: 213–26; Grant 1988a: 1–17.

74 Schoedel 1989: 55–78.
75 Grant 1986a: 221–2.
76 Keresztes 1990: 213–22; Keresztes 1966: 124–33.
77 Guerra 1995: 4–5.
78 Aune 1992: 95.
79 Jordan 1986: 317.
80 Cf. Guerra 1995: 2; Aune 1992: 94; Jordan 1986: 330.
81 Cf. Aune 1992: 97.
82 Jordan 1986: 319–24.
83 Aune 1992: 101.
84 Malherbe 1986: 122; Guerra 1995: 5–6.
85 Jordan 1986: 330.
86 Jordan 1986: 330.
87 On the topic of "conversion to philosophy," see further Nock 1933: 164–86.
88 Jordan 1986: 309; cf. Aune 1992: 96.
89 Jaeger 1961: 9–10.
90 Nock 1933: 78.
91 Aune 1992: 106–7.
92 On this theme, especially on the Christian appropriation of this argument, see Droge 1989.
93 *Jewish War* 2.119; *Jewish Antiquities* 18.11.
94 *The Life* 9–12; cf. Aune 1992: 107.
95 *On the Life of Moses* 2.215–16.
96 Aune 1992: 107.
97 For example, Guerra (1992: 171–87) argues Justin's *First Apology* as a *protreptikos*; Keresztes (1965b: 858–69) also shows the *Second Apology* as a protreptic work; McGehee (1993: 143–58) classifies Tatian's *Oratio* as a *protreptikos*.
98 *Dial.* 1.
99 *De testimonio animae* 1.4.
100 For example, most recently by Buck 1996: 209–26.
101 Representatively, MacMullen 1984: 20–1; MacMullen 1981: 77, 90.
102 Gamble (1995: 112–13) confirms both external and internal audience and propagandist use of the Christian Apologies by their rapid publication and circulation.
103 Grant 1988b: 9.
104 Guerra 1995: 19; Millar 1977: 561–6. For example, see Justin, *1 Apol.* 1.1; Athenagoras, *Leg.* 1.1.
105 Cf. Dihle 1994: 306–8. *Contra* Pervo 1987: 122–3; Schneemelcher 1991: 76.
106 Cf. Thomas 1992: 126, no. 3.
107 Schneemelcher 1991: 76.
108 Bovon 1995a: 168. Bovon (2003: 188–9, no. 135) also points out a connection between the Apocryphal Acts and Q.
109 Pervo 1994: 239–41.
110 Pervo 1992: 47–68.
111 Cf. Pervo (1987: 121–35) considers both the Lucan Acts and the Apocryphal Acts to belong to the genre of the ancient novel and stresses their similarities; *contra* Schneemelcher (1991: 82), who claims that "their

[Apocryphal Acts'] literary model was not Luke's Acts – whether it was known to the authors or not." For a comparative study of Lucan Acts and Apocryphal Acts, see Bovon 2003: 165–94.

112 Bauckham 2000: 799–800.
113 Bauckham 2000: 800; cf. Pervo 1987: 129.
114 See, for example, recent articles in volume 80 (1997) of the journal *Semeia*: Hills 1997: 145–58; Bauckham 1997: 159–68; Marguerat 1997: 169–84; cf. Bauckham 1993: 105–52.
115 Bauckham 2000: 800.
116 Cf. J.K. Elliott 1993a: 74; Bovon 2003: 171–2, 179.
117 Cf. Bovon 2003: 174–7, 181–8.
118 See D.R. MacDonald (1983), where he argues for the polemical relation between the two – the *Acts of Paul* preserving the socially radical Paul of the oral legend and the Pastorals producing the socially conservative Paul against the legend especially in relation to women; cf. Bauckham 1993: 116–30; Bauckham 1997: 165–7.
119 Thomas (1998: 273, no. 1) provides a convenient list of scholars and their works that classify the Apocryphal Acts as Christian fictions.
120 Rohde 1914.
121 Perry 1967.
122 Reardon 1971; cf. Reardon 1969: 291–301.
123 Reardon 1991: especially 169–80. Cf. Kerenyi 1927.
124 Anderson 1984.
125 Pervo 1987: 101.
126 Morgan 1994: 7.
127 Pervo 1987: 105.
128 Pervo 1987: 114.
129 Pervo 1987: 105–8.
130 Pervo 1987: 108.
131 M. Braun 1938.
132 Cf. Pervo 1987: 109; Thomas 1998: 274–87.
133 Pervo 1987: 109.
134 Cf. Pervo 1987: 104.
135 Bowersock 1994: 7–8.
136 *Adversus mathematikos* 1.263–69 (cited by Bowersock 1994: 10).
137 Cf. Bowersock 1994: 10.
138 Bowersock 1994: 143.
139 Pervo 1987: 117.
140 Cf. Pervo 1987: 118.
141 Aune 1988: 110.
142 Cox 1983: xiv.
143 Cox 1983: xiv.
144 Wills 1994: 223–4. For an excellent monograph on the Jewish novels by the same author, see Wills 1995.
145 Pervo 1996; rev. edn 2003: 688.
146 Wills 1994: 224.
147 Wills 1994: 224.
148 Pervo 1996: 688–9; cf. Wills 1994: 234.
149 Cf. Pervo 1987: 120–1.
150 Cf. Pervo 1987: 120.

151 Pervo 1987: 120–1.
152 Pervo 1987: 121.
153 Thomas (1998: 274–87; 1995: 14–18) also argues for the pre-Sophistic "biographical historical novels" as a closer model to the Apocryphal Acts than the Sophistic erotic novels for reasons of chronology and genre development. Cf. Pervo 1996: 709.
154 Acknowledging a close relationship between biographies and novels, Pao (1995: 179–202) places the *Acts of Andrew* within the trajectory of the biographies of philosophers.
155 Söder 1932. Cf. Dihle 1994: 306.
156 Note the examples from the biographical novels previously illustrated.
157 This relation will be examined in detail in Chapter 3.
158 Thomas 1998: 287; Thomas 1995: 17.
159 For example, Stephens 1994: 405–18; Bowie 1994: 435–59.
160 Egger 1988: 33–66. Cf. Bremmer (2001a: 160–70, especially 165–9), who concludes women as the intended and actual readership of the Apocryphal Acts.
161 See MacMullen 1984: 26–30; MacMullen 1983: 174–92; MacMullen 1985–6: 74–5.
162 Cf. Bremmer 2001a: 157, 170. This point will be elaborated in Chapter 3.
163 Schneemelcher 1991: 85.
164 For the Apocryphal Acts as part of "rhetorics of resistance," see Wimbush 1997.
165 Cf. Bisbee 1988: 5.
166 On the prominence of the athletic image in the Martyr Acts and its historical development, see Pfitzner 1967; Pfitzner 1981: 9–17; Brodin 2000: 138–71.
167 There has been a great deal of scholarly debate on the date of Polycarp's death. There is a conflict between the date given by Eusebius, who places it in the (early) reign of Marcus Aurelius (160–80 CE), and the date of proconsul Quadratus mentioned in 21 who was *consul ordinaries* in 142 CE. Barnes (1968b: 511–12), based on the average length of office, suggests three possibilities: 155/6 (possible), 156/7 (most probable), and 157/8 or 158/9 (possible). This is followed by Musurillo (1972: xiii), Grant (1988b: 53–4), and Bisbee (1988: 120–1). The Eusebian date (165–8 CE) is followed by Frend (1965: 240) and von Campenhausen (1957).
168 Here the cult of the martyrs does not refer to the expressions of "worship" directed to the martyrs but, rather, refers to various expressions of respect for their physical remains.
169 Bowersock 1995: 13.
170 Barnes 1968b: 509.
171 Barnes 1968b: 528.
172 Delehaye 1962: 89–94.
173 Bowersock 1995: 26. Cf. his comment on the Martyr Acts as "precious repositories of authentic historical material," 38. Also, see Bowersock 1994: 141.
174 Bisbee 1988: 84.
175 D. Potter 1996: 155.
176 Bisbee 1988: 87. Most clearly, see the contrasting portrayal between Polycarp and Quintus in the *Mart. Pol.*

177 Bisbee 1988: 87.
178 See Frend 1965: especially 31–68.
179 Frend 1965: 44.
180 Frend 1965: 44–9.
181 Frend 1965: 44.
182 Frend 1965: 45.
183 Frend 1965: 59.
184 Frend 1965: 67.
185 Bowersock 1995: 5–8.
186 Bowersock 1995: 28.
187 Bowersock 1995: 54.
188 Bowersock 1995: 8–9.
189 Bowersock 1995: 9–10.
190 Bowersock 1995: 12. Cf. van Henten (1997: 78), who also argues for
     the turn of the century (100 CE) or later period, which is nearly con-
     temporary with the earliest Christian martyr texts. See also van Henten
     and Avemarie 2002: 47–8.
191 Bowersock 1995: 10–13.
192 Boyarin 1999: 93.
193 Boyarin 1998: 593; cf. Boyarin 1999: 94.
194 Boyarin 1999: 126.
195 Boyarin 1999: 95; cf. Boyarin 1998: 593–4.
196 Boyarin 1999: 95; cf. Boyarin 1998: 594.
197 See, for example, Frend 1965: 19–20, 198–9; Dehandschutter 1993:
     507–8; Perler 1949: 47–72; deSilva 1998: 149–52; Lieu 1996: 79–82.
198 Van Henten 1995: 303.
199 Van Henten 1995: 306.
200 See van Henten 1995: 305–6, nos. 9–14 for examples.
201 On the voluntary death in Cynic and Stoic traditions, see Droge and Tabor
     1992: 23–6, 29–39. On noble death in the Greco-Roman thoughts in
     general, see Seeley 1990: 113–41.
202 Lieu 1996: 82; see further van Henten 1997: 146–50; Barton 1989:
     19–23.
203 Pfitzner 1981: 12.
204 Barton: 1994: 41–71. See also Barton 1989: 1–36.
205 See Coleman 1990: 44–73 and Kyle 1998: 242–65.
206 Bowersock 1995: 50.
207 Lieu 1996: 82.
208 Cf. Bisbee 1988: 103–4.
209 See, for example, *Mart. Pol.* 10.1; 12.1; *Mart. Carp.* 23, 34 (Greek); 3.5
     (Latin); *Mart. Lyons* 1.19, 50; *Acts Scill.* 9, 13; *Mart. Apol.* 2; *Mart. Perp.*
     3.2; 6.4. On this topic, see further Bremmer (1991: 12–18), where he
     states, "the only occasion where the followers of Jesus publicly used the
     self-designation 'Christian' was the confrontation with the Roman magis-
     trate" (18). See the section, "Martyr Acts: Christianity as true piety" in
     Chapter 2, pp. 88–102.
210 Mühlenberg 1997: 90.
211 *Mart. Pol.* 1.1.
212 Lieu 1996: 82.
213 Cf. Boyarin 1999: 116–17.

214 Mühlenberg 1997: 87.
215 Boyarin 1999: 101; cf. Boyarin 1998: 595.
216 For a list of these literary features, see Hopkins 2001: 113–14.
217 Clark 1995c: 28, also quoted by Boyarin 1999: 101.
218 See, for example, *Mart. Perp.* 9.1; 16.4; *Mart. Potam.*
219 Nock 1933: 198.
220 Boyarin 1999: 101; cf. Boyarin 1998: 595.
221 *2 Apol.* 12.
222 For example, see *Mart. Carp.* 15–20 (Greek); *Acts Just.* 2.5–6; *Mart. Apol.* 4–22; *Acts Scill.* 4.
223 Weiner and Weiner 1990: 57.
224 Schüssler Fiorenza 1976b: 4.

2 THE SUPERIORITY OF CHRISTIAN MONOTHEISM

1 *Diogn.* 1.1.
2 Cf. Grant 1988b: 31.
3 Middle Platonism is the modern scholarly designation for the Platonic philosophical tradition from the first century BCE to the late second century CE.
4 Daniélou 1973: 107. Specific texts will be mentioned in appropriate places.
5 Daniélou 1973: 75–6.
6 On the negative theology in the Greek Apologists, see Palmer 1983: 234–59. On the influence of Middle Platonism on Justin Martyr, see Andresen 1952: 157–95; Andresen 1955: 312–44.
7 *Didaskalikos (Handbook)*, 10.165. Alcinous was formerly known as Albinus.
8 *2 Apol.* 6, 12; *Dial.* 114.
9 *1 Apol.* 9, 61.
10 *Dial.* 3.7.
11 *1 Apol.* 13.1; *Dial.* 23.2.
12 *Leg.* 10.1; cf. 8.1–3.
13 *Leg.* 4.1.
14 On Tatian in his second-century Greco-Roman philosophical and Syrian Christian context, see a recent study by Hunt (2003). I regret that I have been unable to interact with this work due to the late timing of its release.
15 *Or.* 4.1–3; 7.1; 15.2; 25.2.
16 *Autol.* 1.3.
17 *Oct.* 18.8. *Sensibus maior est, infinitus, inmensus et soli sibi tantus, quantus est, notus.*
18 Cf. Daniélou 1973: 324.
19 Daniélou 1973: 109; e.g. Atticus, *Fragment* 12.
20 Daniélou 1973: 110; cf. Minucius Felix, *Oct.* 19.15; Tatian, *Or.* 4.1; 6.1; 7.1; 32.1.
21 Justin, *1 Apol.* 12.9; 45.1; *2 Apol.* 6.1; 9.2; Clement of Alexandria, *Strom.* 1.28.178.2.
22 Justin, *Dial.* 56.4; Athenagoras, *Leg.* 8.1, 4, 7; Clement of Alexandria, *Strom.* 5.13.86.2; cf. Athenagoras, *Leg.* 10.5.

23 Justin, *2 Apol.* 10.6; *Dial.* 140; Athenagoras, *Leg.* 6.2; Clement of Alexandria, *Protr.* 68.1.
24 Cf. Theophilus, *Autol.* 1.4.
25 Justin, *2 Apol.* 10.6; Athenagoras, *Leg.* 6.2; Clement, *Protr.* 68.1–2; cf. Minucius Felix, *Oct.* 19; Tertullian, *Apol.* 46.9.
26 *Leg.* 6.2.
27 On gnostic (Nag Hammadi) use of this description, see, for example, I,*3 Gospel of Truth*, 20.19; 43.4; I,*3 Apocryphon of John*, 14.21; cf. "Father of the Universe," III,*3 Eugnostos of the Blessed*, 73.2; BG,*3 Sophia of Jesus Christ*, 114.19.
28 *1 Apol.* 10; *2 Apol.* 4.
29 Cf. Chadwick 1966: 46.
30 *1 Apol.* 10.2; cf. Wis. 11.17.
31 *1 Apol.* 59.1.
32 The standard work on this topic is May 1994.
33 Daniélou 1973: 116; cf. Justin, *1 Apol.* 20; *2 Apol.* 6.
34 *Strom.* 5.89.6; 92.3; 126.2.
35 Chadwick 1966: 46, 142.
36 See Daniélou 1973: 116–18. cf. *Strom.* 5.14.93–4.
37 See May 1994: 148–63.
38 *Or.* 5.2.
39 *Or.* 5.3.
40 *Or.* 12.
41 *Or.* 12; cf. Torchia 1993: 195.
42 *Autol.* 1.4; cf. 2.10; Tertullian, *Apol.* 17.1, *de nihilo expressit*.
43 *Autol.* 2.4; cf. Torchia 1993: 195.
44 *Autol.* 2.4; cf. Torchia 1993: 195.
45 Torchia 1993: 196.
46 O'Neill (2002: 449–65) argues for the doctrine of *ex nihilo* as a creed by the time of the New Testament. According to him, the doctrine was formulated in Hellenistic Judaism, including 2 Maccabees 7.28 (quoted by Theophilus), Proverbs 8.24, Philo, and the DSS (1QS 3.15). The contemporary (Jewish) Christian example comes from the *Shepherd of Hermas* (*Herm. Mand.* I.1; cf. *Herm. Vis.* I.1.6).
47 Torchia 1993: 199.
48 *Iliad* 2.204.
49 *Or.* 29.2; cf. Minucius Felix, *Oct.*19.1; Clement of Alexandria, *Strom.* 6.17; 151.5.
50 See also Clement of Alexandria, *Protr.* 74.2.
51 *Leg.* 5.1–2.
52 *Leg.* 6.
53 *Oct.* 19.3–14.
54 *Oct.* 19.15.
55 *Oct.* 20.1.
56 Theophilus, *Autol.* 1.5; Tatian, *Or.* 4.
57 Justin, *Dial.* 3.7; cf. Plato, *Tim.* 52a.
58 Alcinous, *Didaskalikos*, 10.165; Maximus of Tyre, *Diss.* 17.9.
59 *Leg.* 4.1.
60 *Leg.* 10.1.
61 *Leg.* 4.1.

62 Cf. Daniélou 1973: 333–4.
63 *Apol*.17.4–5.
64 Minucius Felix, *Oct*. 17.2–3.
65 *Autol*. 1.5.
66 *Leg*. 6.4; *Or*. 4.2; *Apol*. 17.3–6; *Oct*. 17.2–11; 18.1–7; 32.4–6, respectively.
67 Justin, *1 Apol*. 13.1.
68 Athenagoras, *Leg*. 13.2.
69 Minucius Felix, *Oct*. 32.2; cf. Clement, *Strom*. 5.11.67.1.
70 Praise and thanksgiving: Justin, *1 Apol*. 13; *Dial*. 117.2; 118.2; prayer: Tertullian, *Apol*. 30.5; Clement, *Strom*. 7.6.31.7; eucharist: Justin, *Dial*. 117.1, 3, 5; cf. *1 Apol*. 65–6; and virtuous and righteous life: Justin, *1 Apol*. 10.1; Minucius Felix, *Oct*. 32.1–3; Clement, *Strom*. 7.3.14.1. Martyrdom as sacrifice will be treated in section, "Martyrs as the imitators of Christ: martyrdom as the sacrifice," pp. 95–7, this chapter. For further study on this topic, see Ferguson 1981: 1171–86; Daly 1978: 323–37 (Justin), 466–90 (Clement of Alexandria).
71 Minucius Felix, *Oct*. 19.2.
72 Armstrong and Markus 1960: 19.
73 Cf. Armstrong and Markus 1960: 19.
74 Armstrong and Markus 1960; 18; cf. Plutarch on the Logos and the Ideas in Dillon 1977: 200–2.
75 Barnard 1967: 86.
76 Barnard 1967: 86.
77 Cf. Armstrong and Markus 1960: 18.
78 Cf. Holte 1958: 123; Lilla 1971: 204. See further Wolfson 1947: 200–82, 325–32.
79 Dillon 1977: 159–60.
80 Cf. Daniélou 1973: 346.
81 Daniélou 1973: 354; Lilla (1971: 200–12) presents a similar viewpoint for the doctrine of Logos of Clement of Alexandria.
82 *Leg*. 10.2.
83 *Strom*. 4.155.2; 5.73.3.
84 Daniélou 1973: 348; this is characteristic of Middle Platonism – see Lilla 1971: 202.
85 *Leg*. 24.
86 Barnard 1972: 97.
87 *Leg*. 10.2.
88 Daniélou 1973: 350.
89 Justin, *1 Apol*. 23.2; 32.10; 33.6; 63.4; Athenagoras, *Leg*. 16; Tatian, *Or*. 4, 5; Theophilus, *Autol*. 1.3; Tertullian, *Apol*. 21.11 (*sermo, ratio, virtus*); cf. Daniélou 1973: 350.
90 Cf. Tatian, *Or*. 5.1.
91 *Dial*. 61.1.
92 Cf. Tatian, *Or*. 5.1.
93 Justin, *1 Apol*. 21.1; *Dial*. 129.4; *1 Apol*. 23.2; *2 Apol*. 6.3; *Dial*. 105.1.
94 *1 Apol*. 33.6.
95 Justin, *1 Apol*. 60.1–7; cf. Alcinous, *Didaskalikos* 14.169.
96 Justin, *2 Apol*. 10.8.
97 Justin, *Dial*. 105.1.

98 Justin, *2 Apol.* 6.3.
99 Cf. Clement of Alexandria, *Strom.* 7.7.4; 3.7.9–13.
100 Athenagoras, *Leg.* 10; Tatian, *Or.* 5; Theophilus, *Autol.* 2.10, 13, 18, 22; Tertullian, *Apol.* 21.10–11.
101 Tatian, *Or.* 5.1.
102 Justin, *Dial.* 61; 62; 128; 129; *1 Apol.* 13.3.
103 Tatian, *Or.* 5.2; Justin, *Dial.* 61.2; cf. Philo, *On Giants* 25; *QE* 2.68.
104 Justin, *Dial.* 128.3; cf. Tertullian, *Prax.* 8.
105 Tatian, *Or.* 5.2; Justin, *Dial.* 61.2.
106 *Autol.* 2.2.
107 *Apol.* 21.10–11.
108 Theophilus, *Autol.* 2.22; cf. Justin, *Dial.* 55ff.; 127.2–3.
109 Justin, *1 Apol.* 22.2; Theophilus, *Autol.* 2.10.
110 *2 Apol.* 8.3; 13.3.
111 *2 Apol.* 8.1; 13.5.
112 Note the important distinction between λόγος σπερματικός and σπέρμα τοῦ λόγου. See Andresen 1955: 340–3; Holte 1958: 136–42; Daniélou 1973: 43–4, Lilla 1971: 24.
113 *1 Apol.* 46.2.
114 E.g. Socrates in *1 Apol.* 5.2–4.
115 *2 Apol.* 13.4.
116 *Dial.* 2.1.
117 *2 Apol.* 8.3; 10.1–3; 13.2–6.
118 *Protr.* 98.4.
119 Cf. Lilla 1971: 17.
120 *Protr.* 71.1.
121 *Protr.* 74.7; 68.2; cf. Lilla 1971: 18.
122 *Strom.* 1.37.2–4.
123 *1 Apol.* 21–2. cf. Tertullian, *Apol.* 21.7–9, 14–15, 19–22.
124 *1 Apol.* 22.
125 *1 Apol.* 14.5.
126 *Dial.* 142.3.
127 *2 Apol.* 2.13.
128 The historical argument for Christ will be treated later more in detail in conjunction with Justin's argument from prophecy. See the section, "Antiquity of Christian belief," pp. 66–9.
129 Cf. Wells 1999: 210–15.
130 *Leg.* 11.2; 32.2.
131 See, for example, the way they cite the prologue of the Fourth Gospel in Tatian, *Or.* 5.1; Theophilus, *Autol.* 1.22.
132 *Or.* 21.1; cf. possible reference to the passion, *Or.* 13.3, τὸν διάκονον τοῦ πεπονθότος θεοῦ.
133 E.g. *Autol.* 3.13–14.
134 See Nock 1933: 221–2; Hanson 1980: 934–41; Attridge 1978: 45–78.
135 Cf. S.R.F. Price 1999: 124–6.
136 *Nat.* 2.2–6.
137 *Protr.* 63.1–3; cf. Theophilus, *Autol.* 2.35.
138 *Protr.* 64–5.
139 E.g. Athenagoras, *Leg.* 15.2–4; Tatian, *Or.* 4.2; Theophilus, *Autol.* 1.11.

140 *Nat.* 2.6–7; cf. *Apol.* 10.3. Euhemerus' theory was extensively exploited by the other Apologists as well: Clement, *Protr.* 26.5, 7; 29.1–3; Minucius Felix, *Oct.* 20.5–21; Athenagoras, *Leg.* 28.5–30.2; Theophilus, *Autol.* 1.9.
141 Tertullian, *Apol.* 11.10.
142 *Nat.* 2.6–7.
143 *Apol.* 11.4.
144 *Apol.* 11.11–12.
145 E.g. Clement of Alexandria, *Protr.* 30.1–36.3; Tatian, *Or.* 8–10.
146 Athenagoras, *Leg.* 17.2; 19.1; 21.1; Minucius Felix, *Oct.* 21.3–12; Clement of Alexandria, *Protr.* 36.4–5.
147 Justin, *1 Apol.* 5; *2 Apol.* 10.
148 Clement of Alexandria, *Protr.* 58.4–59.2.
149 Athenagoras, *Leg.* 30.4; cf. Tatian, *Or.* 10.2–3; Justin, *2 Apol.* 5.4–6.
150 Minucius Felix, *Oct.* 22.10; 24.1–2; cf. Justin, *1 Apol.* 23.3; Athenagoras, *Leg.* 13.1–2.
151 Athenagoras, *Leg.* 30.4.
152 *Nat.* 2.8; cf. *Apol.* 24.7–8.
153 Theophilus, *Autol.* 1.1,10; 2.3; Athenagoras, *Leg.* 14.2.
154 Theophilus, *Autol.* 1.10.
155 Minucius Felix, *Oct.* 22.1–5.
156 Tatian, *Or.* 8.1–2; Theophilus, *Autol.* 1.10; cf. demons as offspring of angels and human women in Justin, *2 Apol.* 5.
157 Justin, *1 Apol.* 14.1; Tertullian, *Apol.* 22. 4, 6; Minucius Felix, *Oct.* 26.7–8; 27.1–2; Tatian, *Or.* 8–14.
158 Justin, *1 Apol.* 5; cf. Tertullian, *Apol.* 23.8–11; Minucius Felix, *Oct.* 27.7.
159 Justin, *1 Apol.* 5.
160 Justin, *1 Apol.* 54; cf. *1 Apol.* 22–3; *Dial.* 69–70; 78.
161 Justin, *1 Apol.* 62.
162 Justin, *1 Apol.* 66.
163 Minucius Felix, *Oct.* 28.5–6; Clement of Alexandria, *Protr.* 102.2–103.1; cf. Justin, *1 Apol.* 2, 10; Athenagoras, *Leg.* 22.12; 28.2.
164 Clement of Alexandria, *Protr.* 89.3.
165 Minucius Felix, *Oct.* 16.5–6.
166 Justin, *1 Apol.* 6; Athenagoras, *Leg.* 4.1; Tertullian, *Apol.* 10.2; 24.1–2; cf. Clement of Alexandria, *Protr.* 24.2; 25.1–2.
167 Athenagoras, *Leg.* 30.6; 4.1.
168 *Apol.* 24.2.
169 Tertullian, *Apol.* 24.6.
170 Tertullian, *Apol.* 28.1–2; 24.9–10; cf. Justin, *1 Apol.* 2. On the topic of free will, see Justin, *1 Apol.* 43–4; *2 Apol.* 7; Tatian, *Or.* 7.1.
171 Clement of Alexandria, *Protr.* 95.1. Cf. Tatian, *Or.* 11.2, "'Die to the world' . . . 'live to God.'"
172 Cf. Clement of Alexandria, *Protr.* 68.1–69.4.
173 Justin, *Dial.* 4.6–7; Tatian, *Or.* 3.2; Minucius Felix, *Oct.* 34.6–9.
174 Athenagoras, *Leg.* 22.5; cf. Tatian, *Or.* 3.2; 6.1; Clement of Alexandria, *Protr.* 66.3; Minucius Felix, *Oct.* 34.2.
175 Clement of Alexandria, *Protr.* 66.4; Tatian, *Or.* 2.2; cf. Chadwick 1966: 39.
176 Tatian, *Or.* 25.2; Theophilus, *Autol.* 2.3–4; 3.7; 3.2; Tertullian, *Apol.* 47.5–8, 9–11; Minucius Felix, *Oct.* 34.
177 Theophilus, *Autol.* 3.3; cf. Tatian, *Or.* 3.3.

178 Harnack 1908: 369.
179 Daniélou 1973: 69.
180 Tatian, *Or.* 29.1–2; Theophilus, *Autol.* 2.29–32; Clement of Alexandria, *Protr.* 70.1–72.5; Tertullian, *Apol.* 47.1–4; cf. Minucius Felix, *Oct.* 34.5.
181 Droge 1989: 86; *Or.* 1.1–3.
182 Cf. Droge 1989: 86; *Or.* 1–2. Tatian's catalogue includes a common *topos*: astronomy from the Babylonians; magic from the Persians; geometry from the Egyptians; and the alphabet from the Phoenicians. Cf. Theophilus, *Autol.* 3.30. See "Antiquity of Christian belief" section, pp. 66–9, for the Apologists' chronological argument.
183 *Strom.* 1.74.1–10.
184 See, for example, *Or.* 2.1–3.4; 19.1–4.
185 Athenagoras, *Leg.* 7.2–3; Justin, *2 Apol.* 10; cf. Tatian, *Or.* 20.2; Theophilus, *Autol.* 2.3–4.
186 Justin, *2 Apol.* 10; cf. Tatian, *Or.* 20.2.
187 Justin, *1 Apol.* 33; 36.1; *Dial.* 7.1; 9.1; 61.3–5. For Justin, the Spirit is essentially the "prophetic Spirit," and prophecy is the work of both the Logos and the Spirit; see Barnard 1967: 101–10; Osborn 1973: 87–110. Cf. Athenagoras, *Leg.* 9.1; 10.4; Theophilus, *Autol.* 2.33; 3.11.
188 On the Creator God: Theophilus, *Autol.* 2.34; on the coming of Christ: Justin, *1 Apol.* 30–6; on idolatry: Theophilus, *Autol.* 2.34.
189 Theophilus, *Autol.* 2.35; 3.17.
190 Athenagoras, *Leg.* 9.1; Theophilus, *Autol.* 3.17.
191 E.g. Tertullian, *Apol.* 19.1; 47.1. Cf. Armstrong 1984b: 414–31.
192 For possible literary interactions and reactions, see Droge 1989: 72–81 (Justin and Celsus), 97–101 (Tatian and Celsus), and 119–23 (Theophilus and Celsus), 149–52 (Clement and Cesus).
193 Cf. Droge 1989: 11.
194 On Tertullian's Christian use of history, see Burrows 1988: 209–35; for Clement's historical argument, see Mortley 1980: 186–200, 261–4.
195 Justin, *1 Apol.* 59; cf. Tertullian, *Apol.* 19.1, *Primus enim prophetes Moyses.*
196 *1 Apol.* 44.8–10.
197 Droge 1989: 60.
198 *1 Apol.* 31.8; for a possible explanation, see Droge 1989: 60, no. 41.
199 Cf. Droge 1989: 92.
200 *1 Apol.* 59.
201 *1 Apol.* 60.1.
202 *1 Apol.* 60.5.
203 *Or.* 31.1.
204 *Or.* 36.
205 Egyptians, Chaldaeans, and Phoenicians were considered the most ancient races; cf. Tertullian, *Apol.* 19.5. See also no. 179.
206 *Or.* 36.1–38.2.
207 *Or.* 40.1.
208 Cf. Droge 1989: 96. E.g. according to Tertullian (*Apol.* 19.1), Moses "is about a thousand years earlier than the Trojan War, and consequently earlier than Saturn himself." In *Apol.* 19.3, Tertullian places Moses fifteen hundred years before Homer. Clement, *Strom.* 1.24.162.2, claims that Moses predates Dionysus' deification by 604 years.
209 Cf. Droge 1989: 111.

210 *Autol.* 3.16.

211 *Autol.* 3.17–19.

212 *Autol.* 3.20–1.

213 *Autol.* 3.22.

214 *Autol.* 3.24–8; notice his literal understanding of the biblical chronology.

215 *Autol.* 3.29.

216 F.M. Young 1999: 94.

217 Tertullian, *Apol.* 47.1.

218 Tatian, *Or.* 40.1; Clement of Alexandria, *Strom.* 1.66 ff.; 5.86 ff.; cf. Chadwick 1966: 141, no. 52; Tertullian, *Apol.* 47.1–3, 9–14; Minucius Felix, *Oct.* 34.5.

219 E.g. Tertullian, *Apol.* 37.4; 19.1; Clement of Alexandria, *Protr.* 6.4–5; 88.2–3.

220 E.g. Tertullian, *Apol.* 19.2; 21.7.

221 *Autol.* 3.18.

222 *Autol.* 2.30; 3.26.

223 *Autol.* 3.20.

224 Tatian, *Or.* 21; 13; 29.1–2; Theophilus, *Autol.* 2.10; 3.17.

225 Noah: *Dial.* 138.2; Jacob: *Dial.* 134–5; Moses: *Dial.* 91.4; 94; 131.4; *1 Apol.* 60; Joshua: *Dial.* 111; 113–16.

226 The Pascal lamb: *Dial.* 40.3; the scapegoat: *Dial.* 40.4; Rahab's scarlet rope: *Dial.* 111.4.

227 Justin, *1 Apol.* 30, 31, 33 (virgin birth); 35 (crucifixion); 50 (humiliation); cf. Tertullian, *Apol.* 21.7–9 (incarnation and virgin birth); 21.14–15, 19–22 (death and resurrection).

228 Justin, *Dial.* 100; 103; cf. Chadwick 1965: 290.

229 *Dial.* 43.1.

230 Chadwick 1965: 295.

231 Chadwick 1966: 50.

232 *Strom.* 1. 28.3; 6.58.1.

233 *Strom.* 1. 29.1; cf. 6.42.2.

234 Cf. Justin, *Dial.* 1–2.

235 M. Whittaker 1982: xv.

236 Justin, *Dial.* 8; Tatian, *Or.* 31–3; 35.1. Tatian introduces himself as a "barbarian philosopher" in 42.1.

237 Cf. Tertullian's notorious statement, "What has Jerusalem to do with Athens? The Church with the Academy?" (*Praescr.* 7.9) has been exploited on behalf of his anti-cultural and anti-philosophical stance throughout history without proper attention to its polemical (anti-heretical) context.

238 *Apol.* 21.1–2, 26; 37.3; 38.1; 40.7; 46.2; 50.13.

239 Hanson 1980: 930. On the topic of miracle, see further Remus 1983; Kee 1983; Kee 1986.

240 Origen, *Cels.* 1.71; 1.28; 1.6.

241 Justin, *2 Apol.* 6.

242 Tertullian, *Apol.* 23.4–6.

243 Justin, *2 Apol.* 6; *Dial.* 30; 76.6; Tertullian, *Apol.* 23.15–16; 27.7; cf. Minucius Felix, *Oct.* 27.5–7.

244 Justin, *2 Apol.* 6.

245 *Or.* 18.1–2.

NOTES

246 *1 Apol.* 14.1–2; cf. Tertullian, *Apol.* 22.7; 23.2–5; Minucius Felix, *Oct.* 26.10–11; 27.
247 *1 Apol.* 26.2.
248 For Christian labeling and demarcation of magic from miracles, see Remus 1982: 131–4, 148–50.
249 Justin, *1 Apol.* 19.6; Athenagoras, *Leg.* 36.1–3; Tatian, *Or.* 6; Clement of Alexandria, *Strom.* 5.1.9.4. Mansfeld (1983: 218–33) points out that the Apologists (Athenagoras, Tatian, and Clement) appropriate and appeal to the Stoic doctrine of final conflagration for the support of the resurrection of the flesh.
250 Justin, *1 Apol.* 18–19; Athenagoras, *Leg.* 31.4; 36.1–3; Tatian, *Or.* 6.1–2.
251 Justin, *1 Apol.* 19.5; Theophilus, *Autol.* 1.8.
252 Cf. Theophilus, *Autol.* 1.13.
253 Achtemeier 1976: 149.
254 See Remus 1982: 131–50. Cf. Meeks 1993: 128, "one person's magic is another's miracle."
255 *Conversion*, 83.
256 According to Gallagher (1991: 13–29), of the 29 conversion stories in the Apocryphal Acts, 22 relate the performance of a miracle to the conversion.
257 *Acts Pet.* 7. For the English translation, J.K. Elliott (1993b) will be used throughout this work unless noted otherwise.
258 MacMullen 1983: 174–92; 1985–6: 67–81; 1981: 95–8.
259 Cf. *Acts Thom.* 43, 44; *Acts John* 70.
260 Compare and contrast the way the Apologies and the Apocryphal Acts portray, understand, and deal with the demonic origin of and activities in the pagan religion and culture.
261 *Acts John* 41.
262 *Acts Thom.* 119.
263 *Acts Thom.* 46.
264 Cf. *Acts Pet.* 12, 32.
265 *Acts Thom.* 45; *Acts Andr. Laudatio.* 17; cf. Mark 8.29.
266 MacMullen 1984: 28.
267 MacMullen 1984: 28.
268 D.R. MacDonald 1990.
269 Resurrection of Christ as a topic and understanding of the resurrection as the eschatological reality is confined to the so-called *3 Cor.* in the *Acts Paul*. For the resurrection as future reality see also the beatitudes in the *Acts Paul Thec.* (5) in the *Acts Paul*.
270 From the Latin fragment of the *Epistle of Pseudo-Titus*, in J.K. Elliott 1993b: 398.
271 The spiritual significance of resurrection is usually emphasized for the *Acts John*, which does have a strong spiritualizing tendency (cf. Gallagher 1991: 18–21; Lalleman 1998a: 164–5; Perkins 2002: 6–9). However, the unambiguous correlation between resurrection and conversion in all of the Acts shows that resurrections effect spiritual benefits in all the other Acts as well, as will be further illustrated in the following pages. For the social significance and implications of resurrection, see Perkins 2002: 3–18.
272 *Acts Andr.* 38; *Acts John* 104; *Acts Pet.* 9, 17, 27.

209

273 *Acts John* 79.
274 Cf. *3 Cor.* 3.9; *Acts Pet.* 7; *Acts Paul* 4; *Acts Paul Thec.* 24; *Acts Thom.* 10, 60.
275 Prieur 1991: 113; cf. on several occasions, Jesus is called the Father: the "Father of the souls," *Acts Thom.* 67; cf. 97, 143; see also *Acts John* 77, 94, 98, 112; *Acts Pet.* 39.
276 *Acts Andr.* 16; cf. *Acts Paul* 7.
277 Lalleman 1998a: 168.
278 Lalleman 1998a: 168.
279 See the previous section, "Christian monotheism: greater power through miracles and judgments," pp. 72–9; cf. *Acts Pet.* 21; *Acts Paul* 8; *Acts Thom.* 122, 149.
280 E.g. *Acts Pet.* 39; *Acts Thom.* 20–1, 26, 31, 37, 42, 47, 58, 61, 123, 137.
281 *Acts Thom.* 60, 136.
282 *Acts Andr.* 16; *Acts John* 43, 82, 107; *Acts Paul* 7; *Acts Pet.* 5; *Acts Thom.* 47, 60.
283 *Acts Andr.* 13; *Acts John* 24, 46; *Acts Paul* 10; *Acts Pet.* 19, 28, 32; *Acts Thom.* 37, 54, 167; cf. "My Lord and my God," *Acts Thom.* 10, 81, 144, 159.
284 *Acts Thom.* 42, 69, 73, 78, 123; *Acts John* and *Acts Andr.*
285 Cf. Lalleman 1998a: 184–5.
286 *Acts Pet.* 23.
287 Cf. The high and cosmic Christology of the Apologists in the section, "Christian monotheism: divine Logos," pp. 55–61.
288 R.M. Price 1998: 169.
289 Pervo 1996: 698; see also Pervo 1992: 63–7.
290 Luttikhuizen 1995: 127; cf. *Acts John* 104.
291 See the second point on p. 83, this volume.
292 Cf. Lalleman 1998a: 187.
293 Luttikhuizen 1995: 140.
294 Cf. Lalleman 1998a: 190.
295 Cf. *Acts Andr.* 54 (*Mart. Andr.* 4).
296 Lalleman 1998a: 148, 175.
297 *Acts Andr.* (D.R. MacDonald 1990): 54; *Acts Pet.* 38.
298 *Acts Andr.* (D.R. MacDonald 1990): 54; *Acts John* 99. On the abstract function of the cross in the Apocryphal Acts, see Bolyki 1998: 115–16.
299 *Acts Andr.* (D.R. MacDonald 1990): 54.
300 *Acts Pet.* 38.
301 *Acts Pet.* 38.
302 Lalleman 1998a: 184.
303 Lalleman 1998a: 190.
304 R.M. Price 1998: 172.
305 Lalleman 1995: 99, 102.
306 *Acts Andr.* 47; *Acts John* 87; *Acts Paul Thec.* 21; *Acts Pet.* 22, 35; *Acts Thom.* 11, 27.
307 *Acts Andr.* 32; *Acts John* 73, 75, 76; *Acts Paul* 7; *Acts Pet.* 5; *Acts Thom.* 154.
308 *Acts John* 91–2; Lalleman 1995: 105–6; Lalleman 1998a: 171.
309 *Acts John* 91–2; Lalleman 1995: 105–6; Lalleman 1998a: 171.
310 Cf. Lalleman 1995: 108.

311 Junod and Kaestli 1983: 479.
312 Cartledge 1986: 59, 63.
313 For the possible origin and background of the motif of polymorphy, see Lalleman 1995: 111–17; Cartledge 1986: 53, 66.
314 Cf. Cartledge 1986: 57–8.
315 Cf. *Acts Pet.* 10, 28, 40.
316 *Acts Paul* 10; *Acts Pet.* 24; *Acts Thom.* 59, 80.
317 Cf. Bovon and Junod 1986: 167–8; also see Bovon 1995b: 245–59.
318 Cf. Pesthy (1998: 128) states that "[a]fter Christ's departure from earth, it is the apostle who takes over his role so that in a way he becomes a substitute of Christ."
319 Achtemeier 1976: 174.
320 Bovon 1995a: 169.
321 *Acts Pet.* 23; cf. *Acts Thom.* 139, 160.
322 Cf. *Acts Thom.* 102, 112.
323 Cf. *Acts Paul Thec.* 17; *Acts Andr.* 47, 50.
324 Cf. Bovon 2003: 182, no. 100.
325 Cf. *Acts Pet.* 6, 12. The Logos assumes this title in the Apologies; e.g. Justin, *1 Apol.* 22.2; Theophilus, *Autol.* 2.10.
326 Cf. Again, the Logos functions as the "Sower" of the divine truth in the works of Justin and Clement of Alexandria.
327 Prieur 1991: 111.
328 See, for example, 7–8, 11, 44–7, 52, 59. For the contemporary Christian perception and rejection of (pagan) philosophy, see Wilken 1984: 79; cf. Chadwick 1966: 1–3, 43–4.
329 Cf. Prieur 1991: 111. On the topic of a divine man, see Corrington 1986; Georgi 1976: 27–42; M. Smith 1978: 335–45.
330 For example, people prostrate themselves before the apostles and attempt to worship them (*Acts John* 27; *Acts Pet.* 10; *Acts Thom.* 88, 106); people fear them as gods (*Acts Andr.* 3; *Acts Pet.* 10); Christ appears to people in a form of the apostle in the respective Acts (*Acts Andr.* 47; *Acts John* 87; *Acts Paul Thec.* 21; *Acts Pet.* 22, 35; *Acts Thom.* 11, 27); the apostles possess superhuman strength and characteristics (*Acts Paul Thec.* 3; *3 Cor.* 5; *Acts Andr.* 59; *Acts Thom.* 170); they are called the "blessed one" and the "righteous one," which are the titles used only in reference to Jesus in the canonical Gospels (*Acts Andr.* 4, 8, 15, 26, 51).
331 Prieur 1991: 111.
332 Frend 1965: 255.
333 *Mart. Pol.* 8.2; *Mart. Carp.* 4, 9, 11, 21, 33 (Greek); 6.1, 3 (Latin); *Acts Just.* A.5.6; B.2.1; C.1.4; *Mart. Apol.* 7; *Mart. Perp.* 6.2, 3.
334 *Mart. Pol.* 9.2; 10.1; *Acts Scill.* 3, 5; *Mart. Apol.* 3.
335 *Ep.* 10.96.
336 Cf. R.D. Young 2001: 1–2, 4.
337 *Mart. Carp.* 11–16. The texts and English translations come from Musurillo (1972) unless noted otherwise.
338 *Acts Scill.* 6. *Ego imperium huius seculi non cognosco; sed magis illi Deo seruio quem nemo hominum uidit nec uidere his oculis potest.*
339 *Mart. Apol.* 6.
340 *Acts Just.* 5; *Mart. Apol.* 2.
341 *Mart. Lyons* 1.52.

342 *Mart. Pol.* 14.1; 19.2.

343 *Mart. Carp.* 3.4 (Latin). It is to be noted that the Latin *Mart. Carp.*, while still quoted and used in this study, indicates the Emperor as Decius and thus is later than the Greek edition.

344 *Mart. Carp.* 4.4 (Latin); cf. *Mart. Carp.* 4.5 (Latin); *Mart. Carp.* 40 (Greek); *Mart. Pol.* 11.2; *Mart. Lyons* 1.26; *Mart. Perp.* 18.8; *Mart. Apol.* 25; *Mart. Ptol.* 2.

345 *Acts Just.* A.5.2; *Mart. Apol.* 30, 37, 42; *Mart. Lyons* 1.38, 56.

346 Cf. *Acts Just.* C.2.4.

347 *Mart. Carp.* 6 (Greek).

348 Cf. *Mart. Carp.* 12, 34 (Greek); 6.1 (Latin).

349 *Mart. Pol.* 9.3; 19.2; *Acts Just.* A.6; B.2.2; *Mart. Apol.* 36.

350 E.g. *Mart. Pol.* 19.2; *Mart Carp.* 41, 42 (Greek); 4.6, 5, 7 (Latin); *Mart. Just.* B.2.5; *Mart. Perp.* 21.11; *Mart. Potam.* 6.

351 *Mart. Pol.* 17.3; *Mart. Carp.* 5, 41 (Greek); *Mart. Just.* A.2.7; cf. Jesus Christ as the child of God in *Mart. Pol.* 14.3; 20.2; *Acts Just.* A.2.5.

352 *Acts Just.* A.2.5.

353 *Mart. Carp.* 5 (Greek).

354 Cf. Frend 1965: 316.

355 *Mart. Apol.* 36.

356 Cf. *Mart. Carp.* 5 (Greek).

357 *Mart. Pol.* 14.3.

358 Cf. Hebrews 8.3; 9.12–14, 25–8.

359 *Mart. Lyons* 2.3.

360 Cf. *Mart. Lyons* 1.27, 44; *Mart. Pol.* 17.1.

361 *Mart. Lyons* 1.44.

362 *Mart. Pol.* 2.1.

363 *Mart. Pol.* 1.2.

364 *Mart. Lyons* 1.28, 41; cf. *Mart. Pol.* 2.2; *Mart. Carp.* 3.6 (Latin); *Mart. Apol.* 47; *Mart. Perp.* 15.6.

365 Farkasfalvy 1992: 23.

366 Pagels 1980: 266.

367 *Mart. Pol.* 1.2; *Mart. Lyons* 2.2.

368 *Mart. Pol.* 6.2, my translation.

369 *Mart. Perp.* 18.9; cf. *Mart. Carp.* 41 (Greek).

370 *Contra* Rordorf (1986: 345–6), who distinguishes the "sacrificial" portrayal of martyrdom (i.e. expiatory death) under the Christological argument and the "athletic" portrayal of martyrdom under the apologetic argument. However, these kinds of classifications do not take into account the fact that these "types" of presentation intersected each other and that the athletic imagery in imitation of Christ was clearly a part of the Christological argument. Thus, both athletic and sacrificial themes constitute the Christological and apologetic arguments. Cf. Brodin 2000: 140.

371 *Mart. Lyons* 1.44.

372 *Mart. Carp.* 35 (Greek); 3.5 (Latin), *fortis athleta*; *Mart. Lyons* 1.17, 19, 36.

373 *Mart. Lyons* 1.4; *Mart. Carp.* 4.2 (Latin), *ministry diaboli*.

374 *Mart. Pol.* 3.1; 17.1; *Mart. Carp.* 17, 35 (Greek); *Mart. Lyons* 1.5, 6, 16, 23, 27; 2.6; *Mart. Apol.* 47; *Mart. Perp.* 20.1.

375 This phrase is from Griffin 2002: 139.
376 *Mart. Lyons* 1.37–40.
377 *Mart. Lyons* 1.43.
378 *Mart. Lyons* 1.47.
379 *Mart. Lyons* 1.42; ἵνα διὰ πλειόνων γυμνασμάτων νικήσασα τῷ μὲν σκολιῷ ὄφει ἀπαραίτητον ποιήσῃ τὴν καταδίκην ... μέγαν καὶ ἀκαταγώνιστον ἀθλητὴν Χριστὸν ἐνδεδυμένη, διὰ πολλῶν κλήρων ἐκβιάσασα τὸν ἀντικείμενον καὶ δι᾿ ἀγῶνος τὸν τῆς ἀφθαρσίας στεψαμένη στέφανον.
380 *Mart. Perp.* 7.9.
381 For the translation of *lanista* as a "president of games" equivalent to ἀγωνοθέτης, see den Boeft and Bremmer 1982: 391; Bowersock 1995: 51; cf. Robert 1982: 228–76.
382 *Mart. Perp.* 10.1–14.
383 *Mart. Perp.* 9.2; 10.14, 15; 15.4; 16.1; 19.5; cf. *spectaculum* in 21.2. Cf. Griffin 2002: 179.
384 *Mart. Perp.* 18.3.
385 Cf. Barton 1989: 30, no. 54:

> It is a mistake to think that the opposition of Christians to the gladiatorial games was necessarily or principally a result of their opposition to violence per se or to the public emulation of the bloody figure of the gladiator. As long as martyrdom was of value, violence was of value. The martyr was, in many ways, competing with the gladiator – but for a different *editor* (the producer of the games).

386 Hopkins 1983: 21.
387 Barton 1989: 3; cf. Barton 1994: 51–4.
388 Barton 1989: 5–7.
389 Barton 1989: 13.
390 Barton 1989: 15.
391 Barton 1989: 15.
392 Barton 1989: 1, 5; cf. Barton 1994: 56–7.
393 Cf. *Mart. Pol.* 2. 1–3; *Mart. Lyons* 2.4; *Mart. Apol.* 47; *Mart. Perp.* 21.11.
394 *Mart. Pol.* 12.1; 19.2; *Mart. Carp.* 44 (Greek); 4.1; 6.1 (Latin); *Mart. Lyons* 1.55, 63; 2.7; *Mart. Perp.* 18.1, 3, 9.
395 *Mart. Carp.* 41 (Greek); 4.1 (Latin); *Mart. Ptol.* 19; *Acts Just.* A.6; B.6; *Acts Scill.* 15, 17; *Mart. Apol.* 46.
396 *Mart. Pol.* 12.1; *Mart. Lyons* 1.35.
397 *Mart. Pol.* 2.3; *Mart. Lyons* 1.26.
398 *Mart. Pol.* 17.1; 19.2; *Mart. Lyons* 1.36, 38, 42; *Mart. Perp.* 19.2; *Mart. Potam.* 6; cf. on the eternal life: *Mart. Lyons* 2.7; *Mart. Apol.* 30, 37, "immortality of soul"; *Acts Just.* A.5.2; B.5.2; *Mart. Perp.* 10.13, "the Gate of Life."
399 *Mart. Carp.* 39, 42 (Greek); 4.3 (Latin); *Mart. Lyons* 1.27, 41.
400 *Acts Scill.* 15; *Mart. Perp.* 4.8–10; 11.1–12.7; cf. *Mart. Lyons* 1.55.
401 Cf. *Mart. Carp.* 6.3 (Latin).
402 E.g. *Mart. Lyons* 1.19 ff., 50.
403 *Mart. Lyons* 1.9, 18, 22, 39, 43, 49–50; 2.5, πᾶσι ἀπελογοῦντο; *Mart. Apol.* 4 ff., ἀπολογία; *Acts Scill.* 4, *mysterium simplicitatis*; *Acts Just.* A.3,

τοῖς ἀληθέσι λόγοις τῶν Χριστιανῶν; *Mart. Pol.* 12.2, Polycarp as a διδάσκαλος; *Mart. Perp.* 17.1–2.

404 *Mart. Pol.* 18.3.
405 On this relation, see de Jonge 1991: 135–51; Downing 1963: 279–93; Williams 1975.
406 Barton 1989: 19; cf. Barton 1994: 56.
407 Barton 1989: 19.
408 Barton 1989: 19.
409 Barton 1989: 19.
410 Barton 1989: 20.
411 Cf. Pfitzner 1981: 11.
412 Van Henten (1995: 311, 313) brings to attention the similar sacrificial terminology of the prayer of Azariah in Daniel 3.39–40 (LXX), which to him provides a decisive factor for interrelationship between the Jewish and Christian martyrological literature: προσδεχθείημεν (3.39a); ἐν ὁλοκαυτώμασι (3.39b); κριῶν (3.39b); πιόνων (3.39c); θυσία (3.40a); ἐνώπιόν σου σήμερον (3.40a).
413 On the sacrifice of the martyr as a thank-offering, see F.M. Young 1971: 130, 140.
414 Bowersock 1995: 52.
415 *Mart. Pol.* 21. On the discussion on the Great Sabbath, see Bowersock 1995: 48, appendix.
416 *Mart. Perp.* 7.9; 16.3.
417 *Mart. Potam.* 5–7.
418 *Mart. Carp.* 42–4 (Greek).
419 *Mart. Ptol.* 15, 20.
420 *Apol.* 50.13. *Semen est sanguis Christianorum.*
421 R.D. Young 2001: 12.
422 Cf. Girard 1977: 8.
423 *Mart. Perp.* 18.4–5; cf. Tertullian, *Apol.* 15.4–5.
424 Coleman 1990: 66.
425 *Mart. Perp.* 5.
426 *Acts Just.* C.4.4.
427 *Mart. Pol.* 10.1; *Mart. Carp.* 5, 23, 34 (Greek); 6.1 (Latin); *Mart. Lyons* 1.19, 20, 26, 50; *Acts Scill.* 9, 10, 13; *Mart. Apol.* 2; *Mart. Potam.* 5; cf. *Mart. Perp.* 3.2.
428 *Mart. Ptol.* 10–12, 15, 18; *Acts Just.* A.3.4; 4 *passim*; *Mart. Lyons* 1.10; *Mart. Apol.* 1–2; *Mart. Perp.* 6.4.
429 Cf. *Mart. Lyons* 1.19ff., 33, 50; see p. 95, this volume.
430 F.M. Young 1971: 229.
431 F.M. Young 1971: 229.
432 *Mart. Lyons* 1.23.
433 *Mart. Pol.* 5.1; 8.1.
434 *Mart. Lyons* 2.6.
435 *Mart. Lyons* 2.7.
436 *Mart. Potam.* 3, 6.
437 *Mart. Perp.* 7–8.
438 Hinson 1993: 425.
439 R.D. Young 2001: 10.
440 *Mart. Lyons* 1.24; *Mart. Carp.* 3.6 (Latin).

441 *Mart. Pol.* 5.2; *Mart. Perp.* 4, 7–8, 10–13.
442 E.g. *Mart. Perp.* 9.1.
443 *Mart. Pol.* 2.3; cf. *Acts Scill.* 15.
444 *Mart. Pol.* 16.2.
445 *Mart. Pol.* 12.2, my translation. Referring to the reading of the codex Atheniensis, published by himself, Dehandschutter (1990: 391–4) prefers the reading ἀσεβείας over the reading Ἀσίας for contextual and historical reasons. Thus, "Here is the teacher of atheism . . ." See Dehandschutter 1990: 432.
446 *Mart. Perp.* 17.1.
447 *Mart. Perp.* 17.1.
448 *Mart. Ptol.* 9.
449 *Acts Just.* A.2.2.
450 *Hist. eccl.* 5.21.
451 R.D. Young 2001: 31.
452 Cf. *Mart. Pol.* 17.2.
453 *Mart. Pol.* 17.3.
454 *Mart. Lyons* 2.3.
455 *Mart. Lyons* 1.63.

3 THE SUPERIORITY OF CHRISTIAN SEXUAL MORALITY

1 On the Stoic concept of soul and body, see Long 1996: 224–49.
2 On "right reason" and nature as the basis of Stoic ethics and on the Stoic concept of virtue, see Long 1996; 134–55; cf. Rist 1969: 37–53.
3 See Francis 1995: 33–6.
4 See Francis 1995: 60–6.
5 Cf. Wimbush 1987: 5.
6 Cf. Justin, *1 Apol.* 12, 52–3; Tertullian, *Apol.* 41.3.
7 E.g. *Mart. Carp.* 4.4 (Latin); *Acts Just.* B.5.6; C.4.6; *Mart. Apol.* 26–30.
8 E.g. Athenagoras, *Leg.* 12.1; Minucius Felix, *Oct.* 32.9.
9 See Perkins 1995: 15–40.
10 E.g. Marcus Aurelius, *Meditations* 11.3; cf. Epictetus, *Discourses* 1.29.29; 3.24.96–102. For a concise study of the Stoic position on voluntary death, see Rist 1969: 233–55; Droge and Tabor 1992: 29–39.
11 Perkins 1995: 15.
12 Tertullian, *Apol.* 1.12; *Acts Andr.* 54, 61, 63; *Acts John* 113; *Acts Paul* 10; 11.4; *Acts Pet.* 35, 37; *Acts Thom.* 160, 168; *Mart. Pol.* 12.1; 19.2; *Mart. Carp.* 41; 44 (Greek); 4.1; 6.1 (Latin); *Acts Just.* A.6; B.6; *Mart. Lyons* 1.55, 63; 2.7; *Acts Scill.* 15, 17; *Mart. Apol.* 46; *Mart. Perp.* 18.1, 3, 9; cf. Athenagoras, *Leg.* 12.3; Clement of Alexandria, *Strom.* 7.3.18.
13 Minucius Felix, *Oct.* 8.5.
14 Meeks 1993: 131.
15 See Raditsa 1980: 278–339; cf. Roetzel 2000: 234–8.
16 Galinsky 1996: 130.
17 Galinsky 1996: 130.
18 Rawson 1986b: 9; Dixon 1992: 67.
19 Dixon 1992: 79–80; Grubbs 1994: 380; cf. Raditsa 1980: 319–30.
20 Raditsa 1980: 310.

NOTES

21 Juvenal, *Satires* 6.
22 *Strom.* 2.23.138.
23 Deming 1995: 51. On Stoic-Cynic debate, see also Roetzel 2000: 232–3.
24 *Discourses* 3.22.69.
25 Deming 1995: 54–8.
26 An excerpt in Stobaeus 4.511.15–512.1 (cited in Balch 1983: 432).
27 14.30–9; Lutz 1947: 92. References to Musonius Rufus follow the fragment numbers and lines of the text of Lutz 1947: 3–147; cf. Antipater of Tarsus, *On Marriage*, SVF 3.254.23–257.10 from Stobaeus 4.507.6–512.7 W.-H., in Deming 1995: 226–9.
28 13A.10; Lutz 1947: 89.
29 The same ideology also prevailed in the Greek East and Judaism according to Grubbs 1994: 362.
30 14.35; Lutz 1947: 92.
31 15; Lutz 1947: 96–100.
32 12.5–10; Lutz 1947: 86.
33 12.10–19; Lutz 1947: 87.
34 *On Duties*, 22.21–2, from Malherbe 1986: 100–1.
35 *Discourses* 3.7.19–25.
36 Modestinus, *Dig.* 23.2.1, quoted by Dixon 1992: 61.
37 Dixon 1992: 70. For those references, see Dixon 1992: 206; Treggiari 1991: 229–61.
38 Grubbs 1994: 371.
39 Dixon 1992: 70. See Treggiari 1991: 243–53; cf. Pliny, *Ep.* 8.5.
40 13A.20; Lutz 1947: 88.
41 Shelton 1990: 163–86.
42 *Ep.* 4.19; 7.19.
43 Treggiari 1991: 233; Grubbs 1994: 370.
44 Cooper 1996: 56.
45 Pliny, *Ep.* 4.19; 7.19; Plutarch, *Advice to Bride and Groom*, 139C, 10; 141E, 26.
46 Pagels 1983: 147.
47 For further Stoic and Cynic elements in 1 Corinthians 7, see Deming 1995: 108–210.
48 Cf. Jesus' saying about the eunuch for the kingdom of heaven in Matthew 19.11–12.
49 Martin 1995: 209, for the term "prophylaxis."
50 I am grateful to S. Scott Bartchy for highlighting this aspect during a telephone conversation in May, 2003.
51 For Paul's "theology of calling" and its implications on marriage and celibacy, see Bartchy 1973: 132–55.
52 I am indebted to S.S. Bartchy for this English translation of the Greek word μακαριωτέρα.
53 Justin, *1 Apol.* 27; Athenagoras, *Leg.* 32.1; 34.2–3; 35.6; Tatian, *Or.* 28.1; 29.1; 33–4; Theophilus, *Autol.* 3.6, 8; Tertullian, *Apol.* 9.8; 39.12–14; 46.10–16; Minucius Felix, *Oct.* 30.2–31.4; 37.11–12; 38.57.
54 *1 Apol.* 14.2.
55 *2 Apol.* 2.1–20 (= *Mart. Ptol.*).
56 *Apol.* 39.12; cf. *Diogn.* 5.7.
57 Justin, *1 Apol.* 15; Athenagoras, *Leg.* 33.1; cf. Tertullian, *Marc.* 1.29.

58 Tertullian, *Apol.* 39.11; 46.11; Minucius Felix, *Oct.* 31.5.
59 Justin, *1 Apol.* 15; Athenagoras, *Leg.* 33.4–6; Clement of Alexandria, *Strom.* 2.23.145.3; 3.47.2; Theophilus, *Autol.* 3.13; Minucius Felix, *Oct.* 31.5; cf. Tertullian, *Ux.*; *Exh. cast.*; *Monogamy*. Compare this trend with 1 Corinthians 7.9, 36; 1 Timothy 5.14; Clement of Alexandria, *Strom.* 3.12.82, where a remarriage is allowed or even recommended.
60 Justin, *1 Apol.* 15; Athenagoras, *Leg.* 32.2–3; Theophilus, *Autol.* 3.13; cf. Tertullian, *Apol.* 46.12.
61 Athenagoras, *Leg.* 32.4.
62 Justin, *1 Apol.* 15; Athenagoras, *Leg.* 33.3.
63 Clement of Alexandria, *Strom.* 3.7.57.
64 E.g. Justin, *1 Apol.* 43–4; Tatian, *Or.* 11.2.
65 Cf. Tertullian, *Monogamy*; *Ux.* 1.2.
66 *Autol.* 2.28.
67 *Autol.* 2.28.
68 Stevenson 1980: 414.
69 *Ad uxorem* 2.8.
70 Pagels 1983: 156.
71 *Marc.* 1.29.5.
72 Chadwick 1966: 58.
73 *Strom.* 3.2.5–11.
74 *Strom.* 3.3.12–4.29; 3.3.79–85; cf. Irenaeus, *Haer.* 1.28.1; Eusebius, *Hist. eccl.* 4.29.1–3; 4.28.1; Hippolytus, *Haer.* 8.13. Lloyd-Moffett (2003) rightly argues that "heresy" of encratism or Encratites is a category constructed and developed by the "Western" (Greco-Roman) Church fathers to describe a set of radical ascetic behaviors and orientation of the East Syrian Christians, who considered those practices normal. See also the section, "Tatian and encratism," pp. 123–4.
75 Tertullian also based his defense of marriage against Marcion's radicalism on the theology of creation. See *Marc.* 1.29.
76 See the section, "Tatian and encratism," pp. 123–4.
77 Cf. self-control is a key to celibacy in Paul: 1 Corinthians 7.9, 37.
78 Athenagoras, *Leg.* 33.2; Theophilus, *Autol.* 3.15; cf. Tatian, *Or.* 32.2.
79 *1 Apol.* 15.
80 This phrase is from Grant 1988b: 67; *1 Apol.* 29.
81 *Oct.* 31.5.
82 *Apol.* 9.19.
83 *De exhortatione castatitas* 1. In this treatise sympathetic to the teachings of the New Prophecy (*c*.204–12 CE), practice of monogamy forms the third and the last degree of perfection.
84 *Strom.* 6.12.100.2.
85 *Strom.* 3.7.57.
86 *Strom.* 3.7.57.
87 *Strom.* 3.10.69.
88 *Strom.* 3.10.69.
89 Noted by Vogt 1991: 177.
90 *Strom.* 6.12.100.3. Like most of the early Church fathers, Clement's attitude toward women is ambivalent. On the capacity of asceticism and martyrdom, he recognizes the "gender equality" (e.g. Book 4 of *Strom.*), but on the subject of sexuality, marriage, and domestic life, he is as

traditional and conservative as he can be (e.g. Book 3 of *Strom.*), endorsing and teaching the "Christianized" version of the Stoic ideal of marriage (partnership of the unequals). Tertullian, Clement's close contemporary, shows similar ambivalence toward women.

91 See the section, "Continence as autonomy and authority: portrayal of female converts," pp. 136–42.
92 *Strom.* 6.12.100.3.
93 *Strom.* 6.12.100.
94 Reference in Walzer (1949: 15):

> For their contempt of death (and of its sequel) is patent to us every day, and likewise their restraint in cohabitation. For they include not only men but also women who refrain from cohabiting all through their lives; and they also number individuals who, in self-discipline and self-control in matters of food and drink, and in their keen pursuit of justice, have attained a pitch not inferior to that of genuine philosophers.

95 Cf. Clement of Alexandria, *Strom.* 4.68.2; 58.3; Justin, *1 Apol.* 15; Athenagoras, *Leg.* 33.1–6.
96 Theophilus, *Autol.* 3.15.
97 Clement of Alexandria, *Strom.* 3.12.79; Tertullian, *Marc.* 1.29; cf. Bailey 1959: 22–3.
98 Clement of Alexandria, *Strom.* 3.12.86.
99 *Strom.* 3.12.86; cf. *Strom.* 3.12.88.
100 Cf. Francis 1995: 176.
101 For Tertullian's social conservatism, see Brown 1988: 78–82.
102 *Or.* 8.1.
103 *Or.* 11.1–2; 33.1.
104 *Strom.* 3.6.49; 3.12.81.
105 *Strom.* 3.6.49.
106 *Strom.* 3.12.86.
107 Pagels 1983: 152.
108 Pagels 1983: 152.
109 Brown 1988: 95.
110 Irenaeus, *Haer.* 1.28.1; Eusebius, *Hist. eccl.* 4.29.1–3; cf. 4.28.1; Epiphanius, *Panarion* 45–7.
111 Lloyd-Moffett 2003: 2–9; see Vööbus 1958: 69–103.
112 Vööbus 1958: 31–9.
113 Germond 1996: 352.
114 *Acts Paul Thec.* 5.
115 Coptic papyrus Berlin 8502, pp. 128–32, 135–41, in J.K. Elliott 1993b: 397–8.
116 *Acts John* 113; *Acts Thom.* 144, 146 (*The Mart.*).
117 Fragments from the *Epistle of Pseudo-Titus*, in J.K. Elliott 1993b: 346–7.
118 See further Wagener (1991: 353), where he writes: "For Andrew, the present scenario is a reenactment of the Paradise drama, with himself and Maximilla as the primal human beings."
119 Brown 1988: 98.
120 Cf. Brown 1988: 98–100.
121 Drijvers 1991: 328.

122 Cf. The previously quoted part of the Latin version of the *Acts of John* concludes the paragraph on the earthly marriage by juxtaposing the heavenly marriage: "Hearing this, little children, join yourselves together in an inseparable marriage, holy and true, waiting for the one true incomparable bridegroom from heaven, even Christ, the ever-lasting bridegroom."

123 E.A. Clark 1995b: 509.

124 Schroeder 2000: 114.

125 Cooper 1996: 46; cf. Perkins 1995: 25–30.

126 Perkins 1995: 26, 46–76; Cooper 1996: 20–44; Egger 1994: 260–80; Konstan 1998: 35.

127 Cf. Perkins 1995: 46–50; Cooper 1996: 36–43. Note the fundamental importance of marriage in the romance and compare it with that of Stoic (and Middle Platonic) moralists.

128 Cooper 1996: 55.

129 Cf. Cooper 1996: 51–2.

130 Cooper 1996: 52.

131 Cooper 1996: 55.

132 Cf. Cooper 1996: 50, 52. See *Acts Paul* 7; *Acts Andr.* 23–5, 36–7; *Acts Thom.* 95, 99; *Acts Pet.* 33–4.

133 This rivalry as more of a political conflict will be treated in the next chapter.

134 Cf. *Cels.* 1.6, 26, 71; 3.55; 8.55.

135 S.L. Davies 1980: 32.

136 E.g. *Acts Paul Thec.* 10, 20; *Acts John* 48–55; *Acts Thom.* 13, 16.

137 *Acts Andr.* 25–6, 64.

138 *Acts Paul Thec.* 12; cf. *Acts Thom.* 101.

139 Cf. Perkins 1985: 216; Perkins 1995: 28. Compare and contrast this "Christian continence and marriage disruption" theme with the con- temporary story of a Roman matron recorded by Justin (*2 Apol.* 2 = *Mart. Ptol.*). After her conversion, she embraced chastity (in marriage) and tried to persuade her husband to the same chastity; however, he refused to join her and rather became worse in his "wickedness." Finally, she sent him a bill of divorce (*repudium*), and, annoyed by her action against his will, the husband accused her as a Christian. When she obtained a delay in her trial from the emperor, the husband instead denounced her Christian teacher, Ptolemaeus, and had him executed on account of his Christian identity, which spurred two more to martyrdom. There is a parallel with the Apocryphal Acts that women's conversion leads to the dissolution of marriage and the apostles' martyrdom. However, in this story, the matron embraced not continence but chastity (note the distinction), and the hus- band's moral (sexual) depravity is stressed. While highlighting the moral (sexual) superiority of Christians and illustrating the possible disruptive effect of women's conversion in a mixed marriage, it seems that Justin places a greater emphasis on the injustice of Christian persecution due to the Christian Name. See further Buck 2002: 541–6; M. MacDonald 1990; M. MacDonald 1996: 205–13; cf. Grant 1985: 461–72.

140 *Acts Andr.* 23.

141 *Acts Andr.* 36.

142 Note that in the interrogation of Thomas, King Misdaeus orders Thomas to "bring peace and concord" to the marriage of Charisius and Mygdonia – the very ideal of harmonious partnership (*Acts Thom.* 127).

143 *Acts Thom.* 114.

144 Cooper 1996: 58–9.

145 Perkins 1985: 216; Perkins 1995: 28.

146 E.A. Clark 1995a: 371.

147 See Jacobs 1999: 105–38; cf. Konstan 1998: 15–36.

148 On the early Christian kinship as a surrogate sibling relationship, see Bartchy 1999; Hellerman 2001.

149 Cf. *Acts Paul Thec.* 10, 27–9.

150 *Acts Andr.* 36; *Acts Thom.* 95.

151 See Bremmer 1989: 37–48.

152 Cooper 1996: 64.

153 Germond 1996: 366.

154 S.L. Davies 1980: 53.

155 Meeks 1993: 142.

156 Burrus 1986: 102.

157 On the "one-sex model, " in which "woman does not exist as an onto-logically distinct category (62)," see Laqueur 1990. On Philo's understanding of gender polarity and use of male and female categories, see Baer 1970.

158 Meeks 1993: 140; Baer 1970: 35–44; Harlow 1998: 156.

159 Harlow (1998: 159) summarizes the physician Galen's view on this: "in essence a female offspring was a male who had not achieved its full potential due to being undercooked in the womb."

160 E.g. Philo, *QE* 1.7–8; *On the Cherubim* 50.

161 This point was especially important to Philo. See Philo, *Spec. Laws* 2.56, 64; Baer 1970: 14–35; Aspegren 1990: 84–95; Meeks 1974: 176–7.

162 Cf. *Acts Andr.* 37–9; *Acts Thom.* 12, 15, 43; Philo, *Spec. Laws* 3.178. See Baer 1970: 45–9; Attridge 1991: 410; Gasparro 1991: 138–40; Meeks 1974: 193–7. Also, cf. *Gospel of Thomas*, logion 22:

> When you make the two one, and when you make the inner as the outer and the outer as the inner and the upper as the lower, and when you make the male and the female into a single one, so that the male is not male and the female not female, . . . then you shall enter the kingdom.

163 VIII,1 *Zostrianos* 131.8; cf. *1 Clem.* 55.3–6; Clement of Alexandria, *Strom.* 6.12.100.

164 Aspegren 1990: 98.

165 E.g. Philo, *QE* 2.3; *Worse* 28. cf. Baer 1970: 54.

166 Harlow 1998: 166–7.

167 Cf. Cameron 1989: 196.

168 E.g. Burrus 1987: 108–9; S.L. Davies 1980: 58–63; D.R. MacDonald 1983: 50–3. They all argue for the oral folklores and/or legends as the source of the *Acts Paul Thec.*, and Davies, in fact, claims female authorship for the Acts. Other scholars who regard Thecla as the "heroine of women's liberation" include: Kraemer 1980: 298–307; Ruether 1979: 71–98.

169 Cf. W. Braun 2000: 216. Note the female martyrs in the Martyr Acts.

170 This scene corresponded to reality. The Council of Gangra (340 CE) condemned transvestism of female ascetics. See Yarbrough 1990: 448–55.

171 W. Braun 2000: 216.

172 That Thecla's example was used "as a licence for women's teaching and baptizing" against "the teaching of Paul" is cited by Tertullian in his *On Baptism* 17, who strongly opposed the "liberated" claim and practice for women.

173 In Greek usage, there is a distinction between ἄνθρωπος and ἀνήρ; the former can refer to a human being in general, a person of either male or female sex, or to a male person, whereas the latter specifically denotes a male person. However, as an explanation follows, the use of these two Greek words is to be seen in the specific "male" context with corresponding ideal qualities as opposed to the "female" nature or ways exhibited by Aegeates. Therefore, the use of ἄνθρωπος and ἀνήρ in this context is interchangeable and points to Maximilla's internal masculinization.

174 Cf. Rodman 1997: 38.

175 Rodman 1997: 38, no. 17.

176 This phrase is from Aspegren, *The Male Woman* (1990). Note the paradox in this expression.

177 For the feminist critique of this "liberated" view and the "ideology of virginity," see Castelli 1986: 61–88; cf. Castelli 1991: 33, 46.

178 D.R. MacDonald (1983) provides an intriguing comparison between the Pastorals and the *Acts Paul Thec.* as the contrasting interpretations of Paul in 1 Corinthians 7 in the development of the second century.

179 Cf. Castelli 1991: 45.

180 Brown 1990: 481.

181 Roetzel 2000: 245.

182 Valantasis 1995: 549.

183 *Mart. Apol.* 26.

184 *Mart. Apol.* 26.

185 *Acts Just.* A.4.2; B.4.2.

186 *Mart. Potam.* 1.

187 *Mart. Potam.* 2.

188 *Mart. Potam.* 3.

189 Cardman 1988: 148.

190 In the later Martyr Acts, the threat and sentence of sexual violence have become more prominent for Christian (female) virgins, and the link between the martyrdom and ascetic continence of women is more pronounced. E.g. Sabrina in *The Martyrdom of Pionius*, 7.6; Irene in *The Martyrdom of Agape, Irene, Chione, and Companions*, 4.4; 7.2; Eusebius, *Martyrdom of Palestine*, 5.3; 8.5–8. See Jones 1993: 32; Cardman 1988: 148.

191 See, for example, Jensen 1996: 90; Hinson 1993: 427–28; Jones 1993: 30–1.

192 Jones (1993: 23–34) shows the ironical position of women in Roman law that "in their access to the process of law they found themselves in an inferior position, but in punishment they could expect no such distinction. Under law in death alone were women the equals of men" (34).

193 This aspect is stressed by Cardman 1988: 144–50.

194 Cf. Shaw 1993: 9; Cardman 1988: 148–50.
195 *Mart. Carp.* 6.4–5 (Latin).
196 *Mart. Perp.* 20.2.
197 *Mart. Perp.* 20.3–5.
198 *Mart. Potam.* 4, 2.
199 *Mart. Lyons* 1.56.
200 Shaw 1993: 8.
201 Shaw 1993: 7. In the later *Martyrdom of Crispina*, prior to her decapitation, Crispina's head was shaved that "her beauty might first thus be brought to shame" (3.1).
202 Streete 2002: 2.
203 Streete 2002: 3.
204 Streete 2002: 3.
205 Cf. Streete 2002: 3.
206 *Mart. Lyons* 1.41.
207 *Mart. Lyons* 1.41.
208 I will return to this topic in the section, "Resistance to and reconfiguration of the established social order," pp. 153–6.
209 *Mart. Lyons* 1.20.
210 *Acts Just.* B.4.8.
211 *Mart. Carp.* A.32 (Greek); B.3.2 (Latin).
212 Matthew 12.48–50; Mark 3.33–35; cf. Luke 8.21.
213 Salisbury 1997: 8.
214 *Mart. Carp.* B.6.2 (Latin); cf. A.43 (Greek).
215 *Mart. Carp.* A.44 (Greek); cf. B.6.3–5 (Latin).
216 Salisbury 1997: 116.
217 Harlow 1998: 155, 161.
218 Bartchy 1998: 285.
219 Salisbury 1997: 6. On this topic, see an important study by Hallett 1984.
220 Sullivan 1997: 71.
221 Cf. Dronke 1984: 5.
222 den Boeft and Bremmer 1982: 388–9.
223 See the section, "Resistance to and reconfiguration of the established social order," pp. 153–6.
224 Cf. Perkins 1994a: 840.
225 Sullivan 1997: 71.
226 *Mart. Lyons* 1.55. Further references to the Maccabean mother appear in the *Martyrdom of Marian and James* 13.1 and the *Martyrdom of Montanus and Lucius* 16.4.
227 *Mart. Lyons* 1.55.
228 Cf. Salisbury 1997: 101.
229 Dronke 1984: 5.
230 Cf. Christ in *Acts Just.* B.4.8.
231 As Griffin (2002: 87) notes, although Papylus claimed spiritual children, he did not call himself father and was not called father, *Mart. Carp.* A.32 (Greek); B.3.2 (Latin).
232 Cf. Griffin 2002: 85.
233 Origen, *Cels.* 3.55.
234 *Mart. Lyons* 1.17.
235 Ferguson 1993b: 497.

236 R.D. Young 2001: 13.
237 See Scholer 1989: 10–14.
238 Castelli 1991: 35; cf. Perkins 1994a: 837–47; Lefkowitz 1976: 417–21.
See also Scholer 1989: 11–14; Robeck 1992: 64–5.
239 For a detailed analysis of Perpetua's visions, see Robeck 1992: 19–69.
240 Lefkowitz 1976: 419.
241 Perkins 1994a: 843.
242 See Dronke 1984: 5–6.
243 Cf. Castelli 1991: 36–7; Salisbury 1997: 100.
244 Artemidorus, *Oneirocritica* 1.35; 4.55.
245 Castelli 1991: 40.
246 A curious silence about Perpetua's husband has spawned a wide array of
scholarly speculations and explanations. For a convenient summary of those
conjectures and arguments, see Dronke 1984: 282–3, no. 3; Salisbury
1997: 8. Cf. Osiek (2002: 287–90), who argues that Perpetua's husband
and the father of her child is Saturus.
247 *Contra* Shaw 1993: 30–4.
248 Streete 1997: 102.
249 Brown 1989: 429.
250 Brown 1989: 429.

4 CHRISTIAN LOYALTY TO THE EMPIRE

1 E.g. Tertullian, *Apol.* 29.1–4.
2 For this topic, see Klauck 2000, 2003: 288–330.
3 Beaujeu 1955: 73.
4 Fears 1980: 101.
5 This definition is from Hopkins 1978: 205.
6 Nock 1934: 479.
7 Nock 1934: 475.
8 Fears 1980: 102.
9 See Liebeschuetz 1979: 63–5.
10 Millar 1973: 164.
11 Deissmann 1927: 344.
12 *Domitian* 13.4.
13 *Epigrams* 9.93.
14 See Deissmann 1927: 353–4.
15 Fears 1980: 104–5.
16 "Savior of the world," cf. Deissmann 1927: 364.
17 Ehrenberg and Jones 1955: no. 100 A: Θεοῦ Καίσαρος θεοῦ υἱοῦ Σωτῆρος
Ελευθερίου.
18 Fears 1980: 104.
19 Fears 1980: 103.
20 Fears 1980: 106.
21 See S.R.F. Price 1984: 102–8.
22 See S.R.F. Price 1984: 108–14.
23 Thompson 1990: 162.
24 Cf. Fears 1980: 104.
25 Bowersock 1982: 174.
26 See S.R.F. Price 1987: 77–9.

27 Horsely 1997: 11.
28 See Bowersock 1972: 179–206.
29 *Ep.* 10.96.
30 Cf. Millar 1973: 153.
31 On Menander Rhetor, see Russell and Wilson 1981.
32 See Schoedel 1979b: 71–87; Schoedel 1973: 317–19; cf. Grant 1986a: 219–20.
33 Cf. Guerra 1992: 179.
34 *1 Apol.* 2.
35 *Hist. eccl.* 4.26.10.
36 See Schoedel 1979b: 69–90.
37 Grant 1988b: 102.
38 Eusebius, *Laud. Const.* 3.4–6. On the use of the "Christological" terms, see Grant 1988b: 102; cf. Schoedel 1979b: 86.
39 *1 Apol.* 17.
40 For a critique of Justin's dualistic approach from a Christian ethicist's perspective, see Stassen and Gushee 2003: 128–30.
41 *Autol.* 1.11.
42 *Autol.* 1.11.
43 *Oct.* 29.5.
44 *Or.* 4.1.
45 Bowersock 1982: 175.
46 *1 Apol.* 29.
47 *Apol.* 32.2.
48 A significant exception is Tertullian, *Apol.* 28.1.
49 Bowersock 1982: 175.
50 E.g. Justin, *1 Apol.* 68; cf. 12; Athenagoras, *Leg.* 12.2.
51 Justin, *1 Apol.* 2–5; Athenagoras, *Leg.* 1.3–4; Melito, in Eusebius, *Hist. eccl.* 4.26.5.
52 *1 Apol.* 12, 17.
53 Tax: Tatian, *Or.* 4.1; peace: Athenagoras, *Leg.* 37.3; Tertullian, *Apol.* 37.1–8; prayer: Theophilus, *Autol.* 1.11; Athenagoras, *Leg.* 37.3 (1 Tim. 2.2); Tertullian, *Apol.* 30.4; 32.1.
54 *Apol.* 37.4. Subsequent references to this text appear in parenthesis unless it is noted otherwise. Cf. Celsus' complaint that Christians withdraw from assuming public office in Origen, *Cels.* 8.75.
55 Later, during his so-called "Montanist" period, Tertullian changed his attitude toward Christian military service; see *The Crown*; *Flight in Persecution* 13.3. Cf. Origen, *Cels.* 8.68, 73.
56 *Hist. eccl.* 5.5.1–5.
57 *Hist. eccl.* 5.5.1; cf. Dio Cassius, *Roman History* 71.8.
58 *Hist. eccl.* 5.5.4. According to Dio, the Legion seems to have had this name since the time of Augustus.
59 Cf. Origen, *Cels.* 8.68–9, 73.
60 Bainton 1946: 192. From that time on, the references to Christians in the ranks increase with some conflicting views. Tertullian himself became increasingly opposed to Christian presence in the ranks. See no. 55. On this topic of Christian military service, see further Swift 1983. On the evidence for early Christian pacifism, see, for example, Hornus 1980.
61 *1 Apol.* 12.

62 E.g. Tertullian, *Apol.* 30.5; cf. Frend 1965: 285.
63 *Hist. eccl.* 4.26.
64 *Hist. eccl.* 4.26.7; Frend 1984: 240.
65 *Hist. eccl.* 4.26.7.
66 *Hist. eccl.* 4.26.9.
67 *Hist. eccl.* 4.26.10. Cf. Justin, who attaches (what is supposed to be)
    Hadrian's letter at the end of his *First Apology.*
68 For a succinct study of Tertullian's political ethics, see Forrell 1978:
    27–41.
69 *To Scapula* 2.
70 Grant 1988b: 95. See Cicero, *Nat. d.* 2.8:

> If we care to compare our characteristics with those of foreign
> peoples [*externis*], we shall find that, while in all other respects
> we are only the equals or even the inferiors of others, yet in the
> sense of religion [*religio*], that is in worship of the gods [*cultus
> deorum*], we are far superior.

71 The phrase, "Manifest Destiny" is from Fears 1980: 99.
72 This point is echoed in Minucius Felix, *Oct.* 25.1–7.
73 Cf. *Oct.* 25.12.
74 Cf. Grant 1988b: 95.
75 Justin, *1 Apol.* 32.3–4; *Dial.* 110.6
76 Justin, *Dial.* 46; 92.2.
77 Justin, *1 Apol.* 55.6.
78 Nock 1934: 479.
79 Chadwick 1965: 287.
80 Cf. Tertullian, *Apol.* 24.6, 9; 28.1.
81 Cf. Perkins 1992a: 446.
82 A notable exception is the *Acts of John*, where the apostle faces a natural
    death and a political confrontation is largely missing.
83 Cf. Bremmer 1996a: 50–1.
84 For more detailed accounts of the martyrdom of Peter and Paul, see the
    section, "Christian threat and challenge to the Empire," pp. 176–9.
85 See Stoops 1986: 91–100; Stoops 1992: 143–57; cf. Perkins 1994b:
    300–1, 304.
86 Stoops 1986: 92; Stoops 1992: 146.
87 Stoops 1992: 151–4.
88 Stoops 1992: 149.
89 *Contra* Brock 1999: 145–69, especially 147–52, where she characterizes
    the attitudes of the *Acts of Paul* to political authority as antipathy but
    those of the *Acts of Peter* as accommodation.
90 S.R.F. Price 1984: especially 191–206, 238–44.
91 *Life of Apollonius*, 1.15.
92 Perkins 1994b: 298.
93 Perkins 1994b: 298; cf. *Mart. Perp.* 7.9.
94 Perkins 1994b: 298.
95 Cf. Bolyki 1996: 92; Meeks 1993: 167–9.
96 Bolyki 1996: 101.
97 Tajra 1994: 121.
98 Frend 1965: 285.

99 Barton 1994: 59.
100 *Simplex est religio nostra, et iuramus per genium domni nostri imperatoris et pro salute eius supplicamus.*
101 Cf. *Mart. Carp.* 4; *Acts Just.* B.2.1.
102 *Mart. Pol.* 10.2.
103 *Mart. Pol.* 8.2.
104 *Acts Scill.* 6.
105 *Acts Scill.* 9.
106 *Mart. Apol.* 37.
107 *Mart. Apol.* 6.
108 *Mart. Apol.* 6.
109 *Mart. Carp.* 21.
110 *Mart. Pol.* 9.3.
111 *Mart. Pol.* 21.
112 *Acts Scill.* 6. *Ego imperium huius seculi non cognosco . . . cognosco domnum meum, imperatorem regum et omnium gentium.*
113 *Mart. Potam.* 5.
114 Cf. *Martyrdom of Paul.*
115 *Mart. Apol.* 8.
116 *Mart. Apol.* 9.
117 *Mart. Apol.* 24.
118 D. Potter 1993: 54.
119 D. Potter 1993: 54.
120 See Coleman 1990: 44–73.
121 D. Potter 1993: 65.
122 D. Potter 1993: 53.
123 This reference and following ones in parentheses come from the *Mart. Pol.*
124 This reference and subsequent ones in parentheses come from the *Acts Scill.*
125 See B.D. Shaw 1996: 269–312, especially 291–312.
126 Cf. *Mart. Lyons* 1.34; *Mart. Pol.* 12.1; *Mart. Perp.* 6.6.
127 *Acts Scill.* 17; cf. *Mart. Carp.* 4.1 (Latin); *Mart. Ptol.* 19; *Acts Just.* A.6; B.6; *Mart. Apol.* 46.
128 Coleman 1990: 51.
129 Cf. Coleman 1990: 49.
130 *Mart. Perp.* 18.5.
131 *Mart. Apol.* 27; cf. martyrs' voluntarism in Barton 1994: 56–7.
132 *Mart. Ptol.* 19.
133 See Tertullian, *Apol.*1.10–13; cf. Shaw 1996: 302.
134 *Mart. Perp.* 18.2; *Mart. Pol.* 12.1; *Mart. Lyons* 1.34, 55, 63.
135 *Mart. Perp.* 18.2, 7.
136 *Mart. Perp.* 18.9; *Mart. Lyons* 1.38, 55.
137 *Mart. Carp.* 38–9 (Greek); 4.3 (Latin); *Acts Just.* A.6; B.6; *Mart. Lyons* 1.55–6; *Mart. Pol.* 3.1 (Germanicus); *Mart. Perp.* 21.9 (Perpetua); cf. *Mart. Apol.* 29–30.
138 B.D. Shaw 1996: 302.
139 *Mart. Pol.* 11.2; cf. *Mart. Lyons* 1.26: "eternal punishment in Gehenna."
140 *Mart. Carp.* 4.4 (Latin).
141 *Mart. Carp.* 4.5 (Latin).

142 *Mart. Perp.* 18.8; cf. 17.1.
143 *Mart. Apol.* 25.
144 *Mart. Pol.* 17.3.
145 Kelly 1995: 22.
146 D. Potter 1993: 72.

CONCLUSION

1 Cf. The title of MacMullen (1986), "What Difference Did Christianity Make?"
2 Meeks 1993: 33.
3 Meeks 1993: 36, 33.
4 Frend 1965: 247.
5 Cf. Niebuhr 1951.
6 Osborn 2000: 525.
7 Cf. Markus 1990: 87–95.
8 Cf. Markus 1990: 70–2; Malone 1950.

BIBLIOGRAPHY

Achtemeier, P.J. (1976) "Jesus and the Disciples as Miracle Workers in the
Apocryphal New Testament," in E. Schüssler Fiorenza (ed.) *Aspects of Religious
Propaganda in Judaism and Early Christianity*, Notre Dame, IN and London:
University of Notre Dame Press, pp. 149–86.

Alcinous (1993) *Alcinous: The Handbook of Platonism*, trans. with an introduction and commentary J.M. Dillon, Oxford: Clarendon Press.

Alexander, L. (1998) "'Better to Marry than to Burn': St. Paul and the Greek
Novel," in R.F. Hock, C.J. Bradley, and J. Perkins (eds) *Ancient Fiction and
Early Christian Narrative*, SBL Symposium Series 6, Atlanta, GA: Scholars
Press, pp. 235–56.

Allert, C.D. (2002) *Revelation, Truth, Canon and Interpretation: Studies in Justin
Martyr's Dialogue with Trypho*, Leiden-Boston-Köln: Brill.

Anderson, G. (1984) *Ancient Fiction: The Novel in the Greco-Roman World*,
London: Croom Helm.

Andresen, C. (1952) "Justin und der mittlere Platonismus," *ZNTW* 44:
157–95.

—— (1955) *Logos und Nomos: Die Polemik des Kelsos wider das Christientum*,
Arbeiten zur Kirchengeschichte 30, Berlin: Walter de Gruyter.

—— (1984) "The Integration of Platonism into Early Christian Theology,"
StPatr 15.1: 399–413.

Arbesmann, R., Daly, E.J., and Quain, E.A. (trans.) (1950) *Tertullian: Apolo-
getical Works and Minucius Felix: Octavius*, The Fathers of the Church 10, New
York: Fathers of the Church.

Armstrong, A.H. (1980) "The Self-Definition of Christianity in Relation to
Later Platonism," in B.F. Meyer and E.P. Sanders (eds) *Jewish and Christian
Self-Definition*, vol. 1: *The Shaping of Christianity in the Second and Third
Centuries*, Philadelphia, PA: Fortress, pp. 74–99.

—— (1984a) "Greek Philosophy and Christianity," in M.I. Finley (ed.)
The Legacy of Greece: A New Appraisal, Oxford: Oxford University Press,
pp. 347–67.

—— (1984b) "Pagan and Christian Traditionalism in the First Three
Centuries AD," *StPatr* 15.1: 414–31.

—— and Markus, R.A. (1960) *Christian Faith and Greek Philosophy*, London: Darton, Longman & Todd.

Artemidorus (1975) *Oneirocritica/The Interpretation of Dreams*, trans. R.J. White, Noyes Classical Studies, Park Ridge, NJ: Noyes Press.

Aspegren, K. (1990) *The Male Woman: A Feminine Ideal in the Early Church*, Uppsala: Acta Universitatis Upsaliensis.

Athenagoras (1972) *Legatio and De Resurrectione*, ed. and trans. W.R. Schoedel, OECT 2, Oxford: Clarendon Press.

Attridge, H.W. (1978) "The Philosophical Critique of Religion Under the Early Empire," *ANRW* II.16.1: 45–78.

—— (1991) "'Masculine Fellowship' in the Acts of Thomas," in B.A. Pearson (ed.) *The Future of Early Christianity*, Minneapolis, MN: Fortress Press, pp. 406–13.

Aune, D.E. (1981) "Magic in Early Christianity," *ANRW* II.23.2: 1507–57.

—— (1988) "Greco-Roman Biography," in D.E. Aune (ed.) *Greco-Roman Literature and the New Testament*, SBL Sources for Biblical Study 21, Atlanta, GA: Scholars Press, pp. 107–26.

—— (1992) "Romans as a *Logos Protreptikos* in the Context of Ancient Religious and Philosophical Propaganda," in M. Hengel and U. Heckel (eds) *Paulus und das antike Judentum*, Tübingen: J.C.B. Mohr (Paul Siebeck), pp. 91–121.

—— (1994) "Mastery of the Passions: Philo, 4 Maccabees and Earliest Christianity," in W.E. Helleman (ed.) *Hellenization Revisited: Shaping a Christian Response within the Greco-Roman World*, Lanham, MD: University Press of America, pp. 125–58.

Aurelius, M. (1916) *The Communings with Himself of Marcus Aurelius Antoninus, Emperor of Rome, Together with Speeches and Sayings*, rev. and trans. C.R. Haines, LCL, Cambridge, MA: Harvard University Press.

Baer, R.A., Jr (1970) *Philo's Use of the Categories of Male and Female*, Arbeiten zur Literatur und Geschichte des hellenistischen Judentums 3, Leiden: Brill.

Bailey, D.S. (1959) *Sexual Relation in Christian Thought*, New York: Harper & Brothers.

Bainton, R.H. (1946) "The Early Church and War," *HTR* 39: 189–212; rpt in E. Ferguson (ed.) (1993) *Studies in Early Christianity: A Collection of Scholarly Essays*, vol. 16: *Christian Life: Ethics, Morality, and Discipline in the Early Church*, New York and London: Garland, pp. 193–216.

Balch, D.L. (1972) "Backgrounds of 1 Cor. 7: Sayings of the Lord in Q; Moses as an Ascetic *Theios Aner* in 2 Cor. 3," *NTS* 18: 351–64.

—— (1983) "1 Cor. 7.32–35 and Stoic Debate about Marriage, Anxiety, and Distractions," *JBL* 102/3: 429–39.

Barclay, W. (1937–8) "Church and State in the Apologists," *Expository Times* 49: 360–2.

Barnard, L.W. (1967) *Justin Martyr: His Life and Thought*, Cambridge: Cambridge University Press.

—— (1968) "The Heresy of Tatian – Once Again," *JEH* (1968): 1–10.

—— (1972) *Athenagoras: A Study in Second Century Christian Apologetic*, Theologie Historique 18, Paris: Beauchesne.

Barnes, T.D. (1968a) "Legislation against the Christians," *JRS* 58: 32–50.

—— (1968b) "Pre-Decian *Acta Martyrum*," *JTS* 19: 509–31.

—— (1971) *Tertullian: A Historical and Literary Study*, Oxford: Clarendon Press.

—— (1975) "The Embassy of Athenagoras," *JTS* 26: 111–14.

Bartchy, S.S. (1973) *Mallon Chresai: First-Century Slavery and the Interpretation of 1 Corinthians 7:21*, SBL Dissertation Series 11, Atlanta, GA: Scholars Press.

—— (1987) "Issues of Power and a Theology of the Family: Part I," *Mission Journal* 21/1: 3–15, 32; (1987) "Part II," *Mission Journal* 21/2: 3–11; (1987) "Part III," *Mission Journal* 21/3: 9–11, 18.

—— (1998) "Families in the Greco-Roman World," in H. Anderson, D. Browning, I.S. Evison, and M.S. Van Leeuwen (eds) *The Family Handbook*, Louisville, KY: Westminster John Knox Press, pp. 282–6.

—— (1999) "Undermining Ancient Patriarchy: The Apostle Paul's Vision of a Society of Siblings," *Biblical Theology Bulletin* 29/2: 68–78.

Barton, C.A. (1989) "The Scandal of the Arena," *Representations* 27: 1–36.

—— (1994) "Savage Miracles: The Redemption of Lost Honor in Roman Society and the Sacrament of the Gladiator and the Martyr," *Representations* 45: 41–71.

Bauckham, R. (1993) "The Acts of Paul as a Sequel to Acts," in B.C. Winter and A.D. Clarke (eds) *The Book of Acts in Its First Century Setting*, vol. 1: *The Book of Acts in Its Ancient Literary Setting*, Grand Rapids, MI: Eerdmans, pp. 105–52.

—— (1997) "The *Acts of Paul*: Replacement of Acts or Sequel to Acts," *Semeia* 80: 159–68.

—— (2000) "Imaginative Literature," in P. Esler (ed.) *The Early Christian World*, vol. 2, London and New York: Routledge, pp. 791–812.

Bauer, W. (1934) *Rechtgläubigkeit und Ketzerei im ältesten Christentum*, Beiträge zur historischen Theologie 10, Tübingen: J.C.B. Mohr (Paul Siebeck); trans. R.A. Kraft and G. Krodel (eds) (1972) *Orthodoxy and Heresy in Earliest Christianity*, London: SCM Press.

Baus, K. (1980) *History of the Church* (H. Jedin and H. Dolan, eds), vol. 1: *From the Apostolic Community to Constantine*, New York: The Seabury Press.

Beaujeu, J. (1955) *La religion romaine à l'apogée de l'empire*, Paris: Belles Lettres.

Behr, J. (1993) "Shifting Sands: Foucault, Brown and the Framework of Christian Asceticism," *Heythrop Journal* 34: 1–21.

—— (2000) *Asceticism and Anthropology in Irenaeus and Clement*, Oxford and New York: Oxford University Press.

Benko, S. (1980) "Pagan Criticism of Christianity during the First Two Centuries AD," *ANRW* II.23.2: 1055–118.

—— (1984) *Pagan Rome and the Early Christians*, Bloomington, IN: Indiana University Press.

Bisbee, G.A. (1988) *Pre-Decian Acts of Martyrs and Commentarii*, Harvard Dissertations in Religion 22, Philadelphia, PA: Fortress.

Bolyki, J. (1996) "Events after the Martyrdom: Missionary Transformation of an Apocalyptic Metaphor in Martyrium Pauli," in J.N. Bremmer (ed.) *The Apocryphal Acts of Paul and Thecla*, Studies on the Apocryphal Acts of the Apostles 2, Kampen: Kok Pharos, pp. 92–106.

—— (1998) "'Head Downwards': The Cross of Peter in the Light of the Apocryphal Acts, of the New Testament and of the Society-transforming Claim of Early Christianity," in J.N. Bremmer (ed.) *The Apocryphal Acts of Peter: Magic, Miracles and Gnosticism*, Studies on the Apocryphal Acts of the Apostles 3, Leuven: Peeters, pp. 111–22.

Boughton, L.C. (1991) "From Pious Legend to Feminist Fantasy: Distinguishing Hagiographical License from Apostolic Practice in the Acts of Paul/Acts of Thecla," *Journal of Religion* 71/3: 362–83.

Bovon, F. (1988) "The Synoptic Gospels and the Noncanonical Acts of the Apostles," *HTR* 81: 19–36.

—— (1994) "The Words of Life in the Acts of the Apostle Andrew," *HTR* 87: 139–54.

—— (1995a) "The Life of the Apostles: Biblical Traditions and Apocryphal Narratives," in F. Bovon (ed.) *New Testament Traditions and Apocryphal Narratives*, Allison Park, PA: Pickwick, pp. 159–75.

—— (1995b) "Miracles, magie et guérison dans tes Actes apocryphes des apôtres," *JECS* 3/3: 245–59.

—— (2003) "Canonical and Apocryphal Acts of Apostles," *JECS* 11/2: 165–94.

—— and Junod, E. (1986) "Reading the Apocryphal Acts of the Apostles," *Semeia* 38: 163–71.

—— , Brock, A.G., and Matthews, C.R. (eds) (1999) *The Apocryphal Acts of the Apostles*, Harvard Divinity School Studies, Cambridge, MA: Harvard University Press.

Bowersock, G.W. (1972) "Greek Intellectuals and the Imperial Cult," in W. den Boer (ed.) *Le culte des souverains dans l'empire romain*, Geneva: Fondation Hardt, pp. 179–206.

—— (1982) "Imperial Cult: Perceptions and Persistence," in B.F. Meyer and E.P. Sanders (eds) *Jewish and Christian Self-Definition*, vol. 3: *Self-Definition in the Greco-Roman World*, Philadelphia, PA: Fortress, pp. 171–82.

—— (1994) *Fiction as History*, Berkeley, CA: University of California Press.

—— (1995) *Martyrdom and Rome*, Cambridge: Cambridge University Press.

Bowie, E.L. (1985) "The Greek Novel," in P.E. Easterling and B.M.W. Knox (eds) *The Cambridge History of Classical Literature*, Cambridge: Cambridge University Press, pp. 683–99.

—— (1994) "The Readership of Greek Novels in the Ancient World," in J. Tatum (ed.) *The Search for the Ancient Novel*, Baltimore, MD: Johns Hopkins University Press, pp. 435–59.

Boyarin, D. (1998) "Martyrdom and the Making of Christianity and Judaism," *JECS* 6/4: 577–627.

—— (1999) *Dying for God: Martyrdom and the Making of Judaism and Christianity*, Stanford, CA: Stanford University Press.

Bradley, D.J.M. (1974) "The Transformation of the Stoic Ethic in Clement of Alexandria," *Augustinianum* 14: 41–66; rpt in E. Ferguson (ed.) (1993) *Studies in Early Christianity: A Collection of Scholarly Essays*, vol. 16: *Christian Life: Ethics, Morality, and Discipline in the Early Church*, New York and London: Garland, pp. 43–68.

Braun, M. (1938) *History and Romance in Graeco-Oriental Literature*, Oxford: Blackwell.

Braun, W. (2000) "Physiotherapy of Femininity in the Acts of Thecla," in S.G. Wilson and M. Desjardins (eds) *Text and Artifact in the Religions of Mediterranean Antiquity: Essays in Honor of Peter Richardson*, Studies in Christianity and Judaism 9, Waterloo, Ontario: Wilfrid Laurier University Press, pp. 209–30.

—— (2002) "Body, Character and the Problem of Femaleness in Early Christian Discourse," *Religion & Theology* 9/1–2: 108–17.

Bremmer, J.N. (1989) "Why Did Early Christianity Attract Upper Class Women?," in A. Bastiaensen, A. Hilhorst, and C.H. Kneepkens (eds) *Fructus Centesimus*, Mél. G. Bartelink, Instrumenta Patristica 19, Dordrecht: Kluwer, pp. 37–48.

—— (1991) " 'Christianus Sum': The Early Christian Martyrs and Christ," in G.J.M. Bartelink, A. Hilhorst, and C.H. Kneepkens (eds) *Eulogia*, Instrumenta Patristica 24, Hague: Nijhoff International, pp. 11–20.

—— (ed.) (1995) *The Apocryphal Acts of John*, Studies on the Apocryphal Acts of the Apostles 1, Kampen: Kok Pharos.

—— (1996a) "Magic, Martyrdom and Women's Liberation in the Acts of Paul and Thecla," in J.N. Bremmer (ed.) *The Apocryphal Acts of Paul and Thecla*, Studies on the Apocryphal Acts of the Apostles 2, Kampen: Kok Pharos, pp. 37–59.

—— (ed.) (1996b) *The Apocryphal Acts of Paul and Thecla*, Studies on the Apocryphal Acts of the Apostles 2, Kampen: Kok Pharos.

—— (ed.) (1998) *The Apocryphal Acts of Peter: Magic, Miracles and Gnosticism*, Studies on the Apocryphal Acts of the Apostles 3, Leuven: Peeters.

—— (ed.) (2000) *The Apocryphal Acts of Andrew*, Studies on the Apocryphal Acts of the Apostles 5, Leuven: Peeters.

—— (2001a) "The Apocryphal Acts: Authors, Place, Time and Readership, in J.N. Bremmer (ed.) *The Apocryphal Acts of Thomas*, Studies on the Apocryphal Acts of the Apostles 6, Leuven: Peeters, pp. 149–70.

—— (ed.) (2001b) *The Apocryphal Acts of Thomas*, Studies on the Apocryphal Acts of the Apostles 6, Leuven: Peeters.

Brock, A.G. (1994) "Genre of the *Acts of Paul*: One Tradition Enhancing Another," *Apocrypha* 5: 119–36.

—— (1999) "Political Authority and Cultural Accommodation: Social Diversity in the *Acts of Paul* and the *Acts of Peter*," in F. Bovon, A.G. Brock, and C.R. Matthews (eds) *The Apocryphal Acts of the Apostles*, Harvard Divinity School Studies, Cambridge, MA: Harvard University Press, pp. 145–69.

Brock, S.P. (1973) "Early Syrian Asceticism," *Numen* 20: 1–19.

Brodin, K.L. (2000) "Athletic Exemplars in the New Testament and Early Christian Martyrological Literature," unpublished dissertation, Fuller Theological Seminary, Pasadena, CA.

Brooten, B.J. (1985) "Early Christian Women and Their Cultural Context: Issues of Method in Historical Reconstruction," in A.Y. Collins (ed.) *Feminist Perspectives on Biblical Scholarship*, Chico, CA: Scholars Press, pp. 65–91.

Brown, P. (1988) *The Body and Society: Men, Women and Sexual Renunciation in Early Christianity*, New York: Columbia University Press.

—— (1989) "The Notion of Virginity in the Early Church," in B. McGinn, J. Meyendorff, and J. Leclerq (eds) *Christian Spirituality: Origins to the Twelfth Century*, London: SCM, pp. 427–44.

—— (1990) "Bodies and Minds: Sexuality and Renunciation in Early Christianity," in D.M. Halpern, J.J. Winkler, and F.I. Zeitlin (eds) *Before Sexuality: The Construction of Erotic Experience in the Ancient World*, Princeton, NJ: Princeton University Press, pp. 479–93.

Brunt, P.A. (1975) "Stoicism and the Principate," *Papers of the British School at Rome* 43/30: 7–35.

—— (1979) "Marcus Aurelius and the Christians," in C. Deroux (ed.) *Studies in Latin Literature and Roman History*, Brussels: Collection *Latomus* no. 164.1, pp. 483–520.

Buck, P.L. (1996) "Athenagoras's Embassy: A Literary Fiction," *HTR* 89/3: 209–26.

—— (2002) "The Pagan Husband in Justin, *2 Apology* 2:1–20," *JTS* 53/2: 541–6.

Burrows, M.S. (1988) "Christianity in the Roman Forum: Tertullian and the Apologetic Use of History," *VC* 42: 209–35.

Burrus, V. (1986) "Chastity as Autonomy: Women in the Stories of the Apocryphal Acts," *Semeia* 38: 101–17.

—— (1987) *Chastity as Autonomy: Women in the Apocryphal Acts*, Studies in Women and Religion 23, Lewiston, NY: Edwin Mellen Press.

Bynum, C.W. (1995) *The Resurrection of the Body in Western Christianity, 200–1336*, Lectures on the History of Religions, New Series 15, New York: Columbia University Press.

Cameron, A. (1986) "Redrawing the Map: Early Christian Territory after Foucault," *JRS* 76: 266–71.

—— (1989) "Virginity as Metaphor: Women and Rhetoric of Early Christianity," in A. Cameron (ed.) *History as Text: The Writing of Ancient History*, London: Duckworth, pp. 181–205.

—— (1991) *Christianity and the Rhetoric of the Empire*, Berkeley, CA: University of California Press.

—— (1996) "Neither Male Nor Female," in I. McAuslan and P. Walcot (eds) *Women in Antiquity*, Oxford: Oxford University Press, pp. 26–35.

Cardman, F. (1988) "Acts of the Women Martyrs," *ATR* 70: 144–50; rpt in D.M. Scholer (ed.) (1993) *Studies in Early Christianity: A Collection of Scholarly Essays*, vol. 14: *Women in Early Christianity*, New York and London: Garland, pp. 98–104.

Cartledge, D.R. (1986) "Transfigurations of Metamorphosis Traditions in the Acts of John, Thomas and Peter," *Semeia* 38: 53–66.

Casey, R.P. (1925) "Clement of Alexandria and the Beginnings of Christian Platonism," *HTR* 18: 39–101; rpt in E. Ferguson with D.M. Scholer and P.C. Finney (eds) (1993) *Studies in Early Christianity: A Collection of Scholarly Essays*, vol. 8: *The Early Church and Greco-Roman Thought*, New York and London: Garland, pp. 83–145.

Cassius Dio (1914–27) *Dio's Roman History*, trans. E. Cary, 9 vols, LCL, London: Heinemann; New York: Macmillan.

Castelli, E. (1986) "Virginity and Its Meaning for Women's Sexuality in Early Christianity," *JFSR* 2: 61–88.

—— (1991) "'I Will Make Mary Male': Pieties of the Body and Gender Transformation of Christian Women in Late Antiquity," in J. Epstein and K. Straub (eds) *Body Guards: The Cultural Politics of Gender Ambiguity*, London and New York: Routledge, pp. 29–49.

Celsus (1987) *On the True Doctrine: A Discourse against the Christians*, trans. with an introduction R.J. Hoffmann, Oxford and New York: Oxford University Press.

Chadwick, H. (1947) "Origen, Celsus, and the Stoa," *JTS* 48: 34–49.

—— (1948) "Origen, Celsus, and the Resurrection of the Body," *HTR* 41: 83–102.

—— (trans.) (1953) *Contra Celsum*, Cambridge: Cambridge University Press.

—— (1965) "Justin Martyr's Defence of Christianity," *BJRL* 47: 275–97; rpt in E. Ferguson with D.M. Scholer and P.C. Finney (eds) *Studies in Early Christianity: A Collection of Scholarly Essays*, vol. 8: *The Early Church and Greco-Roman Thought*, New York and London: Garland, pp. 23–45.

—— (1966) *Early Christian Thought and the Classical Tradition*, Oxford: Oxford University Press.

Cicero, Markus Tullius (1933) *De natura deorum/Academia*, trans. H. Rackham, LCL, Cambridge, MA: Harvard University Press.

Clark, E.A. (ed.) (1983) *Women in the Early Church*, Message of the Fathers of the Church 13, Wilmington, DE: Michael Glazier.

—— (1995a) "Antifamilial Tendencies in Ancient Christianity," *Journal of the History of Sexuality* [Chicago] 5/3: 356–80.

—— (1995b) "The Ascetic Impulse in Religious Life: A General Response," in V.L. Wimbush and R. Valantasis (eds) *Asceticism*, Oxford and New York: Oxford University Press, pp. 505–10.

—— (1995c) "A Response," in E. Castelli (ed.) *Visions and Voyeurism: Holy Women and the Politics of Sight in Early Christianity*, Protocol of the Colloquy of the Center for Hermeneutical Studies, New Series 2, Berkeley, CA: Center for Hermeneutical Studies, pp. 28–34.

Clark, G. (1998) "The Old Adam: The Fathers and the Unmaking of Masculinity," in L. Foxhall and J. Salmon (eds) *Thinking Men: Masculinity and Its Self-Representation in the Classical Tradition*, London and New York: Routledge, pp. 170–82.

Clarke, G.W. (1964–5) "The Literary Setting of the Octavius of Minucius Felix," *JRH* 3: 195–211; (1966–7), 4: 267–86; rpt in E. Ferguson (ed.) (1993) *Studies in Early Christianity: A Collection of Scholarly Essays*, vol. 2: *Literature of the Early Church*, New York and London: Garland, pp. 127–43.

—— (1967a) "The Date of the Oration of Tatian," *HTR* 60: 122–6.

—— (1967b) "The Historical Setting of the Octavius of Minucius Felix," *JRH* 4: 267–86; rpt in E. Ferguson (ed.) (1993) *Studies in Early Christianity: A Collection of Scholarly Essays*, vol. 2: *Literature of the Early Church*, New York and London: Garland, pp. 145–64.

Clement of Alexandria (1919) *Exhortation to the Greeks*, trans. G.W. Butterworth, LCL, Cambridge, MA: Harvard University Press.

—— (1954) *Stromata III and VII*, in J.E.L. Oulton and H. Chadwick (eds) *Alexandrian Christianity*, trans. H. Chadwick, Library of Christian Classics, vol. 2, London: SCM.

—— (1991) *Stromateis: Books 1–3*, trans. J. Ferguson, The Fathers of the Church 85, Washington DC: Catholic University of America Press.

—— (1995) *Clementis Alexandrini Protrepticus*, ed. M. Marcovich, Supplements to Vigiliae Christianae 34, Leiden and New York: E.J. Brill.

—— (1999) *Les Stromates: Stromate VI*, ed. and trans. P. Descourtieux with an introduction and notes, Sources Chrétiennes 446, Paris: Éditions du Cerf.

Cloke, G. (1996) "*Mater* or Martyr: Christianity and the Alienation of Women within the Family in the Later Roman Empire," *Theology and Sexuality* 5: 37–57.

—— (2000) "Women, Worship and Mission," in P. Esler (ed.) *The Early Christian World*, vol. 2, London and New York: Routledge, pp. 422–51.

Coleman, K.M. (1990) "Fatal Charades: Roman Executions Staged as Mythological Enactments," *JRS* 80: 44–73.

Contreras, C.A. (1980) "Christian Views of Paganism," *ANRW* II.23.2: 974–1022.

Cooper, K. (1996) *The Virgin and the Bride: Idealized Womanhood in Late Antiquity*, Cambridge, MA: Harvard University Press.

—— (1998) "The Voice of the Victim: Gender, Representation and Early Christian Martyrdom," *BJRL* 80: 147–57.

Corrington, G.P. (1986) *The "Divine Man": His Origin and Function in Hellenistic Popular Religion*, New York and Frankfurt: Peter Lang.

—— (1988) "The 'Divine Woman'? Propaganda and the Power of Celibacy in the New Testament Apocrypha: A Reconsideration," *ATR* 70: 207–20; rpt in D.M. Scholer (ed.) (1993) *Studies in Early Christianity: A Collection of Scholarly Essays*, vol. 14: *Women in Early Christianity*, New York and London: Garland, pp. 169–82.

Cox, P. (1983) *Biography in Late Antiquity: A Quest for Holy Man*, Berkeley, CA: University of California Press.

Daly, R.J. (1978) *Christian Sacrifice: The Judaeo-Christian Background before Origen*, Washington, DC: Catholic University of America Press.

Daniélou, J. (1973) *A History of Early Christian Doctrine before the Council of Nicaea*, vol. 2: *Gospel Message and Hellenistic Culture*; trans. J.A. Baker, London: Darton, Longman & Todd/Philadephia, PA: The Westminster Press.

Davies, E.L. (1984) "Ascetic Madness," in R.C. Smith and J. Lounibos (eds) *Pagan and Christian Anxiety: A Response to E. R. Dodds*, Lanham, MD, New York and London: University Press of America, pp. 13–26.

Davies, J. (1999) *Death, Burial and the Rebirth in the Religions of Antiquity*, London and New York: Routledge.

Davies, S.L. (1980) *The Revolt of the Widows: Social World of the Apocryphal Acts*, Urbana, IL: Southern Illinois University Press.

Davis, J.G. (1972) "Factors Leading to the Emergence of Belief in the Resurrection of the Flesh," *JTS* 23: 448–55.

Davis, S.J. (2000) "A 'Pauline' Defense of Women's Right to Baptize? Intertextuality and Apostolic Authority in the Acts of Paul," *JECS* 8/3: 453–9.

Dehandschutter, B. (1990) "A 'New' Text of the Martyrdom of Polycarp," *ETL* 66: 391–4.

—— (1993) "*The Martyrium Polycarpi*: A Century of Research," *ANRW* II.27.1: 485–522.

—— (1999a) "Example and Discipleship: Some Comments on the Biblical Background of the Early Christian Theology of Martyrdom," in J. den Boeft and M.L. van Poll-van de Lisdonk (eds) *The Impact of Scripture in Early Christianity*, Leiden, *et al.*: E.J. Brill, pp. 20–6.

—— (1999b) "The *Martyrdom of Polycarp* and the Outbreak of Montanism," *ETL* 75/4: 430–7.

Deissmann, A. (1927) *Light from the Ancient East*, New York: Harper & Brothers.

de Jonge, M. (1991) "Jesus' Death for others and the Death of the Maccabean Martyrs," in M. de Jonge (ed.) *Jewish Eschatology, Early Christian Christology and the Testaments of the Twelve Patriarchs: Collected Essays of M. de Jonge*, Leiden: E.J. Brill, pp. 135–51.

Delehaye, H. (1962) *The Legends of the Saints*, trans. D. Attwater, New York: Fordham University Press.

Deming, W. (1995) *Paul on Marriage and Celibacy: The Hellenistic Background of 1 Corinthians 7*, Society for New Testament Studies Monograph Series 83, Cambridge: Cambridge University Press.

den Boeft, J. and Bremmer, J. (1981) "Notiunculae Martyrologicae," *VC* 35: 43–56.

—— and —— (1982) "Notiunculae Martyrologicae II," *VC* 36: 383–402.

—— and —— (1985) "Notiunculae Martyrologicae III," *VC* 39: 110–30.

—— and —— (1991) "Notiunculae Martyrologicae IV," *VC* 45: 105–22.

deSilva, D.A. (1998) *4 Maccabees*, Sheffield: Sheffield Academic Press.

des Places, É. (1977) *Atticus: Fragments*, Collection des Universités de France (Budé), Paris: Société d'Édition "Les Belles Lettres."

—— (1984) "Platonisme moyen et apologétique chrétienne an IIe siècle ap. J.-C. Numénius, Atticus, Justin," *StPatr* 15.1: 432–41.

Desprez, V. (1991) "Christian Asceticism between the New Testament and the Beginning of Monasticism: The Second Century," *American Benedictine Review* 42/2: 163–78.

de Ste Croix, G.E.M. (1963) "Why Were the Early Christians Persecuted?," *Past and Present* 26: 6–38.

—— (1964) "Why Were the Early Christians Persecuted? – A Rejoinder," *Past and Present* 27: 28–33.

de Vos, C. (2000) "Popular Greco-Roman Responses to Christianity," in P. Esler (ed.) *The Early Christian World*, vol. 2, London and New York: Routledge, pp. 869–89.

Dihle, A. (1994) *Greek and Latin Literature of the Roman Empire: From Augustus to Justinian*, London and New York: Routledge.

Dillon, J.M. (1977) *The Middle Platonists: 80 BC to AD 220*, Ithaca, NY: Cornell University Press.

Dixon, S. (1992) *The Roman Family*, Baltimore, MD, and London: Johns Hopkins University Press.

Downing, J. (1963) "Jesus and Martyrdom," *JTS* 14: 279–93.

Drijvers, H.J.W. (1982) "Facts and Problems in Early Syriac-Speaking Christianity," *SecCent* 2: 157–75; rpt in H.J.W. Drijvers (1984) *East of Antioch: Studies in Early Syriac Christianity*, London: Variorum.

—— (1984) *East of Antioch: Studies in Early Syriac Christianity*, London: Variorum.

—— (1991; rev. edn 1992) "The Acts of Thomas: Introduction," in W. Schneemelcher (ed.) and R.McL. Wilson (trans.) *New Testament Apocrypha*, vol. 2: *Writings Relating to Apostles, Apocalypses and Related Subjects*, Louisville, KY: Westminster/John Knox, pp. 322–39.

Droge, A.J. (1987) "Justin Martyr and the Restoration of Philosophy," *Church History* 56: 303–19; rpt in E. Ferguson with D.M. Scholer and P.C. Finney (eds) (1993) *Studies in Early Christianity: A Collection of Scholarly Essays*, vol. 8: *The Early Church and Greco-Roman Thought*, New York and London: Garland, pp. 65–81.

—— (1989) *Homer or Moses? Early Christian Interpretation of the History of Culture*, Hermeneutische Untersuchungen zur Theologie 26, Tübingen: J.C.B. Mohr (Paul Siebeck).

—— and Tabor, J.D. (1992) *A Noble Death: Suicide and Martyrdom among Christians and Jews in Antiquity*, San Francisco, CA: HarperCollins.

Dronke, P. (1984) *Women Writers of the Middle Ages: A Critical Study of Texts from Perpetua to Marguerite Porete*, Cambridge: Cambridge University Press.

Dunn, J.D.G. (1977) *Unity and Diversity in the New Testament: An Inquiry into the Character of Earliest Christianity*, Philadelphia, PA: Westminster.

Dunn, P.W. (1993) "Women's Liberation, the Acts of Paul, and other Apocryphal Acts of the Apostles: A Review of Some Recent Interpreters," *Apocrypha* 4: 245–61.

Edwards, M.J. (1995) "Justin's Logos and the Word of God," *JECS* 3/3: 261–80; rpt in E. Ferguson (ed.) (1999) *Recent Studies in Early Christianity*, vol. 2: *Christianity in Relation to Jews, Greeks, and Romans*, New York and London: Garland, pp. 85–104.

—— Goodman, M., and Price, S.R.F. (eds) (1999) *Apologetics in the Roman Empire: Pagans, Jews, and Christians*, Oxford: Oxford University Press.

Egger, B. (1988) "Zu den Frauenrollen im griechischen Roman: Die Frau als Heldin und Leserin," in H. Hofmann (ed.) *Groningen Colloquia on the Novel I*, Groningen: Egbert Forsten, pp. 33–66.

—— (1994) "Women and Marriage in the Greek Novels: The Boundaries of Romance," in J. Tatum (ed.) *The Search for the Ancient Novel*, Baltimore, MD: Johns Hopkins University Press, pp. 260–80.

Ehrenberg, V. and Jones, A.M. (eds) (1955) *Documents Illustrating the Reigns of Augustus and Tiberius*, Oxford: Clarendon Press.

Ehrhardt, A. (1953) "Justin Martyr's Two Apologies," *JEH* 4: 1–12.

Elliott, A.G. (1987) *Roads to Paradise: Reading the Lives of the Early Saints*, Hanover and London: University Press of New England for Brown University Press.

Elliott, J.K. (1993a) "The Apocryphal Acts," *Expository Times* 105: 71–7.

—— (1993b) *The Apocryphal New Testament*, Oxford: Clarendon Press.

Epictetus (1928) *The Discourses as Reported by Arrian, the Manual and Fragments*, trans. W.A. Oldfather, 2 vols, LCL, Cambridge, MA: Harvard University Press; rpt 1978.

Epiphanius (1987–94) *The Panarion of Epiphanius of Salamis*, trans. F. Williams, 2 vols, Leiden–New York: E.J. Brill.

Esler, P. (ed.) (2000) *The Early Christian World*, 2 vols., London and New York: Routledge.

Eusebius of Caesarea (1926–32) *The Ecclesiastical History*, trans. K. Lake, LCL, Cambridge, MA: Harvard University Press.

—— (1998) *Eusebius' Ecclesiastical History*, trans. C.F. Cruse, new updated edn, Peabody, MA: Hedrickson Publishers.

Farkasfalvy, D. (1992) "Christological Content and Its Biblical Basis in the Letter of the Martyrs of Gaul," *SecCent* 9: 5–25; rpt in E. Ferguson (ed.) (1999) *Recent Studies in Early Christianity*, vol. 2: *Christianity in Relation to Jews, Greeks, and Romans*, New York and London: Garland, pp. 279–99.

Fears, J.R. (1980) "Rome: The Ideology of Imperial Power," *Thought* 55/216: 98–109.

Ferguson, E. (1976) "Voices of Religious Liberty in the Early Church," *ResQ* 19: 13–22.

—— (1981) "Spiritual Sacrifice in Early Christianity and its Environment," *ANRW* II.23.2: 1152–92.

—— (1984) *Demonology of the Early Christian World*, Symposium Series 12, New York and Toronto: Edwin Mellen Press.

—— (1993a) "Early Christian Martyrdom and Civil Disobedience," *JECS* 1/1: 73–83; rpt in E. Ferguson (ed.) (1999) *Recent Studies in Early Christianity*, vol. 2: *Christianity in Relation to Jews, Greeks, and Romans*, New York and London: Garland, pp. 267–77.

—— (1993b) "Women in the Post-Apostolic Church," in C.D. Osburn (ed.) *Essays on Women in Earliest Christianity*, vol. 1, Joplin, MO: College Press, pp. 493–513.

Fiedrowicz, M. (2000) *Apologie im frühen Christentum: Die Kontroverse um den christlichen Wahrheitsanspruch in den ersten Jahrhunderten*, Paderborn and Zürich: Ferdinand Schöningh.

Fischler, S. (1998) "Imperial Cult: Engendering the Cosmos," in L. Foxhall and J. Salmon (eds) *When Men Were Men: Masculinity, Power and Identity in Classical Antiquity*, London: Routledge, pp. 165–83.

Fitzgerald, M.L. (1969) "The Apologists and Evangelization," *Euntes Docete* 22: 481–520.

Forrell, G. (1978) "Christ against Culture: A Re-examination of the Political Ethics of Tertullian," in *1978 Selected Papers of the American Society of Christian Ethics*, Newton Center, MA: American Society of Christian Ethics, pp. 27–41.

Foucault, M. (1985) *The History of Sexuality*, vol. 3: *The Care of the Self*, trans. R. Hurley, New York: Pantheon.

Fowler, F.W. (1911) *The Religious Experience of the Roman People*, London: MacMillan & Co.

Francis, J.A. (1995) *Subversive Virtue: Asceticism and Authority in the Second-Century Pagan World*, University Park, PA: Pennsylvania State University Press.

Frend, W.H.C. (1965) *Martyrdom and Persecution in the Early Church: A Study of Conflict from the Maccabees to Donatus*, Oxford: Blackwell.

—— (1973) "The Old Testament in the Age of the Greek Apologists AD 130–180," *Scottish Journal of Theology* 26: 129–50.

—— (1974) "Open Questions concerning Christians and the Roman Empire in the Age of the Severi," *JTS* 25: 334–43.

—— (1978) "Blandina and Perpetua," in M. LeGlay (ed.) *Les Martyrs de Lyons (177)*, Paris: Centre national de la recherche scientifique, pp. 167–77; rpt in D.M. Scholer (ed.) (1993) *Studies in Early Christianity: A Collection of Scholarly Essays*, vol. 14: *Women in Early Christianity*, New York and London: Garland, pp. 87–97.

—— (1984) *The Rise of Christianity*, Philadelphia, PA: Fortress.

—— (1997) "Christianity in the Second Century: Orthodoxy and Diversity," *JEH* 48/2: 302–13.

Futrell, A. (1997) *Blood in the Arena: The Spectacle of Roman Power*, Austin, TX: University of Texas Press.

Gager, J.G. (1982) "Body-Symbols and Social Reality: Resurrection, Incarnation, and Asceticism in Early Christianity," *Religion* 12: 345–63.

Galinsky, K. (1996) *Augustan Culture: An Interpretive Introduction*, Princeton, NJ: Princeton University Press.

Gallagher, E.V. (1982) *Divine Man or Magician? Celsus and Origen on Jesus*, SBL Dissertation Series 64, Chico, CA: Scholars Press.

—— (1991) "Conversion and Salvation in the Apocryphal Acts of the Apostles," *SecCent* 8: 13–29.

Gamble, H.Y. (1995) *Books and Readers in the Early Church: A History of Early Christian Texts*, New Haven, CT, and London: Yale University Press.

Gardner, J.F. and Wiedermann, T. (1991) *The Roman Household: A Sourcebook*, London and New York: Routledge.

Gasparro, G.S. (1991) "Image of God and Sexual Differentiation in the Tradition of Enkrateia: Protological Motivations," in K.E. Børresen (ed.) *Image of God and Gender Models in Judaeo-Christian Tradition*, Oslo: Solum Forlag, pp. 138–71.

—— (1995) "Asceticism and Anthropology: Enkrateia and 'Double Creation' in Early Christianity," in V.L. Wimbush and R. Valantasis (eds) *Asceticism*, Oxford and New York: Oxford University Press, pp. 127–46.

Georgi, D. (1971) "Forms of Religious Propaganda," in H.J. Schultz (ed.) *Jesus in His Time*, Philadelphia, PA: Fortress, pp. 124–31.

—— (1976) "Socioeconomic Reasons for the 'Divine Man' as a Propagandistic Pattern," in E. Schüssler Fiorenza (ed.) *Aspects of Religious Propaganda in Judaism and Early Christianity*, Notre Dame, IN, and London: University of Notre Dame Press, pp. 27–42.

Germond, P. (1996) "A Rhetoric of Gender in Early Christianity: Sex and Salvation in the *Acts of Thomas*," in S.E. Porter and T.H. Olbricht (eds) *Rhetoric, Scripture and Theology: Essays from the 1994 Pretoria Conference*, Journal for the Study of the New Testament Supplement Series 131, Sheffield: Sheffield Academic Press, pp. 350–68.

Girard, R. (1977) *Violence and the Sacred*, trans. P. Gregory, Baltimore, MD: Johns Hopkins University Press.

Gleason, M.W. (1990) "The Semiotics of Gender: Physiognomy and Self-Fashioning in the Second Century CE," in D.M. Halpern, J.J. Winkler, and F.I. Zeitlin (eds) *Before Sexuality: The Construction of Erotic Experience in the Ancient World*, Princeton, NJ: Princeton University Press, pp. 389–416.

González, J.L. (1974) "Athens and Jerusalem Revisited: Reason and Authority in Tertullian," *CH* 43: 17–25; rpt in E. Ferguson with D.M. Scholer and P.C. Finney (eds) (1993) *Studies in Early Christianity: A Collection of Scholarly Essays*, vol. 8: *The Early Church and Greco-Roman Thought*, New York and London: Garland, pp. 147–55.

Goodspeed, E.J. (1966) *A History of Early Christian Literature*, rev. R.M. Grant, Chicago, IL: University of Chicago Press.

Grant, R.M. (1947) "Theophilus of Antioch to Autolycus," *HTR* 40: 227–56.

—— (1950) "The Problem of Theophilus," *HTR* 43: 179–96.

—— (1953) "The Date of Tatian's Oration," *HTR* 46: 99–101.

—— (1955) "The Chronology of the Greek Apologists," *VC* 8: 25–33.

—— (1958) "Studies in the Apologists," *HTR* 51: 123–34.

—— (1959) "Scripture, Rhetoric and Theology in Theophilus," *VC* 13: 33–45.

—— (1971) "Early Alexandrian Christianity," *CH* 40: 133–44.

—— (1980) "The Social Setting of Second-Century Christianity," in B.F. Meyer and E.P. Sanders (eds) *Jewish and Christian Self-Definition*, vol. 1: *The Shaping of Christianity in the Second and Third Centuries*, Philadelphia, PA: Fortress, pp. 16–29.

—— (1981) "Charges of 'Immorality' against Various Religious Groups in Antiquity," in R. van den Broek and M.J. Vermaseren (eds) *Studies in Honor of Gilles Quispel*, Leiden: Brill, pp. 161–70.

—— (1985) "A Woman of Rome: Justin, *Apol.* 2,2," *CH* 54: 461–72.

—— (1986a) "Forms and Occasions of the Greek Apologists," *SMSR* 52: 213–26.

—— (1986b) *Gods and the One God*, Philadelphia, PA: The Westminster Press.

—— (1988a) "Five Apologists and Marcus Aurelius," *VC* 42: 1–17; rpt in E. Ferguson with D.M. Scholer and P.C. Finney (eds) (1993) *Studies in Early Christianity: A Collection of Scholarly Essays*, vol. 8: *The Early Church and Greco-Roman Thought*, New York and London: Garland, pp. 47–63.

—— (1988b) *Greek Apologists of the Second Century*, Philadelphia, PA: Westminster.

—— (1990) *Jesus after the Gospels*, Louisville, KY: Westminster/John Knox Press.

Griffin, M.H. (2002) "Martyrdom as a Second Baptism: Issues and Expectations for the Early Christian Martyrs," unpublished dissertation, University of California, Los Angeles.

Grubbs, J.E. (1994) "'Pagan' and 'Christian' Marriage: The State of the Question," *JECS* 2/3: 361–412.

Guerra, A.J. (1992) "The Conversion of Marcus Aurelius and Justin Martyr: The Purpose, Genre, and Content of the First Apology," *SecCent* 9/3: 171–87.

—— (1995) *Romans and the Apologetic Tradition: The Purpose, Genre and Audience of Paul's Letter*, Cambridge: Cambridge University Press.

Hall, S.G. (1993) "Women among the Early Martyrs," *Studies in Church History* 30: 1–21; rpt in E. Ferguson (ed.) (1999) *Recent Studies in Early Christianity*, vol. 2: *Christianity in Relation to Jews, Greeks, and Romans*, New York and London: Garland, pp. 301–21.

Hallett, J.P. (1984) *Fathers and Daughters in Roman Society: Women and the Elite Family*, Princeton, NJ: Princeton University Press.

Hanson, R.P.C. (1980) "The Christian Attitude to Paganism up to the Time of Constantine," *ANRW* II.23.2: 910–73.

Hargis, J.W. (1999) *Against the Christians: The Rise of Early Anti-Christian Polemic*, New York: Peter Lang.

Harlow, M. (1998) "In the Name of the Father: Procreation, Paternity and Patriarchy," in L. Foxhall and J. Salmon (eds) Thinking Men: Masculinity and Its Self-Representation in the Classical Tradition, London and New York: Routledge, pp. 155–69.

Harnack, A. (1908) *The Mission and Expansion of Christianity in the First Three Centuries*, 2 vols, trans. J. Moffatt, New York: G.P. Putnam's Sons; rpt (1972) Gloucester, MA: Peter Smith.

Hawthorne, G.F. (1964) "Tatian and His Discourse to the Greeks," *HTR* 54: 161–88.

Heinrichs, A. (1970) "Pagan Ritual and the Alleged Crimes of the Early Christians," in P. Granfield and J. Jungmann (eds) *Kyriakon: Festschrift Johannes Quasten*, Munster: Aschendorff, pp. 18–35.

Hegeland, J. (1974) "Christians and the Roman Army AD 173–337," *CH* 43: 149–63.

——, Daly, R.J., and Burns, J.P. (1985) *Christians and the Military: The Early Experience*, Philadelphia, PA: Fortress.

Helleman, W.E. (1994) "Tertullian on Athens and Jerusalem," in W.E. Helleman (ed.) *Hellenization Revisited: Shaping a Christian Response within the Greco-Roman World*, Lanham, MD: University Press of America, pp. 361–81.

Hellerman, J.H. (2001) *The Ancient Church as Family*, Minneapolis, MN: Fortress Press.

Hilhorst, A. (2000) "The Apocryphal Acts as Martyrdom Texts: The Case of the Acts of Andrew," in J.N. Bremmer (ed.) *The Apocryphal Acts of Andrew*, Studies on the Apocryphal Acts of the Apostles 5, Leuven: Peeters, pp. 1–14.

Hills, J. (1997) "The *Acts of Paul* and the Legacy of the Lukan Acts," *Semeia* 80: 145–58.

Hinson, E.G. (1993) "Women among the Martyrs," *StPatr* 25: 423–8.

Hippolytus (1868) *The Refutation of All Heresies*, trans. J.H. MacManon, Ante-Nicene Fathers, vol. 6, 9, Edinburgh: T&T Clark.

Hock, R.F., Bradley, C.J., and Perkins, J. (eds) (1998) *Ancient Fiction and Early Christian Narrative*, SBL Symposium Series 6, Atlanta, GA: Scholars Press.

Holmes, M.W. (ed. and rev.) (1999) *The Apostolic Fathers: Greek Texts and English Translations*, Grand Rapids, MI: Baker Books.

Holte, R. (1958) "Logos Spermatikos: Christianity and Ancient Philosophy according to St. Justin's Apologies," *StTheol* 12: 109–68.

Holzberg, N. (1995) *The Ancient Novel: An Introduction*, trans. C. Jackson-Holzberg, London and New York: Routledge.

Hopkins, K. (1978) *Sociological Studies in Roman History*, vol. 1: *Conquerors and Slaves*, Cambridge and London: Cambridge University Press.

—— (1983) *Sociological Studies in Roman History*, vol. 2: *Death and Renewal*, Cambridge and London: Cambridge University Press.

—— (1998) "Christian Number and Its Implications," *JECS* 6/2: 185–226.

—— (2001) *A World Full of Gods: The Strange Triumph of Christianity*, New York: A Plume Book.

Hornus, J.-M. (1980) *It Is Not Lawful for Me to Fight*, Scottdale, PA: Herald; (1960) French original.

Horsely, R.A. (1997) "The Gospel of Imperial Salvation: Introduction," in R.A. Horsely (ed.) *Paul and Empire: Religion and Power in Roman Imperial Society*, Harrisburg, PA: Trinity Press International, pp. 10–24.

Hunt, E.J. (2003) *Christianity in the Second Century: The Case of Tatian*, London and New York: Routledge.

Irenaeus of Lyons (1992) *St. Irenaeus of Lyons Against the Heresies, Book I*, trans. D.J. Unger and J.J. Dillon, ACW 55, New York: Paulist Press.

Jacobs, A.S. (1999) "A Family Affair: Marriage, Class, and Ethics in the Apocryphal Acts of the Apostles," *JECS* 7/1: 105–38.

Jaeger, W. (1961) *Early Christianity and Greek Paideia*, Cambridge, MA: Harvard University Press.

Janssen, L.F. (1979) "'Superstitio' and the Persecution of the Christians," *VC* 33: 131–59.

Jeanes, G. (1993) "Baptism Portrayed as Martyrdom in the Early Church," *Studia Liturgia* 23/2: 158–76.

Jensen, A. (1996) *God's Self-Confident Daughters: Early Christianity and the Liberation of Women*, trans. O.C. Dean, Louisville, KY: Westminster John Knox.

Jones, C. (1993) "Woman, Death, and the Law during the Christian Persecutions," in D. Wood (ed.) *Martyrs and Martyrologies*, Studies in Church History 30, Oxford: Blackwell, pp. 23–34.

Jones, D.L. (1980) "Christianity and the Roman Imperial Cult," *ANRW* II.23.2: 1023–54.

Jordan, M.D. (1986) "Ancient Philosophic Protreptic and the Problem of Persuasive Genres," *Rhetorica* 4: 309–33.

Junod, E. and Kaestli, J.-D. (eds) (1983) *Acta Iohannis*, Corpus Christianorum Series Apocryphorum 1 and 2, Turnhout: Brepols.

Justin Martyr (1908) *Dialogue with Trypho, First Apology*, and *Second Apology*, ed. A.C. Coxe, The Ante-Nicene Fathers, vol. 1, New York: Charles Scribner's Sons.

—— (1948) *Writings of Saint Justin Martyr*, trans. T.B. Falls, The Fathers of the Church 6, New York: Christian Heritage.

—— (1994) *Iustini Martyris Apologiae pro Christianis*, ed. M. Marcovich, Patristische Texte und Studien 38, Berlin and New York: Walter de Gruyter.

—— (1997a) *Dialogus cum Typhone*, ed. M. Marcovich, Patristische Texte und Studien 47, Berlin and New York: Walter de Gruyter.

—— (1997b) *The First and Second Apologies*, trans. with introduction and notes by L.W. Barnard, ACW 56, New York: Paulist Press.

Juvenal (1918) *Juvenal and Persius*, trans. G.G. Ramsay, LCL, London: W. Heinemann; New York: G.P. Putnam's Sons.

Kaufman, P.I. (1991) "Tertullian on Heresy, History, and the Reappropriation of Revelation," *CH* 60: 167–79; rpt in E. Ferguson (ed.) (1999) *Recent Studies in Early Christianity*, vol. 6: *History, Hope, Human Language, and Christian Reality*, New York and London: Garland, pp. 38–51.

Kee, H.C. (1983) *Miracle in the Early Christian World*, New Haven, CT: Yale University Press.

—— (1986) *Medicine, Miracle, and Magic in New Testament Times*, Cambridge: Cambridge University Press.

Kelly, C. (1995) "Butchered to Make a Roman Holiday," *Times Literary Supplement*, 22.

Kennedy, E.J. (1982) "Books and Readers in the Roman World," in E.J. Kennedy (ed.) *The Cambridge History of Classical Literature*, vol. 2: *Latin Literature*, Cambridge: Cambridge University Press, pp. 3–32.

Kerenyi, K. (1927) *Die griechisch-orientalische Romanliteratur in religions-geschichtlicher Beleuchtung*, Tübingen: Mohr; 2nd edn (1973), Wissenschaftliche: Darmstadt.

Keresztes, P. (1964) "Law and Arbitrariness in the Persecution of the Christians and Justin's First Apology," VC 18: 204–14.

—— (1965a) "The Literary Genre of Justin's First Apology," VC 19: 99–110.

—— (1965b) "The 'So-Called' Second Apology of Justin," Latomus 24: 858–69.

—— (1966) "Tertullian's Apologeticus: A Historical and Literary Study," Latomus 25: 124–33.

—— (1968) "Marcus Aurelius a Persecutor?" HTR 61: 321–41.

—— (1971) "The Emperor Antoninus Pius and the Christians," JEH 22: 1–18.

—— (1979) "The Imperial Roman Government and the Christian Church I: From Nero To the Severi," ANRW II.23.1: 247–315.

—— (1990) "Classical Literary Genres: The Traditional Forms and Means of Christian Apologetics," in La Tradizione: Forme e Modi. XVIII Incontro di studiosi dell'antichità cristiana, Roma 7–9 maggio 1989, Studia ephemeridis Augustinianum, 31, Rome: Institutum Patristicum Augustinianum, pp. 213–22.

Kinzig, W. (1989) "Der 'Sitz im Leben' der Apologie in der Alten Kirche," ZKG 100: 291–317.

—— (1997) "The Greek Christian Writers," in S.E. Potter (ed.) Handbook of Classical Rhetoric in the Hellenistic Period (330 BC–AD 400), Leiden and New York: E.J. Brill, pp. 633–70.

Klauck, H.-J. (2000, 2003) The Religious Context of Early Christianity: A Guide to Graeco-Roman Religions, trans. B. McNeil, Edinburgh: T&T Clark; Minneapolis, MN: Fortress; (1995, 1996) German original.

Klawiter, F.C. (1980) "The Role of Martyrdom and Persecution in Developing the Priestly Authority of Women in Early Christianity: A Case Study of Montanism," Church History 49: 251–61; rpt in D.M. Scholer (ed.) (1993) Studies in Early Christianity: A Collection of Scholarly Essays, vol. 14: Women in Early Christianity, New York and London: Garland, pp. 105–15.

Klijn, A.F.J. (1962) The Acts of Thomas, Leiden: Brill.

Kolenkow, A.B. (1976) "A Problem of Power: How Miracle Workers Counter Charges of Magic in the Hellenistic World," Society of Biblical Literature Seminar Papers 1: 105–10.

—— (1981) "Relationship between Miracle and Prophecy in the Greco-Roman World and Early Christianity," ANRW II.23.2: 1470–506.

Konstan, D. (1998) "Acts of Love: A Narrative Pattern in the Apocryphal Acts," JECS 6/1: 15–36.

Kraemer, R.S. (1980) "The Conversion of Women to Ascetic Forms of Christianity," Signs 6: 298–307; rpt in D.M. Scholer (ed.) (1993) Studies in Early Christianity: A Collection of Scholarly Essays, vol. 14: Women in Early Christianity, New York and London: Garland, pp. 252–61.

—— (1992) Her Share of the Blessings: Women's Religions among Pagans, Jews, and Christians in the Greco-Roman World, Oxford and New York: Oxford University Press.

Kreitzer, L. (1990) "Apotheosis of the Roman Emperor," *Biblical Archaeologist* 53: 210–17.

Krill, R.M. (1978) "Roman Paganism under the Antonines and the Severans," *ANRW* II.16.1: 27–44.

Kyle, D.G. (1998) *Spectacles of Death in Ancient Rome*, London and New York: Routledge.

Lacey, W.K. (1986) "*Patria Potestas*," in B. Rawson (ed.) *The Family in Ancient Rome: New Perspectives*, Ithaca, NY: Cornell University Press, pp. 121–44.

Lalleman, P.J. (1995) "Polymorphy of Christ," in J.N. Bremmer (ed.) *The Apocryphal Acts of John*, Studies on the Apocryphal Acts of the Apostles 1, Kampen: Kok Pharos, pp. 95–118.

—— (1998a) "Christology," in P.J. Lalleman (ed.) *The Acts of John: A Two-stage Initiation into Johannine Gnosticism*, Studies on the Apocryphal Acts of the Apostles 4, Leuven: Peeters, pp. 153–215.

—— (1998b) *The Acts of John: A Two-stage Initiation into Johannine Gnosticism*, Studies on the Apocryphal Acts of the Apostles 4, Leuven: Peeters.

Lane Fox, R. (1987) *Pagans and Christians*, New York: Alfred A. Knopf.

Laqueur, T.W. (1990) *Making Sex: Body and Gender from the Greeks to Freud*, Cambridge, MA: Harvard University Press.

Lawrence, P. (2001) "Eglise, femmes et pouvoir dans les Actes de Thomas," *Revista Agustiniana* [Madrid] 42/127: 193–220.

Lefkowitz, M. (1976) "The Motivations for Saint Perpetua's Martyrdom," *JAAR* 44: 417–21.

Levick, B. (1978) "Concordia at Rome," in R.A.C. Carson and C.M. Kraay (eds) *Scripta Nummaria Romana: Essays Presented to Humphrey Sutherland*, London: Spink, pp. 217–33.

Liebeschuetz, J.H.W.G. (1979) *Continuity and Change in Roman Religion*, Oxford: The Clarendon Press.

Lieu, J. (1996) *Image and Reality: The Jews in the World of the Christians in the Second Century*, Edinburgh: T&T Clark.

—— (1998) "The 'Attraction of Women' into Early Judaism and Christianity: Gender and Politics of Conversion," *JSSR* 72: 5–22.

—— (2002) " 'Impregnable Ramparts and Wall of Iron': Boundary and Identity in Early 'Judaism' and 'Christianity,'" *NTS* 48: 297–313.

Lilla, S.R.C. (1971) *Clement of Alexandria: A Study in Christian Platonism and Gnosticism*, Oxford: Oxford University Press.

Lipsius, R.A. and Bonnet, M. (eds) (1891–1903) *Acta Apostolorum Apocrypha*, 3 vols, Leipzig: Mendelssohn.

Lloyd-Moffett, S.R. (2003) "The 'Heresy' of Encratism and the History of Christianity in Eastern Syria," paper presented at the annual meeting of the SBL, Atlanta, GA, November.

Long, A.A. (1996) *Stoic Studies*, Cambridge and New York: Cambridge University Press.

Lucian of Samosata (1921–67) *Lucian*, trans. A.M. Harmon, K. Kilburn, and M.D. Macleod, 8 vols, LCL, Cambridge, MA: Harvard University Press.

Luttikhuizen, G. (1995) "A Gnostic Reading of the Acts of John," in J.N. Bremmer (ed.) *The Apocryphal Acts of John*, Studies on the Apocryphal Acts of the Apostles 1, Kampen: Kok Pharos, pp. 119–52.

Lutz, C.E. (1947) "Musonius Rufus: The Roman Socrates," *Yale Classical Studies* 10: 3–147.

MacDonald, D.R. (1983) *The Legend and the Apostle: The Battle for Paul in Story and Canon*, Philadelphia, PA: Westminster.

—— (ed.) (1990) *The Acts of Andrew and The Acts of Andrew and Matthias in the City of the Cannibals*, SBL Texts and Translations 33, Christian Apocrypha 1, Atlanta, GA: Scholars Press.

—— (1994) *Christianizing Homer: The Odyssey, Plato, and the Acts of Andrew*, Oxford and New York: Oxford University Press.

—— (1997) "Which Came First? Intertextual Relationships among the Apocryphal Acts of the Apostles," *Semeia* 80: 11–41.

MacDonald, M. (1990) "Early Christian Women Married to Unbelievers," *Studies in Religion* 19/2: 221–34.

—— (1996) *Early Christian Women and Pagan Opinion: The Power of the Hysterical Woman*, Cambridge: Cambridge University Press.

McGehee, M. (1993) "Why Tatian Never 'Apologized' to the Greeks," *JECS* 1/2: 143–58.

McKechnie, P. (1996) "'Women's Religion and Second-Century Christianity," *JEH* 47: 409–31; rpt in E. Ferguson (ed.) (1999) *Recent Studies in Early Christianity*, vol. 1: *Christianity and Society: The Social World of Early Christianity*, New York: Garland, pp. 31–53.

MacMullen, R. (1981) *Paganism in the Roman Empire*, New Haven, CT: Yale University Press.

—— (1983) "Two Types of Conversion to Early Christianity," *VC* 37: 174–92.

—— (1984) *Christianizing the Roman Empire (AD 100–400)*, New Haven, CT: Yale University Press.

—— (1985–6) "Conversion: A Historian's View," *SecCent* 5: 67–81.

—— (1986) "What Difference Did Christianity Make?" *Historia* 35: 322–43.

McNamara, J.A. (1976) "Sexual Equality and the Cult of Virginity in Early Christian Thought," *Feminist Studies* 3: 145–58; rpt in D.M. Scholer (ed.) (1993) *Studies in Early Christianity: A Collection of Scholarly Essays*, vol. 14: *Women in Early Christianity*, New York and London: Garland, pp. 219–32.

—— (1983) *A New Song: Celibate Women in the First Three Christian Centuries*, New York: Institute for Research in History/Haworth.

Malherbe, A.J. (1963) "Apologetic and Philosophy in the Second Century," *ResQ* 7: 19–32.

—— (1968) "Towards Understanding the Apologists: A Review Article," *ResQ* 11: 215–24.

—— (1969a) "Athenagoras on Christian Ethics," *JEH* 20: 1–5; rpt in E. Ferguson (ed.) (1993) *Studies in Early Christianity: A Collection of Scholarly Essays*, vol. 16: *Christian Life: Ethics, Morality, and Discipline in the Early Church*, New York and London: Garland, pp. 37–41.

—— (1969b) "Structure of Athenagoras, 'Supplicatio pro christianis,'" *VC* 23: 1–20.

—— (ed.) (1986) *Moral Exhortation, A Greco-Roman Sourcebook*, Library of Early Christianity, Philadelphia, PA: Westminster.

Malone, E.E. (1950) *The Monk and the Martyr: The Monk as the Successor of the Martyr*, Washington, DC: Catholic University of America Press.

Mansfeld, J. (1983) "Resurrection Added: The Interpretatio Christiana of a Stoic Doctrine," *VC* 37: 218–33.

Marguerat, D. (1997) "The Acts of Paul and the Canonical Acts: A Phenomenon of Rereading," *Semeia* 80: 169–83.

Markus, R.A. (1980) "The Problem of Self-Definition: From Sect to Church," in B.F. Meyer and E.P. Sanders (eds) *Jewish and Christian Self-Definition*, vol. 1: *The Shaping of Christianity in the Second and Third Centuries*, Philadelphia, PA: Fortress, pp. 1–15.

—— (1990) *The End of Ancient Christianity*, Cambridge and New York: Cambridge University Press.

Martial (1993) *Epigrams*, ed. and trans. D.R. Shackleton Baily, LCL, Cambridge, MA: Harvard University Press.

Martin, D.B. (1995) *The Corinthian Body*, New Haven, CT: Yale University Press.

Maximus of Tyre (1997) *The Philosophical Orations*, trans. with an introduction and notes M.B. Trapp, Oxford: Clarendon Press.

May, G. (1994) *Creatio ex nihilo: The Doctrine of 'Creation Out of Nothing' in Early Christian Thought*, trans. A.S. Worrall, Edinburgh: T&T Clark.

Meeks, W. (1974) "The Image of the Androgyne: Some Uses in Earliest Christianity," *History of Religions* 13: 165–208.

—— (1993) *The Origins of Christian Morality: The First Two Centuries*, New Haven, CT: Yale University Press.

Melito of Sardis (1979) *On Pascha and Fragments*, ed. and trans. S.G. Hall, OECT 6, Oxford: Clarendon Press.

Millar, F. (1973) "The Imperial Cult and the Persecutions," in W. den Boer (ed.) *Le culte des souverains dans l'empire romain*, Geneva: Vandouevres, pp. 145–65.

—— (1977) *The Emperor in the Roman World (31BC–AD 337)*, Ithaca, NY: Cornell University Press.

Miller, P.C. (1992) "The Devil's Gateway: An Eros of Difference in the Dreams of Perpetua," *Dreaming* 2/1: 45–63.

Minucius Felix (1931) *Octavius*, trans. G.H. Rendall, LCL, Cambridge, MA: Harvard University Press.

—— (1974) *The Octavius of Marcus Minucius Felix*, trans. G.W. Clarke, ACW 39, New York: Newman Press.

Misset-van de Weg, M. (1998) "'For the Lord Always Takes Care of His Own': The Purpose of the Wondrous Works and Deeds in the Acts of Peter," in J.N. Bremmer (ed.) *The Apocryphal Acts of Peter: Magic, Miracles and Gnosticism*, Studies on the Apocryphal Acts of the Apostles 3, Leuven: Peeters, pp. 97–110.

Morgan, J.R. (1994) "Introduction," in J.R. Morgan and R. Stoneman (eds) *Greek Fiction: The Greek Novel in Context*, London: Routledge, pp. 1–10.

Moriarty, R. (1997a) "The Claims of the Past: Attitudes to Antiquity in the Introduction to Passio Perpetuae," *StPatr* 31: 307–13.

—— (1997b) "The Faith of Our Fathers: The Making of the Early Christian Past," *Studies in Church History* 33: 5–17; rpt in E. Ferguson (ed.) (1999) *Recent Studies in Early Christianity*, vol. 6: *History, Hope, Human Language, and Christian Reality*, New York and London: Garland, pp. 25–37.

Mortley, R. (1980) "The Past in Clement of Alexandria: A Study of an Attempt to Define Christianity in Socio-Cultural Terms," in B.F. Meyer and E.P. Sanders (eds) *Jewish and Christian Self-Definition*, vol. 1: *The Shaping of Christianity in the Second and Third Centuries*, Philadelphia, PA: Fortress, pp. 186–200, 261–4.

Moxnes, H. (ed.) (1997) *Constructing Early Christian Families: Family as Social Reality and Metaphor*, London and New York: Routledge.

Mühlenberg, E. (1997) "The Martyr's Death and Its Literary Presentation," *StPatr* 29: 85–93.

Murray, R. (1975) "The Exhortation to Candidates for Ascetic Vows at Baptism in the Ancient Syriac Church," *NTS* 21: 59–80.

Musurillo, H. (ed.) (1972; rpt 2000) *The Acts of the Christian Martyrs*, Oxford: Oxford University Press.

Nagy, A.A. (2001) "La forme originale de l'accusation d'anthropophagie contre les chrétiens, son dévelopement et les changements de sa représentation au IIe siècle," *REAug* 47: 223–49.

Niebuhr, H.R. (1951) *Christ and Culture*, New York: Harper & Row.

Nock, A.D. (1933) *Conversion: The Old and the New in Religion from Alexander the Great to Augustine of Hippo*, Oxford: Oxford University Press.

—— (1934) "Religious Development from the Close of the Republic to the Death of Nero," in S.A. Cook, F.E. Adcock and M.P. Charlesworth (eds) *The Cambridge Ancient History*, vol. 10: *The Augustan Empire*, Cambridge: Cambridge University Press, pp. 465–511.

O'Neill, J.C. (2002) "How Early is the Doctrine of *Creation ex Nihilo*?," *JTS* 52/2: 449–65.

Origen (2001) *Contra Celsum*, ed. M. Marcovich, Boston, MA: Brill.

Osborn, E.F. (1972) "From Justin to Origen: The Pattern of Apologetic," *Prudentia* 4: 1–22; rpt in E. Ferguson with D.M. Scholer and P.C. Finney (eds) (1993) *Studies in Early Christianity: A Collection of Scholarly Essays*, vol. 8: *The Early Church and Greco-Roman Thought*, New York and London: Garland, pp. 1–22.

—— (1973) *Justin Martyr*, Tübingen: J.C.B. Mohr (Paul Siebeck).

—— (1994) "Arguments for Faith in Clement of Alexandria," *VC* 48: 1–24; rpt. in E. Ferguson (ed.) (1999) *Recent Studies in Early Christianity*, vol. 2: *Christianity in Relation to Jews, Greeks, and Romans*, New York and London: Garland, pp. 105–28.

—— (1997) *Tertullian: The First Theologian of the West*, Cambridge and New York: Cambridge University Press.

—— (2000) "The Apologists," in P. Esler (ed.) *The Early Christian World*, vol. 2, London and New York: Routledge, pp. 525–51.

Osiek, C. (2002) "Perpetua's Husband," *JECS* 10/2: 287–90.

Pagels, E. (1980) "Gnostic and Christian Views of Christ's Passion," in B. Layton (ed.) *The Rediscovery of Gnosticism*, vol. 1, Leiden: Brill, pp. 262–83.

—— (1981) *The Gnostic Gospels*, New York: Vintage Books.

—— (1983) "Adam and Eve, Christ and the Church: A Survey of Second Century Controversies concerning Marriage," in A.H.B. Logan and A.J.M. Wedderburn (eds) *The New Testament and Gnosis: Essays in Honour of Robert McL. Wilson*, Edinburgh: T&T Clark, pp. 146–75.

—— (1985) "Christian Apologists and 'The Fall of the Angels': An Attack on Roman Imperial Power?," *HTR* 78: 301–25.

Palmer, D.W. (1983) "Atheism, Apologetic, and Negative Theology in the Greek Apologists of the Second Century," *VC* 37: 234–59.

Pao, D.W. (1995) "The Genre of the Acts of Andrew," *Apocrypha* 6: 179–202.

Pellegrino, M. (1958) "L'Imitation du Christ dans les Actes des martyrs," *La Vie Spirituelle* 98: 38–54; rpt in E. Ferguson (ed.) (1993) *Studies in Early Christianity: A Collection of Scholarly Essays*, vol. 17: *Acts of Piety in the Early Church*, New York and London: Garland, pp. 2–18.

Perkins, J. (1985) "The Apocryphal Acts of the Apostles and the Early Christian Martyrdom," *Arethusa* 18: 211–30.

—— (1992a) "The Apocryphal *Acts of Peter*: A Roman à Thèse?" *Arethusa* 25: 445–55.

—— (1992b) "The 'Self as Sufferer,'" *HTR* 85: 245–72.

—— (1994a) "The Passion of Perpetua: A Narrative of Empowerment," *Latomus* 53: 837–47.

—— (1994b) "The Social World of the *Acts of Peter*," in J. Tatum (ed.) *The Search for the Ancient Novel*, Baltimore, MD: Johns Hopkins University Press, pp. 296–307.

—— (1995) *The Suffering Self: Pain and Narrative Representation in the Early Christian Era*, London and New York: Routledge.

—— (1997) "This World or Another? The Intertextuality of the Greek Romances, the Apocryphal Acts and Apuleius' *Metamorphoses*," *Semeia* 80: 247–60.

—— (2002) "Resurrection in the Apocryphal *Acts of Peter* and *Acts of John*," paper presented at the annual meeting of the SBL, Toronto, Canada, November.

Perler, O. (1949) "Das vierte Makkabäerbuch, Ignatius von Antiochien und die ältesten Martyrerberichte," *RAC* 25: 47–72.

Perry, B. (1967) *The Ancient Romances: A Literary-Historical Account of Their Origins*, Berkeley, CA: University of California Press.

Pervo, R.I. (1987) *Profit with Delight: The Literary Genre of the Acts of the Apostles*, Philadelphia, PA: Fortress.

—— (1992) "Johannine Trajectories in the *Acts of John*," *Apocrypha* 3: 47–68.

—— (1994) "Early Christian Fiction," in J.R. Morgan and R. Stoneman (eds) *Greek Fiction: The Greek Novel in Context*, London: Routledge, pp. 239–54.

249

—— (1996; rev. edn 2003) "The Ancient Novel Becomes Christian," in G.L. Schmeling (ed.) *The Novel in the Ancient World*, Leiden: Brill, pp. 685–709.

—— (1997a) "Egging on the Chickens: A Cowardly Response to Dennis MacDonald and Then Some," *Semeia* 80: 43–56.

—— (1997b) "Rhetoric in the Christian Apocrypha," in S.E. Potter (ed.) *Handbook of Classical Rhetoric in the Hellenistic Period (330 BC–AD 400)*, Leiden and New York: Brill, pp. 793–805.

Pesthy, M. (1998) "Cross and Death in the Apocryphal Acts of the Apostles," in J.N. Bremmer (ed.) *The Apocryphal Acts of Peter: Magic, Miracles and Gnosticism*, Studies on the Apocryphal Acts of the Apostles 3, Leuven: Peeters, pp. 123–33.

Pettersen, A. (1987) "Perpetua – Prisoner of Conscience," *VC* 41: 139–53.

Pfitzner, V.C. (1967) *Paul and the Agon Motif: Traditional Athletic Imagery in the Pauline Literature*, Supplements to Novum Testamentum 16, Leiden: Brill.

—— (1981) "Martyr and Hero: The Origin and Development of a Tradition in the Early Christian Martyr-Acts," *Lutheran Theological Journal* 15: 9–17.

Philo (1929–62) *Philo*, trans. F.H. Colson and G.H. Whitaker, 10 vols, LCL, London: Heinemann; New York: Putnam's.

Philostratus (1912) *Life of Apollonius*, trans. F.C. Conybeare, LCL, Cambridge, MA: Harvard University Press; rpt 1917, 1927, 1948.

Plato (1959) *Timaeus*, trans. F.M. Cornford, ed. O. Piest, New York: Liberal Arts Press.

Plescia, J. (1971) "On the Persecution of the Christians in the Roman Empire," *Latomus* 30: 120–32.

Pliny, Caecilius Secundus (1961, 1963) *Letters*, trans. W. Melmoth, 2 vols, rev. W.M.L. Hutchinson, LCL, Cambridge, MA: Harvard University Press.

Plutarch (1927) *Plutarch's Moralia*, vol. 2: *Advice to Bride and Groom*, trans. F.C. Babitt, LCL, Cambridge, MA: Harvard University Press.

—— (1959) *Consolation to His Wife*, vol. 7: *Plutarch's Moralia*, trans. P.H. De Lacy and B. Einarson, LCL, Cambridge, MA: Harvard University Press.

—— (1999) *Plutarch's Advice to the Bride and Groom and A Consolation to His Wife*, ed. S.B. Pomeroy, Oxford: Oxford University Press.

Potter, D. (1993) "Martyrdom and Spectacle," in R. Scodel (ed.) *Theater and Society in the Classical World*, Ann Arbor, MI: University of Michigan Press, pp. 53–88.

—— (1996) "Performance, Power, and Justice in the High Empire," in W.J. Slater (ed.) *Roman Theater and Society*, E. Togo Salmon Papers I, Ann Arbor, MI: University of Michigan Press, pp. 129–60.

Potter, S.E. (ed.) (1997) *Handbook of Classical Rhetoric in the Hellenistic Period (330 BC–AD 400)*, Leiden and New York: Brill.

Poupon, G. (1981) "L'accusation de magie dans des Actes apocryphes," in F. Bovon (ed.) *Les Actes Apocryphes des Apôtres: Christianisme et monde païen*, Publications de la Faculté de Théologie de l'Université de Genève 4, Geneva: Labor et Fides, pp. 71–93.

Price, R.M. (1998) "Docetic Epiphanies: A Structuralist Analysis of the Apocryphal Acts," *JHC* 5/2: 163–87.

Price, S.R.F. (1984) *Rituals and Power: The Roman Imperial Cult in Asia Minor*, Cambridge: Cambridge University Press.

—— (1987) "From Noble Funerals to Divine Cult," in D. Cannadine and S.R.F. Price (eds) *Rituals of Royalty*, Cambridge: Cambridge University Press, pp. 56–105.

—— (1999) "Latin Christian Apologetics: Minucius Felix, Tertullian, and Cyprian," in M.J. Edwards, M. Goodman, and S.R.F. Price (eds) *Apologetics in the Roman Empire: Pagans, Jews, and Christians*, Oxford: Oxford University Press, pp. 124–6.

Prieur, J.-M. (1981) "La figure de l'apôtre dans les Actes apocryphes d'André," in F. Bovon (ed.) *Les Actes Apocryphes des Apôtres: Christianisme et monde païen*, Publications de la Faculté de Théologie de l'Université de Genève 4, Geneva: Labor et Fides, pp. 121–39.

—— (ed.) (1989) *Acta Andreae*, Corpus Christianorum Series Apocryphorum 3 and 4, Turnhout: Brepols.

—— (1991; rev. edn 1992) "The Acts of Andrew: Introduction," in W. Schneemelcher (ed.) and R.McL. Wilson (trans.) *New Testament Apocrypha*, vol. 2: *Writings Relating to Apostles, Apocalypses and Related Subjects*, Louisville, KY: Westminster/John Knox, pp. 101–18.

—— (1999) "La croix vivante dans la littérature chrétienne du IIe siècle," *RHPR* 79/4: 435–44.

Raditsa, L.F. (1980) "Augustus' Legislation concerning Marriage, Procreation, Love Affairs and Adultery," *ANRW* II.13: 278–339.

Rawson, B. (1986a) "Children in the Roman *Familia*," in B. Rawson (ed.) *The Family in Ancient Rome: New Perspectives*, Ithaca, NY: Cornell University Press, pp. 170–200.

—— (1986b) "The Roman Family," in B. Rawson (ed.) *The Family in Ancient Rome: New Perspectives*, Ithaca, NY: Cornell University Press, pp. 1–57.

Reardon, B.P. (1969) "The Greek Novel," *Phoenix* 23: 291–309.

—— (1971) *Courants littéraires grecs des IIe et IIIe siècles après J.-C.*, Paris: Les belles Lettres.

—— (1991) *The Form of Greek Romance*, Princeton, NJ: Princeton University Press.

Remus, H. (1982) "'Magic or Miracle'? Some Second-Century Instances," *SecCent* 2: 127–56.

—— (1983) *Pagan-Christian Conflict over Miracle in the Second Century*, Patristic Monograph Series 10, Cambridge, MA: Philadelphia Patristic Foundation.

—— (1999) "'Magic', Method, Madness," *Method & Theory in the Study of Religion* 11: 258–98.

Reydams-Schils, G.J. (1999) *Demiurge and Providence: Stoic and Platonist Readings of Plato's Timaeus*, Turnhout: Brepols.

Rist, J.M. (1969) *Stoic Philosophy*, Cambridge: Cambridge University Press.

Rives, J. (1995) "Human Sacrifice among Pagans and Christians," *JRS* 85: 65–85.

Robeck, C.M., Jr (1992) *Prophecy in Carthage: Perpetua, Tertullian and Cyprian*, Cleveland, OH: The Pilgrim Press.

Robert, L. (1982) "Une vision de Perpétue martyre à Carthage en 203," *Comptes rendus de l'Académie des inscriptions et belles-lettres*: 228–76.

Roberts, A. and Donalson, J. (eds) (1885) *The Fathers of the Second Century: Hermas, Tatian, Athenagoras, Theophilus, and Clement of Alexandria (Entire)*, The Ante-Nicene Fathers, vol. 2, New York: Charles Scribner's Sons.

Robinson, J.M. (ed.) (1977; 4th edn 1996) *The Nag Hammadi Library in English*, Leiden: E.J. Brill.

Rodman, R.C. (1997) "Who's on Third? Reading Acts of Andrew as a Rhetoric of Resistance," *Semeia* 79: 27–43.

Roetzel, C.J. (2000) "Sex and the Single God: Celibacy as Social Deviancy in the Roman Period," in S.G. Wilson and M. Desjardins (eds) *Text and Artifact in the Religions of Mediterranean Antiquity: Essays in Honor of Peter Richardson*, Studies in Christianity and Judaism 9, Waterloo, Ontario: Wilfrid Laurier University Press, pp. 231–48.

Rohde, E. (1914) *Der griechische Roman und seine Vorläufer*, 3rd edn, Leipzig: Breitkopf and Härtel.

Rordorf, W. (1969) "Marriage in the New Testament and in the Early Church," *JEH* 20: 193–210; rpt in E. Ferguson (ed.) (1993) *Studies in Early Christianity: A Collection of Scholarly Essays*, vol. 16: *Christian Life: Ethics, Morality, and Discipline in the Early Church*, New York and London: Garland, pp. 141–58.

—— (1972) "Aux origins du culte des martyrs," *Irenikon* 45: 315–31; rpt in E. Ferguson (ed.) (1993) *Studies in Early Christianity: A Collection of Scholarly Essays*, vol. 17: *Acts of Piety in the Early Church*, New York and London: Garland, pp. 79–95.

—— (1986) "L'ésperance des martyrs chrétiens," in *Liturgie, foi et vie des premiers chrétiens: Études patristiques*, Paris: Beauchesne, pp. 345–61.

Rossi, M.A. (1984) "The Passion of Perpetua, Everywoman of Late Antiquity," in R.C. Smith and J. Lounibos (eds) *Pagan and Christian Anxiety: A Response to E.R. Dodds*, New York: University Press of America, pp. 53–86.

Rousselle, A. (1988) *Porneia: On Desire and the Body in Antiquity*, trans. F. Pheasant, New York: Basil Blackwell.

Ruether, R. (1974) "Virginal Feminism in the Fathers of the Church," in R. Ruether (ed.) *Religion and Sexism*, New York: Simon & Schuster, pp. 150–83.

—— (1979) "Mothers of the Church: Ascetic Women in the Late Patristic Age," in R. Ruether (ed.) *Women of Spirit: Female Leadership in the Jewish and Christian Traditions*, New York: Simon & Schuster, pp. 71–98.

Russell, D.A. and Wilson, N.G. (eds) (1981) *Menander Rhetor*, Oxford: Clarendon Press.

Ryan, E.A. (1952) "The Rejection of Military Service by the Early Christians," *Theological Studies* 13: 1–32; rpt in E. Ferguson (ed.) (1993) *Studies in Early Christianity: A Collection of Scholarly Essays*, vol. 16: *Christian Life: Ethics,*

Morality, and Discipline in the Early Church, New York and London: Garland, pp. 217–48.

Salisbury, J.E. (1997) *Perpetua's Passion: The Death and Memory of a Young Roman Woman*, London and New York: Routledge.

Saller, R.P. (1999) "*Pater Familias, Mater Familias*, and the Gendered Semantics of the Roman Household," *Classical Philology* 94: 182–97.

Sanders, J.T. (2000) *Charisma, Converts, Competitors: Societal and Sociological Factors in the Success of Early Christianity*, London: SCM Press.

Schneemelcher, W. (1991; rev. edn 1992) *New Testament Apocrypha*, vol. 2: *Writings Relating to Apostles, Apocalypses and Related Subjects*, trans. R.McL. Wilson, Louisville, KY: Westminster/John Knox.

Schneider, P.G. (1991a) "A Perfect Fit: The Major Interpolation in the Acts of John," in E.H. Lovering, Jr (ed.) *Society of Biblical Literature Seminar Papers 30*, Atlanta, GA: Scholars Press, pp. 518–32.

—— (1991b) *The Mystery of the Acts of John*, Lewiston, NY: Edwin Mellen Press.

—— (1994) "The Acts of John: The Gnostic Transformation of a Christian Community," in W.E. Helleman (ed.) *Hellenization Revisited: Shaping a Christian Response within the Greco-Roman World*, Lanham, MD: University Press of America, 241–69.

Schoedel, W.R. (1973) "Christian 'Atheism' and the Peace of the Roman Empire," *CH* 42: 309–19.

—— (1979a) "Enclosing, Not Enclosed: The Early Christian Doctrine of God," in W.R. Schoedel and R.L. Wilken (eds) *Early Christian Literature and the Classical Intellectual Tradition: In Honorem Robert M. Grant*, Paris: Beauchesne, pp. 75–86.

—— (1979b) "In Praise of the King: A Rhetorical Pattern in Athenagoras," in D.F. Winslow (ed.) *Disciplina Nostra: Essays in Memory of Robert F. Evans*, Patristic Monograph Series, 6, Cambridge, MA: Philadelphia Patristic Foundation, pp. 69–90, 199–203.

—— (1989) "Apologetic Literature and Ambassadorial Activities," *HTR* 82: 55–78.

—— (1993) "Polycarp of Smyrna and Ignatius of Antioch," *ANRW* II.27.1: 272–358.

Scholer, D.M. (1989) "And I Was a Man: The Power and Problem of Perpetua," *Daughters of Sarah* 15/5: 10–14; rpt in D.M. Scholer (ed.) (2001) *Selected Articles on Hermeneutics and Women and Ministry in the New Testament*, Pasadena, CA: Fuller Theological Seminary, pp. 203–7; rpt also in R. Finger and K. Sandhaas (eds) (2001) *The Wisdom of Daughters: Two Decades of the Voice of Christian Feminism*, Philadelphia, PA: Innisfree, pp. 244–8.

—— (ed.) (1993) *Studies in Early Christianity: A Collection of Scholarly Essays*, vol. 14: *Women in Early Christianity*, New York and London: Garland.

Schroeder, C.T. (2000) "Embracing the Erotic in the Passion of Andrew: The Apocryphal Acts of Andrew, the Greek Novel, and Platonic Philosophy," in J.N. Bremmer (ed.) *The Apocryphal Acts of Andrew*, Studies on the Apocryphal Acts of the Apostles 5, Leuven: Peeters, pp. 110–26.

Schüssler Fiorenza, E. (ed.) (1976a) *Aspects of Religious Propaganda in Judaism and Early Christianity*, Notre Dame, IN and London: University of Notre Dame Press.

—— (1976b) "Miracles, Mission, and Apologetics: An Introduction," in E. Schüssler Fiorenza (ed.) *Aspects of Religious Propaganda in Judaism and Early Christianity*, Notre Dame, IN and London: University of Notre Dame Press, pp. 1–25.

—— (1984) *In Memory of Her: A Feminist Theological Reconstruction of Christian Origins*, New York: Crossroad.

—— (ed.) (1994) *Searching the Scriptures*, vol. 2: *A Feminist Commentary*, New York: Crossroad.

Seeley, D. (1990) *The Noble Death: Graeco-Roman Martyrology and Paul's Concept of Salvation*, Journal for the Study of the New Testament Supplement Series 28, Sheffield: Sheffield Academic Press.

Shaw, B.D. (1993) "The Passion of Perpetua," *Past and Present* 139: 3–45.

—— (1996) "Body/Power/Identity: Passions of the Martyrs," *JECS* 4/3: 269–312.

Shaw, T.M. (2000) "Sex and Sexual Renunciation," in P. Esler (ed.) *The Early Christian World*, vol. 2, London and New York: Routledge, pp. 401–21.

Shelton, J. (1990) "Pliny the Younger and the Ideal Wife," *Classica et Medievalia* 41: 163–86.

—— (1998) *As the Romans Did: A Sourcebook in Roman Social History*, 2nd edn, Oxford and New York: Oxford University Press.

Sherwin-White, A.N. (1966, 1985) *The Letters of Pliny: A Historical and Social Commentary*, Oxford: Clarendon Press.

Sider, R.D. (1971) *Ancient Rhetoric and the Art of Tertullian*, London: Oxford University Press.

Siker, J.S. (2000) "Christianity in the Second and Third Centuries," in P. Esler (ed.) *The Early Christian World*, vol. 1, London and New York: Routledge, pp. 231–57.

Simmons, M.B. (2000) "Graeco-Roman Philosophical Opposition," in P. Esler (ed.) *The Early Christian World*, vol. 2, London and New York: Routledge, pp. 840–68.

Simon, M. (1973) "Early Christianity and Pagan Thought: Confluences and Conflicts," *Religious Studies* 9: 385–99.

Simpson, A.D. (1941) "Epicureans, Christians, Atheists in the Second Century," *Transactions and Proceedings of the American Philosophical Association* 72: 372–81.

Skarsaune, O. (1987) *The Proof from Prophecy: A Study in Justin Martyr's Prooftext Tradition*, Leiden: E.J. Brill.

Smith, J.Z. (1978) "Towards Interpreting Demonic Powers in Hellenistic and Roman Antiquity," *ANRW* II.16.1: 425–39.

Smith, M. (1978) "On the History of the Divine Man," in *Paganisme, Judaisme, Christianisme: Influences et affrontements dans le monde antique*, Mélanges offerts à Marcel Simon, Paris: de Boccard, pp. 335–45.

Söder, R. (1932) *Die apokryphen Apostelgeschichten und die romanhafte Literatur der Antike*, Stuttgart: W. Kohlhammer.

Sordi, M. (1986) *The Christians and the Roman Empire*, trans. A. Benini, London: Croom Helm.

Stark, R. (1996) *The Rise of Christianity*, Princeton, NJ: Princeton University Press.

Stassen, G.H. and Gushee, D.P. (2003) *Kingdom Ethics: Following Jesus in Contemporary Context*, Downers Grove, IL: InterVarsity Press.

——, Yeager, D.M., and Yoder, J.H. (1996) *Authentic Transformation: A New Vision of Christ and Culture*, with a previously unpublished essay by H.R. Niebuhr, Nashville, TN: Abingdon Press.

Stephens, S.A. (1994) "Who Read Ancient Novels?'" in J. Tatum (ed.) *Search for the Ancient Novel*, Baltimore, MD: Johns Hopkins University Press, pp. 405–18.

Stevenson, K. (1980) "The Origins of Nuptial Blessing," *Heythrop Journal* 21: 412–16; rpt in E. Ferguson (ed.) (1993) *Studies in Early Christianity: A Collection of Scholarly Essays*, vol. 16: *Christian Life: Ethics, Morality, and Discipline in the Early Church*, New York and London: Garland, pp. 160–4.

Stoops, R.F., Jr (1986) "Patronage in the Acts of Peter," *Semeia* 38: 91–100.

—— (1992) "Christ as Patron in the Acts of Peter," *Semeia* 56: 143–57.

—— (1997) "The Acts of Peter in Intertextual Context," *Semeia* 80: 57–86.

Streete, G.C. (1997) "Outrageous (Speech) Acts and Everyday (Performative) Rebellions: A Response to Rhetorics of Resistance," *Semeia* 79: 97–105.

—— (1999) "Women as Sources of Redemption and Knowledge in Early Christian Traditions," in R.S. Kraemer and M.R. D'Angelo (eds) *Women and Christian Origins*, Oxford: Oxford University Press, pp. 330–54.

—— (2002) "Speaking and Silencing: The Woman Martyr's 'Voice,'" paper presented at the annual meeting of the SBL, Toronto, Canada, November.

Suetonius (1951) *Suetonius*, vol. 1, trans. J.C. Rolfe, LCL, Cambridge, MA: Harvard University Press.

Sullivan, L.M. (1997) "I Responded, 'I Will Not . . .': Christianity as Catalyst for Resistance in the Passio Perpetuae et Felicitatis," *Semeia* 79: 63–73.

Swift, L.J. (ed.) (1983) *The Early Fathers on War and Military Service*, Message of the Fathers of the Church 19, Wilmington, DE: Michael Glazier.

Tabbernee, W. (1985) "Early Montanism and Voluntary Martyrdom," *Colloquium* 17: 33–44.

—— (1997) *Montanist Inscriptions and Testamonia: Epigraphic Sources Illustrating the History of Montanism*, Patristic Monograph Series 16, Macon, GA: Mercer University Press.

Tacitus (1937) *The Annals*, trans. J. Jackson, 2 vols, LCL, Cambridge, MA: Harvard University Press.Tajra, H.W. (1994) *The Martyrdom of St. Paul: Historical and Judicial Context, Traditions and Legends*, Tübingen: J.C.B. Mohr (Paul Siebeck).

Talbert, C.H. (1978) "Biographies of Philosophers and Rulers as Instrument of Religious Propaganda in Mediterranean Antiquity," *ANRW* II.16.2: 1619–51.

Tatian (1982) *Oratio ad Graecos and Fragments*, ed. and trans. M. Whittaker, OECT 8, Oxford: Clarendon Press.

Tatum, J. (ed.) (1994) *The Search for the Ancient Novel*, Baltimore, MD: Johns Hopkins University Press.

Tertullian (1931) *Apology and De Spectaculis*, trans. T.R. Glover, LCL, Cambridge, MA: Harvard University Press.

—— (1948) *Tertullian's Treatise against Praxeas*, ed. and trans. E. Evans, London: SPCK.

—— (1954) *Tertulliani Opera, Pars I: Opera Catholica Adversus Marcionem*, Corpus Christianorum Series Latina, Turnholti: Typographi Brepols Editores Pontificii.

Theissen, G. (1983) *The Miracle Stories of the Early Christian Tradition*, trans. F. McDonagh, Philadelphia, PA: Fortress.

Theophilus of Antioch (1980) *Ad Autolycum*, trans. R.M. Grant, OECT 10, Oxford: Clarendon Press.

Thomas, C.M. (1992) "Word and Deed: The *Acts of Peter* and Orality," *Apocrypha* 3: 125–64.

—— (1995) "The Acts of Peter, the Ancient Novel, and Early Christian History," unpublished dissertation, Harvard University.

—— (1998) "Stories without Texts and without Authors: The Problem of Fluidity in Ancient Novelistic Texts and Early Christian Literature," in R.F. Hock, C.J. Bradley, and J. Perkins (eds) *Ancient Fiction and Early Christian Narrative*, SBL Symposium Series 6, Atlanta, GA: Scholars Press, pp. 273–91.

—— (2001) *The Acts of Peter, Gospel Literature, and the Ancient Novel: Rewriting the Past*, Oxford and New York: Oxford University Press.

Thompson, L. (1990) *The Book of Revelation: Apocalypse and Empire*, Oxford: Oxford University Press.

Tilley, M.A. (1991) "The Ascetic Body and the (Un)Making of the World of the Martyr," *JAAR* 59/3: 467–79.

Tissot, Y. (1981) "Encratisme et Actes Apocryphes," in F. Bovon (ed.) *Les Actes Apocryphes des Apôtres: Christianisme et monde païen*, Publications de la Faculté de Théologie de l'Université de Genève 4, Geneva: Labor et Fides, pp. 109–19.

—— (1988) "L'encratisme des Actes de Thomas," *ANRW* II.25.6: 4415–30.

Torchia, N.J. (1993) "Theories of Creation in the Second Century Apologists and their Middle Platonic Background," *StPatr* 26: 192–9.

Treggiari, S. (1991) *Roman Marriage: Iusti Coniuges from the Time of Cicero to the Time of Ulpian*, Oxford: Clarendon Press.

Trevett, C. (1996) *Montanism: Gender, Authority and the New Prophecy*, Cambridge: Cambridge University Press.

Valantasis, R. (1995) "A Theory of the Social Function of Asceticism," in V.L. Wimbush and R. Valantasis (eds) *Asceticism*, New York and Oxford: Oxford University Press, 544–54.

van Eijk, T.H.J. (1972) "Marriage and Virginity, Death and Immorality," in J. Fontaine and C. Kannengiesser (eds) *Epektasis: Mélanges offerts au cardinal J. Daniélou*, Paris: Beauchesne, pp. 209–35.

van Henten, J.W. (1995) "The Martyrs as Heroes of the Christian People: Some Remarks on the Continuity between Jewish and Christian Martyrology, with Pagan Analogies," in M. Lamgerigts and P. van Deun (eds) *Martyrium in Multidisciplinary Perspective*, Memorial Louis Reekmans, Louvain: Louvain University Press, pp. 303–22.

—— (1997) *The Maccabean Martyrs as Saviours of the Jewish People: A Study of 2 and 4 Maccabees*, Supplements to the Journal for the Study of Judaism 57, Leiden, New York and Köln: E.J. Brill.

—— and Avemarie, F. (eds) (2002) *Martyrdom and Noble Death: Selected Texts from Graeco-Roman, Jewish and Christian Antiquity*, London and New York: Routledge.

Veyne, P. (1987) "The Roman Empire," in P. Veyne (ed.) *A History of Private Life*, vol. 1: *From Pagan Rome to Byzantium*, trans. A. Goldhammer, Cambridge, MA: Harvard University Press, pp. 6–233.

Vogt, K. (1991) "'Becoming Male': A Gnostic and Early Christian Metaphor," in K.E. Børrensen (ed.) *Image of God and Gender Models in Judaeo-Christian Tradition*, Oslo: Solum Forlag, pp. 172–87.

von Campenhausen, H. (1957) "Bearbeitungen und Interpolationen des Polykarpmartyriums," *Sitzungsberichte der Heidelberger Akad., Phil.-hist. Kl.*, Abhnad. 3, pp. 5–48; rpt in *Aus der Frühzeit des Christentums* (1963), pp. 197–301.

—— (1968) "Early Christian Asceticism," in *Tradition and Life in the Church*, Philadelphia, PA: Fortress Press, 90–122; rpt in E. Ferguson (ed.) (1993) *Studies in Early Christianity: A Collection of Scholarly Essays*, vol. 17: *Acts of Piety in the Early Church*, New York and London: Garland, pp. 178–210.

Vööbus, A. (1958) *History of Asceticism in the Syrian Orient*, vol. 1: *The Origin of Asceticism*, Corpus Scriptorum Christianorum Orientalium (CSCO) 184, Subsidia 14, Louvain: CSCO.

Wagener, K.C. (1991) "'Repentant Eve, Perfected Adam': Conversion in *The Acts of Andrew*," in E.H. Lovering, Jr (ed.) *Society of Biblical Literature Seminar Papers 30*, Atlanta, GA: Scholars Press, pp. 348–56.

Walsh, J.J. (1991) "On Christian Atheism," *VC* 45: 255–77.

Walzer, R. (1949) *Galen on Jews and Christians*, Oxford Classical & Philosophical Monographs, London: Oxford University Press.

Ward, R.B. (1990) "Musonius and Paul on Marriage," *NTS* 36: 281–9.

Weiner, E. and Weiner, A. (1990) *The Martyr's Conviction: A Sociological Analysis*, Brown Judaic Studies 203, Atlanta, GA: Scholars Press.

Weinrich, W.C. (1981) *Spirit and Martyrdom: A Study of the Work of the Holy Spirit in Contexts of Persecution and Martyrdom in the New Testament and Early Christian Literature*, Washington, DC: University Press of America.

Wells, G.A. (1999) "Doing without Jesus: Some Aspects of Second-Century Christianity," *JHC* 6/2: 210–15.

Whittaker, J. (1975) "Tatian's Educational Background," *StPatr* 13: 57–9.

—— (1979) "Christianity and Morality in the Roman Empire," *VC* 33: 209–25; rpt in E. Ferguson (ed.) (1993) *Studies in Early Christianity: A Collection of Scholarly Essays*, vol. 16: *Christian Life: Ethics, Morality, and Discipline in the Early Church*, New York and London: Garland, pp. 18–35.

Whittaker, M. (1982) "Introduction," in M. Whittaker (ed.) *Oratio ad Graecos and Fragments*, Oxford: Clarendon, 1982.

Wicker, K. O'Brien (1975) "First Century Marriage Ethics: A Comparative Study of the Household Codes and Plutarch's Conjugal Precepts," in J.W. Flanagan and A.W. Robinson (eds) *No Famine in the Land*, Chico, CA: Scholars Press, 141–53.

Wilken, R.L. (1970) "Toward a Social Interpretation of Early Christian Apologetics," *CH* 39: 436–58.

—— (1979) "Pagan Criticism of Christianity: Greek Religion and Christian Faith," in W.R. Schoedel and R.L. Wilken (eds) *Early Christian Literature and the Classical Intellectual Tradition: In Honorem Robert M. Grant*, Theologie Historique 53, Paris: Beauchesne, pp. 17–34.

—— (1980) "The Christians as the Romans (and Greeks) Saw Them," in B.F. Meyer and E.P. Sanders (eds) *Jewish and Christian Self-Definition*, vol. 1: *The Shaping of Christianity in the Second and Third Centuries*, Philadelphia, PA: Fortress, pp. 100–25, 234–6.

—— (1981) "Diversity and Unity in Early Christianity," *SecCent* 1: 101–10.

—— (1984) *The Christians as the Romans Saw Them*, New Haven, CT: Yale University Press.

Williams, S.K. (1975) *Jesus' Death as Saving Event: The Background and Origin of a Concept*, Harvard Dissertations in Religion 2, Missoula, MO: Scholars Press.

Wills, L.M. (1994) "The Jewish Novellas," in J.R. Morgan and R. Stoneman (eds) *Greek Fiction: The Greek Novel in Context*, London: Routledge, pp. 223–38.

—— (1995) *The Jewish Novel in the Ancient World*, Ithaca, NY: Cornell University Press.

Wimbush, V.L. (1987) *Paul the Worldly Ascetic: Response to the World and Self-Understanding according to 1 Corinthians 7*, Macon, GA: Mercer University Press.

—— (ed.) (1990) *Ascetic Behavior in Greco-Roman Antiquity: A Sourcebook*, Minneapolis, MN: Fortress.

—— (1993a) "The Ascetic Impulse in Ancient Christianity," *Theology Today* 50: 417–28.

—— (1993b) "The Ascetic Impulse in Early Christianity: Some Methodological Challenges," *StPatr* 25: 462–78.

—— (ed.) (1997) *Semeia 79: Rhetorics of Resistance: A Colloquy on Early Christianity as Rhetorical Formation*, Atlanta, GA: SBL.

Wimbush, V.L. and Valantasis, R. (eds) (1995) *Asceticism*, Oxford and New York: Oxford University Press.

Wolfson, H.A. (1947) *Philo: Foundations of Religious Philosophy in Judaism, Christianity, and Islam*, vol. 1, Cambridge, MA: Harvard University Press.

Wypustek, K. (1999) "Un aspect ignoré des persécutions des chrétiens dans l'Antiquité: les accusations de magie érotique imputees aux chrétiens aux IIe et III siècles," *Jahrbuch für Antike und Christentum* 42: 50–71.

Yarbrough, O.L. (1990) "Canons from the Council of Gangra," in V.L. Wimbush (ed.) *Ascetic Behavior in Greco-Roman Antiquity: A Sourcebook*, Minneapolis, MN: Fortress, pp. 448–55.

Young, F.M. (1971) *The Use of Sacrificial Ideas in Greek Christian Writers from the New Testament to John Chrysostom*, Patristic Monograph Series 5, Philadelphia, PA: Philadelphia Patristic Foundation.

—— (1999) "Greek Apologists of the Second Century," in M.J. Edwards, M. Goodman, and S.R.F. Price (eds) *Apologies in the Roman Empire: Pagans, Jews, and Christians*, Oxford: Oxford University Press, pp. 81–104.

Young, R.D. (1990) "Recent Interpretations of Early Christian Asceticism," *Thomist* 54/1: 123–40.

—— (2001) *In Procession before the World: Martyrdom as Public Liturgy in Early Christianity*, Milwaukee, WI: Marquette University Press.

INDEX

Acts, canonical *see* Lucan Acts
Acts of Andrew 2, 3, 29, 30, 37, 74,
    75, 77, 79–80, 85, 87, 103,
    128–9, 131, 140–1, 174
Acts of John 2, 3, 29, 30, 37, 73, 75,
    77, 79, 81–2, 83–4, 85, 103,
    128, 135, 138
Acts of Justin and Companions 3, 40,
    144
Acts of Paul 2, 3, 29, 30, 37, 38, 72,
    80, 85, 86, 173, 178–9
Acts of Paul and Thecla 37, 38,
    125–7, 130, 135, 140, 172
Acts of Peter 2, 3, 29, 30, 76, 77,
    78–9, 80, 82, 83, 84–5, 86, 127,
    133, 175, 176–8
Acts of the Scillitan Martyrs 3, 40,
    180
Acts of Thomas 2, 29, 37, 74, 76, 80,
    83, 85, 86, 124, 129–30, 131,
    135, 141, 175
Ad nationes (Tertullian) 23, 61
Agathonicê 98, 145, 147, 151
Alcinous 50, 53, 54, 57
Alexander Romance 31, 33, 35
ancient novels: comic 33; historical
    33–4, 36; idea romances *see* Greek
    romances; Jewish 35–6
Anderson, Graham 32
antiquity, Christian 66–9
apocalyptic 19, 79, 108, 172, 179,
    182, 188

Apocryphal Acts: and the ancient
    novels 4, 31, 36–8, 131–2; and
    the canonical Gospels 29–30; and
    Christian monotheism 71–87; as a
    Christian polemic 87–8; as a
    corpus 2–4, 29; genre and
    purpose 6, 29–39; historical
    reliability 6, 36–7; and the Lucan
    Acts 30–1; politically subversive
    171–9; relation to the Apologies
    and Martyr Acts 4–5, 48; socially
    subversive 125–58; *see also*
    continence; encratism; Greek
    romances
Apocryphal Acts of the Apostles see
    Apocryphal Acts
Apollinaris 22, 168
Apollonius 90, 91, 143, 180, 181,
    182, 183, 186
Apologies 1–2; against paganism
    61–4; against philosophers 64–5;
    Christian loyalty to the Empire
    159, 164–71; Christian
    monotheism 50–71; Christian
    sexual morality 117–23; genre
    and purpose 21–9; relation to the
    Apocryphal Acts and Martyr Acts
    4–5, 48; as a unit 3
Apologists *see* Apologies; *see also*
    individual Apologists such as
    Apollinaris; Athenagoras; Clement
    of Alexandria; Justin Martyr;